Technical C Programming

Vincent Kassab
Erie Community College

PRENTICE HALL, Englewood Cliffs, New Jersey 07632

Library of Congress Cataloging-in-Publication Data
Kassab, Vincent.
Technical C programming.

Includes index.
1. C (Computer program language) I. Title.
QA76.73.C15K37 1989 005.13'3 88-5939
ISBN 0-13-898339-9

Editorial/production supervision: *Raeia Maes*
Cover design: *Joel Mitnick Design, Inc.*
Manufacturing buyer: *Robert Anderson*

Printed in the United States of America

10 9 8 7 6 5 4 3

ISBN 0-13-898339-9

PRENTICE-HALL INTERNATIONAL (UK) LIMITED, *London*
PRENTICE-HALL OF AUSTRALIA PTY. LIMITED, *Sydney*
PRENTICE-HALL CANADA INC., *Toronto*
PRENTICE-HALL HISPANOAMERICANA, S.A., *Mexico*
PRENTICE-HALL OF INDIA PRIVATE LIMITED, *New Delhi*
SIMON & SCHUSTER SOUTHEAST ASIA PTE. LTD., *Singapore*
EDITORA PRENTICE-HALL DO BRASIL, LTDA., *Rio de Janeiro*

To my dear wife Karen
and my lovely daughters
Lisa and Monica

Contents

Preface

The **C** language has been the language of choice among professional programmers for years. Today, it is increasingly popular with beginners and those who want to move from other languages into one that offers greater speed, versatility, portability, and compactness of code.

Although it was originally developed as a compiler type language, **C** is now available in interpreted form. Interpreted **C** is ideal for learning the language. It is also useful for the development of relatively short programs or complex functions. Compiled **C** performs faster than the interpreted form. Moreover, students should be exposed to the process of compilation. The best of both worlds would be obtained by using both an interpreter and a compiler.

As is the case with any programming text, you will find that learning is easier and you will be able to retain more by making extensive use of the computer. Try each example and problem encountered in the text. Experiment by modifying the programs and observing if the expected results are obtained. You will find that the computer is your best teacher!

This book is specifically directed to students in the technologies and includes examples and problems that are mathematical, scientific, or technological in nature. It emphasizes practical methods of applied mathematical analysis, graphics, and system interfaces.

Technical C Programming is organized into two parts. Part I can be used as an introductory course in the second year of a community college technical program. It can also be used in the second or third year of a four-year technical program. Part I presents the fundamentals of the **C** language with relatively simple applications. Part II covers more advanced aspects of the language. The applications in Part II are also more involved. These topics can be covered in an advanced course or be used as a reference by the student, practicing technician, engineer, or programmer.

Students using this text should have some previous computer experience. A general knowledge of computer architecture, use of an operating system, and the ability to work with binary and hexadecimal number systems is recommended. A prior course in assembly language programming is useful. Students with some assembly language exposure generally have a better appreciation of pointers, memory allocation, and other concepts that are important in **C.**

ACKNOWLEDGMENTS

I would like to thank all the reviewers who have contributed to the production of this text. Special thanks go to Tori Basford of the Computer Science Department of Pima College in Tucson, Arizona, for meticulous editorial work and technical contributions. I also thank John Uffenbeck of Wisconsin Indianhead Technical Institute in Ashland, Wisconsin, for his helpful comments and suggestions. Last but not least, I would like to thank my wife Karen for giving me the time to complete the manuscript and always providing moral support.

Vincent Kassab

chapter 1

Introduction

1.1 HISTORY OF C

The **C** language was developed at Bell Laboratories by Dennis M. Ritchie during the period 1969 to 1972. At the time, Dennis was working with Ken Thompson, also of Bell Labs, on the development of the UNIX operating system for the PDP-7 minicomputer. (An *operating system* is a program that facilitates use of the computer's resources.) The original UNIX was written in a language called **B**, a predecessor to **C**, by Ken Thompson. **C** was developed primarily as a tool for rewriting the UNIX operating system to run on newer minicomputers.

In 1979, Brian W. Kernigan and Dennis M. Ritchie wrote a book called *The C Programming Language*. This book became the definition and de facto standard for the **C** language. An American National Standards Institute (ANSI) standard for the language is now available. It closely follows the original version of **C**.

Although UNIX and **C** were designed for use on powerful minicomputers, their popularity, coupled with the increasing power of microcomputers, has lead to implementations of UNIX and **C** on the larger microcomputers. Today, **C** is also running on popular operating systems designed specifically for microcomputers, such as the MS-DOS, CP/M, and OS-9.

1.2 THE C ADVANTAGE

Many high-level programming languages are in use today, each with its own particular niche. FORTRAN is the original high-level language for scientific programming. COBOL was developed for business applications. BASIC was introduced as an easy-to-learn language for students who are not computer majors. Pascal was designed to be a teaching language. These are but a few examples.

At the other extreme, we have assembly language. It is a tedious language in which to work. Furthermore, every central processor has a unique assembly language. But assembly language provides the ultimate in compactness of programs, speed of execution, and flexibility.

Which languages should you learn? Which languages should you use? Ideally, it would be nice to have one language that could be used for all programming jobs and on all computers. The language that comes closest to this universal ideal is **C**. Why? Because **C** is block structured, portable, fast, compact, and versatile. Let's take a look at each of these virtues in more detail.

- *Block structured:* Unlike languages such as BASIC in which program flow is from one program line or statement to another, **C** programs consist of blocks of program lines called *functions*. Each function is clearly defined and performs a specific task. This block structure, also common to other languages such as Pascal, Modula II, and Ada, makes a program easier to read and more manageable.
- *Portable:* A program written in **C** for one computer can be *ported* (carried over) to another with little or no modification. Other languages may make this claim, but **C** is the most portable of computer languages available today.
- *Fast:* **C** programs execute at a speed approaching that of assembly language, which is unquestionably the fastest.
- *Compact:* The size of a program generated in **C** is generally less than that obtained by using other compiler-type languages.
- *Versatile:* **C** is used for writing virtually all types of programs, from *system programs* such as operating systems, compilers, assemblers, and editors, to *applications programs,* including computer-aided design (CAD), animations, business programs, and scientific applications.

1.3 USING C COMPILERS

Procedure for Non-UNIX Systems

The basic steps for compiling a **C** program are illustrated in Fig. 1.1. If you are already familiar with other language compilers, you will notice that the procedures are similar. The original text of our program is called the *source code*. It is prepared using a *text editor*. This is the first step. Any text editor may be used to generate the source code. Some compiler programs include a text editor as part of the package.

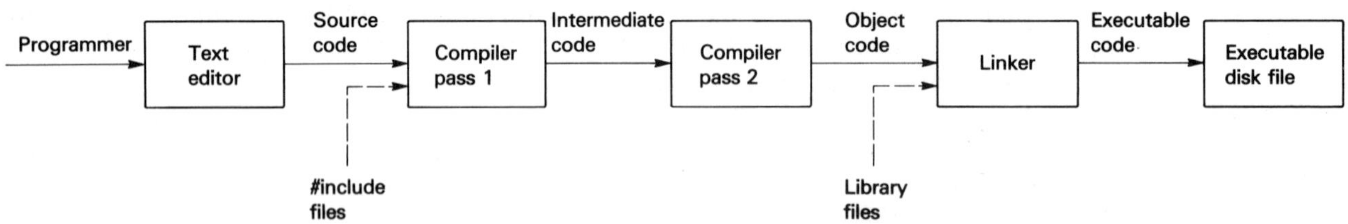

Figure 1.1 Compiling a program.

The source code is normally saved using a file name having a **.c** extension. This identifies it as a **C** program. The compiler will take the source code and convert it into an intermediate form, which may be in assembly language. (Additional source code files, called **#include** files, may be added here.) This procedure is called the *first pass* of the compiler. The *intermediate code* is a temporary file and will normally be destroyed by the compiler when it is no longer needed. The compiler generates many other temporary files in the process of compiling our program.

The *second pass* of the compiler will generate what is called *relocatable object code*. It is written to the disk file using the same file name given to the source file, but having an extension such as **.o** or **.obj** to identify it as object code. The compiler will not destroy this file since it is required to produce the final executable program.

We can compile a **C** program in separate modules, each producing its own object code. These modules are bound together into an executable program by another program called the *linker*. The output of the linker is machine language. It will normally be saved to the disk file with the same name as the source file, but having an extension such as **.exe** or **.com** to identify it as executable code.

The linker also permits us to include what are called *library modules*. Each of these modules consists of code that performs some standardized task needed by our program. They may be included with the compiler, purchased separately, or developed by the user.

In the process of converting your program from source code to executable machine language, the compiler will most likely detect some errors. These errors are reported to you in a format that is unique to each compiler. You must then correct the mistakes in the program at the source code level and recompile. Herein lies the major weakness of compiler-type languages. The cycle of compile, find errors, correct, and then compile again is very time consuming. However, if you persevere, the final program will run faster than the equivalent interpreted program.

The exact procedure for running any given compiler will be described by a manual that accompanies the software. Also included will be a listing of error messages and other useful information. You should read the manual provided with the compiler before attempting to use the program.

Procedure for UNIX Systems

If you are using a **C** compiler on a computer running the UNIX operating system, the procedure for compiling a program is much simpler. The standard text editors for UNIX are **ed** and **vi**. After composing the source program, save it with the **.c** extension. At the command line, type **cc**, followed by the name of the source file. All the steps of compilation are combined under UNIX. The final executable machine code is written to the disk file under the file name **a.out**.

You may wonder why the executable file is not saved using the source code file name. The **a.out** notation is a carry-over from a predecessor of the **C** language called **a-natural.** The output of this compiler was more logically called **a.out**. You should rename the output file to something more suggestive of the function of the program.

1.4 USING C INTERPRETERS

C was originally a compiled language. In most applications, the final form of a **C** program should be compiled. However, for learning purposes and also for developing complex program segments, the newer interpreted forms of **C** have several definite advantages. First, they eliminate the delays involved in debugging a program due to repeated recompilations. Second, mistakes are detected sooner, providing faster feedback. Also, you need only store the source code version of a program. This eliminates cluttering the disk with object and executable files.

Interpreted **C** programs are handled very much like their interpreted BASIC counterparts. Once you have completed composing the program, you simply type RUN or some equivalent command and the program executes automatically. If mistakes are encountered, they are corrected using the editor, and the program is immediately ready for testing.

Of course, the major disadvantage of interpreters is their slowness of execution. Each line must be translated during program execution. The speed of execution is usually not a problem during the learning or development process. Wherever it is, you may easily switch from the interpreter to the compiler without having to do any significant rewriting of the source code.

1.5 ELEMENTARY C PROGRAMS

In this section, we will look at some simple **C** programs. Each program will introduce more detail of **C** program structure and some new definitions. This approach will allow you to try what you have just learned on a computer to reinforce the concepts and give you more confidence.

A Simple Program: Printing a Message

Figure 1.2(a) shows a simple but complete **C** program that prints a message on the screen. The same program is repeated for comparison in Fig. 1.2(b) in the BASIC language. If you are not familiar with BASIC, ignore any references to that langauge. They are included here as an additional aid.

```
/* printing a message */
#include <stdio.h>
main()
     {
     printf("This is a complete C program.\n");
     }
```

(a)

```
100 REM PRINTING A MESSAGE IN BASIC
110 PRINT "This is a complete BASIC program."
```

(b)

Figure 1.2 Printing a message.

The first program line constitutes a program comment, similar to the REM statement in the BASIC version of the program. In **C**, a comment begins with the /* character sequence and ends with the reverse sequence of */. As is the case with BASIC, comments are included to clarify the program for the reader. The computer will completely ignore all comments.

The second line in the **C** version of the program

```
#include(stdio.h)
```

is referred to as a *preprocessor directive*. All preprocessor directives begin with the # symbol. They give the compiler information on how to handle some aspect of the program before the compiling actually begins. In this case, the directive says to include a file called **stdio.h** before compiling the program.

The **stdio.h** file is the *standard input/output file header*. It includes information that the compiler may need in processing any input/output statements within your program. This preprocessor directive is not needed by all programs. Different compilers may or may not require it for the same program. If the **stdio.h** file for your compiler includes a reference to a standard input/output function you are using in your program, then you should add the **#include⟨stdio.h⟩** preprocessor directive to your program.

Angle brackets enclose the header file name to indicate that this file is in the standard library directory. If the file is located in some other directory, double quote marks replace the angle brackets. Thus, a header file named **other.h** which is in a different directory would have a preprocessor **include** directive that looks like

```
#include "other.h"
```

C programs are composed of one or more blocks called *functions*. Each function must be assigned a name. The name of the first function to be executed is always called **main**. Notice in Fig. 1.2(a) that parentheses immediately follow the function name. Later we will see why these parentheses are needed for all functions.

The line

```
printf("This is a complete C program.\n");
```

is called a *statement*. It constitutes a complete instruction to the computer. Every function consists of one or more statements. You may have guessed that the **printf()** statement in this example prints the message "This is a complete C program." It is very similar to the PRINT statement in BASIC. How are they different? Notice that the **C** version includes the message to be printed within parentheses and terminates the line with a semicolon. Also, the character sequence **\n** has been added at the end of the message.

The use of parentheses in conjunction with the **printf()** statement is due to the fact that **printf()** is itself a function, just like **main()**. It is part of a collection of functions called the *standard I/O library*. More will be said about this library later.

In the **C** language, all statements are terminated with a semicolon. The location of a statement on a line is not critical but should follow a consistent style. You should have only one statement per line.

The sequence **\n** at the end of the message is called an escape sequence. It forces the next program output to be printed on a new line. Other escape sequences, each beginning with the \ character, perform operations such as tabbing **(\t)**, backspacing **(\b)**, and so on. The **\n** characters are not printed as part of the output.

The program *statements* that constitute a function are enclosed within *braces*. The function *body* begins with the open brace ({) and ends with the close brace (}). Braces can also be used to group statements within a function, as we will see in later examples. All **C** programs have an equal number of open and close braces. The closing brace of **main()** marks the end of a program.

Let's Do Some Computation

The **C** program of Fig. 1.3(a) computes an area, given the length and width. The same program is repeated in Fig. 1.3(b) using BASIC.

```
/* doing some computation */
#include <stdio.h>
main()
     {
     int length, width, area;

     length = 20;
     width = 16;
     area = length * width;
     printf("The area equals %d", area);
     }
```

(a)

```
100 REM DOING SOME COMPUTATION IN BASIC
110 LENGTH = 20
120 WIDTH = 16
130 AREA = LENGTH*WIDTH
140 PRINT "The area equals ";AREA
```

(b)

Figure 1.3 Doing some computation.

The variables used in the program are **length**, **width**, and **area**. In the **C** language, the type of data that each variable represents must be *declared*, usually within the function. In this program, the line

```
int  length, width, area;
```

declares the three variables as being integer (whole) numbers. Here, **int** is a *keyword* used to specify integer-type data. The keywords of a computer language are reserved for expressing some concept or operation within the language. They may not be used for variable names. Thus, you should never have a variable named **int** within your program.

Variable declarations within a function occur immediately after the open brace of the function body. A variable can never be used before it is declared.

The program lines

```
length = 20;
width = 16;
```

assign values to the variables **length** and **width**. The area is computed from the expression **length*width** and assigned to the variable **area**. In this case, the area equals 320. Notice that the asterisk (*) is used to indicate multiplication.

The last statement of the program prints the message

```
The area equals 320
```

Here, the **printf()** function is used for output of data and text. Previously, we used this function for printing text only. In this case, the output includes a message and the value of the variable **area**. The **%d** character sequence is a *conversion specifier* that tells the **printf()** function that the data to be printed is a decimal integer. It also tells the function exactly where to insert the value within the output message, in this case after the blank that follows the word "equals." The variable **area** is listed after the message to indicate which variable's value is to be filled in at the **%d**.

Using Keyboard Input

Now let's look at a program that accepts input data from the keyboard. We will make use of the **scanf()** function from the standard I/O library to accomplish the input function. The program of Fig. 1.4(a) is a **C** program that converts weight in pounds into weight in kilograms. The BASIC version is included in Fig. 1.4(b).

```
/* conversions using input and output */
#include <stdio.h>
main()
    {
    float weight, metric_weight;

    printf("Enter your weight in pounds\n");
    scanf("%f", &weight);
    metric_weight = weight / 2.2;
    printf("You weigh %f kilograms\n", metric_weight);
    }
```

(a)

```
100 REM Conversions using INPUT and PRINT in BASIC
110 PRINT "Enter your weight in pounds"
120 INPUT WEIGHT
130 METRIC_WEIGHT = WEIGHT/2.2
140 PRINT "You weigh ";METRIC_WEIGHT;" kilograms"
```

(b)

Figure 1.4 Conversions using input and output.

The keyword **float** in the variable declaration defines the variables **weight** and **metric_weight** as representing *real numbers*. Real numbers may include a decimal component. An example of a real number is the value of pi, or 3.141592654.

All keyboard inputs should be preceded by a *prompt message* on the screen, indicating which input item is required. The line

```
printf("Enter your weight in pounds\n");
```

is a statement that prints the prompt message

```
Enter your weight in pounds
```

on the screen. The user now knows what is being asked for by the program. Immediately after the prompt, the **scanf()** statement

```
scanf("%f",&weight);
```

will wait for a keyboard input followed by a carriage return. It will then assign the entered value to the variable **weight**. The **%f** character sequence is a conversion specifier indicating that the data to be input will be of type **float**. The ampersand symbol (**&**) is used as a prefix to the variable weight. It actually defines another quantity, **&weight**, whose value is the location in memory of the variable **weight**. Variables that contain the location of other variables are called *pointers*. This is an important concept that will be discussed in detail in Chapter 7.

When the value of **metric_weight** is output, the **%f** conversion specifier is used, since we are dealing with a variable of type **float**. The rest of the program is straightforward. A run of the program produces the following input and output:

```
Enter your weight in pounds
200
You weigh 90.909088 kilograms
```

Repetition

Computers excel at doing repetitive computation. This is achieved by repeated execution of a block of statements under a predetermined set of conditions. Various methods exist for implementing this repetitive execution, which is generally referred to as a *program loop*.

One way that **C** provides for this ability is through the **while** statement. The program of Fig. 1.5 uses the **while** statement to print a table of squares for whole numbers from 1 to 10.

```
/* table of squares */
#include <stdio.h>
main()
    {
    int i;

    i = 1;
    while (i <= 10)
        {
        printf("%d\t%d\n", i, i*i);
        i = i+1;
        }
    }
```

```
1       1
2       4
3       9
4       16
5       25
6       36
7       49
8       64
9       81
10      100
```

Figure 1.5 Repetition using while.

The variable **i** represents the number to be squared. It is initialized to a value of 1 to start the table at that point. Had we wanted to start the table at some other value, **i** would have been adjusted accordingly.

The keyword **while** directs **C** to repeat all the statements enclosed within the braces that follow, as long as **i** is *less than or equal to* 10. The condition *less than* *or equal to* is written in **C** as <=. On each pass through this block of statements, the value of **i** and its square are printed, and **i** is incremented by 1 through the statement

```
i = i+1;
```

This statement can be read as "set **i** to its current value plus 1." Finally, when **i** is incremented to 11, the test condition (i <= 10) fails and execution of the **while** loop terminates.

Observe that all the statements included within the **while** loop are indented. This allows you to immediately notice the extent of the loop and all the statements it controls.

The shaded region of Fig. 1.5 shows the output screen obtained from execution of this program. This shading is used here and throughout the text to differentiate the program listing from the program input and output generated during execution.

Selection

Another statement that takes some action dependent on a test condition is the **if else** statement. In the program of Fig. 1.6, the block of statements within the braces following the **if** will be executed if the test condition is true; otherwise, the block of statements within the braces following the **else** keyword will be executed. Indentation is used to easily identify the extent of these blocks and the keyword they follow.

```
/* selection using if else */
#include <stdio.h>
main()
      {
      int i;

      printf("What is the square root of 256?\n");
      scanf("%d", &i);
      if (i == 16)
            {
            printf("That is correct!\n");
            printf("You certainly know your roots.\n");
            }
      else
            {
            printf("Sorry, that's the wrong answer.\n");
            printf("The correct value is 16.\n");
            }
      }
```

Figure 1.6 Selection using if else.

The response to the question "What is the square root of 256?" is assigned to the variable **i**. The test condition (i == 16) checks for equality of **i** with the number 16. Notice the double equal sign that is used for testing equality. If the condition is true, the message

```
That is correct!
You certainly know your roots.
```

which follows the **if** keyword, is printed. Otherwise, the message

```
Sorry, that's the wrong answer.
The correct value is 16.
```

which follows the **else** keyword, is printed.

1.6 PROGRAM FORMAT

As we mentioned earlier, all **C** programs consist of a series of functions. Program execution must begin with a function called **main()**. Other functions included in the program are named by the programmer. The name is normally suggestive of the operation performed by the function.

When the name of a function appears as a statement in a program, program execution transfers to that function. This procedure is referred to as *calling* a function. After the *called* function has been completely executed, a *return* is made to the *calling* function. If you are familiar with other programming languages, you probably have detected a similarity between functions in **C** and subroutines in BASIC or assembly language or functions and procedures in Pascal.

When one function calls another function, the second function is said to be *nested* inside the first. The second function may include a call to a third function, and so on. It is possible to have a very large number of functions all nested within one another.

In many cases, when a function is called, information is passed to it. This information is included within the parentheses after the function name. The called function may also return a single value to the calling function. Again, this arrangement is similar to the behavior of subroutines or procedures in other languages.

Naming Variables and Functions

Variable names in **C** may include any number of letters, digits, or the underscore (_) symbol. A space is not permitted. The first character must not be a digit. Only a fixed number of characters in a variable name are significant, usually 31. But if your **C** compiler only recognizes eight characters, it would not distinguish between variables named **perimeter1** and **perimeter2**.

You may use upper- or lowercase letters. By convention, lowercase letters are used for variable names and uppercase letters are used for symbolic constants. **C** will differentiate between a variable name in uppercase and one in lowercase having the same spelling. Thus, **pi** is not the same as **PI**.

The underscore symbol is often used for compounding words in a variable name to make it more readable. Examples of valid and invalid variable names are given in Fig. 1.7.

Valid	*Invalid*
frequency	2_harmonic
period_1	@table
max_mode	new-size

Figure 1.7 Variable names in **C**.

Keywords may not be used as variable names. A list of **C** keywords is given in Fig. 1.8. It is permissible to have a keyword appear as part of a valid variable name. For example, all the following are valid variable names:

```
in_char
get_switch
long_pulse
```

Function names follow the same restrictions as variable names. However, it is common to use only lowercase letters for naming functions. Remember, parentheses must immediately follow a function name. If any information is passed to the called function, then arguments will be included within the parentheses.

auto	double	if	static
break	else	int	struct
case	enum	long	switch
char	extern	register	typedef
continue	float	return	union
default	for	sizeof	unsigned
do	goto	short	while

Figure 1.8 **C** keywords.

Program Style

C is referred to as a *free-form* language. It is not very restrictive of the placement of comments, declarations, statements, or white space (blanks, tabs, and new lines). However, certain conventions are used in the language to help you create a program that is more readable.

- Use comments to explain anything in your program that may not be obvious to someone reading it for the first time. Comments can be used to explain:
  1. What a program will do
  2. How to use a program
  3. What a variable represents
  4. What a function will do
  5. The operation performed by a complex statement
- Locate comments in a consistent fashion throughout your program. They may be included after a statement or on a separate line, or you may have one comment spanning several lines. Examples of each style are:
  1. main()   /* Here is a comment on the same line */
  2. /* Here is a comment preceding a function */
     main()
  3. /*
     *   A comment using this style
     *   should be reserved for explaining
     *   anything that requires more than
     *   one line
     */
- Use braces to mark the beginning and end of functions. Braces are also used to identify the beginning and end of logically grouped statements, referred to as a *block*. The exact location of braces is not prescribed by **C**. However, by convention, the opening and closing braces for a function are always aligned in the same column. The opening and closing braces for blocks of statements need not be aligned, but their location should be

consistent from one occurrence to another. Figure 1.9(a) and (b) illustrates two commonly used styles for the use of braces surrounding a block.

```
while (expression) {
      statements
      .
      .
      .
      }
```

(a)

```
while (expression)
      {
      statements
      .
      .
      .
      }
```

(b)

Figure 1.9 Use of braces to identify blocks: (a) style 1; (b) style 2.

- Use white space to provide a clear, clean layout for your program. The following rules will help you achieve this goal:
  1. Place only one statement on a line.
  2. Skip a line between the last variable declaration and the first statement in each function.
  3. Place the opening and closing braces of a function on separate lines. Nothing else should appear on these lines.
  4. Use indentation to identify statements that follow a **while**, **if else**, or other control structure in a consistent style.

You may find it helpful to create a style sheet illustrating how you will handle each of the elements we have discussed. Referring to the style sheet will assure consistency throughout your programs.

Variable Declarations

All the variables used within a program must be declared. The declaration defines the type of data that the variable represents. The **C** language supports the following basic types of data.

int	integer (whole numbers)
char	character (a byte)
float	single-precision floating point (real numbers)
double	double-precision floating point

So far, we have encountered **int** and **float** in our examples. More will be said about these and other data types in Chapter 2.

Calling Your Own Function

The simple program of Fig. 1.2 included a call to the function **printf()**, which we said was part of the standard I/O library. Let's look at another program that calls a function created by the programmer. Figure 1.10 lists a program that calls a function that will produce a pause. Pressing the *return* or *enter* key will force continuation of the program.

```
/* calling your own function */
#include <stdio.h>
main()
      {
      printf("What's my favorite computer language?\n");
      pause();
      printf("C!");
      }

pause()                         /* a function that produces a pause */
      {
      int keypress;

      printf("Press return for the answer\n");
      scanf("%d", &keypress);
      }
```

Figure 1.10 Calling your own function.

The **main()** function first prints the message

```
What's my favorite computer language?
```

on the screen. It then calls the function **pause()**. The line

```
pause();
```

invokes the function. The parentheses after the function name remain empty, since we are not passing any information to the function. Notice that the function call is followed by a semicolon, as would be the case for any other statement. **pause()** prints the message

```
Press return for the answer
```

The actual pause is produced by the **scanf** statement, which waits for a keyboard entry terminated by a press of the enter or return key. In this case, we are not trying to enter any data, so the value of the variable **keypress** is not important. After pressing the return key, the end of the function is reached and control returns to the line in **main()** immediately following the function call. This line prints the message **"C!"**. Program execution then terminates, since the close brace of **main()** is encountered.

The preceding example demonstrates how functions are called. In later chapters, we will see the real utility of using functions.

QUESTIONS

1.1. Define the term *block structured* as it relates to computer languages.

1.2. Define the term *portable* as it relates to computer languages.

1.3. Compare compilers and interpreters, indicating where each may have an advantage over the other.

1.4. Describe the steps involved in compiling a **C** program.

1.5. What is the name of the first function to be executed in a **C** program?

1.6. Define the term *keyword*.

1.7. Define the term *statement*. Which character is used to terminate each statement?

1.8. What is a *preprocessor directive*? Give an example.

1.9. What does the **stdio.h** file header include?

1.10. What is a *prompt message*? Why is it used?

1.11. Name a **C** function used for printing output.

1.12. Name a **C** function used for keyboard input.

1.13. Name a **C** statement used for repetition of a program block.

1.14. Name a **C** statement used for selection.

1.15. Describe the restrictions on variable names in **C**.

1.16. Where are braces used in **C** programs?

1.17. How are the beginning and end of *comments* identified?

1.18. What are the four basic data types in **C**?

PROBLEMS

1.1. What is printed by each of the following **printf()** statements?

```
(a) printf("one two three\n");
(b) printf("one\ntwo\nthree\n");
(c) printf("one\ttwo\tthree\n");
(d) printf("1\b2\b3\n");
(e) printf("The answer is %d\n",400);
```

1.2 What is printed by the following program?

```
#include <stdio.h>
main()
    {
    float x,y;

    x = 3;
    y = x*x;
    printf("For x = %f, y = %f\n",x,y);
    }
```

1.3. What is printed by the following program?

```
#include <stdio.h>
main()
    {
    int i;

    i = 10;
    while (i>0)
          {
          printf("%d\n",i);
          i = i-1;
          }
    }
```

chapter 2

Data Types, Operators, and Expressions

2.1 THE C DATA TYPES

In Chapter 1, we briefly mentioned the basic **C** data types. They are **int**, **char**, **float**, and **double**. Here we will look at each of these types in detail, as well as the variations of type **int**, which include **short**, **long**, and **unsigned**. There are other, more complex data types. They will be covered in later chapters.

Binary Measure

All information inside the computer is represented in terms of *binary*, or base 2, numbers. The most elementary quantity of information in the binary system is the *bit*, which stands for *binary digit*. One bit of information is stored inside one memory cell inside the computer. Each bit may take on a value of either 0 or 1, corresponding to the state of the memory cell.

When we enter information into the computer, whether it is a decimal number, text, or anything else, that information is eventually represented internally as a binary number. Figure 2.1 shows the binary patterns that are obtained by storing the integers 0 through 15 inside the computer.

Decimal	*Binary*	*Decimal*	*Binary*
0	00000000	8	00001000
1	00000001	9	00001001
2	00000010	10	00001010
3	00000011	11	00001011
4	00000100	12	00001100
5	00000101	13	00001101
6	00000110	14	00001110
7	00000111	15	00001111

Figure 2.1 Binary representation of integer numbers.

Notice that we only needed 4 bits to represent the numbers 0 through 15. Four bits is referred to as a *nibble*. The largest number that can be stored in n bits is given by

$$2^n - 1$$

A *byte* is equal to 8 bits. The largest number that a byte can represent is equal to

$$2^8 - 1$$

or 255. You cannot store a very large number inside a byte, but it is just right for storing characters, including letters, decimal digits, and special symbols. How do you store characters in binary memory? The answer is that you don't. What we really store is a coded representation of the original character. A partial listing of the American Standard Code for Information Interchange, or ASCII code, is shown in Figure 2.2. (A complete listing may be found in Appendix B.) It is the

ASCII	*Dec*	*Hex*	*Octal*	*Binary*	*ASCII*	*Dec*	*Hex*	*Octal*	*Binary*
NUL	00	00	00	000 0000	@	64	40	100	100 0000
BEL	07	07	07	000 0111	A	65	41	101	100 0001
BS	08	08	10	000 1000	B	66	42	102	100 0010
HT	09	09	11	000 1001	C	67	43	103	100 0011
LF	10	0A	12	000 1010	D	68	44	104	100 0100
FF	12	0C	14	000 1100	E	69	45	105	100 0101
CR	13	0D	15	000 1101	F	70	46	106	100 0110
SP	32	20	40	010 0000	G	71	47	107	100 0111
!	33	21	41	010 0001	H	72	48	110	100 1000
"	34	22	42	010 0010	I	73	49	111	100 1001
#	35	23	43	010 0011	J	74	4A	112	100 1010
$	36	24	44	010 0100	K	75	4B	113	100 1011
%	37	25	45	010 0101	L	76	4C	114	100 1100
&	38	26	46	010 0110	M	77	4D	115	100 1101
'	39	27	47	010 0111	N	78	4E	116	100 1110
(	40	28	50	010 1000	O	79	4F	117	100 1111
)	41	29	51	010 1001	P	80	50	120	101 0000
*	42	2A	52	010 1010	Q	81	51	121	101 0001
+	43	2B	53	010 1011	R	82	52	122	101 0010
,	44	2C	54	010 1100	S	83	53	123	101 0011
–	45	2D	55	010 1101	T	84	54	124	101 0100
.	46	2E	56	010 1110	U	85	55	125	101 0101
/	47	2F	57	010 1111	V	86	56	126	101 0110
0	48	30	60	011 0000	W	87	57	127	101 0111
1	49	31	61	011 0001	X	88	58	130	101 1000
2	50	32	62	011 0010	Y	89	59	131	101 1001
3	51	33	63	011 0011	Z	90	5A	132	101 1010
4	52	34	64	011 0100	[	91	5B	133	101 1011
5	53	35	65	011 0101	\	92	5C	134	101 1100
6	54	36	66	011 0110	]	93	5D	135	101 1101
7	55	37	67	011 0111	^	94	5E	136	101 1110
8	56	38	70	011 1000	_	95	5F	137	101 1111
9	57	39	71	011 1001	`	96	60	140	110 0000
:	58	3A	72	011 1010					
;	59	3B	73	011 1011					
<	60	3C	74	011 1100					
=	61	3D	75	011 1101					
>	62	3E	76	011 1110					
?	63	3F	77	011 1111					

Figure 2.2 ASCII code.

most widely accepted code for representing characters in the computer industry. Notice that all the entries fit nicely inside a byte-sized piece of memory. When character data are entered into the computer, they are represented internally by the ASCII code equivalent. When they are output to the video screen or printer, the data are converted back to their original form.

The byte is the basic building block for data types used in **C**. An *integer* is a whole number usually 2 bytes long. (Some larger computers may define integer numbers as being longer than 2 bytes.) The largest number that can be represented by a 2-byte integer is $2^{15} - 1$ or 32,767. Since integer numbers use 1 bit for storing the sign of the number, the largest number is given by $2^{15} - 1$ and not $2^{16} - 1$. The smallest number that can be represented by type **int** is -2^{15} or $-32{,}768$.

The *unsigned integer* data type is an integer without a sign bit. This provides one extra bit for the magnitude of positive numbers. Therefore, the largest unsigned 2-byte integer is given by $2^{16} - 1$ or 65,535. The unsigned type cannot represent negative numbers, so the smallest value it can represent is zero.

A *long integer* data type is usually twice the size of an ordinary integer, or 4 bytes long. Since it is a signed data type, the largest 4-byte long number is $2^{31} - 1$ or 2,147,483,647. The smallest value is $-2{,}147{,}483{,}648$.

Numbers that have a fractional component are referred to as *real* or *floating-point* numbers. The value of pi (3.141592654) is an example of a floating-point number. **C** provides a data type called *float* to represent such numbers.

For very large or very small numbers, **C** makes use of an alternate method for printing float numbers called *exponential notation*. This is essentially the same as the scientific notation you learned in high-school mathematics or physics. The number 1234.567 is written in scientific notation as 1.234567×10^3. The same number in exponential notation is written as 1.234567E3. The equivalence can be seen if you read E3 as "multiplied by 10 raised to the 3."

The float data type is usually 4 bytes long. A portion of this memory space is used to specify the *mantissa*, or digits of the number, and the balance is used to specify the *exponent*. The value of the exponent locates the position of the decimal point. Floating-point numbers in **C** usually provide 6 to 7 digits of precision and an exponent range of at least ± 38.

Specifying Data Type

Whenever a variable is created for use in a function, we must declare its type before using it. This is done by using a **C** *type specifier*, followed by a list of all the variables that we wish to declare as having that type. The **C** type specifiers are as follows:

Type specifiers	*Description*
char	A byte, contains one character of data
short	A short integer (see **int**)
int	An integer number, usually 2 bytes long
long	A long integer, usually 4 bytes long
unsigned	An integer without sign; largest value is twice that of type **int**
float	A floating-point number
double	A double-precision floating-point number
struct	A complex or mixed data structure
union	Declares different types as sharing the same memory space
typedef	Renames or labels a data type

To declare variables named **i**, **j**, and **k** as type **int**, we would include a *declaration statement* in our function as follows:

```
int i,j,k;
```

The declaration statement must occur after the open brace of the function and before any use of the variables. In most cases, we will have a variety of data types to declare. We must then include a type specifier for each type used and follow each specifier with a list of all the variables of that type. For example,

```
char      alpha,c;
int       i = 256;
long      big_number;
unsigned  speed;
float     x,gnp;
```

will declare the variables **alpha** and **c** as being of type **char** or character data, **i** as integer, **big_number** as a **long** integer, **speed** as an **unsigned** integer, and **x** and **gnp** as floating-point numbers. Notice the equal sign after the variable **i**. It is used to initialize a variable at the time it is declared. In this case, **i** is set equal to 256.

Type Conversion

Whenever we input or output data using the **scanf()** or **printf()** functions, the format of the data must be specified by a *control string*. The control string consists of two double quotes containing the *conversion specifiers*. As we saw in the examples in Chapter 1, the conversion specifiers start with the % character. This is immediately followed by a character indicating the desired conversion. Figure 2.3 lists the conversion specifiers that are used with **printf()** or **scanf()** and their description.

		Used with:	
Specifiers	*Description*	*printf*	*scanf*
Numeric			
%d	Decimal or base 10 integer	×	×
%o	Octal or base 8 integer	×	×
%x	Hexadecimal or base 16 integer	×	×
%u	Unsigned decimal integer	×	
%f	Floating-point decimal	×	×
%e	Exponential (scientific) notation	×	
%g	Shortest of %e or %f	×	
%h	Short integer		×
Character			
%c	Single character	×	×
%s	String of characters	×	×

Figure 2.3 Conversion specifiers.

The example of Fig. 2.4 illustrates the use of the numeric conversion specifiers in their simplest form. (The character specifiers will be covered in the next section.) In this example, we have declared the variable **i** as integer and **f** as float. The value of **i** has been set to 12, while the value of **f** is 12.0. These two quantities have the same value, but **C** looks for a decimal point in all floating-point numbers. The first **printf()** statement outputs the number 12 in decimal format. We are already familiar with using **%d** for integer data.

```
/* demonstration of type conversion */
#include <stdio.h>
main()
    {
    int i;
    float f;

    i = 12;
    f = 12.0;
    printf("The integer 12 is printed as %d using d for decimal\n", i);
    printf("The integer 12 is printed as %o using o for octal\n", i);
    printf("The integer 12 is printed as %x using x for hexadecimal\n", i);
    printf("The integer 12 is printed as %u using u for unsigned\n", i);
    printf("The number 12.0 is printed as %f using f for float\n", f);
    printf("The number 12.0 is printed as %e using e for exponential\n", f);
    printf("The number 12.0 is printed as %g for smallest of f or e\n", f);
    }
```

```
The integer 12 is printed as 12 using d for decimal
The integer 12 is printed as 14 using o for octal
The integer 12 is printed as c using x for hexadecimal
The integer 12 is printed as 12 using u for unsigned
The number 12.0 is printed as 12.000000 using f for float
The number 12.0 is printed as 1.200000e+01 using e for exponential
The number 12.0 is printed as 12.000000 for smallest of f or e
```

Figure 2.4 Converting numeric data.

The second and third **printf()** statements use the **%o** and **%x** specifiers. These lines will output the value of 12 in octal (base 8) and hexadecimal (base 16) format. The octal equivalent of 12 is 14, and its hexadecimal equivalent is 0C.

The next **printf()** statement outputs the value of 12 using the **%u** specifier for **unsigned** data. The actual output will be the same as that obtained using the **%d** specifier as long as the number being printed is positive and less than the maximum size for integer data. An attempt to print a negative number using the unsigned specifier will produce an erroneous output. Of course, the unsigned data type has a maximum value that is twice the maximum for integer data.

The next two **printf()** statements output the value of 12.0 in floating point and exponential-format floating point. Here, the **%f** is used for **float** and **%e** for **exponential**. The last **printf()** statement uses the **%g** specifier to output the shortest of **%f** or **%e**. In this case, the floating-point representation is shorter. If the value of **f** is changed to a large number, such as 12345678.0, the exponential form would be printed, since it is shorter.

2.2 WORKING WITH THE C DATA TYPES

Character Data

Data of the type **char** have a size of 1 byte or 8 bits. It is used to store one character of information. The largest **unsigned** number that can be stored in **char** data type is 255.

A character constant can be defined several ways. The first method is to include the character within single quote (') marks. For example, **'a'** is a character constant representing the letter *a*. A second method of representing the letter *a* is to use an *escape sequence*. In **C**, an escape sequence is defined by the backslash character followed by a octal code number or letter. Using the ASCII octal code for the lowercase *a*, the escape sequence would be \141 and the character constant would be written as **'\141'**. The first method is generally preferred since it is code independent. An **'a'** works equally well for ASCII or any other code.

Some characters do not have a printable form, such as the *bell*, *linefeed*, or *carriage return*. In such cases, we are forced to use an escape sequence to represent the character. Thus, a bell is represented as **'\007'**, a linefeed as **'\012'**, and so on.

Since certain escape sequences occur frequently within a program, **C** provides a special notation for them. They are summarized in Fig. 2.5.

ASCII	*Description*	*C escape sequence*
LF	Linefeed (newline)	\n
HT	Horizontal tab	\t
BS	Backspace	\b
CR	Carriage return	\r
FF	Form feed	\f
\	Backslash	\\
'	Single quote	\'
"	Double quote	\"

Figure 2.5 **C** escape sequences.

You will find it much easier to remember and use a linefeed represented as **'\n'** instead of **'\102'**. It is also code independent and thus the preferred method.

Whenever the **scanf()** or **printf()** functions are used for entering or printing character data, the conversion specifier **%c** specifies that the data are of type character. For example, the letter *A* is printed as

```
printf("%c", 'A');
```

String Data

A collection of characters contained within double quotation marks (") is defined as a *character string* or simply a *string*. Thus the sentence "This is my first C program." is a string. The string includes all the characters within the double quotes but not the quote marks themselves. In **C**, strings are of type **char**. Since a character is stored in 1 byte of memory, an array or collection of type **char** is needed to contain a string. We will defer further discussion of strings until Chapter 5.

Integer Data

Integer data are 2 or 4 bytes long in most versions of **C**. On larger systems, they will usually be 4 bytes long. The variations of type **int** are **short**, **unsigned**, and **long**. **Short** is either the same or half the length of **int**, and **long** is usually twice its length. On some systems, **long** may be the same size as **int**. Your compiler or interpreter reference manual will define the exact size of these types for the **C** you are using. The examples in this text assume that **short**, **int**, and **unsigned** are 2 bytes long and that **long** is 4 bytes long.

Integer constants can be expressed in decimal, octal, or hexadecimal form. We can also specify an integer constant as being **long**. Figure 2.6 is a program that

```
/* four common ways to express integer constants */
#include <stdio.h>
main()
    {
    int i1, i2, i3;
    long i4;

    i1 = 100;                                   /* decimal */
    i2 = 0100;                                  /* octal */
    i3 = 0x100;                                 /* hex */
    i4 = 1234567890L;                           /* long */
    printf("%d %d %d %ld", i1, i2, i3, i4);
    }
```

```
100 64 256 1234567890
```

Figure 2.6 Integer constants.

defines the number 100 as being a decimal, octal, and hex constant. It then prints the decimal equivalent of each number. It also defines the number 1234567890 as a **long** integer and prints its value in decimal.

Notice that an integer constant beginning with a nonzero digit is assumed to be decimal. If it begins with zero, it is octal. If it begins with 0x or 0X, it is hexadecimal. An integer constant ending with **l** or **L** is defined as **long**.

The output of this program is a series of numbers, all of which are expressed in decimal form. From this we can see that a decimal 64 equals an octal 100 and that a decimal 256 equals a hexadecimal 100.

The conversion specifier for type **long** is **%ld** or **%Ld**. If the **l** is omitted, then any integer longer than type **int** will not be printed correctly. Also, if an attempt is made to express a constant such as 1234567890 without using the **l** or **L** suffix, an *overflow* error will occur.

Float and Double Data

Floating-point numbers can be represented in either decimal or exponential format. In either form, you must include the decimal point. Therefore, a number like 1 million is written in floating point as either 1000000.0 or 1.0e6. No spaces are allowed on either side of the **e** in the exponential form. A capital may be used to express the number as 1.0E6.

You cannot use commas in representing a floating-point number (or any number for that matter). Thus 1,000,000.0 is illegal. You may include a sign in the exponent of the exponential form. One-millionth is written as 0.000001 or 1.0e-6. The range on the exponent is usually ± 38, and fractional exponents are not allowed.

As you can see, very small or large numbers are more conveniently expressed in exponential notation. Your choice of decimal or exponential form for computation does not restrict the form of the program output. The conversion specifiers dictate how the output will be expressed. *Caution*! If you specify that an output is to be **float** and the number is too small to be expressed as a 6- or 7-digit number following the decimal point, an erroneous output will appear. Thus, if we try to output the number 1.0e-10 with the statement

```
printf("%f",1.0e-10)
```

a value of zero will be printed. You must know beforehand if a potential problem will occur.

A floating-point constant is stored as a double-precision number. All floating-point computations in **C** are done in double precision. The output will normally have six or seven decimal places and as many digits before the decimal point as are needed to express the number. Chapter 5 will introduce *conversion format modifiers* that permit more precise control over the output.

Symbolic Constants

Wherever a constant appears within a program, we have the choice of printing the actual value of the constant or representing it symbolically. For example, the expression 2*3.1415927 can be written as 2*pi provided that the variable **pi** has been previously declared and initialized to 3.1415927. A better way to represent constants symbolically uses the **C** preprocessor directive *#define*. Thus, we can write

```
#define PI 3.1415927
```

at the beginning of our program, before **main()**, and then express the quantity 2*3.1415927 as 2*PI wherever it is needed. The advantage of using the #define directive is that the preprocessor will substitute the value of PI before the program is actually compiled. Using the variable **pi** will force substitution to occur during program execution, a time-consuming operation.

The use of symbolic constants makes a program easier to comprehend. For example, if you encountered the number 80 within an equation, its significance may not be obvious. However, if you encountered a preprocessor directive written as

```
#define MAX_COLS 80 /* maximum number of columns */
```

and then **MAX_COLS** within the equation, the meaning would be clearer.

Another advantage of using symbolic constants is that we can alter the value of the constant by changing only the #define. If the actual constant is used throughout a program, we would have to change each occurrence. Thus #define **MAX_COLS** 40 automatically changes the value used for each occurrence of **MAX_COLS** to 40.

2.3 ARITHMETIC OPERATORS

The arithmetic operators used in C are

+	addition
−	subtraction
*	multiplication
/	division
%	modulus

We have already encountered the +, −, *, and / operators in previous examples. The *modulus* operator is used to obtain the remainder of an integer division operation. For example, 20%8 equals 4, since the remainder of 20 divided by 8 is 4.

All these operators belong to a group referred to as *binary operators* because they have two operands. Operators that have only one operand are referred to as *unary operators*. The minus (−) sign, used to change the sign of a term, is an example of a unary operator.

Whenever an expression contains more than one operator, care must be taken to ensure that the expression is being evaluated in the proper order. The expression 12 + 6/3 equals 14, not 6. Why? The division operator is defined as having a higher priority than the addition operator. Therefore, 6/3 yields 2. This result added to 12 yields 14.

We can force the addition of 12 + 6 to occur first by placing these numbers within parentheses, since parentheses have the highest priority of all the operators in **C**. The expression would then yield 6. Figure 2.7 lists the arithmetic operators and the parentheses in the *order of precedence* in which they are evaluated. Entries occurring on the same line have equal priority. Operations of equal priority will be evaluated in a left to right order.

Priority	*Operator*	*Description*
1	()	Parentheses
2	−	Minus sign (unary)
3	* / %	Multiplication, division, modulus
4	+ −	Addition, subtraction

Figure 2.7 Order of precedence for arithmetic operators.

Assignment

The assignment operator in **C** is the equal (=) sign. When used in a statement like

$$y = 1;$$

it indicates that the variable **y** is being *assigned* a value of 1. The *associativity* of this operator is from right to left. In other words, the quantity on the right side is first evaluated, and its value is given to the variable on the left side. An expression may be placed on the right side, but not the left. Therefore,

```
y = x*x - 15   (valid)
```

is valid but

```
x*x - 15 = y   (invalid)
```

is not. In the first case, the expression x*x − 15 is evaluated and its value is given to **y**. In the second case, an expression was used in place of a variable on the left side.

Do not read the = sign as meaning "equal to." In **C**, a statement like

```
i = i + 1;
```

is perfectly valid. It says that the variable **i** is being assigned its original value plus 1. In algebra it would be incorrect, since **i** cannot equal $i + 1$.

2.4 RELATIONAL OPERATORS

The relational operators used in **C** are listed in Fig. 2.8. They are binary operators that test a relationship between two operands. The result of the test is either *true* or *false*. For example, if we test

```
(5 > 2)
```

the result is true, whereas

```
(2 > 5)
```

gives a false result.

Symbol	*Meaning*
<	Less than
<=	Less than or equal to
>	Greater than
>=	Greater than or equal to
==	Equal to
!=	Not equal to

Figure 2.8 Relational operators.

The relational operators are used with the **while** and **if else** statements to test a condition. In the **while** loop, a block of statements will be repeated as long as the test condition is true. For the **if else** statement, a decision is made to execute one or another block of statements based on the test condition.

To illustrate the use of rational operators, consider the following program segment.

```
/* use of relational operators */
i = 10
while (i>0)
  {
  printf("%d\n",i);
  i = i-1;
  }
```

As long as the test condition (i>0) is true, the statements within the braces following the **while** keyword will be repeated. In this example they will print the value of **i** and then decrement **i** by 1. The value of **i** starts at 10. On each pass through the loop, its value is decreased by 1. Finally, when **i** equals 0, the test condition will no longer be true and the loop execution will terminate. The output will include all integers from 10 to 1.

C will replace any true test condition with a 1 and any false condition with a 0. Therefore, the decision as to whether or not to repeat the loop is actually based on the result of the test being 1 or 0. Actually, **C** considers any nonzero result to be true. We could have therefore written the program segment as follows:

```
/* an alternate form */
i = 10;
while (i)
  {
  printf("%d\n",i);
  i = i-1;
  }
```

The test condition being used in this version is that **i** has a value different from 0. Initially, its value is 10. Therefore, the test condition is true, since **i** has a value that is nonzero. When the value of **i** is finally decremented to 0, the test condition will be false and the loop execution will terminate.

A common mistake for beginners is to mistakenly use the assignment operator (=) in place of the equality operator (==). What happens here can be illustrated by the following program segment:

```
x=1;
y=2;
if (x=y)
  printf ("x equals y\n");
else
  prinf ("x does not equal y\n");
```

The value of **y** is mistakenly *assigned* to **x** by x=y, producing a result of 2 from the test, which is a true condition. Therefore, the statement "x equals y" is erroneously printed, since 2 does not equal 1. The correct form for the test condition would be (x == y), which *compares* **x** to **y**. This test would produce a false or 0 result, which would print the correct output of "x does not equal y."

The order of precedence for the relational operators is shown in Fig. 2.9. They are divided into two groups. The <, <=, >, and >= operators have an equal priority, which is higher than that for the == and != operators.

All the relational operators have a *lower* priority than the arithmetic operators and a *higher* priority than the assignment operator. This permits abbreviated and sometimes difficult to discern test conditions. For example,

Priority	*Operators*
1	<, <=, >, >=
2	==, !=

Figure 2.9 Order of precedence for relational operators.

```
z == (y-1)
```

can be written as

```
z == y-1
```

since the equality operator has a lower priority than the arithmetic subraction operator. In both cases, we are testing to see if **z** is equal to **y−1**.

Another example is

```
result = x*x == y
```

which is the same as

```
result = (x*x == y)
```

Here, the assignment operator has a lower priority than the equality operator. Therefore, the parentheses are redundant, except for clarity. The value of **result** in either case is the true or false (1 or 0) outcome of the equality test **x*x == y**. If **x*x** equals **y**, then **result** will be true; otherwise, **result** will be false.

The relational operators have a left to right associativity. Therefore, the test

```
x == y != z
```

tests to see if **x** equals **y** first. The result of that test, true or false, is then compared to **z** for inequality. Thus, if **x** and **y** are true and **z** is false, the result of the test will be true.

If you're not too sure about the operation of a test like the one just presented, try it out on the computer. A test of the outcome of (x == y != z) can be easily implemented as shown in Fig. 2.10.

```
/* Test of x == y != z */
#include <stdio.h>
main()
          {
          int x = 2, y = 2, z = 0;

          if (x == y != z)
                  printf("true\n");
          else
                  printf("false\n");
          }
```

Figure 2.10 Test of relational operators.

For the given values of x, y, and z, the output of the program will be "true". If the test is changed to ((x == y) != z), the same result will be obtained. Note that (x == (y != z)) would yield "false". Do you see why?

2.5 LOGICAL OPERATORS

The logical operators in **C** allow us to perform multiple tests within the **while** or **if else** statements. These operators are listed in Fig. 2.11 along with their relative priority ranking. The **not** operator (!) has a priority that is just below the parentheses and above the arithmetic operators. The other two logical operators, the **and** (&&) and **or** (¦¦), have a priority that is below the relational operators and above the assignment operator.

Priority	*Symbol*	*Logical operator*
1	!	Not
2	&&	And
3	¦¦	Or

Figure 2.11 Logical operators.

Suppose that we want two or more test conditions to be met simultaneously; then each of these conditions should be joined by the **and** operator as follows:

```
if (test_1 && test_2 && test_3 ...)
```

Likewise, if we want any one or any combination of a group of conditions to make a test true, then all the tests are joined by the **or** operator as follows:

```
if (test_1 ¦¦ test_2 ¦¦ test_3 ...)
```

Figure 2.12 illustrates the use of multiple test conditions. In this program, four **if** statements test various combinations of conditions for the values of **a** and **b**. The first test (a == 2 && b == 4) is true since both test conditions are true. In the second test, (a == 3 && b == 4) is not true, since **a** is not equal to 3. In the

```
/* multiple tests */
#include <stdio.h>
main()
     {
     int a = 2, b = 4;

     /* test 1 */
     if (a == 2 && b == 4)
          printf("(a == 2 && b == 4) is true\n");
     else
          printf("(a == 2 && b ==4) is not true");

     /* test 2 */
     if (a == 3 && b == 4)
          printf("(a == 3 && b == 4) is true\n");
     else
          printf("(a == 3 && b == 4) is not true\n");

     /* test 3 */
     if (a == 3 || b == 4)
          printf("(a == 3 || b == 4) is true\n");
     else
          printf("(a == 3 || b == 4) is not true\n");

     /* test 4 */
     if (a == 3 || b == 5)
          printf("(a == 3 || b == 5) is true\n");
     else
          printf("(a == 3 || b == 5) is not true");
     }
```

```
(a == 2 && b == 4) is true
(a == 3 && b == 4) is not true
(a == 3 || b == 4) is true
(a == 3 || b == 5) is not true
```

Figure 2.12 Multiple tests using the logical operators.

third test (a == 3 ¦ ¦ b == 4) is true, since one of the test conditions, b == 4, is true. For the last test, (a == 3 ¦ ¦ b == 5) is not true since neither test is true.

The **not** operator preceding a test condition will make a true test condition false, and vice-versa. For example, if **a** is true, then **!a** is false. Likewise, if **a** is false, then **!a** is true.

2.6 INCREMENT AND DECREMENT OPERATORS

The increment (++) and decrement (−−) operators provide a shorthand notation for incrementing or decrementing the value of a variable. Thus, we can replace **i** = **i+1** with **i++** or **i** = **i−1** with **i−−**. Use of the increment or decrement operators is preferred, since it is more compact and also speeds up execution of the program. The priority of these operators is just below the parentheses.

The increment or decrement operators may be placed before or after the variable. When placed before the variable, they are referred to as *prefix* operators. If they occur after the variable, they are called *postfix* operators.

A prefixed increment or decrement will cause the variable to be incremented or decremented before its value is used. Postfixing will cause the value of the variable to be used before it is changed. Therefore,

```
x = 1;
y = ++x;
```

will produce a final value of 2 for **x** and **y**, whereas

```
x = 1;
y = x++;
```

will produce a final value of 2 for **x** and 1 for **y**.

Let's see how the decrement operator behaves in a **while** loop. Our program segment for printing all values of **i** while i > 0 is repeated here for reference.

```
/* decrement using i = i-1 */
i = 10;
while (i>0)
  {
  printf("%d\n",i);
  i = i-1;
  }
```

Using the decrement operator to replace the statement i = i−1, we get

```
/* decrement using i-- */
i = 10;
while (i>0)
  {
  printf("%d\n",i);
  i--;
  }
```

The output of both program segments will be identical. However, the latter form will execute faster. We could have used the prefix decrement operator in place of the postfix operator in this case without affecting the program. *Caution*! This is not always the case, as we will see in the next example.

Figure 2.13 shows a program that performs the decrement operation inside the while test condition. The output of this program is identical to that of the two previous programs. Notice that the initial value of **i** has been changed to 11. This is necessary because the decrement operation occurs before the first **printf()** statement.

What happens to the program output if the postfix decrement operator is used in place of the prefix operator? In that case, **i** will be decremented after the test condition is applied. Therefore, when **i** equals 1, the test condition will still be

```
/* using --i inside the test condition */
#include <stdio.h>
main()
      {
      int i = 11;

      while (--i > 0)
            printf("%d\n", i);
      }
```

Figure 2.13 Using prefixed decrement in a test condition.

true and the **printf** statement will be executed. However, since **i** is decremented after the test and before execution of the loop, the program will print 0 as the last value instead of 1. Test this program yourself using both prefix and postfix operators to see the difference in output.

2.7 ADVANCED OPERATOR TOPICS

Bitwise Logical Operators

The bitwise logical operators perform bit manipulation on integer or character data. They are listed in Fig. 2.14 along with a description of their action.

Symbol	*Operation*
&	AND
¦	OR
^	Exclusive OR
<<	Shift left
>>	Shift right
~	One's complement

Figure 2.14 Bitwise logical operators.

To visualize what is happening to the data as a result of these bitwise operations, it is best to convert the numbers from decimal to binary and carry out the operation in binary form. The result can then be converted back to decimal for comparison to the output that **C** will produce.

Bitwise AND

The statement

```
printf("%d",67 & 63);
```

will output the number 3. How does this make sense? By converting 67 and 63 into binary and performing the logical AND (&) operation on a bit by bit basis, we see what happens.

$$
\begin{aligned}
67_{10} = 43_{16} &= 01000011_2 \\
63_{10} = 3F_{16} &= \underline{00111111}_2 \\
67 \text{ and } 63 &= 01111111 \quad \text{which equals 3 in decimal}
\end{aligned}
$$

Bitwise OR

Likewise, the statement

```
printf("%d",67 ¦ 63);
```

will output the number 127. Converting each of the operands into binary and performing the bitwise or (¦) operation, we get

$$
\begin{aligned}
67_{10} = 43_{16} &= 01000011_2 \\
63_{10} = 3F_{16} &= \underline{00111111}_2 \\
67 \mid 63 &= 01111111 \quad \text{which equals 127 in decimal}
\end{aligned}
$$

Utilizing the bitwise logical operators, we can *selectively set* one or more bits in a binary number to 1 by a process called *OR masking*. A mask is a special bit pattern used to operate on another number. In general, to force any bit position within a number to a 1, we OR that number with a mask having 1's only in the positions to be affected. For example, to force the three least significant bits of a number to the 1 state, we can OR that number with a mask having a value of 7. To force the most significant bit of an 8-bit number to 1, we would OR that number with 128.

We can *selectively clear* bits from a number by using *AND masking*. Here, we AND the number with a mask taht has 0's in all the positions to be forced to 0. All the other bit positions in the mask contain 1's.

Bitwise Complement

The unary operator ~ will perform a 1's complement operation on an integer number. The statement

```
printf("%u",~128 & 255);
```

will print the number 127. The & 255 is an AND mask that restricts the output to 8 bits. To check the effect of the complement operation, we observe that 128 in binary equals 10000000. Inverting all the bits gives 01111111, which equals 127. Without the AND mask, the output would be 65407 (assuming unsigned numbers are 2 bytes long). Why?

Bitwise Exclusive OR

The exclusive OR operator (^) will produce a 1 in each bit position where the two operands differ. For example, the statement

```
printf("%d", 9 ^ 5);
```

will output a 12. To see how this happens, we write the two operands in binary and perform the exclusive OR operation on each bit position.

```
    9 = 00001001
    5 = 00000101
        --------
9 ^ 5 = 00001100 which is 12 in decimal
```

Bitwise Shift Operators

The left shift operator (<<) will perform a shift of the left-side operand by a number of bit positions specified by the right-side operand. For example, 1 << 3 will shift the number 1 three positions to the left. Zeros will be added to the right side in the process. Thus, the number that results from this operation is equal to 8. Notice that this is equivalent to multiplying the left operand by 2 raised to a power equal to the right operand.

The shift right operator (>>) will perform a similar shift operation, moving bits toward the right. For unsigned numbers, zeros will be added from the left side to fill in.

The program of Figure 2.15 illustrates the use of the bitwise logical operators by producing truth tables for **a & b**, **a ¦ b**, and **a ^ b**.

```
/* truth tables */
#include <stdio.h>
main()
	{
	int a, b;

	printf("a\tb\ta & b\ta | b\ta ^ b\n\n");
	a = 0;
	b = 0;
	printf("%d\t%d\t%d\t%d\t%d\n", a, b, a & b, a | b, a ^ b);
	b = 1;
	printf("%d\t%d\t%d\t%d\t%d\n", a, b, a & b, a | b, a ^ b);
	a = 1;
	b = 0;
	printf("%d\t%d\t%d\t%d\t%d\n", a, b, a & b, a | b, a ^ b);
	b = 1;
	printf("%d\t%d\t%d\t%d\t%d\n", a, b, a & b, a | b, a ^ b);
	}
```

a	b	a & b	a | b	a ^ b
0	0	0	0	0
0	1	0	1	1
1	0	0	1	1
1	1	1	1	0

Figure 2.15 Truth tables using bitwise logical operators.

Conditional Expression Operator

The **if else** was introduced in Chapter 1. Its format is

```
if (expression_1)
  expression_2;
else
  expression_3;
```

where **expression_1** is a test condition. If **expression_1** is true, then **expression_2** is executed; otherwise, **expression_3** is executed. A shorthand method of implementing the preceding is given by the *conditional expression* operator (?:). It has the format

```
expression_1 ? expression_2 : expression_3
```

where the ? and : are separators for the three expressions. Again, if **expression_1** is true, then **expression_2** is executed; otherwise, **expression_3** is executed. The conditional expression operator is also called a *ternary* operator since it has three operands.

To illustrate the use of this operator, consider the following statement for finding the absolute value of **a**.

```
a = (a < 0) ? -a : a;
```

The assignment made to **a** will be determined by the conditional expression. Here, **a < 0** is **expression_1**. If it is true, then **a** is assigned a value of **−a**, making it positive. If **a < 0** is false, it is assigned a value of **a**. This statement can be replaced by an **if else** statement as follows:

```
if (a < 0)
  a = -a;
else
  a = a;
```

You can see that the conditional expression is a much more compact way of representing this relationship. This operator can also be used in places where the **if else** cannot. The program of Fig. 2.16 accepts an integer from the keyboard and prints the word false if the number is 0; otherwise, it prints the word true. The conditional expression operator is used within the **printf()** statement to test the input and return one of the strings "true" or "false". The returned value then becomes the argument of the **printf()** statement.

```
/* use of conditional expression */
#include <stdio.h>
main()
      {
      int i;

      printf("? ");
      scanf("%d",&i);
      printf("%s", i ?"true" :"false");
      }
```

```
? 1
true
```

Figure 2.16 Use of the conditional expression.

Assignment Shorthand

The increment and decrement operators encountered in Section 2.6 represented a shorthand form for adding or subtracting 1 from the value of a variable. They provided both compact representation and faster execution speed. Another shorthand technique is provided by the combination of a binary operator and the assignment operator. The resulting compound has the same priority as the assignment operator itself. For example, the binary operator +, representing simple addition, can be combined with the assignment operator (=) to produce the += operator. Used in a statement such as

```
i += 10;
```

it means that **i** is incremented by 10 and is equivalent to

```
i = i + 10;
```

We can use the −= combination as follows:

```
i -= 10;
```

in place of the equivalent form

```
i = i - 10;
```

In fact, any of the compound operators in Fig. 2.17 can be used in a statement. The term **a** in this figure may represent a constant, a variable, or an expression. For example, we can write

```
x *= y-1
```

to mean

```
x = x*(y-1)
```

Compound Operator	*Operation*	*Example*	*Equivalent to*
+=	Plus equals	x += a	x = x + a
-=	Minus equals	x -= a	x = x - a
*=	Times equals	x *= a	x = x*a
/=	Divide equals	x /= a	x = x/a
%=	Modulus equals	x %= a	x = x % a
<<=	Left shift equals	x <<= a	x = x << a
>>=	Right shift equals	x >>= a	x = x >> a
&=	Bitwise and equals	x &= a	x = x & a
^=	Bitwise exclusive OR equals	x ^= a	x = x ^ a
¦=	Bitwise or equals	x ¦= a	x = x ¦ a

Figure 2.17 Assignment shorthand combinations.

2.8 TYPE CONVERSIONS AND CAST

Type Conversion

Normally, expressions involve the same data type throughout. Some languages, such as Pascal, insist on this. **C** will permit a limited mixing of data types and handles them according to a fixed set of rules. In general, any binary operator having two types of operands will *promote* the *lower* type to the *higher* type. The result will have the higher type. The ranking of data types from lowest to highest is

Character
Short
Unsigned short
Integer
Unsigned integer
Long
Unsigned long
Float
Double

To illustrate the *promotion* process, assume **ch** is of type **char** and **i** is of type **int**, and **sum** is of type **char**. The statement

```
sum = ch + i;
```

would promote **ch** to integer data, perform the addition, and make the result an integer data type. But **sum** is of type character! In any assignment operation, **C** will convert the evaluation of the right side into the data type of the variable on the left. In this case, a *demotion* takes place, since the integer result on the right is converted into character data. There is no danger in the promotion process, but a demotion produces problems if the data will not fit the lower type. In this example, if the integer result on the right had a value greater than 255, it would not fit into the **char** data type for **sum**.

The program of Fig. 2.18 illustrates the promotion and demotion of data types. The character entered from the keyboard is assigned to a variable that is of type **int** by the line

```
i = ch;
```

The integer **i** now has a value equal to that of character **ch**. Likewise, the **float** variable **f** takes on the same value from the line

```
f = ch;
```

The first **printf()** statement prints the value of the **int** and **float** forms of the input character. This shows that the promotion process took place without any problems. The second **printf()** statement converts **i** to type **char** and prints the result. However, the attempt to convert **f** to type **char** fails.

```
/* promotion and demotion */
#include <stdio.h>
main()
     {
     float f;
     int i;
     char ch;

     printf("Enter a letter\n");
     scanf("%c", &ch);
     i = ch;
     f = ch;
     printf("%d %f\n", i, f);
     printf("%c %c\n", i, f);
     }
```

```
Enter a letter
a
97 97.000000
a
```

Figure 2.18 Promotion and demotion of data types.

Cast Operator

The *cast* operator is used to force a type conversion. It has the form

```
(type) expression
```

For example, to convert **ch** from character to integer type, we can write

```
(int) ch
```

In the program of Fig. 2.18, the conversion from **float** to **char** in the last **printf()** statement can be made to work by using the cast operator as follows:

```
printf("%c %c\n",i,(char) f);
```

2.9 SUMMARY OF OPERATOR PRECEDENCE

The order of precedence for each of the operator types discussed has been presented in this chapter. Here we can look at all the operators and see exactly where any given operator lies in term of its precedence. The table of Fig. 2.19 lists all the **C** operators along with their name, precedence, and associativity. All operators having the same precedence number share an equal precedence. The highest precedence starts at the top of the table.

Precedence	*Name*	*Symbol*	*Associativity*
1	Parentheses	`() []`	L to R
1	Structure access	`-> .`	L to R
2	Unary (see Fig. 2.20)	`! ~ ++ -- -`	R to L
2		`(type) * & sizeof`	R to L
3	Multiply, divide, modulus	`* / %`	L to R
4	Add, subtract	`+ -`	L to R
5	Shift left, shift right	`<< >>`	L to R
6	Less than, less than or equal	`< <=`	L to R
6	Greater than, greater than or equal	`> >=`	L to R
7	Equal, not equal	`== !=`	L to R
8	Bitwise AND	`&`	L to R
9	Bitwise exclusive OR	`^`	L to R
10	Bitwise OR	`¦`	L to R
11	Logical AND	`&&`	L to R
12	Logical OR	`¦¦`	L to R
13	Conditional expression	`? :`	R to L
14	Assignment	`= += -= *= /= %=`	R to L
14		`>>= <<= &= ^= ¦=`	R to L
15	Comma	`,`	L to R

Figure 2.19 Operator precedence.

We have not yet discussed some of the operators listed. Those unmentioned to this point will be covered in later chapters. The unary operators are listed along with their names in Fig. 2.20 for the purpose of identification.

Name	*Operator*
Unary negative	!
One's Complement	~
Increment	++
Decrement	--
Unary minus	-
Cast	(type)
Indirection	*
Address of	&
Size of	sizeof

Figure 2.20 Unary operators and their names.

QUESTIONS

2.1. Define the terms bit, nibble, and byte. What is the size, in bits, of a nibble or byte?

2.2. What is the ASCII code? What is it used for?

2.3. Describe the data types **char**, **int**, **unsigned**, **long**, **float**, and **double**.

2.4. What is a character string?

2.5. What is a symbolic constant?

2.6. Describe the situation where **C** will *promote* a data type.

2.7. When will **C** *demote* a data type? Under what conditions might a problem arise in demotion? How can the problem be resolved?

2.8. What is the largest number that can be stored in a type **char**?

PROBLEMS

2.1. Write a **printf()** statement using the appropriate conversion specifier to output the value of each of the following variables:
(a) **char** alpha;
(b) **int** digit;
(c) **long** big_num;
(d) **unsigned** date;
(e) **float** pi;
(f) **double** gnp;
(h) **int** hex; (output in base 16)
(i) **int** octal; (output in base 8)
(j) **double** mass_e; (output in exponential form)

2.2. Express the number 200 as a hexadecimal constant.

2.3. Express the number 450000000 as a **long** constant.

2.4. Define the value of **TWO_PI** (6.283185307) as a symbolic constant.

2.5. Evaluate the following **int** expressions applying the rules of operator precedence:
(a) `1+5/2`
(b) `10/3*9`
(c) `(2+6)/(4+12)`
(d) `10+16%3`
(e) `48%10/2`

2.6. Which of the following relational tests are true?

(a) `(1 !=2)`

(b) `(8 <= 10)`

(c) `((a = 2*2) == 2)`

(d) `(x = (1+1) == 2)`

2.7. What is printed by the following program segment?

```
int x = 5;
int y = 10;

printf("%d\n",x++);
printf("%d\n",++y);
```

2.8. What is output from the following bitwise operations?

(a) `printf("%x\n", 0xFF >> 1);`

(b) `printf("%x\n", 7 | 15);`

(c) `printf("%x\n", 7 ^ 15);`

(d) `printf("%x\n", 0x3F & 0xAA);`

chapter 3

Loop Control and Selection

3.1 WHILE AND DO WHILE

While

The **while** statement, introduced in Chapter 1, is used to force repetition of a statement or block of statements while some condition is true. The format of the while statement is

```
while (condition)
    {
    statement;
    .
    .
    .
    }
```

where *condition* is a test condition that must be *true* in order to execute the statement or block of statements contained within the braces that follow. If the *condition* is *not true,* the program exits the **while** loop. As long as the *condition* is *true,* the statements contained within this loop will be repeated. If there is only one statement within the **while** loop, the braces are not needed.

The test condition normally makes use of the relational operators. If multiple test conditions must be met, then the logical operators will also be used. Figure 3.1 illustrates the use of the **while** statement.

The programs of Fig. 3.1(a) and (b) print the value of the integer **i** as long as the test condition **i** < **9** is true. Notice that the output of the program in Fig. 3.1(a) prints the numbers 1 through 8, while that of Fig. 3.1(b) prints the numbers 1 through 9. This is due to the fact that the first program uses the prefixed increment operator, while the second uses the postfixed increment operator. With the pre-

```
/* prefixed increment while loop */
#include <stdio.h>
main()
        {
        int i = 0;

        while (++i < 9)
                printf("%d", i);
        }
```

```
12345678
```

(a)

```
/* postfixed increment while loop */
#include <stdio.h>
main()
        {
        int i = 0;

        while (i++ < 9)
                printf("%d", i);
        }
```

```
123456789
```

(b)

Figure 3.1 **While** loop.

fixed increment operator, the increment is performed before testing for **i** < **9**. Thus, after the value of 8 is printed and the next increment occurs, the test condition is false and the program exits the **while** loop.

With the postfixed increment of Fig. 3.1(b), after the value of 8 is printed the test condition is true. The value of **i** is then incremented to 9 and printed. On the next pass, the test condition will be false, thus ending execution of the loop.

When using **while** loops that do something for a certain range of values of a variable, you must include a means of incrementing or decrementing the variable so that it will proceed from one limit to the other. Otherwise, the loop will execute indefinitely with a fixed value of the variable. Figure 3.2(a) illustrates a **while** loop whose execution never ends, since the value of **i** is not decremented. In Fig. 3.2(b), provision is added for proper decrementing of **i**. Notice that the test condition (i) will be true as long as **i** has a nonzero value.

Do While

The **while** loop tests a condition before execution of the statement(s) contained within. Sometimes it is desirable to cause execution of a block of statements first and test for some condition at the end of the block. The **do while** statement is provided in **C** to handle this situation. It has the format

```
do  {
    statement;
    .
    .
    .
    }
while (condition);
```

```
/* endless while loop */
#include <stdio.h>
main()
        {
        int i = 9;

        while (i)
                printf("%d",i);
        }
```

```
99999999999999999999...(forever)
```

(a)

```
/* a while loop that terminates */
#include <stdio.h>
main()
        {
        int i = 9;

        while (i--)
                printf("%d",i);
        }
```

```
876543210
```

(b)

Figure 3.2 Endless and finite **while** loops.

The program of Fig. 3.2(b) is modified to use a **do while** loop in Fig. 3.3 to illustrate the difference between the two methods of implementing a loop. Notice that the output of the **do while** loop starts with 9, whereas the **while** loop output starts with 8. This is due to the fact that the test condition in a **do while** occurs at the end of the loop, and the decrementing of **i** is contained within the test condition.

You must be careful not to misinterpret the **while** keyword at the end of a **do while** loop as being the beginning of a **while** loop. Any **while** keyword that is not followed by a block of indented statements should be suspect as being the end of a

```
/* do while */
#include <stdio.h>
main()
        {
        int i = 9;

        do      {
                printf("%d", i);
                }
        while (i--);
        }
```

```
9876543210
```

Figure 3.3 **Do while** loop.

do while loop. Further examination of the preceding code will clearly identify the use of the **while** statement.

An important difference between the **while** and **do while** is that the **do while** must be executed as least once. This fact makes the **while** loop more desirable in the majority of situations.

3.2 FOR

The **for** loop in **C** provides an alternative method to the **while** loop for controlling repetitive execution. Although it is slightly more complex, it also offers more versatility. In fact, **for** loops in **C** are much more versatile than their counterparts in BASIC or Pascal. The format of the **for** statement is

```
for (initialize variable(s); test condition(s);increment/decrement variable(s))
    {
    statement;
    .
    .
    .
    }
```

The semicolons inside the **for** statement's parentheses are required as separators. However, all the other entries within the parentheses are optional. The simplest form of the **for** statement is therefore

```
for ( ; ; )
    {
    statement;
    .
    .
    .
    }
```

In this case, there is no initialization, no test condition, and no increment or decrement. Therefore, the loop continues indefinitely unless terminated by some statement contained within the loop.

Using For in Place of While

The **for** loop may be a simple alternative to the **while** loop. For example,

```
/* simple for loop */
for (i = 0;i < 10; i++)
    printf("%d",i);
```

is equivalent to the **while** loop

```
/* equivalent while loop */
i = 0;
while (i < 10)
    {
    printf("%d",i);
    i++;
    }
```

Notice that the **for** loop was written more concisely than its **while** equivalent. The **while** loop requires initialization of the variable **i** within its declaration or in a separate statement preceding the loop. It also uses a separate line for incrementing the value of **i** after the **printf()** statement. If an attempt is made to increment **i** within the test condition, such as

```
while (i++ <10)
```

or

```
while (++i < 10)
```

the first value printed would be one more than the initialized value. In the **for** loop, the initialized value of **i** is always the first to be used.

For Loop Parameters

The **for** loop permits the use of multiple initializations, test conditions, or increment/decrement operations within the parentheses. The program of Fig. 3.4 uses multiple initializations for printing a table of powers of 2. The loop variable **p** takes on integer values that equal the power to which the number 2 will be raised. **p** takes on an initial value of 0 and increments up to the value of the variable **n**, which is entered from the keyboard. The value of **n** represents the largest power to which the number 2 will be raised. The variable **val** is defined by **val** = $\mathbf{2^p}$.

The initial values of **p** and **val** are 0 and 1, since $2^0 = 1$. Both of these variables are initialized within the **for** statement. The test condition, **p** <= **n**, says that the loop will continue to execute while **p** is less than or equal to the value of **n**.

```
/* powers of 2 */
#include <stdio.h>
main()
     {
     int n, p, val;

     printf("Enter the largest power to print: ");
     scanf("%d", &n);
     printf("power\tvalue");
     for (p=0, val=1; p <= n; p++)
          {
          printf("\n%d\t%d", p, val);
          val = val*2;
          }
     }
```

```
Enter the largest power to print: 7
power   value
0       1
1       2
2       4
3       8
4       16
5       32
6       64
7       128
```

Figure 3.4 **For** loop with multiple initializations.

The body of the loop prints the current value of **p** and **val**. It then determines the next value of **val** as being the current value multiplied by 2. At this point, **p** is incremented and the test condition is applied before the next pass through the loop. The order of the two statements in the body of the loop is important, since reversing them would print the current value of **p** with the next value of **val**. When **p** > **n**, the test condition fails and the program exists the **for** loop.

The test condition in the program of Fig. 3.4 tested the value of the loop variable **p**. We can use a test condition that is not directly or explicitly related to the loop variable. The program of Fig. 3.5 repeats the power of 2 table using a different test condition. Instead of entering the largest power to be used, we enter the largest value of a power of 2 to be printed. This number is assigned to the variable **n**. The test condition now becomes **val** <= **n**, which does not directly involve the loop variable **p**.

```
/* another powers of 2 */
#include <stdio.h>
main()
        {
        int n, p, val;

        printf("Enter the largest value to be printed: ");
        scanf("%d", &n);
        printf("power\tvalue");
        for (p=0, val = 1; val <= n; p++)
                {
                printf("\n%d\t%d", p, val);
                val = val*2;
                }
        }
```

Figure 3.5 **For** loop with test conditions not using the loop variable.

Nested Loops

When one **for** (or **while**) loop is contained within another, the loops are said to be nested. In this case, the inner loop will be executed completely for each pass through the outer loop. You can draw an analogy between the operation of nested loops and a clock or counter. The *seconds* hand on a clock measures or counts 60 seconds for each increment of the *minutes* hand. Likewise, the loop variable for the inner loop will go through a complete cycle, from starting to ending value, for each increment of the loop variable in the outer loop.

The program of Fig. 3.6(a) uses nested **for** loops to print a two-dimensional array of subscripted variables **x** and **y**. One line of output is generated for each complete execution of the inner or **x** loop. During this time, the value of **y** does not change. After each completion of the **x** loop, the value of **y** is incremented by 1. The last pass through the inner loop will occur for a **y** value of 4.

Each **printf()** output is terminated with a *tab* (**\t**) escape sequence to space the array entries. The *new line* (**\n**) escape sequence is printed after each completion of the inner loop to force the next output to be printed on the next line.

The program of Fig. 3.6(b) produces the same output as that of Fig. 3.6(a) using nested **while** loops. Notice that the inner loop variable, **x**, must be initialized within the outer loop and before the beginning of the inner loop. This is due to the fact that after each completion of the inner loop the value of **x** will be 4.

```
/* nested for loops */
#include <stdio.h>
main()
	{
	int x, y;

	for (y = 1;y <= 4; y++)
		{
		for (x = 1; x <= 3; x++)
			printf("y%dx%d\t", y, x);
		printf("\n");
		}
	}
```

```
y1x1	y1x2	y1x3
y2x1	y2x2	y2x3
y3x1	y3x2	y3x3
y4x1	y4x2	y4x3
```

(a)

```
/* nested while loops */
#include <stdio.h>
main()
	{
	int x, y;

	y = 1;
	while (y <= 4)
		{
		x = 1;
		while (x <= 3)
			{
			printf("y%dx%d\t", y, x);
			x++;
			}
		printf("\n");
		y++;
		}
	}
```

(b)

Figure 3.6 Nested loops: (a) nested **for** loop; (b) nested **while** loop.

3.3 LOOP TIMING

It is often desirable or necessary to know the execution time of a program segment, such as a **for** or **while** loop. This may arise from the need to produce a fixed time delay or perhaps to optimize a loop for minimum execution time. The use of integer data types within a loop will result in the fastest execution time. Float or double types, on the other hand, result in a much slower response, typically over 100 times slower than integer loops in **C**.

The program of Fig. 3.7(a) can be used for timing a **while** loop. The procedure used here is to have the program sound the bell (or speaker) once before the start of the loop and again at the end. A stopwatch can be used to determine elasped time. (You could modify the program to use the computer's real-time clock, if it has one.) If the loop time is too short to be measured during a single execution, as is the case here, we simply nest the loop inside another. The overall

```
/* time a while loop */
#include <stdio.h>
#define BELL   007
main()
     {
     int i, j = 0;

     printf("%c", BELL);
     while (j++ < 10)
          {
          i = 0;
          while (i++ < 30000)
               ;
          }
     printf("%c", BELL);
     }
```

(a)

```
/* time a for loop */
#include <stdio.h>
#define BELL   007
main()
     {
     int i, j = 0;

     printf("%c", BELL);
     while (j++ < 10)
          {
          for (i = 0; i < 30000; i++)
               ;
          }
     printf("%c", BELL);
     }
```

(b)

Figure 3.7 Loop timing: (a) timing a **while** loop; (b) timing a **for** loop.

execution time will then be a multiple of the desired time. The multiple will equal the number of passes through the outer loop.

The **#define** statement in Fig. 3.7(a) sets the value of **BELL** to **007**. Printing this character will produce a beep on most terminals or computers that have this capability. The outer or **j** loop will execute ten times. The inner loop will execute completely for each pass through the outer loop. For each value of **j**, the value of **i** will be incremented 30,000 times. After completion of the nested loops, the **BELL** character is printed again to mark the time interval.

A popular **C** compiler produces executable code from the program of Fig. 3.7(a) and runs in 6 seconds on the IBM Personal Computer. This means that each complete execution of the inner loop takes 0.6 seconds or that one pass through the inner loop takes 0.6/30000 or 2×10^{-5} second (20 microseconds).

An equivalent integer loop in IBM PC interpreted BASIC using the FOR NEXT statement runs in 24 seconds or 40 times slower than compiled **C**. Do not interpret this to mean that all BASIC programs run 40 times slower than **C** programs. Some BASIC statements actually execute faster than their **C** equivalent!

The program of Fig. 3.7(b) replaces the inner **while** loop of Fig. 3.7(a) with a **for** statement. The execution time using **for** is about equal to that using the **while** statement. Changing the data type for a loop or the method of incrementing the loop variable will have a significant effect on the execution time. You can experiment using this technique to measure the execution time of **C** statements or complete loops.

3.4 IF ELSE

The **if else** statement is used to choose between alternative actions within a program. It has the format

```
if (test condition)
   {
   statement;
   .
   .
   .
   }
else
   {
   statement;
   .
   .
   }
```

If the *test condition* is true, the statement(s) following the **if** will be executed. If the *test condition* is not true, the statement(s) following the **else** will be executed. When only one statement is present, the braces are not needed.

The **else** portion of the **if else** statement is optional. When the **else** is not used, a false result on the test condition for the **if** will result in no action being taken. For example,

```
if (a < b)
    printf("a < b");
```

will print **a < b** when the value of **a** is less than the value of **b**. If the value of **a** is greater than the value of **b**, then nothing will happen as a result of this statement.

Nesting of **if else** statements results in a construction referred to as **else if** or *multiway decision*. The following program segment illustrates multiway decision:

```
if (a < b)
     printf("a < b");
else if (a == b)
     printf("a == b");
else if (a > b)
     printf("a > b");
else
     printf("error");
```

Only one of the **printf()** statements will be executed. If the indicated test condition is true, the corresponding **printf()** will be executed; otherwise, the program flow moves to the next test condition. The last **else** is the default condition, which will be executed if none of the other conditions is true. It is sometimes used to trap errors or impossible situations. In our example, **a** must be less than, equal to, or greater than **b**. If none of the first three test conditions is true, clearly an error condition exists.

The general format for multiway decision is

```
if (test condition 1)
     statement_1;
else if (test condition 2)
     statement_2;
```

```
else if (test condition 3)
     statement_3;
.
.
.
else [if (test condition n)]
     statement_n;
```

where the test condition associated with the last else is optional. If the last test condition is excluded, then **statement_n** is always executed when none of the other test conditions is true.

If any of the **else**'s are missing in nested **if else** statements, an ambiguity results. For example, in the program segment

```
if (a > 0)
     if (a < 10)
          printf("a is greater than 0 and less than 10");
     else
          printf("a is greater than or equal to 10");
```

is the **else** associated with the second **if** or the first? The answer is the second. In general, an **else** is associated with the nearest preceding **if** unless indicated otherwise by the use of braces. The second **printf()** statement is therefore correct as it stands.

We can associate the **else** with the first **if** by adding braces as follows:

```
if (a > 0)
    {
    if (a < 10)
        printf("a is greater than 0 and less than 10");
    }
else
    printf("a is less than or equal to 0");
```

3.5 SWITCH

In the previous section, we saw how nested **if else** statements could be used for multiway selection. Although this construction could be used for any number of choices, a more convenient alternative exists for multiway decisions where the options are based on the evaluation of an integer expression. This is the **switch** statement. It has the format

```
switch (expression)
    {
     case constant1 :
          statement(s);
          break;
     case constant2 :
          statement(s);
          break;
     .
     .
     default :
          statement(s);
     }
```

where *expression* is an integer (or character) expression whose value is compared to the *constants* associated with each **case**. If there is a match, the statements following the **case** are executed. The last statement within each **case** is usually the **break**. It forces termination of the switch statement. If the last statement within a **case** is not a **break**, all the following cases will be executed unless another statement is encountered that will force termination of the **switch**.

The use of **default** is optional. It is normally used to trap errors. If *expression* does not match any of the choices, then **default** will be executed if it is present; otherwise, the **switch** execution will terminate.

The program of Fig. 3.8 illustrates the use of the **switch** statement. It is a simple calculator program that accepts a first operand, an operator, and a second operand. The switch is then used to decide whether to perform addition, subtraction, multiplication, or division based on the operator being +, −, *, or /. Notice that the argument of the switch, **operator,** is a character data type.

```
/* calculator program using switch */
#include <stdio.h>
main()
      {
      float x, y;
      char operator;

      printf("Enter x, operator, y: ");
      scanf("%f%c%f", &x, &operator, &y);
      switch (operator)
        {
        case '+':
            printf("%f plus %f equals %f", x, y, x+y);
            break;

        case '-':
            printf("%f minus %f equals %f", x, y, x-y);
            break;
        case '*':
            printf("%f times %f equals %f", x, y, x*y);
            break;
        case '/':
            printf("%f divide by %f equals %f", x, y, x/y);
            break;
        default:
            printf("Invalid operation");
        }
      }
```

```
Enter x, operator, y: 2+3
2.000000 plus 3.000000 equals 5.000000
```

Figure 3.8 Calculator program using switch.

The **scanf** statement is used to input both data values and the value of **operator**. The choices for the four **cases** are '+', '−', '*', and '/'. These are character constants that will be compared to the value of **operator**. If there is a match, that particular **case** will be executed. Since each **case** ends with a **break**, only one will be executed. Should the value of **operator** not match any of the **case** values, then **default** will be executed. This choice prints the message "Invalid operation."

When a particular **case** has been selected, the appropriate operation is performed. For example, if **operator** equals '+', the statement

```
printf("%f plus %f equals %f",x,y,x+y);
```

will be executed. The **switch** execution then terminates.

Program Menus Using Switch

The **switch** statement is often used to permit the selection of program options. A *menu* of choices is printed on the screen with a number or letter code assigned to each choice. The operator is then prompted to enter the code corresponding to his or her selection. The **switch** statement is used to compare the entered code value to all the available choices. If a match occurs, that particular selection is executed. Any program that uses menus for option selection is said to be *menu driven*.

The listing of Fig. 3.9 is a menu-driven program that offers the following options:

1. Find the square of a number
2. Find the cube of a number
3. Find the sum of squares of two numbers

These are relatively trivial options, but they serve to illustrate the use of menus. The sequence used in such a program is as follows:

1. Print the menu options.
2. Prompt the user to enter a selection.
3. Get the response.
4. Use the **switch** statement to call a function or series of functions that implement the selection.

The program uses numbers as the code values to identify each selection. The **switch** variable **select** will be assigned a value of 1, 2, or 3. We have the option of making **select** either a character or integer data type. It is made an integer type here. Therefore, all the **case** constants will be integer.

Case 1 corresponds to finding the square of a number. If **select** equals 1, a call is made to the function **square()**. This function accepts keyboard input of a number and prints the square of that number. The **return** statement at the end of the function transfers control back to the statement following the function call, which is **break**. Since no value is passed from the function to the main program, we could have omitted the **return** statement and achieved the same result.

The **break** statement ends execution of **switch**, and the program terminates upon reaching the closing brace of **main()**. A similar sequence occurs for the other menu selections, with the appropriate function being called on to implement a particular choice.

```
/* menu driven program using switch */
#include <stdio.h>
main()
      {
      char select;

      printf("1.  Find square of a number\n");
      printf("2.  Find cube of a number\n");
      printf("3.  Find sum of squares for two numbers\n\n");
      printf("Enter your selection: ");
      scanf("%c", &select);
      switch (select)
        {
        case '1':
            square();
            break;
        case '2':
            cube();
            break;
        case '3':
            sumofsqr();
            break;
        default:
            printf("Not a valid selection\n");
        }
      }

square()
      {
      int n;

      printf("Enter a number ");
      scanf("%d", &n);
      printf("The square of %d is %d", n, n*n);
      return;
      }

cube()
      {
      int n;

      printf("Enter a number ");
      scanf("%d", &n);
      printf("The cube of %d is %d", n, n*n*n);
      return;
      }

sumofsqr()
      {
      int x, y;

      printf("Enter two numbers ");
      scanf("%d%d", &x, &y);
      printf("The sum of squares of %d and %d is %d", x, y, x*x + y*y);
      return;
      }
```

```
1.  Find square of a number
2.  Find cube of a number
3.  Find sum of squares for two numbers

Enter your selection: 2
Enter a number 3
The cube of 3 is 27
```

Figure 3.9 Menu-driven program using switch.

3.6 BREAK AND CONTINUE

Break

The **break** statement is used for early termination of a **while**, **do while**, or **for** loop, as well as for exiting a **switch case**. It is used extensively with **switch**, as we have seen in the previous section. As a rule, you should avoid use of the **break** statement to exit a loop. However, there are times when its use makes the program more understandable.

A break can be used within nested structures. It will always force an exit from the loop in which it occurs to the next outer level or block. Execution will continue with the statement following the exited loop. **Break** cannot be used to exit a function.

In the following program segment, the **break** statement is used for early termination of a **for** loop.

```
for (i=0;i <= 20;i++)
    {
    if (i*i > 150)
        break;
    printf("%d\t%d\n",i,i*i);
    }
```

The **for** statement indicates that the loop will be executed for **i** ranging from 0 to 20. However, if the test condition within the **if** statement is true, a **break** will occur. For **i** = 13, **i*i** = 169, and the test condition is true. Therefore, the largest value of **i** for which its square will be printed is 12.

The use of break could have been easily avoided by incorporating the **if** test condition into the **for** test condition as follows:

```
for (i=0;i <=20 || (i*i) > 150;i++)
    printf("%d\t%d\n",i,i*i);
```

In fact, in almost every case we can avoid the use of **break** to terminate a loop. When should we use it? If combining the test condition for a **break** with that of the **for** statement makes the resulting test condition difficult to read, then keep the **break** within the loop. This will usually be advisable when there are a large number of test conditions or several operator types within the test conditions.

Continue

The **continue** statement causes termination of the current iteration of a loop. When this statement is encountered, the balance of the current pass through a loop is aborted. The next pass is then started if the loop *test conditions* are true. The continue statement is used only with **while**, **do while**, and **for**. As is the case with **break**, you should try to avoid the use of **continue** wherever it does not offer any advantage.

In the program of Fig. 3.10, **continue** is used to avoid a division by zero error. The same result can be achieved without the use of **continue**. This is left as an exercise for the reader.

```
/* use of continue */
#include <stdio.h>
main()
      {
      int a = 100, b = 4, c, d;

      for (c = 1; c <= 10; c++)
            {
            if (b-c == 0)
                  {
                  printf("skip c = %d to avoid division by zero\n", c);
                  continue;
                  }
            d = a/(b-c);
            printf("%d\t%d\n", c, d);
            }
      }
```

```
1       33
2       50
3       100
skip c = 4 to avoid division by zero
5       -100
6       -50
7       -33
8       -25
9       -20
10      -16
```

Figure 3.10 Use of continue.

3.7 GOTO

The **goto** statement is used for unconditional transfer of program control to a program line referenced by a *label*. The jump must be to a line within the same function. The beginning of the label must be the first character encountered on its logical line, and the label must end with a colon. The rules for naming the label are the same as those for variable names.

The use of **goto** in **C** is similar to its use in BASIC or FORTRAN. However, since **C** is a highly structured block language, a **goto** should seldom, if ever, be necessary. The problem with the **goto** statement is that it can make your program less structured and harder to follow.

A situation where a **goto** may offer an advantage is within a deeply nested function where it is necessary to escape to some outer level. This might be in response to a detected error condition. Using **break** will only permit escape to the next outer loop or block, whereas the **goto** will permit transfer to any location within the function.

The format of the **goto** is

```
        goto label;
        .
        .
        .
label:  statement;
```

where **label:** may be anywhere within the same function. The following program segment illustrates the use of **goto**.

```
        while (x)
            {
            while (y)
                {
                if (error)
                    goto fix;
                .
                .
                .
                }
            }
    fix:
        /* error processing routine */
```

PROBLEMS

3.1. What is the output of the following program?

```
#include <stdio.h>
main()
    {
    int low = 0;
    int high = 10;
    int collect = 0;

    while (low < high)
          {
          collect= collect + low;
          low++;
          }
    printf("%d\n",collect);
    }
```

3.2. What is the output of the following program?

```
#include <stdio.h>
main()
    {
    int i;
    int x = 1;

    for (i = 0;i < 5;i++)
          x *= 2;
    printf("%d\n",x);
    }
```

3.3. What is the output of the following program?

```
#include <stdio.h>
main()
    {
    int i,j;
```

```
for (i=1;i<5;i++)
      {
      for (j=1;j<4;j++)
            printf("%d\t",i*j);
      printf("n\n");
      }
}
```

3.4. Write a program that produces the following output. Use a **for** or **while** loop to produce each horizontal row of asterisks.

```
**************************************************
*                                                *
*                                                *
**************************************************
```

3.5. Write a program that accepts an integer input from the keyboard and tests to see if that number is less than or greater than zero. It should output the value of the number followed by the message "is less than zero" for the first case or "is greater than zero" for the second.

3.6. Modify the calculator program of Fig. 3.8 to include a modulus operation. A typical input would be "15%4," for which the output should be "15 modulus 4 = 3."

chapter 4

Using the Math Library

4.1 INTRODUCTION

The **C** language *math library*, like the *I/O library*, is not a part of the language proper but is included in the *standard library*. What this really means is that the formal definition of the **C** language does not consider either the math or I/O functions. However, the math and I/O libraries that were developed for **C** have become a de facto standard for use with the language. The ANSI standard for **C** has also standardized these libraries. A quick look into your **C** compiler or interpreter manual will tell you if these libraries are included.

Figure 4.1 lists the most common **C** math library functions and gives a brief description of their purpose. They are classified into groups including arithmetic, trigonometric, logarithmic, and random-number functions. We will consider each group separately. The arguments for the functions and the numbers that the functions return are all double precision.

Many implementations of **C** require the inclusion of a math header file, usually called "math.h". This file declares all the math functions as being of type **double**. All the programs in this text that make use of the math library will have the line

```
#include <math.h>
```

as a preprocessor directive for including the math header.

All the functions in Fig. 4.1 accept an *argument,* the quantity within the parentheses. The functions will compute a result and pass it back to the user. The value that is passed back is said to be *returned.* Both the argument and the returned value for these functions are of type **double**. You must declare the argument as **double** before calling the function. The returned result is normally assigned to a variable that is also **double**.

Group	Math function	Description
Arithmetic	`ceil(x)`	Returns the nearest whole number above *x*
	`fabs(x)`	Returns the absolute value of *x*
	`floor(x)`	Returns the nearest whole number below *x*
	`pow(x,y)`	Returns *x* raised to the *y* power
	`sqrt(x)`	Returns the square root of *x*
Trigonometric	`acos(x)`	Returns the arc cosine of *x*
	`asin(x)`	Returns the arc sine of *x*
	`atan(x)`	Returns the arc tangent of *x*
	`atan2(y,x)`	Returns the arc tangent of *y*/*x*
	`cos(x)`	Returns the cosine of *x*
	`cosh(x)`	Returns the hyperbolic cosine of *x*
	`sin(x)`	Returns the sine of *x*
	`sinh(x)`	Returns the hyperbolic sine of *x*
	`tan(x)`	Returns the tangent of *x*
	`tanh(x)`	Returns the hyperbolic tangent of *x*
Logarithmic	`exp(x)`	Returns the value of the exponential e^x
	`log(x)`	Returns the value of the natural logarithm ln (*x*)
	`log10(x)`	Returns the value of the common logarithm log(x)
Random number	`frand(x)`	Returns a pseudo random number between 0.0 and 1.0
	`rand(x)`	Returns a pseudo random whole number
	`srand(x)`	Reseeds the random generator with a value of x

Figure 4.1 Math library in **C**.

4.2 ROUNDING OFF

The math function **floor(x)** will return the nearest whole number below the value of the argument **x**. For example, the program segment

```
y = floor(3.141593);
printf("%f",y);
```

will output the number 3.000000. Notice that although the returned value is a whole number it is still a floating-point data type. If the argument of **floor(x)** is negative, the same rule applies. For example, **floor(−3.141593)** will return a value of −4.000000.

The **ceil(x)** returns the nearest whole number above the value of the argument **x**. For example, **ceil(3.141593)** returns a value of 4.000000 and **ceil (−3.141593)** returns −3.000000. The program of Fig. 4.2 illustrates the use of **floor()** and **ceil()**.

The function **floor()** effectively *truncates* the argument. It returns a floating-point number with the decimal component reset to zero, regardless of its value. To convert **floor()** to a function that performs a roundoff, simply add 0.5 to the argument. Figure 4.3 illustrates the difference between truncation and roundoff. Here we have declared the variables **t** and **r** as integer types that represent the truncated and rounded values of a number, respectively. The assignments

```
t = floor(x);
r = floor(x+0.5);
```

demote the double type returned from **floor()** to integer type. Notice that the **floor(3.737)** equals 3, while the **floor(3.727+0.5)** equals **floor(4.227)**, which has a value of 4.

```
/* ceilings and floors */
#include <stdio.h>
#include <math.h>
main()
        {
        double x = 3.14159265;

        printf("ceiling for %f is %f\n", x, ceil(x));
        printf("floor for %f is %f\n", x, floor(x));
        }
```

```
ceiling for 3.141593 is 4.000000
floor for 3.141593 is 3.000000
```

Figure 4.2 Ceilings and floors.

```
/* truncation and roundoff */
#include <stdio.h>
#include <math.h>
main()
        {
        double x = 3.727;
        int t, r;

        t = floor(x);
        r = floor(x + 0.5);
        printf("truncated value of %f is %d\n", x, t);
        printf("rounded value of %f is %d\n", x, r);
        }
```

```
truncated value of 3.727000 is 3
rounded value of 3.727000 is 4
```

Figure 4.3 Truncation and roundoff.

4.3 ABSOLUTE VALUE

The absolute value of any floating-point number can be found by using the function **fabs()**. The argument of this function can be a floating-point constant, variable, or expression. Thus, the value of **fabs(−1234.56789)** is 1234.56789. The value of **fabs(y)**, where **y** is a floating-point variable, will always be positive regardless of the sign of **y**. Likewise, the **fabs()** of any floating point expression such as **(x−y)/2.0** will always be positive.

We can use the **fabs()** function to determine if some quantity is within a predetermined range. Suppose that a computation yields a result that we wish to compare to a reference value. If exact equality is not required, we may assign a range for an acceptable result and test to see if the computation is within that range.

The program of Fig. 4.4 accepts the *nominal* or typical value of some data item, the *actual* value encountered, and the allowable *tolerance*. The tolerance is expressed as a decimal number. It then computes the *percent error* of the actual value from the nominal value. The **fabs()** function is used to express this quantity as a positive number. (We are not concerned with the direction of an error, only

```
/* percent tolerance */
#include <stdio.h>
#include <math.h>
main()
      {
      double nom_val,act_val,error,tolerance;

      printf("Enter nominal value: ");
      scanf("%lf",&nom_val);
      printf("Enter actual value: ");
      scanf("%lf",&act_val);
      printf("Enter tolerance: ");
      scanf("%lf",&tolerance);
      error = fabs((act_val-nom_val)/nom_val)
      if (error <= tolerance)
            printf("Within tolerance\n");
      else
            printf("Out of tolerance\n");
      }
```

```
Enter nominal value: 100
Enter actual value: 103
Enter tolerance: .05
Within tolerance
```

Figure 4.4 Checking tolerance.

its magnitude.) If the percent error is less than or equal to the allowable tolerance, the program prints the message ''Within tolerance''; otherwise, it prints the message ''Out of tolerance''.

4.4 POWERS AND ROOTS

Powers

To find the value of any floating-point number raised to a power, we use the math function **pow(x,y)**. This is read as **x** raised to the **y** power and is written in algebra as $\mathbf{x}^{\mathbf{y}}$. The values of **x** and **y** can be any floating-point numbers, including negative numbers, with the following restrictions. Either **x** or **y** may be zero, but they cannot both be zero since 0^0 is undefined. If **x** is negative, **y** must not be less than 1.0; otherwise, we would be attempting to find the root of a negative number.

Thus **pow(2.0,3.0)** returns 8.000000 and **pow(2.0,0.5)** returns 1.414214. Notice that we can use the **pow()** function to find a root, in this case the square root as indicated by the 0.5 value for **x**. The call **pow(2.0,−2.0)** returns 0.250000, demonstrating the use of a negative power.

The program of Fig. 4.5 illustrates the use of **pow()**. It accepts values for **x** and **y** from the keyboard, computes **pow(x,y)**, and prints the result.

Roots

The **sqrt()** function is used to find the square root of a floating-point constant, variable, or expression. The argument of this function cannot be negative. To find the square root of a negative number, you must first find the square root of its absolute value and then label the result as an *imaginary* number. This is usually done by preceding the number with a lowercase **j** (used in engineering) or **i** (used in mathematics).

```
/* power of a number */
#include <stdio.h>
#include <math.h>
main()
      {
      double x, y;

      printf("Enter a number and its power: ");
      scanf("%lf %lf", &x, &y);
      printf("%f raised to the %f equals %f", x, y, pow(x, y));
      }
```

```
Enter a number and its power: 2 8
2.000000 raised to the 8.000000 equals 256.000000
```

Figure 4.5 Raising a number to a power.

The program listing of Fig. 4.6 demonstrates computation of the square root of an expression when it can take on negative values. The **if else** statement tests to see if **y** is negative. When **y** is less than 0.0, it is made positive by preceding it with the unary minus operator. After the square root is taken, the result is labeled as imaginary by printing a **j** before its value. If **y** is not negative, the **else** part will simply take the square root of **y** and print the result.

A practical application in which we must consider the case of imaginary roots occurs in finding the roots of a quadratic equation. The roots are given by

$$x_1 = \frac{-b + \sqrt{b^2 - 4ac}}{2a}$$

and

$$x_2 = \frac{-b - \sqrt{b^2 - 4ac}}{2a}$$

```
/* square root of an expression */
#include <stdio.h>
#include <math.h>
main()
      {
      double x, y;

      for (x = 1.0;  x <= 5.0;  x++)
            {
            y = 3.0*x - 10.0;
            if (y < 0.0)
                  printf("%f\tj%f\n", y, sqrt(-y));
            else
                  printf("%f\t%f\n", y, sqrt(y));
            }
      }
```

```
-7.000000      j2.645751
-4.000000      j2.000000
-1.000000      j1.000000
2.000000       1.414214
5.000000       2.236068
```

Figure 4.6 Square root of an expression.

The quantity under the square root in these equations is called the *discriminant*. When the discriminant is positive or zero, the roots will be real numbers. When it is not positive, the roots will be *complex numbers*. Complex numbers have both a real and imaginary part. If we let the discriminant be represented by the variable **d**, then **d** < **0** defines the condition of complex roots.

The program of Fig. 4.7 finds the roots of a quadratic. The procedure for finding real roots differs from that for complex roots. The program must therefore detect which condition is present and proceed accordingly. To do this, the value of the discriminant is found. If **d** is less than zero, the procedure for finding complex roots is followed; otherwise, the procedure for finding real roots is used.

For the case of complex roots, the real part is given by **−b/(2*a)**. This quantity is assigned to the variable **re**. The magnitude of the imaginary part of the root is given by **sqrt(−d)/(2*a)**. The value of **−d** will be positive since **d** is known to be negative. This component of the root is assigned to the variable **im**. In printing the value of **x1**, we precede the imaginary part with **+j**. The imaginary part of **x2** will have a magnitude equal to that in **x1**, but the opposite sign. It is thus preceded with a **−j**.

```
/* roots of a quadratic */
#include <stdio.h>
#include <math.h>
main()
	{
	double a, b, c, d, x1, x2, re, im;

	printf("Enter coefficients a,b,c: ");
	scanf("%lf %lf %lf", &a, &b, &c);
	d = b*b - 4*a*c;
	if (d < 0)
		{
		/* complex roots */
		re = -b/(2*a);
		im = sqrt(-d)/(2*a);
		printf("x1= %f +j%f\n", re, im);
		printf("x2= %f -j%f\n", re, im);
		}
	else {
		/* real roots */
		x1 = (-b + sqrt(d))/(2*a);
		x2 = (-b - sqrt(d))/(2*a);
		printf("x1 = %f\tx2 = %f", x1, x2);
		}
	}
```

```
Enter coefficients a,b,c: 1.0 2.0 3.0
x1= -1.000000 +j1.414214
x2= -1.000000 -j1.414214
```

Figure 4.7 Roots of a quadratic.

4.5 TRIGONOMETRIC FUNCTIONS

The **C** math library provides functions for computation of the sine, cosine, and tangent of an angle. It also provides the inverse of these functions, referred to as the arc sine, arc cosine, and arc tangent. All arguments and returned values are of type double, and all angles are in radians. If you wish to work with degrees instead of radians, the conversion

```
1 degree = 3.14159265/180.0 radian
```

is used. All input angles in degrees must first be converted to radians before using the sine, cosine, or tangent. Also, the values returned by arc sine, arc cosine, and arc tangent must be converted from radians to degrees before they are output.

The program of Fig. 4.8 computes the sine, cosine, and tangent of an angle entered in degrees. A **#define** preprocessor directive defines **PI** as 3.14159265. The entered angle is assigned to the variable **deg**. Conversion to radians is performed by the statement

```
rad = deg*PI/180.0;
```

Notice that this statement occurs after the **scanf()**, which assigns a value to **deg**. The **printf()** statements output the angle in degrees and the **sin(rad)**, **cos(rad)**, and **tan(rad)**.

```
/* sine, cosine, and tangent */
#define PI  3.14159265
#include <math.h>
#include <stdio.h>
main()
      {
      double deg, rad;

      printf("Enter an angle in degrees: ");
      scanf("%lf", &deg);
      rad = deg*PI/180;
      printf("The sine of %f degrees is %f\n", deg, sin(rad));
      printf("The cosine of %f degrees is %f\n", deg, cos(rad));
      printf("The tangent of %f degrees is %f\n", deg, tan(rad))
      }
```

```
Enter an angle in degrees: 30
The sine of 30.000000 degrees is 0.500000
The cosine of 30.000000 degrees is 0.866025
The tangent of 30.000000 degrees is 0.577350
```

Figure 4.8 Sine, cosine, and tangent.

Computation of the inverse trig functions is straightforward. The argument passed to the arc sine or arc cosine functions must be within the range from -1.0 to $+1.0$. The arc tangent function can have any real number as an argument. The program of Fig. 4.9 finds the inverse sine, cosine, and tangent of the value of **x**. Notice that the **asin(x)**, **acos(x)**, and **atan(x)** are all multiplied by **180.0/PI** to convert the resulting angle from radians to degrees.

Hyperbolic Functions

The hyperbolic functions are a part of the **C** math library. These include the hyperbolic sine, cosine, and tangent written as **sinh()**, **cosh()**, and **tanh()** respectively. The hyperbolic functions are defined by the equations

```
/* inverse trig functions */
#define PI  3.14159265
#include <stdio.h>
#include <math.h>
main()
    {
    double x;

    printf("Enter a number between 0 and 1: ");
    scanf("%lf", &x);
    printf("The arc sine of %f is %f degrees\n", x, asin(x)*180/PI);
    printf("The arc cosine of %f is %f degrees\n", x, acos(x)*180/PI);
    printf("The arc tangent of %f is %f degrees\n", x, atan(x)*180/PI);
    }
```

```
Enter a number between 0 and 1: 0.5
The arc sine of 0.500000 is 30.000000 degrees
The arc cosine of 0.500000 is 60.000000 degrees
The arc tangent of 0.500000 is 26.565051 degrees
```

Figure 4.9 Inverse trig functions.

$$\sinh(x) = \frac{e^x - e^{-x}}{2}$$

$$\cosh(x) = \frac{e^x + e^{-x}}{2}$$

$$\tanh(x) = \frac{\sinh(x)}{\cosh(x)}$$

where x may take on any real value. From these equations, it can be seen that the **sinh(x)** can take on any real value, where the **cosh(x)** will always be positive. Also, the **tanh(x)** will always lie in the range from -1.0 to $+1.0$.

A table of values for the hyperbolic functions is generated by the program of Fig. 4.10. The **for** loop sets the range of **x** from -2.0 to $+2.0$ in increments of 0.2. The upper limit for **x** is actually set to 2.1 to compensate for the slight error that can occur when summing with floating-point increments. Notice that the **sinh(0)** and **tanh(0)** equal 0, whereas the **cosh(0)** equals 1. For positive values of **x**, as **x** gets larger, the **sinh(x)** and **cosh(x)** approach each other in magnitude, but have opposite signs. For negative **x**, the **sinh(x)** and **cosh(x)** will have the same sign.

Finding the Resultant of Vectors: An Application

A common application that uses the trigonometric functions is the computation of the resultant for a series of vectors. Figure 4.11 shows a system of vectors having arbitrary length and angle. They may represent forces acting on an object where it is necessary to find the resultant force. In electrical circuits, they could represent voltage phasors that must be resolved into a single voltage at some phase angle.

You are probably familiar with the procedure for finding the resultant of vectors from your trigonometry and physics courses. The component of the resultant in the direction of the **x** axis is equal to the sum of the **x** components of each of the vectors. Likewise, the component of the resultant in the direction of the **y** axis is equal to the sum of the **y** components of each of the vectors.

```
/* hyperbolic functions */
#include <stdio.h>
#include <math.h>
main()
	{
	double x;

	printf("x\t\tsinh\t\tcosh\t\ttanh\n");
	for (x = -2.0;  x <= 2.1;  x = x + 0.2)
		printf("%f\t%f\t%f\t%f\n", x, sinh(x), cosh(x), tanh(x));
	}
```

x	sinh	cosh	tanh
-2.000000	-3.626860	3.762196	-0.964028
-1.800000	-2.942174	3.107473	-0.946806
-1.600000	-2.375568	2.577464	-0.921669
-1.400000	-1.904302	2.150898	-0.885352
-1.200000	-1.509461	1.810656	-0.833655
-1.000000	-1.175201	1.543081	-0.761594
-0.800000	-0.888106	1.337435	-0.664037
-0.600000	-0.636654	1.185465	-0.537050
-0.400000	-0.410752	1.081072	-0.379949
-0.200000	-0.201336	1.020067	-0.197375
-0.000000	-0.000000	1.000000	-0.000000
0.200000	0.201336	1.020067	0.197375
0.400000	0.410752	1.081072	0.379949
0.600000	0.636654	1.185465	0.537050
0.800000	0.888106	1.337435	0.664037
1.000000	1.175201	1.543081	0.761594
1.200000	1.509461	1.810656	0.833655
1.400000	1.904302	2.150898	0.885352
1.600000	2.375568	2.577464	0.921669
1.800000	2.942174	3.107473	0.946806
2.000000	3.626860	3.762196	0.964028

Figure 4.10 Hyperbolic functions.

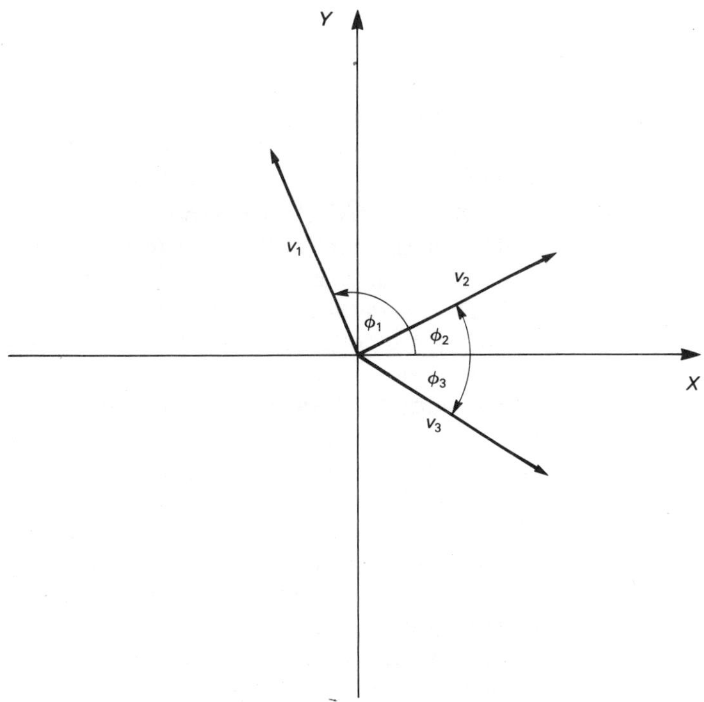

Figure 4.11 Vector diagram.

Finding the **x** and **y** components of any given vector is accomplished by using the relationships

$$v_x = v \cos(\phi)$$

$$v_y = v \sin(\phi)$$

where the original vector has a magnitude **v** and an angle ϕ. The **x** component is found by solving for $\mathbf{v_x}$ and the **y** component by solving for $\mathbf{v_y}$. A vector described by its magnitude and angle is said to be in *polar form*. If it is described by **x** and **y** components, it is said to be in *rectangular form*.

The procedure for finding the resultant of a series of vectors represented in polar form can now be described as consisting of the following steps:

1. Determine the number of vectors, **n**.
2. Set up a loop to perform the following steps **n** times:
   2.1 Enter a vector in polar form.
   2.2 Find its **x** and **y** components.
   2.3 Add the **x** component to the current value of the **x** component of the resultant.
   2.4 Add the **y** component to the current value of the **y** component of the resultant.
3. Output the value of the **x** and **y** components of the resultant.
4. Convert the resultant to polar form.
5. Output the polar form of the resultant.

The program of Fig. 4.12 implements this procedure. The lines

```
x_result = x_result + mag*cos(rad);
y_result = y_result + mag*sin(rad);
```

perform the summation of the **x** and **y** components of the vectors (steps 2.3 and 2.4). On each pass through the loop, the **x** component of the current vector, **mag*cos(rad)**, is added to the **x** component of the current value of the resultant, **x_result**. Likewise, the **y** component of the current vector, **mag*sin(rad)**, is added to the **y** component of the current value of the resultant, **y_result**. After *n* passes through the loop, **x_result** and **y_result** will take on their final values.

The magnitude of the resultant is found by taking the square root of the sum of the squares of **x_result** and **y_result**. Its angle is given by the arc tangent of **y_result/x_result**. Several problems arise here. If the resultant is in the second or third quadrants, the arc tangent will give an angle that is referenced to the negative **x** axis. By convention, all angles must be measured relative to the positive **x** axis. To correct this error, we add 180 degrees to all angles whenever the **x** component of the resultant is less than zero. (An **x** value less than 0 detects a vector in the second or third quadrant). Adding 180 degrees will make the resulting angle referenced to the positive **x** axis.

The other problem arises whenever the **x** component of the resultant equals zero (a rare occurrence). This causes a division by zero in the arc tangent formula. The correction of this problem is left as an exception for the reader.

```
/* resultant of vectors */
#define PI  3.14159265
#include <stdio.h>
#include <math.h>
main()
     {
     int i, n;
     double mag, deg, rad, mag_result, deg_result;
     double x_result = 0.0, y_result = 0.0;

/* Enter the vectors and sum components */
     printf("\nHow many vectors? ");
     scanf("%d", &n);
     for (i = 1;  i <= n;  i++)
          {
          printf("Enter vector %d: ", i);
          scanf("%lf %lf", &mag, &deg);
          rad = deg*PI/180.0;
          x_result = x_result + mag*cos(rad);
          y_result = y_result + mag*sin(rad);
          }
/* Print the resultant in rectangular form */
     printf("\nThe resultant in rectangular form is:\n");
     printf("x component = %f\n", x_result);
     printf("y component = %f\n", y_result);
/* convert resultant to polar form */
     mag_result = sqrt(x_result*x_result + y_result*y_result);
     deg_result = atan(y_result/x_result)*180/PI;
     if (x_result < 0.0)
          deg_result = deg_result + 180.0;
/* print resultant in polar form */
     printf("The polar form of the resultant is:\n");
     printf("Magnitude = %f\n", mag_result);
     printf("Angle = %f degrees\n", deg_result);
     }
```

```
How many vectors? 3
Enter vector 1: 12 45
Enter vector 2: 6.2 -115
Enter vector 3: 14 120

The resultant in rectangular form is:
x component = -1.134952
y component = 14.990529
The polar form of the resultant is:
Magnitude = 15.033432
Angle = 94.329675 degrees
```

Figure 4.12 Resultant of vectors.

4.6 *EXPONENTIALS AND LOGARITHMS*

Exponentials

The exponential function **exp(x)** returns the value of **e**^{x}, where **e** is the base of the natural logarithm, or 2.718281828. The argument of the **exp()** function is a constant, variable, or expression of type **double**. The value of the argument may be any real number.

The exponential function occurs in many applications, a common one being the equation for the charging of a capacitor. The voltage across the capacitor in Fig. 4.13 at any time **t** after the closing of the switch is given by

$$v(t) = E[1 - e^{-t/(RC)}]$$

where **E** is the battery voltage, **R** is the circuit resistance, and **C** is the value of capacitance.

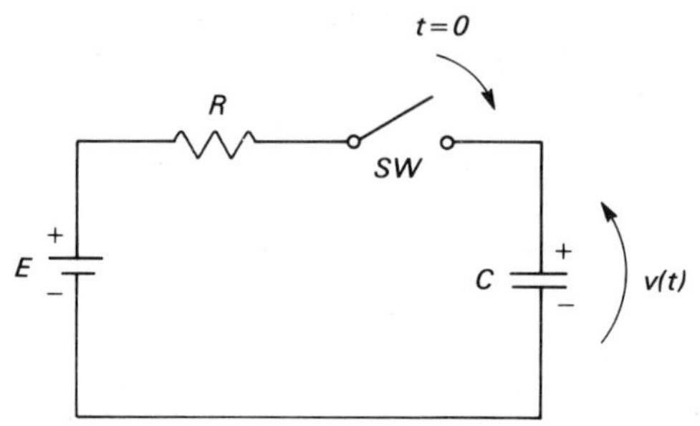

Figure 4.13 Charging of a capacitor.

Suppose **E** = 100, **R** = 1000, and **C** = 0.0005. The program of Fig. 4.14 tabulates the voltage across the capacitor for **t** ranging from 0 to 3 seconds in increments of 0.5 second. From these data, we can see how the capacitor voltage builds up as a function of elapsed time.

```
/* evaluate exponential function */
#include <stdio.h>
#include <math.h>
main()
     {
     double t, v;

     printf("t\t\tv\n");
     for (t = 0.0;  t <= 3.1;  t = t + 0.5)
          {
          v = 100*(1 - exp(-2*t));
          printf("%f\t%f\n", t, v);
          }
     }
```

```
t                 v
0.000000          0.000000
0.500000          63.212056
1.000000          86.466472
1.500000          95.021293
2.000000          98.168436
2.500000          99.326205
3.000000          99.752125
```

Figure 4.14 Exponential function.

Natural Logarithms

If **y** = $\mathbf{e}^{\mathbf{x}}$, then the *natural logarithm of* **y**, written as **ln y**, is given by **x**. Expressed in words, we can say that the natural logarithm of a number is given by the power of **e** that yields a value equal to that number. In **C**, the natural logarithm of a number is returned by the function **log()**. The value of the argument must be a positive number of type **double**.

From the definition of the exponential and natural logarithm, it can be seen that the two functions are inversely related. Thus **log(exp(x))** returns the value of **x**. The exponential can be called the *antilogarithm* of the natural logarithm.

If an equation contains exponentials, we can use the natural logarithm function to solve for the value of the exponent. Let's return to our example of the charging of a capacitor. If it is desired to solve for the time at which the voltage reaches a certain level, we can rearrange the equation to give

$$\mathbf{e}^{-\mathbf{t}/(\mathbf{RC})} = 1 - \frac{\mathbf{v}}{\mathbf{E}}$$

Taking the natural logarithm of both sides yields

$$\frac{-\mathbf{t}}{\mathbf{RC}} = \ln\left(1 - \frac{\mathbf{v}}{\mathbf{E}}\right)$$

Solving for **t** gives

$$\mathbf{t} = -\mathbf{RC}\ln\left(1 - \frac{\mathbf{v}}{\mathbf{E}}\right)$$

It may look as if the time will be a negative number in this equation. This is not the case since the natural logarithm of the expression will be a negative number, yielding a positive value for **t**.

The program of Fig. 4.15 makes use of the natural logarithm function to solve for the time at which the voltage across the capacitor reaches 50 volts.

```
/* solve for t in charging of a capacitor */
#include <stdio.h>
#include <math.h>
main()
    {
    double t, v = 50.0, E = 100.0, R = 1000.0, C = 0.0005;

    t = -R*C*log(1 - v/E);
    printf("The time at which the voltage drops to 50.0 volts is %f", t);
    }
```

```
The time at which the voltage drops to 50.0 volts is 0.346574
```

Figure 4.15 Solving for **t** in the charging of a capacitor.

Common Logarithms

The *common logarithm* of a number is equal to the power of 10 that yields a result equal to that number. This may be written as $\mathbf{y} = 10^{\mathbf{x}}$, where **x** is called the common logarithm of **y**. In **C**, the common logarithm function is **log10()**. The argument of this function must be a positive number.

If your particular math library does not include the **log10(x)** function, it can be expressed in terms of the natural logarithm by

```
common_log = log(x)/log(10);
```

Stated in words, the common logarithm of a number is equal to the natural logarithm of that number divided by the natural logarithm of 10.

The *decibel* is a unit of measure originally used to describe acoustical power ratios, but it has since been adopted in the electrical field as well. It is defined by

$$dB = 10 \log \frac{\mathbf{p}_2}{\mathbf{p}_1}$$

where $\mathbf{p}_2/\mathbf{p}_1$ is a power ratio, and ten times the common logarithm of the power ratio is equal to the decibel power level, or dB level. The program of Fig. 4.16 uses the common logarithm function and the definition of the decibel to generate a table of power ratios and their corresponding decibel values.

```
/* decibel power table */
#include <stdio.h>
#include <math.h>
main()
        {
        double x;

        printf("p2/p1\t\tdB\n");
        for (x = 1.0;  x <= 10.1;  x = x + 1)
                printf("%f\t%f\n", x, 10*log10(x));
        }
```

```
p2/pl               dB
1.000000            0.000000
2.000000            3.010300
3.000000            4.771213
4.000000            6.020600
5.000000            6.989700
6.000000            7.781513
7.000000            8.450980
8.000000            9.030900
9.000000            9.542425
10.000000           10.000000
```

Figure 4.16 Decibel power table.

4.7 RANDOM NUMBER FUNCTION

The **C** function **rand()** returns an integer random number. Actually, the number that is returned is not quite random. It comes from a predictable sequence called a *pseudorandom* sequence. However, since this sequence appears to be random and does not repeat for a very large number of calls, we can use it for generating random numbers within a program.

Each time we execute a program containing calls to the **rand()** function, the same sequence of random numbers will be generated. We can have what appears to be a unique sequence of random numbers on each execution by starting at a different point within the pseudorandom sequence. This is accomplished by using a different *seed* value before we make the first call to **rand()**.

The function **srand(x)** reseeds the random-number generator with a new seed value **x**. The argument **x** is an integer number. Any given value of **x** will produce a unique sequence of values returned by repeated calls to **rand()**.

The program of Fig. 4.17 illustrates the use of **rand()**. A seed value is entered from the keyboard to select a random starting point for the sequence. Five random numbers are generated by repeated calls to **rand()**. If the program is repeated using the same seed value, the same numbers will be returned. A different seed value will produce a different sequence.

```
/* pseudorandom number generation */
#include <stdio.h>
#include <math.h>
main()
      {
      int i,x;
      unsigned seed;

      printf("Enter seed value: ");
      scanf("%u",&seed);
      srand(seed);
      for (i = 1; i <= 5; i++)
            {
            x = rand();
            printf("%d\t%d\n", i, x);
            }
      }
```

```
Enter seed value: 10000
1       32694
2       12743
3       11816
4       20150
5       935
```

Figure 4.17 Pseudorandom number generation.

An application of random numbers is given in the program of Fig. 4.18. This program simulates repeated tosses of a pair of dice. The random numbers required for such a simulation must range from 1 to 6. This is accomplished by applying the modulus operator to **rand()** and adding 1 to the result. The value of

```
rand()%6
```

will be a number from 0 to 5. (An integer number divided by 6 will produce a remainder from 0 to 5.) Adding 1 to the result produces a random number within the desired range.

Two random numbers are required for each toss. To do this, we make two calls to **rand()** within a **for** loop and assign the scaled random numbers to the variables **die_1** and **die_2**. The values of these variables are printed on each pass through the loop.

```
/* simulation of the toss of a pair of dice */
#include <stdio.h>
#include <math.h>
main()
     {
     int i, die_1, die_2;
     unsigned u;

/* seed the random number generator */
     printf("Enter seed value: ");
     scanf("%u", &u);
     srand(u);
     printf("\n");

/* generate dice toss */
     printf("toss\tdie_1\tdie_2\n\n");
     for (i = 1; i <= 5; i++)
          {
          die_1 = rand()%6 + 1;
          die_2 = rand()%6 + 1;
          printf("%d\t%d\t%d\n", i, die_1, die_2);
          }
     }
```

```
Enter seed value: 1000

toss    die_1   die_2

1       5       2
2       6       5
3       4       2
4       3       3
5       3       3
```

Figure 4.18 Simulation of the toss of a pair of dice.

PROBLEMS

4.1. What is the value of each of the following expressions?
(a) `ceil(18.1)`
(b) `ceil(18.7 + 0.5)`
(c) `floor(18.1)`
(d) `floor(-4.4)`
(e) `ceil(-4.4)`

4.2. What is the value of each of the following expressions?
(a) `pow(2.0, 3.0)`
(b) `pow(2.0, -3.0)`
(c) `pow(-2.0, 3.0)`
(d) `pow(-2.0, 4.0)`
(e) `pow(2.0, 0.0)`
(f) `pow(2.2, 2.5)`

4.3. Write a program that evaluates

$$\mathbf{y}^2 = (25 - \mathbf{x}^2)$$

for **x** from 1.0 to 10.0 in unit increments. It should output the value of each **x, y** pair, using the **j** operator to identify imaginary **y** values.

4.4. Components are manufactured to some nominal value of a particular parameter. This includes a *make tolerance,* which is an allowable error range from the nominal value due to the precision limitations of the process. Often, when the parameter values are measured, the components are categorized into groups having various tolerance ranges. Write a program that accepts the serial number and parameter value for each component listed in the following table. It should then establish the percent error from the nominal value of 40.0 and output the serial number followed by one of three tolerance ranges: 1%, 5%, or 10%.

Serial number	*Parameter value*
100	41.4
101	37.3
102	39.8
103	43.6
104	39.2

4.5. Write a program that prints a table of angles from 0.0 to 90.0, degrees in steps of 10.0, degrees along with the corresponding values of the sine, cosine, and tangent for each angle. Devise a method of handling the problem that arises in finding the tangent of 90.0 degrees. (*Hint:* Output a message such as INFINITE.)

4.6. Write a program that generates a table of common and natural logarithms for numbers ranging from 1.0 to 10.0 in unit increments.

4.7. Write a program that simulates 100 flips of a coin by using the **rand()** function. It should output an H for each head and a T for each tail, and output the total number of heads or tails.

4.8. Assume that the capacitor of Figure 4.13 is to be charged from 0 to 100 volts and that the **RC** time constant is 0.10 second. Write a program that tabulates the voltage across the capacitor for **t** = 0 to **t** = 0.10 second in increments of 0.010 second.

4.9. Modify Problem 4.8, solving for the time at voltages from 0 to 90 volts (0.9*E) in uniform increments of 10 volts.

4.10. Use the program of Figure 4.12 to solve for the resultant of the four vectors given next:

Vector	**x** *Component*	**y** *Component*
1	12.0	22.5
2	−7.7	8.6
3	4.8	−5.5
4	−10.0	−8.0

4.11. Improve the program of Figure 4.12 to solve the problem associated with a zero value for the **x** component of the resultant. You must avoid division by zero in finding the polar form of the resultant and still obtain the correct answer.

chapter 5

Input and Output

5.1 INTRODUCTION

We have already used the **scanf()** and **printf()** functions to perform elementary input and output. The **scanf()** function has been used for entering numeric data and single characters. The **printf()** function has been used to output all types of data, but only in a partially formatted arrangement.

In this chapter, we look further into I/O (input/output) alternatives in **C**. This includes the handling of string data, character data, and formatted I/O for all data types using **scanf()** and **printf()**.

To this point, we have considered all input as coming from the keyboard and all output as going to the screen. This is not always the case. The combination of the keyboard and screen is referred to as the *console,* also called a *terminal.* Although there are functions in **C** that permit *direct* I/O to the console, most I/O is passed through a *buffer*. This is a memory region used for the temporary storage of data being passed between two devices. The **C** functions that perform buffered I/O often have a counterpart that performs direct I/O. Unless otherwise specified, all I/O functions presented here are of the buffered type.

The input buffer is called the *standard input*, and the output buffer is called the *standard output*. We will assume that the standard input and standard output are connected to the console. In Chapter 13, we will see how to *redirect* the standard input or output to connect with other devices.

5.2 STRING INPUT/OUTPUT

In Chapter 2, the character data type (**char**) was defined as having a length of 1 byte. A *string* was defined as a collection of characters contained within double quotation marks. Strings are stored in memory as an array of characters. The **NULL** character ('\0') marks the end of the character string. (It is a binary zero, not an ASCII zero.) Thus, the string "Enter units for data:" would appear in memory as shown in Fig. 5.1.

E	n	t	e	r		u	n	i	t	s		f	o	r		d	a	t	a	:	\0			
1	2	3	4	5	6	7	8	9	10	11	12	13	14	15	16	17	18	19	20	21	22			

Figure 5.1 Storage of character strings.

The characters forming the string are stored in consecutive memory addresses and are said to form a *contiguous* array. Any spaces within the string actually store information as well. They contain the ASCII **SP** (space bar) character, which has a value of 32_{10} or 20_{16}. The **NULL** character is not considered to be a part of the string and is thus excluded when determining the string length.

C does not provide a special data type for strings. (String variables in BASIC, terminated by a $ character, do not have an equivalent in **C**.) Instead, a character array is used to represent strings. An *array* is a collection of elements of the same data type. In **C**, variables that represent character arrays are given a name followed by square brackets. When we declare a variable as a character array, a number is placed within the square brackets to define the length of the array. Thus,

```
char units[40];
```

is used to declare the variable **units** as being an array of type **char** and having a length of 40. Note that 40 includes room for the NULL character.

A character array may be initialized within its declaration. For example, the array units is initialized by

```
char units[40] = "Enter units for data:";
```

or

```
char units[] = "Enter units for data:";
```

In the first declaration, the array is defined as having a length of 40 and is only partially filled by the string data. In the second declaration, since the array length was not specified, it is set to the length of the string data to which it was initialized plus 1. The extra character position is required for the NULL terminator ('\0').

String Input/Output Using Scanf() and Printf()

The program of Fig. 5.2 illustrates string input/output using **scanf()** and **printf()**. Notice that the unary & operator is not used as a prefix to **units** in the **scanf()** statement. This is due to the fact that array variables are handled in a different manner than nonarray variables in **C**. The reason for this will be seen in Chapter 7. Observe also that the array name **units** appears without the square brackets in both the **scanf()** and **printf()** statements.

The **scanf()** statement will terminate entry of a string when it reaches the first space or newline character. Therefore, our entry for **units** can consist of only one word or a string of characters excluding the space bar (SP). An entry such as "volts dc" would be cut off at the first space so that it becomes simply "volts". How do you enter a string that is longer than one word? There are several ways of doing this. The simplest method uses the **C** function **gets()**.

```
/* string I/O using scanf and printf */
#include <stdio.h>
main()
    {
    char units[20];
    int data;

    printf("Enter data value:");
    scanf("%d", &data);
    printf("Enter units for data:");
    scanf("%s", units);
    printf("The data value in units of %s is %d", units, data);
    }
```

```
Enter data value:120
Enter units for data:volts
The data value in units of volts is 120
```

Figure 5.2 String I/O using **scanf** and **printf**.

String Input/Output Using Gets() and Puts()

The functions **gets()** and **puts()** are **C** library functions that are used for string input and output, respectively. The string input is from the standard input, usually connected to the console. The string output is to the standard output, which is also normally routed to the console.

The **gets()** function will input characters until it encounters the newline character (return or enter). The newline character is dropped from the input and replaced with the **NULL** ('\0') character to properly terminate the string. The argument of the **gets()** function is the variable name used as a reference to the storage location of the character array. Thus, if a character array is declared as

```
char message[80];
```

then the statement

```
gets (message);
```

will input a string and assign it to the array **message[]**.

The **puts()** is used to output a string. The contents of **message[]** can be printed by the statement

```
puts(message);
```

The **puts()** function differs from **printf()** in that it automatically inserts a newline character at the end of the string that it outputs. Thus,

```
puts(message);
```

is equivalent to

```
printf("%s\n",message);
```

The **printf()** function offers more versatility at the expense of having a more complicated syntax.

The program of Fig. 5.3 makes use of **gets()** and **puts()** for string input/output. The **#define** directive is used here to set the maximum size of **message [MAXLEN]** to 81 characters. This actually permits only 80 characters of input, since the **NULL** character must be appended to the input string.

```
/* string I/O using gets and puts */
#define MAXLEN 81
#include <stdio.h>
main()
      {
      char message[MAXLEN];

      puts("Enter your message");
      gets(message);
      puts("Your message is:");
      puts(message);
      }
```

```
Enter your message
A character string
Your message is:
A character string
```

Figure 5.3 String I/O using **gets** and **puts.**

Puts() is first used to print the prompt "Enter your message". The **gets()** function is then used to get the input string and assign it to the character array **message[ ]**. The second **puts()** statement prints the contents of **message[ ]**.

Sizeof() and Strlen()

The **sizeof()** operator returns the length in bytes of its argument. Valid arguments for **sizeof()** include basic data types like **char**, **int**, **float**, or **double**. They also include variables, arrays, and structures (see Chapter 12). We can use this operator to find the actual size of the basic data types for a particular **C** compiler or interpreter with a simple **printf()** statement as follows:

```
printf("The size of float is %d\n",sizeof(float));
```

The **sizeof()** operator can also tell us the size of an array within our program. In Fig. 5.4, two arrays are declared with different sizes. A **printf()** statement containing the **sizeof()** operator is then used to output the size of each array.

```
/* find the size of arrays */
#include <stdio.h>
main()
      {
      char small[20], large[500];

      printf("The size of small is %d\n", sizeof (small));
      printf("The size of large is %d\n", sizeof (large));
      }
```

```
The size of small is 20
The size of large is 500
```

Figure 5.4 Measuring the size of an array.

When the **sizeof()** operator is applied to arrays, it returns the size of the allocated space for the array, not the size of the data it contains. For character arrays, the **strlen()** function will return the length of the string data actually contained within the array. It does this by counting all the characters up to but not including the NULL terminator. [The **strlen()** function is similar to the **LEN (string)** in BASIC].

The program of Fig. 5.5 declares the same two arrays as found in Fig. 5.4. The **gets()** function is used to input data that are placed into these arrays. The length of the string data in these arrays is found by using the **strlen()** function with the array name as an argument. Notice that, although the **small[]** array is allocated 20 bytes (0 to 19), the string length for the run shown is only 1. Also, the string length for **large[]** is 50 for the same run.

```
/* find the length of strings */
#include <stdio.h>
main()
      {
      char small[20], large[500];

      puts("Enter a small string:");
      gets(small);
      puts("Enter a large string:");
      gets(large);
      printf("The length of your small string is %d\n", strlen(small));
      printf("The length of your large string is %d\n", strlen(large));
      }
```

```
Enter a small string:
A
Enter a large string:
The length of this string will soon be determined.
The length of your small string is 1
The length of your large string is 50
```

Figure 5.5 Measuring the length of a string.

5.3 CHARACTER INPUT/OUTPUT

A very useful feature of the **C** language is its ability to perform single character I/O. While this may seem like a rather tedious way of moving data, it offers a degree of control that cannot be provided by working with a larger unit of data.

The **getchar()** function inputs a single character from the standard input (the keyboard). **Getchar()** does not accept an argument. In some implementations, the character is returned immediately upon entry, while in others the **Enter** or **Return** key must be pressed following the character entry. You can determine which of these two methods is used on your system by experimentation or reference to the compiler manual.

The program of Fig. 5.6 uses **getchar()** to enter a character from the standard input. The returned character is assigned to the variable **ch**. The **printf()** function uses the **%c** conversion specifier to print the value of **ch** to the screen (the standard output).

It is worth mentioning that, although **ch** was declared as type **char**, **getchar()** actually returns an integer. This is necessary, since **getchar()** must be able to return a −1 upon detecting a particular condition in the standard input. (A demo-

```
/* input a character using getchar */
#include <stdio.h>
main()
      {
      char ch;

      printf("Enter a character\n");
      ch = getchar();
      printf("\nYour character is: %c\n", ch);
      }
```

```
Enter a character
+

Your character is: +
```

Figure 5.6 Input a character using **getchar()**.

tion from **int** to **char** occurs here.) For most applications, we will assign the value returned by **getchar()** to a variable of type **int**.

The **putchar()** function is the output counterpart of **getchar()**. It will output a single character argument to the standard output (screen). Thus, **putchar('a')** will print the lowercase letter **a**. Notice that the character constant is surrounded by a pair of single quote marks. An integer argument for **putchar()** will print its character equivalent to the standard output. For example, **putchar(97)** will also print the lowercase letter **a** (which has an ASCII value of 97). Other possible arguments for **putchar()** include character variables or expressions and escape sequences.

Let's see how **getchar()** and **putchar()** work together. The program in Fig. 5.7(a) is used to echo characters entered from the standard input until an END character is detected. The **#define** directive equates END to the asterisk ('*'). Each character read by **getchar()** is tested by the **while** loop condition (**ch != END**). If the character is not the END character, it will be printed to the standard output and another character will be read. If **ch == END**, the program terminates without printing the value of **ch**.

```
/* echo characters */
#include <stdio.h>
#define END        '*'
main()
      {
      int ch;

      ch = getchar();
      while (ch != END)
            {
            putchar(ch);
            ch = getchar();
            }
      }
```

```
Testing echo. * is the last character read.
Testing echo.
```

(a)

Figure 5.7 Echo characters with **putchar()**.

```
/* echo characters */
#include <stdio.h>
#define END         '*'

main()
      {
      int ch;

      while ((ch = getchar()) != '*')
            putchar(ch);
      }
```

```
Testing echo. * is the last character read.
Testing echo.
```

(b)

Figure 5.7 (continued).

The run shows how this program executes on a system with buffered input. A line containing the asterisk is typed from the keyboard and printed onto the screen. However, it is not read by the program until the **Enter** or **Return** key is pressed. At that point, the program reads the input characters and **putchar()** prints all the entered characters up to but not including the asterisk.

If the same program is run on a system with unbuffered input, each keystroke will be read and processed without waiting for the **Enter** or **Return** key. Thus, the characters echoed by **putchar()** will be printed immediately after they are entered, producing an output that appears as follows:

```
TTeessttiinngg eecchhoo.. *
```

Careful design of a program can prevent undesirable results such as these double characters printed by the unbuffered input.

There are times when it is desirable to have the input unbuffered. This permits single keystroke response for quick and convenient interaction. Many systems include a **getchar()** that is buffered and another character input function that is unbuffered to provide the programmer with a choice.

A more compact way of writing our echo program is shown in Fig. 5.7(b). Here we have placed the assignment

```
ch = getchar();
```

within the **while** test condition as

```
while ((ch=getchar())!=END)
```

Notice that parentheses have been placed around **ch=getchar()** and that the semicolon is deleted. **C** will first execute **getchar()**, assigning the returned character to **ch**. The value of **ch** is then used in the test condition **ch != END**. In **C**, any assignment can be placed within an expression. The value used within the expression is always the value assigned to the left side.

Many of the functions in the standard **C** library can be derived or substituted with our own equivalent program segment. For example, we can use the **getchar()** function to input a string, performing a rough equivalent of **gets()**. This is done in Fig. 5.8. The input string is stored in the array **string[MAX+1]**, where **MAX** has been set to 80 by the #**define** preprocessor directive. The size of **string[]** has been

```
/* input a string using getchar */
#define MAX 80
#include <stdio.h>
main()
      {
      char string[MAX + 1], ch;
      int i;

      printf("Enter a string\n");
      for (i = 0; (ch = getchar()) != '\n'; i++)
            {
            string[i] = ch;
            if (i == MAX)
                  break;
            }
      string[i] = '\0';
      printf("Your string is: %s\n", string);
      }
```

```
Enter a string
A one liner.
Your string is: A one liner.
```

Figure 5.8 Input a string using **getchar()**.

set to **MAX+1** to allow 80 characters of input and still provide for the required **NULL** character.

The value of **i** is initialized to 0 within its declaration. The program uses a **while** loop to enter characters until the newline character is encountered. The characters returned by **getchar()** are assigned to **ch**. On the first pass through the loop, **i** equals 0, and the value of **ch** is assigned to **string[0]**, the first element in the **string[]** array. At the bottom of the loop, **i** is incremented, and the loop repeats. On the next pass, the value returned by **getchar()** is assigned to **string[1]**, and so on, until the newline character is entered.

The number of input characters assigned to **string[]** cannot exceed **MAX** or an error will occur. The statement

```
if (i==MAX)
      break;
```

will force exit of the loop before this can happen. Once the loop is terminated, the statement

```
string[i] = '/0';
```

appends a **NULL** character to **string[]**. If the loop terminated because the newline character was encountered, this character is replaced with **NULL**. If the termination was due to **i==MAX**, the last character entered is replaced with **NULL**. The final **printf()** statement outputs the entire string.

Character-level Control of Input/Output

The following examples illustrate some of the things that can be done for character-level control of input/output. In the first program, shown in Fig. 5.9, an input string is scanned, a character at a time, with each character being printed on a separate line. This has the effect of printing the string vertically instead of horizontally.

```
/* scanning a string for processing characters */
#include <stdio.h>
main()
      {
      char string[81];
      int i;

      printf("Enter a string\n");
      gets(string);
      for (i = 0; string[i] != '\0'; i++)
            printf("%c\n", string[i]);
      }
```

```
Enter a string
voltage
v
o
l
t
a
g
e
```

Figure 5.9 Scanning a string for processing characters.

String is entered using **gets()**. The **for** loop starts with the value **i=0** and prints the first character of the string, **string[0]**. The value of **i** is incremented until **string[i] =='\0'**, with each corresponding character being printed on a separate line. The **NULL** terminator will not be printed.

The relatively simple procedure used in this example forms the basis for examining any string to perform character-level operations. These could include searching for a particular character within the string, performing character conversions, and so on. In the next program, Fig. 5.10, an input string is searched for ' ' (space bar) characters. We will use this information to identify words in the input string and print these words in a single column.

The **gets()** function is used again to enter the value of **string**. The scanning operation is performed in the same manner as the previous example. Instead of printing each character on a separate line, we first examine the character to see if it is a ' '. The statement

```
if (string[i]==' ')
    putchar('\n');
else
    putchar(string[i]);
```

will start a new line whenever a ' ' is detected. Otherwise, the character **string[i]** is printed on the current line. When the value of **string[i]** is '\0', the end of the string has been reached and the program terminates.

Our last example of character-level control of I/O is shown in Fig. 5.11. This program will accept a character string consisting of a decimal number followed by the letter 'h' or 'o'. If the letter is 'h', the hexadecimal equivalent of the number will be printed. If the letter is 'o', the octal equivalent will be printed. An 'e' followed by a newline (**Enter** or **Return**) will end the program execution.

The number to be converted is entered using **gets()** and assigned to the string **input[]**. After conversion to decimal, the number will be assigned to **n**, a long

```
/* print words in a column */
#include <stdio.h>
main()
      {
      char string[81];
      int i;

      printf("Enter four words\n");
      gets(string);
      for (i = 0;  string[i] != '\0';  i++)
            {
            if (string[i] == ' ')
                  putchar('\n');
            else
                  putchar(string[i]);
            }
      }
```

```
Enter four words
first second third fourth
first
second
third
fourth
```

Figure 5.10 Print words in a column.

integer. This number will then be output using either the **long** hexadecimal (**%lx**) or **long** octal (**%lo**) specifier.

After the instructions for using the program are printed, the value of **input[0]** is initialized to something different from 'e'. We have arbitrarily selected the '*' character. The **while** loop that follows will continue conversions as long as the first character entered is different from 'e'.

We must convert the decimal characters in the **input[]** string into a long integer. This is done a character at a time. The **for** loop scans the string while the characters of **input[i]** are decimal numbers. As soon as a nondecimal character is encountered, the loop terminates. The **for** loop test conditions are

```
input[i] >='0' && input[i] <='9'
```

These test conditions will be true until the 'h', 'o', or 'e' is encountered.

Each decimal character is converted into a decimal number by taking the difference **input[i]−'0'**. A subtraction of character data is valid, the result being the difference of the ASCII code values. The difference given here will equal the decimal number that corresponds to the character of **input[i]**. It is assigned to the variable **digit**.

Since the most significant digit of the input is entered first, we must shift each value of **digit** left by one position before adding it to the next. (You observe this action on the display of a calculator as each digit is entered).) This is accomplished by multiplying the current value of the converted number, **n**, by 10 before adding it to **digit**. The result then becomes the new current value of the converted number. When a nondecimal character is encountered, the loop terminates with **n** equal to the decimal value of the input.

After exiting the **for** loop, **i** will have a value such that **input[i]** will be the last character of the string (before the **NULL**). The **if** statement tests this character

```
/* convert decimal to hex or octal */
#include <stdio.h>
main()
      {
      int i, digit;
      long n;
      char input[12];

      puts("Enter a decimal number followed by 'h' to convert to hex");
      puts("Enter a decimal number followed by 'o' to convert to octal");
      puts("Enter an 'e' to end");
      input[0] = '*';

      while (input[0] != 'e')
            {
            puts("\nEnter a number or e to end: ");
            gets(input);
            n = 0;
            for (i = 0; input[i] >= '0' && input[i] <= '9'; i++)
                  {
                  digit = input[i] - '0';
                  n = 10*n + digit;
                  }
            if (input[i] == 'h')
                  printf("%ld in hex equals %lx", n, n);
            else if (input[i] == 'o')
                  printf("%ld in octal equals %lo", n, n);
            }
      }
```

```
Enter a decimal number followed by 'h' to convert to hex
Enter a decimal number followed by 'o' to convert to octal
Enter an 'e' to end

Enter a number or e to end:
1000000000h
1000000000 in hex equals 3b9aca00
Enter a number or e to end:
24o
24 in octal equals 30
Enter a number or e to end:
e
```

Figure 5.11 Convert decimal string to integer hex or octal.

and makes the appropriate conversion to either hexadecimal or octal. The **while** loop then repeats until the character 'e' is entered. An 'e' entry for the **gets()** will bypass both the **for** and **if** statements because **input[0]** is neither a digit nor the characters 'h' or 'o'. On the next pass, the **while** loop test condition will terminate the program.

5.4 FORMATTED I/O USING PRINTF() AND SCANF()

In our previous use of **scanf()** and **printf()**, we controlled the format of the I/O with the conversion specifiers presented in Fig. 2.3 and the **C** escape sequences listed in Fig. 2.5. We will now look at how **C** facilitates more precise control over the I/O using **scanf()** and **printf()**.

Printf()

The **printf()** statement is formally defined by

```
printf(control string, arg1, arg2, ...);
```

where the *control string* is an expression contained within double quotation marks. It includes characters and a number of conversion specifiers equal to the number of arguments (*arg1*, *arg2*, and so on) in the list that follows.

In its simplest form, **prinft()** may have no arguments at all, in which case it merely prints the control string. Whenever arguments are included, they are substituted for the conversion specifiers within the control string in the order in which the arguments are listed. The arguments may be constants, variables, or mathematical expressions. When mathematical expressions are included, they are first evaluated, and then the result is printed. Spaces included within the control string are preserved in the output.

The conversion specifier consists of the % character followed by one of the conversion characters as listed in Fig. 2.3. An additional conversion format modifier, taken from the list in Fig. 5.12, may be inserted between the % character and the conversion character. These format modifiers control the *field width* or space allocated for a print item and how the item is to be printed within its field.

Modifier	*Description*
− (minus)	Print with left adjustment. Causes the print item to begin at the left of its field. The default condition is right adjustment.
Digit string (field width)	Sets the minimum field width for the print item. If the print item is larger, more space will be used. If it is smaller, blank spaces will be filled in at the left. A leading zero in the field width digit string will cause a fill with zeros instead. The − modifier will force the fill to occur at the right side.
(period)	A separator between the field width digit string and the precision digit string.
Digit string (precision)	Following the period separator, it specifies the number of digits to be printed to the right of the decimal point for float or double data. When used with character strings, it specifies the maximum number of characters to be printed.
l (letter ell)	Specifies that the print item is **long** instead of **int**.

Figure 5.12 Conversion format modifiers.

The program of Fig. 5.13 illustrates the use of the field width digit string, as well as the left adjustment (−) modifier. This program prints powers of 2 in the range from 1 to 1000. Each value of **i**, a power of 2, is printed twice on the same line. Both outputs have a field width of six. The first output is right adjusted within its field, whereas the second is left adjusted.

Note that the two blank spaces between the conversion specifications within the control string are preserved in the output. The second column of numbers is separated from the end of the first by two spaces. Since the field width is six, there are five spaces printed before the single digit numbers of the first column, which is right adjusted. Four spaces are printed before the two digit numbers, and so on.

The total space occupied by the two fields plus the two spaces printed in between is 14 print positions or columns. If another print item were added on each line, it would begin at column 15.

```
/* left and right justification */
#include <stdio.h>
main()
          {
          int i;

          for (i = 1; i <= 10000; i *= 2)
                    printf("%6d  %-6d\n", i, i);
          }
```

```
     1  1
     2  2
     4  4
     8  8
    16  16
    32  32
    64  64
   128  128
   256  256
   512  512
  1024  1024
  2048  2048
  4096  4096
  8192  8192
```

Figure 5.13 Field width and alignment using **printf**.

To illustrate the effect of the precision digit strings within a float conversion specifier, we will produce a table of numbers using only the **%f** specifier and compare its output to that obtained using the digit string modifier. The program of Fig. 5.14(a) produces a table of angles and their corresponding tangents for angles from 0 to 85 degrees in steps of 5 degrees. Notice that the decimal points do not align in either column and that all the numbers carry six decimal places.

In Fig. 5.14(b), we have used the conversion specifier **%2.0f** to eliminate the decimal component of the angles in the output. The **2** specifies a minimum field width of two positions. The **0** after the decimal point indicates that no decimal places are to be printed. Leaving the **.0** out could cause six decimal places to be printed within a correspondingly larger field. If the angles within the table were expected to be 100 degrees or larger, then a specifier of **%3.0f** would be needed to maintain alignment of the data.

The specifier for the tangent values is **%10.4f**. This indicates that we want its output to carry four decimal places and have a minimum field width of ten. We could have used a specifier of **%7.4f**. This would have provided for four decimal places, a decimal point position, and two positions to the left of the decimal point. However, in order not to crowd the data too close to the first column, we chose a larger value. A minimum of three spaces between the two columns will be kept blank with the **%10.4f**. In general, the minimum field width should be selected to fit the largest expected data value and also provide for column spacing. Notice that this technique of column spacing offers more control over the location of the columns than the use of the tab (\t).

The tangent values in the previous examples were of type **double**. The maximum number of decimal places that can be printed in the output is not limited to six. A conversion specifier of **%20.10f** is perfectly valid and will provide an output having ten decimal places.

```
/* formatting float data */
#define D_TO_R    (3.1415927/180)
#include <stdio.h>
#include <math.h>
main()
      {
      double d;

      for (d = 0.0; d < 90; d = d + 5)
            printf("%f\t%f\n", d, tan(d*D_TO_R));
      }
```

```
0.000000         0.000000
5.000000         0.087489
10.000000        0.176327
15.000000        0.267949
20.000000        0.363970
25.000000        0.466308
30.000000        0.577350
35.000000        0.700208
40.000000        0.839100
45.000000        1.000000
50.000000        1.191754
55.000000        1.428148
60.000000        1.732051
65.000000        2.144507
70.000000        2.747477
75.000000        3.732051
80.000000        5.671281
85.000000        11.430051
```

(a)

```
/* formatting float data */
#define D_TO_R    (3.1415927/180)
#include <stdio.h>
#include <math.h>
main()
      {
      double d;

      for (d = 0.0; d < 90; d = d + 5)
            printf("%2.0f%10.4f\n", d,
            tan(d * D_TO_R));
      }
```

```
 0    0.0000
 5    0.0875
10    0.1763
15    0.2679
20    0.3640
25    0.4663
30    0.5774
35    0.7002
40    0.8391
45    1.0000
50    1.1918
55    1.4281
60    1.7321
65    2.1445
70    2.7475
75    3.7321
80    5.6713
85   11.4301
```

(b)

Figure 5.14 Printing float data: (a) unformatted; (b) formatted.

Figure 5.15 shows how string data can be formatted. It contains four **printf()** statements. Each statement outputs a string consisting of the digits 1234567890. Using digits makes it easier to see the relative position of each output. A character conversion specifier outputs the exclamation mark after each string to show the extent of the string field.

```
/* string formatting */
#include <stdio.h>
main()
      {

      printf("%15.10s%c\n", "1234567890", '!');
      printf("%15.5s%c\n", "1234567890", '!');
      printf("%5s%c\n", "1234567890", '!');
      printf("%15s%c\n", "1234567890", '!');
      }
```

```
     1234567890!
          12345!
1234567890!
     1234567890!
```

Figure 5.15 String formatting.

The first **printf()** statement contains the specifier %**15.10s**, which defines a minimum field width of 15 character positions and permits printing ten characters at the right side of this field. Since the string contains only ten characters, the five leading spaces are left blank. The exclamation mark is printed immediately after the 0 digit in the string, indicating that the field ends at that point. This is also true of the other output lines in this program.

The second **printf()** statement uses %**15.5s**, which permits only five of the ten digits in the string argument to be printed. The other ten spaces within the field are left blank. The next statement uses %**5s** without limiting the number of characters to be printed. As a result, the field is extended to ten positions to print the entire string. The last statement includes a %**15s** specifier. This says that the minimum field length is 15 positions, without limiting the number of characters that can be printed. Since the string argument only contains ten characters, the output will be identical to that of the first statement.

In the previous example, all the strings were printed having right adjustment within their fields. By using the − modifier, we can force the strings to be printed with left adjustment. The program of Fig. 5.16 outputs the same string of digits using three different left-adjusted conversion specifiers.

```
/* string formatting using - modifier */
#include <stdio.h>
main()
      {
      printf("%-15s%c\n", "1234567890", '!');
      printf("%-5s%c\n", "1234567890", '!');
      printf("%-15.5s%c\n", "1234567890", '!');
      }
```

```
1234567890     !
1234567890!
12345          !
```

Figure 5.16 String formatting using the - modifier.

In the first **printf()** statement, the specifier %**−15s** forces left adjustment, sets a minimum field width of 15 positions, and does not limit the number of characters that can be printed. Since there are only ten characters within the string, five spaces are left blank at the right. Notice that the exclamation mark is printed in column 16, confirming that the string field is indeed 15 character positions long. The next statement uses %**−5s**, which sets up a left-adjusted field width of five but does not limit the number of characters to be printed. The string will therefore extend the field to ten positions. The last statement uses %**−15.5s**. This forces left adjustment within a minimum field width of 15 positions and limits the output to five characters. Therefore, only the first five digits of the string are printed, the balance of the field being left as blank spaces.

Long constants must be identified by an **l** or **L** suffix. The capital form is preferred since it cannot be confused with the digit 1. To print data that are a **long** integer, the conversion modifier **l** or **L** must be used. The program of Fig. 5.17 illustrates that the correct output is obtained using the %**ld** specifier and that an erroneous output is printed if the %**d** specifier is used.

The next example shows how we can combine number and string formatting to obtain a table of numbers with column headings that is properly arranged. The program of Fig. 5.18 uses string fields and floating-point fields that are each 20 positions long. The quantity being tabulated and its units are printed in right-adjusted string fields using a specifier of %**20s**. The floating-point data are printed

```
/* print very long integers */
#include <stdio.h>
main()
      {
      long big = 123456789L;

      printf("%ld\n", big);
      printf("%d\n", big);
      }
```

```
123456789
-13035
```

Figure 5.17 Printing long integers.

```
/* putting it all together */
#include <stdio.h>
main()
      {
      int j;
      float v, i, r;

      line();
      printf("%20s%20s%20s\n", "VOLTAGE", "RESISTANCE", "CURRENT");
      printf("%20s%20s%20s\n", "(volts)", "(ohms)", "(amperes)");
      line();
      v = 100;
      for (r = 1; r <= 100; r = 2*r)
            {
            i = v/r;
            printf("%20.3f%20.3f%20.3f\n", v, r, i);
            }
      line();
      }

line()                                    /* draw a line */
      {
      int j;

      for (j = 0; j <= 10; j++)
            putchar(' ');
      for (j = 11; j <= 60; j++)
            putchar('_');
      putchar('\n');
      }
```

VOLTAGE (volts)	RESISTANCE (ohms)	CURRENT (amperes)
100.000	1.000	100.000
100.000	2.000	50.000
100.000	4.000	25.000
100.000	8.000	12.500
100.000	16.000	6.250
100.000	32.000	3.125
100.000	64.000	1.563

Figure 5.18 Putting it all together.

with a specifier of **%20.3f**, thus aligning the numbers underneath the column headings.

The function **line()** is used to draw a line that separates the heading from the data and also to identify the extent of the table. The function is called once before the headings are printed, again before the data are printed, and finally after the data are output. Two **for** loops are used in the **line()** function. The first prints a series of blank spaces up to the start of the table. The second prints the underscore (_) character across the data table.

Scanf()

The **scanf()** function is formally defined by

```
scanf(control string, arg1, arg2,...);
```

where the *control string* includes the conversion specifiers listed in Fig. 2.3. The arguments **(arg1, arg2,...)** in the list are pointers to where the converted inputs will be stored. This necessitates using the **&** operator before each variable name in the list except those that refer to string data. The number of conversion specifiers in the control string must equal the number of arguments in the list.

The **scanf()** function uses *white space* characters to determine where one input ends and the next begins. White space characters include the space (SP or spacebar), tab (\t), and newline (\n). An input extends to the next white space character that is encountered. Thus, if we have a **scanf()** statement that expects four inputs, there must be at least three separators between the inputs that are either spaces, tabs, or newlines. This also means that there cannot be any white space within an input item. Thus, a string input using **scanf()** cannot be a sentence since the input would terminate when the space is encountered at the end of the first word.

The **%c** specifier is the only one that will read white space as a valid input. All other conversion specifiers will ignore single or multiple occurrences of white space between inputs.

The **%d** specifier will stop reading an input at the first nondigit entry. This includes the decimal point. Thus, an input such as **12.34** that is associated with a **%d** specifier will assign **12** to the integer variable. An input of **12a** will likewise assign **12** to the variable. An invalid character that occurs within any input item will terminate that input. The unaccepted characters will be read by the next input routine, whether it is another **scanf()** conversion specification, a **getchar()**, or any other type.

To enter a **long** integer, the conversion specifier must be **%ld**. Likewise, for type **double**, the specifier **%lf** is used to denote a **long float**, or double precision. Of course, we may enter numbers in octal or hexadecimal by using the specifiers **%o** or **%x**, respectively.

Sometimes it is desirable to permit entry of characters that are not actually data items. This can be done by inserting the input characters to be ignored within the control string. For example, to enter two decimal numbers that are separated by a comma, the control string is **"%d,%d"**. (Users of BASIC will appreciate this feature, since multiple entries are separated by commas instead of white space in that language.) Whenever additional characters are inserted in the control string, they must appear in the input stream.

When all the data items within the **scanf()** have been read, a return is made to the function from which it was called. If an input does not match the conversion specification, the **scanf()** function will stop reading the inputs and return with an error. The program of Fig. 5.19 illustrates the use of **scanf()** for formatted input. Two calls are made to the **scanf()** function. The first inputs a character and a string. The second inputs an integer and float number. The two calls to **scanf()** could have been combined into one without any change in operation on most systems. Some **C** implementations require a newline character at the end of the **scanf()** input. On these systems, two calls to **scanf()** would require two newline characters.

The program is executed three times. In the first run, valid inputs are entered and printed. In the second run, a **float** number is entered for the integer conversion specifier. This results in the whole number portion (**123**) being assigned to the integer variable **i** and the decimal portion (**.456**) being read for the next conversion specifier, which assigns the decimal to the **float** variable **n**. There will be no error indication, even though a wrong assignment has been made for **n**. The value of **3.14159** will not be read.

In the third run, a value of **abc** is entered for the character. This results in the first character **a** being assigned to the variable **c** and the characters **bc** to the variable **string**. An attempt to assign the string **Vince** to an **int** variable results in an error that terminates the **scanf()** function, with no assignment made for either of the variables **i** or **n**. Both of these variables will contain garbage values.

```
/* formatted input using scanf() */
#include <stdio.h>
main()
      {
      char c, string[80];
      int i;
      float n;

      puts("Enter a character, your name, age, and the value of pi");
      scanf("%c %s", &c, string);
      scanf("%d %f", &i, &n);
      printf("%c\n", c);
      printf("%s\n", string);
      printf("%d\t%f\n", i, n);
      }
```

```
Enter a character, your name, age, and the value of pi
z Vincent 46 3.14159
z
Vincent
46      3.141590

Enter a character, your name, age, and the value of pi
q Vince 123.456 3.14159
q
Vince
123     0.456000

Enter a character, your name, age, and the value of pi
abc Vince 46 3.14159
a
bc
-22239  0.000000
```

Figure 5.19 Input formatting with **scanf()**.

PROBLEMS

5.1. What is output from the following program?

```
#include <stdio.h>
#define MESSAGE "Hello"
main()
    {
    printf("%d\n",strlen(MESSAGE));
    printf("%s\n",MESSAGE);
    }
```

5.2. What is output from the following program?

```
#include <stdio.h>
#define STR1 "first"
#define STR2 "second"
#define STR3 "and third"
main()
      {
      puts(STR1);
      printf("%s",STR2);
      puts(STR3);
      }
```

5.3. What is output from the following program (assuming one word is entered in lowercase for the **scanf()** function)?

```
#include <stdio.h>
main()
      {
      char text[10];
      int i;

      scanf("%s",text);
      for (i = 0; i < strlen(text); i++)
            putchar(text[i] - 32);
      }
```

5.4. What is output by each of the following **printf()** statements?
(a) `printf("%10.4f\n",123.456789);`
(b) `printf("%-10.4f\n",123.456789);`
(c) `printf("%8d\n",1234);`
(d) `printf("%-8d\n",1234);`
(e) `printf("%20.5s\n","abcdefg");`

5.5. What input character will cause the following loop to terminate?

```
while ((c = getchar())!= 32)
      putchar(c);
```

5.6. Modify Problem 4.5 to format the output data. The angles should be whole numbers (no decimal places). The sine, cosine, and tangent values should each have four digits to the right of the decimal point.

chapter 6

Functions and Program Development

6.1 FUNCTIONS IN C

A function in **C** is a named block of statements that performs a specific task. As we mentioned earlier, **C** programs consist of a series of functions. The first function to be executed must be named **main()**. It generally contains a series of calls to other functions. Since function calls may be nested, a function that is called from **main()** may in turn make a series of calls to other functions. This hierarchy allows us to structure a program so that the more general functions are called from **main()**. These functions will then call other functions that perform more specific subtasks.

The highly specific functions within a program may already exist in one of the following sources:

1. The standard input/output (**stdio**) library. This includes functions such as **printf()**.
2. Other libraries, such as the math library or custom libraries.
3. Functions already written for other parts of the program that may be used again.

A function that is not available from one of these sources must be developed for the given task. It can then be placed into some library of functions for future use.

The format of functions in **C** is shown in Fig. 6.1. We will give a brief description of each component of a **C** function in this section and look at some aspects of functions in more detail in later sections.

Function Name

From our earlier examples, we have seen that each function has a name followed by a set of parentheses. Names for functions follow the same rules as names for variables. They may contain only letters, digits, or the underscore character. The first character must be a letter or the underscore. **C** compilers and interpreters typically provide for 8 to 32 significant characters for a function name. Additional characters may be permitted, but they will not be significant.

```
preprocessor directives                         ⎫
                                                ⎬ Function header
type name(argument list)                        ⎪
argument declarations                           ⎭

     {                                          ⎫
     variable declarations                      ⎪
                                                ⎬ Function body
     statements                                 ⎪
     }                                          ⎭
```

Figure 6.1 Format of **C** functions.

When a function is being defined, the function name is not followed by a semicolon. However, when a function is being called from another function, the semicolon is used after the function call, just as it would be after any statement.

Function-type Declaration

The *function-type declaration* determines the type of the data that the function will return. If no data are returned, it is customary to specify a **void** function type. When the type is not included, the default will be **int**. A function that returns **char** type data need not be declared, since **char** data are converted to **int** in expressions.

A function that should return a **float** or **double** value must have a **float** or **double** function type declaration. Otherwise, the returned data may not be readable. In fact, a function that returns anything other than **int** or **char** must have a type declaration. It is good practice to use a function-type declaration for all functions.

Argument List

If a function does not receive any data from the calling function, then the parentheses will not inclose any arguments. When data are to be received, then the *argument list* includes the variable names that pass the data to the function. For example, the math library function **pow(x,y)** receives the number **x** and the power to which it is to be raised, **y**, from the calling function. All the variables in the argument list are separated by commas.

Argument Declarations

The *argument declarations* are listed after the function name, but before the open brace of the function body. They specify the data type of the variables in the argument list. The declarations are written in the same manner as those used within the function body. The variables declared in the argument declarations are not declared again within the function body.

Function Body

The first open brace after the function name marks the beginning of the function body. The body includes the declaration of all the variables used in the function and the statements that implement the task of the function. It is common practice to separate the declarations from the function statements by a blank line. The body ends with a close brace.

Function Header

The *function header* is the name given to the collection of lines that precede the function body. These lines include any preprocessor commands associated with the function, the function name, and the declaration of the function arguments.

6.2 HOW FUNCTIONS PASS PARAMETERS

Passing Parameters to a Function

The arguments specified within a function call are referred to as the *actual parameters*. The arguments specified in a function header are referred to as the *formal parameters*. In **C**, when a function call is made, the values of the actual parameters are copied into the formal parameters. This process is referred to as *passing parameters by value*. It is important to note that the function receives a temporary copy of the actual parameters. Any alteration of the value of the formal parameters within the called function will not affect the value of the actual parameters in the calling function.

The alternative method of passing data to a function is called *passing parameters by reference*. In this procedure, the addresses of the variables that are the actual parameters are passed to the called function. Any alteration of the value of these variables within the called function will affect their values within the calling function.

Array variables in **C** are passed by reference. When an array name is given as an argument in a function call, the address of the beginning of the array is passed to the function. This is a practical arrangement, since copying the value of all the elements in an array would be a time- and memory-consuming process.

It is possible to have **C** functions pass parameters by reference. This is done by passing a pointer to a variable, rather than the variable itself. This process is discussed in Chapter 7.

Returning a Value from a Function

If a function does not return a value, it can be terminated either by a **return** statement or simply by encountering the close brace of the function body. In either case, control is returned to the calling function.

A **return**(*expression*) statement that includes the optional parentheses returns the value of *expression* to the calling function. When the parentheses are used, an argument must be included. The type of the returned value is the same as the type of the function.

Passing Parameters: An Example

The program of Fig. 6.2 illustrates how parameters are passed when a function call is made. This program includes a function **cube(x)**, which returns the cube of its argument **x**.

```
/* passing arguments by value */
#include <stdio.h>
main()
      {
      int x = 4;
      int y;

      y = cube(x);
      printf("The value of y in main() is %d\n", y);
      printf("The value of x in main() after calling cube() is %d\n", x);
      }

int cube(x)               /* cube a number passed by value */
int x;
      {
      x = x * x * x;
      printf("The value of x returned by cube() is %d\n", x);
      return (x);
      }
```

```
The value of x returned by cube() is 64
The value of y in main() is 64
The value of x in main() after calling cube() is 4
```

Figure 6.2 Passing arguments by value.

The value of **x** in **main()** is initialized to 4. The statement

```
y = cube(x);
```

will result in a call to the function **cube(x)**, with the value of 4 being passed to the function. The value returned by the function will be assigned to **y**. The value of **y** and the value of **x** in **main()** after calling **cube()** are then printed by the pair of **printf()** statements.

The function **cube(x)** contains the statement

```
x = x*x*x;
```

which replaces the value of **x** within **cube()** by its cubed value. This cubed value is printed to show the value of **x** in **cube()** that will be returned to **main()**. The statement

```
return(x);
```

returns the cubed value to **main()**.

A run of the program shows that the value of **x** returned by **cube()** is 64. The value of **y** in **main()** is also 64, indicating that the statement **y = cube(x);** performed the correct assignment of the returned value. The value of **x** in **main()** after calling **cube()** still equals 4. This proves that **cube(x)** received a copy of **x**, since its value in **main()** was unaffected.

The name of the formal parameter used by **cube()** does not have to be the same as the name of the actual parameter passed to it. We could just as well have defined the function as **cube(z)** or made calls to **cube(x)** with statements like

```
cube(10);
cube(a);
cube(a+b);
```

6.3 STORAGE CLASS AND SCOPE OF VARIABLES

The **C** language provides four classes of storage for variables. Each class has unique properties that make it suitable for storage of certain types of data. The four classes are

1. Automatic (auto)
2. External (extern)
3. Static
4. Register

The storage class of a variable is declared by prefixing the variable type with a *storage class* identifier. For example, to declare the integer variable **x** as being **static**, we would use

```
static int x;
```

If a storage class identifier is not given to a variable declared within a function; it defaults to **auto**. For variables defined outside a function, the default is **extern**.

The *scope* of a variable is the extent within a program to which the variable is available. A variable that is defined and available only within a function is referred to as a *local variable*. A variable that is available to a function but defined outside the function is referred to as a *global variable*. In **C**, we can control the scope of a variable. It may be restricted to one function, a group of functions, or the entire program.

Automatic Variables

Automatic variables have a scope that is limited to the function in which they are declared. They are thus local variables. Two or more functions can have automatic variables with the same names. Such identically named variables are totally independent of each other, just as if their names were unique.

An automatic variable has a limited longevity. It comes into existence when the function in which it is declared is called. After a return from the function, the variable is no longer defined. Thus, automatic variables cannot maintain their values from one call to the next call of the same function.

Any variable declared within a function that does not have a specified storage class will be **auto** by default. The following declarations are therefore equivalent:

```
auto int x;
     int x;
```

External Variables

Any variable defined outside a function is **external** by default. Such a variable is available without declaration to any function that follows its definition within the same source file. It is also available to any function in the entire program that declares the variable using the keyword **extern**. It is good practice to always declare the use of an **external** variable, even when it is not necessary.

The program of Fig. 6.3 illustrates the use of **external** variables. We have defined the **external** variable **x_pos** as **int** outside any function and initialized its value to 100. The definition occurs after the function **pre_1()** and before **main()**. The functions **post_1()** and **post_2()** both follow the definition of **x_pos** as well.

```
/* use of external variables */
#include <stdio.h>

int pre_1()                     /* declares x_pos as extern */
      {
      extern int x_pos;

      printf("x_pos in pre_1 is %d\n", x_pos);
      }

int x_pos = 100;                /* x_pos is defined as extern */

main()
      {
      extern int x_pos;           /* declares x_pos as extern */

      printf("x_pos in main is %d\n", x_pos);
      pre_1();
      post_1();
      post_2();
      }

int post_1()                    /* uses x_pos without declaration */
      {
      printf("x_pos in post_1 is %d\n", x_pos);
      }

int post_2()                    /* declares x_pos as auto */
      {
      auto int x_pos;

      printf("x_pos in post_2 is %d\n", x_pos);
      }
```

```
x_pos in main is 100
x_pos in pre_1 is 100
x_pos in post_1 is 100
x_pos in post_2 is -25575
```

Figure 6.3 External variables.

All the functions within the program print the value of a variable called **x_pos**. The functions **pre_1()** and **main()** both declare the variable as **extern int x_pos**. These functions access the same external variable **x_pos** and print a value of 100. The function **post_1()** also has access to the same variable, even though it does not include any declarations at all. This is due to the fact that **post_1()** occurs after the definition of **x_pos**.

The function **post_2()** does not have access to the same **x_pos** variable. It has declared an **int x_pos**, which defaults to a storage class of **auto**. The **auto** declaration overrides the external definition. Thus **post_2()** has created a unique variable of the same name. The value of **x_pos** in **post_2()** is undefined. It will not contain 100, but some garbage value instead.

Static Variables

The **static** storage class may be applied to local or external variables. It has a different effect on local variables than it does on external variables. Local variables that are declared **static** have permanent storage within the function in which they are defined. They retain their value from one function call to the next. They are initialized only once during compilation, whereas automatic variables must be initialized during each function call. The scope of local **static** and automatic variables is the same.

When the **static** storage class is applied to external variables, the scope of these variables becomes the remainder of the same source file. In other words, these variables are hidden from other source files that make up the same program. All functions have an external storage class. We can declare a function **static** as well. It then takes on a degree of privacy in that it is only known or available to other functions within the same source file.

A variable or function is declared **static** by prefixing its name with the keyword **static**. For example, **i** is declared as a **static** integer by

```
static int i;
```

If the declaration occurs within a function, it becomes a local **static int**. If it occurs outside any function, it becomes an external **static int**. Likewise, the function **secret()** is declared static by

```
static secret();
```

Register Variables

The **register** storage class is restricted to automatic variables and the formal parameters of a function. It is applied to variables that are used frequently within a function. The compiler will make an attempt to store **register** variables in the central processor unit registers, thus speeding up execution. It will also provide for more compact machine code.

There is a physical limit to the number of variables within a function that may be given the **register** storage class. Those that cannot be included will be treated as if they do not have this specification. In fact, many of the smaller microcomputer **C** compilers totally ignore the **register** storage class specifier.

Selecting a Storage Class

The most fundamental decision to be made in selecting a storage class is whether to make a variable local or global. The primary advantage of local variables is that their privacy affords a degree of protection. No other function in a program can inadvertently destroy the value of a local variable. This is a very important factor, especially in larger programs.

Normally, local variables will be automatic. This is the default storage class. If permanence of data is needed, then the choice should be local **static**. Another advantage of local **static** variables is that they are automatically initialized to zero if there is no explicit initialization. When speed of execution is important and there are frequently used variables within the function, then the **register** class may be used for these variables.

The primary advantage of global variables is that they facilitate communicating data between functions. If two or more functions must share or communicate a large number of variables or data values, then the external storage class eliminates the need for large function argument lists. Another advantage is that external arrays can be initialized. This is not permitted for automatic arrays.

6.4 THE C PREPROCESSOR

The **C** *preprocessor* is a language extension that provides useful tools for program processing before actual compilation. It is a standard part of the **C** environment. The preprocessor's action takes place as the first step of the compilation process, and its operation is automatic, not requiring any user intervention. The preprocessor provides the following services:

1. *Macro* definition:	This allows substitution of a user-defined *identifier* with a *replacement string*.
2. File inclusion	Normally used for inclusion of *header* files, which contain commonly used declarations, definitions, and constants for the compilation process.
3. Conditional compilation	Provides for selective compilation of a program based on test conditions.

The preprocessor instructions, called *directives*, can be used anywhere within a program. The scope of preprocessor directives is from the line in which they are located to the end of the source file in which they are included. They must start in the first or leftmost column and begin with the **#** symbol. Preprocessor directives are not **C** statements and therefore are not terminated by the semicolon.

Macro Definition

The preprocessor directive **#define** is used for macro definition. Its format is

#define *identifier re placement string*

where the *identifier* is a string of characters that do not include spaces. The *replacement string* is substituted for each occurrence of the identifier by the preprocessor. This string may be a constant or an expression containing parameters. The replacement string may contain spaces. It normally extends to the end of the line, but appending a backslash, \, allows extension to the next line.

We have already seen the **#define** directive used for symbolic constant replacement. For example,

```
#define PI 3.14159
#define MAX 80
```

will replace each occurrence of **PI** and **MAX** within the source file with their respective values. The use of symbolic constants makes the source file more readable. It also simplifies editing a program. Changing the definition of **MAX** to **50** would automatically change its value to **50** everywhere that **MAX** occurs throughout the file.

Macro substitutions do not take place within quotation marks. For example, using the previous definition of **MAX**,

```
printf("There are %d tabs and MAX columns.\n",6);
```

will print

```
There are 6 tabs and MAX columns.
```

Another use of symbolic constants is for shorthand representation of long strings. For example,

```
#define PROMPT "Press enter to continue the program."
```

may be useful for repeated printing of the prompt message without having to type it each time. The statement

```
puts(PROMPT);
```

is equivalent to

```
puts("Press enter to continue the program.");
```

Macros with Arguments

A macro containing arguments is somewhat like a function. However, function calls involve processor activity that adds to the execution time. The simple in-line code provided by a macro with arguments offers a speed advantage for repetitive code whenever the macro has a relatively short execution time. Also, the macro is useful for any data type, whereas a function must be type specific.

Consider the definition

```
#define SSQ(a,b) ((a)*(a) + (b)*(b))
```

which finds the sum of squares of **a** and **b**. Wherever the identifier **SSQ(a,b)** occurs within the source file, the macro is expanded by replacing the identifier with the substitution string. This is done before compilation. The resulting in-line code executes considerably faster than the equivalent function call. Notice that the macro definition does not specify a data type. It may be used for **int**, **float**, or any other type without modification or duplication.

The parentheses around the arguments in the macro **SSQ(a,b)** are needed to prevent errors due to improper association. To illustrate this, let's expand the macro both ways. Using **SSQ_1(a,b) = a*a + b*b** with **a = x+1** and **b = 2** gives

```
x+1*x+1 + 2*2
```

which equals **2x + 5**. Substituting the same values into **SSQ(a,b)** gives

```
((x+1)*(x+1) + (2)*(2))
```

which equals $\mathbf{x^2+2x+5}$. If **x=2**, then the sum of squares of **3** and **2** equals **13**. The expansion without parentheses erroneously gives **9**, whereas using the parentheses correctly gives **13**.

Let's look at some examples of correct usage of the macro **SSQ(a,b)**. The statement

```
printf("The sum of squares of %d and %d is %d\n",3,4,SSQ(3,4));
```

will output

```
The sum of squares of 3 and 4 is 25
```

We can use a macro as an argument within a function call. In such a case, care must be taken to provide the function call with the correct data type. For example,

```
printf("The square root of the sum of squares of %f and %fis",3.0,4.0);
printf("%f \n",sqrt(SSQ(3.0,4.0));
```

will output

```
The square root of the sum of squares of 3.0 and 4.0 is 5.0
```

The decimal points in the arguments for **SSQ(a,b)** were needed, since the **sqrt()** function requires a **double** argument.

File Inclusion

The preprocessor directive

```
#include "filename" or
#include <filename>
```

is used to include the listed *filename* during the compilation process. The included filename is usually a *header file,* with an extension of **.h** at the end. Header files consist of commonly used **#define** directives, declarations for **external** variables, functions that return a type other than **int** or **char**, and so on. Some commonly used **#include** files that we have already encountered are **stdio.h** and **math.h**. These are ASCII files included with your compiler that you may examine. Typical **stdio.h** and **math.h** headers are shown in Fig. 6.4.

The **stdio.h** header consists of definitions of symbolic constants that normally include **stdin**, **stdout**, and **stderr**, which are the standard input, standard output, and standard error file names. Also typical are the symbolic constants that define **NULL**, **TRUE**, **FALSE**, and **EOF**. Macros may also be included in the **stdio.h** file. These are used in lieu of functions for speed and flexibility.

The **math.h** header simply declares all the functions in the math library as being **extern double**. Including the **math.h** header saves you the chore of having to make these declarations within your program when it includes calls to the math functions.

Conditional Compilation

The conditional compilation facility of the preprocessor allows us to configure a program based on test conditions. The **#if**, **#ifdef**, and **#ifndef** instructions are used to test some condition. The subsequent action taken by these instructions may be to **#include** other files or headers and/or to **#define** a list of constants and expressions.

The **#if** instruction is typically used to test the value of a symbolic constant. For example,

```
#if DEVICE == "MOUSE"
#include mouse.h
#endif
```

tests to see if the symbolic constant **DEVICE** equals **"MOUSE"**. If it does, the **mouse.h** header will be included for compilation. The **#endif** instruction identifies

```
/* stdio.h header file */

#define     stdin   0
#define     stdout  1
#define     stderr  2

#define     NULL    0
#define     TRUE    1
#define     FALSE   0
#define     EOF     (-1)
#define     ERROR   (-1)
#define     BUFSIZ  512

#define     getchar()   getc(stdin)
#define     putchar(c)  putc(c,stdout)

#define     abs(x)      ((x) < 0 ? -(x) : (x))
#define     max(a,b)    ((a) > (b) ? (a) : (b))
#define     min(a,b)    ((a) <= (b) ? (a) : (b))
```

(a)

```
/* math.h header file */

extern  double sqrt(), sin(), cos(), tan(), cot(), asin(), acos(), atan();
extern  double atan2(), exp(), exp10(), log(), log10(), pow(), fabs();
extern  double frand(), floor(), ceil();
```

(b)

Figure 6.4 Typical header files: (a) **stdio.h**; (b) **math.h**.

the end of the block of instructions following the #**if**. (Braces are not used by the preprocessor.)

The #**ifdef** instruction will be true if its argument has been previously defined. For example.

```
#ifdef TABLET
#include tablet.h
#define BUFSIZ 1024
#else
#include keyboard.h
#define BUFSIZ 512
#endif
```

will #**include tablet.h** and #**define BUFSIZE 1024** if **TABLET** has been defined. The #**else** instruction terminates the list following the #**ifdef**, just as a close brace would for the **if else** statement. It also indicates that if **TABLET** is not defined #**include keyboard.h** and #**define BUFSIZ 512**. The #**endif** instruction terminates the #**else** list.

If you wish to test for the absence of a particular macro definition, the #**ifndef** will do just that. The instruction

```
#ifndef TABLET
```

will be true if **TABLET** is not currently defined.

The preprocessor includes the instruction **#undef** to undefine a macro. For example,

```
#undef TABLET
```

will delete a previously defined macro for **TABLET**. This may be used to control the scope of a macro definition.

6.5 PROGRAM DEVELOPMENT AND PSEUDOCODE

How do you proceed from the definition of what a software program should do toward the final product? An architect has a design or blueprint that follows certain design rules for the construction of a building. So, too, a systems analyst, computer engineer, or programmer must have a design or plan for the construction of a program. The more complex the programming task, the more extensive will be the design or planning involved. The steps involved in going from a general description of what is needed to the completion of the project include:

1. Definition of the problem
2. Design of the program
3. Coding in a computer language
4. Debugging the program until it appears error free
5. Testing or validating the program to determine if it meets the functional specifications under all conditions
6. Documentation of the program
7. Maintenance and user support for the program

In this section, we will briefly consider problem definition and focus on the design of the program and coding. Chapter 8 will deal primarily with debugging a program. It will also consider, to a lesser extent, the remaining steps in the development process.

Definition of the Problem

The problem definition must specify completely what the program will do. All inputs and outputs must be defined. All the desired features of the program must be completely specified. Any special handling of errors must be included. The problem definition is the blueprint from which the program will be constructed.

Design of the Program

The design of the program is the process of converting the definition into a detailed plan for the solution. The output of the design process should be detailed enough so that the coding phase is simply a conversion into a particular computer language. The tools and processes of the design phase are discussed in the following sections.

Algorithms and Pseudocode

An *algorithm* is a well-defined procedure that can be used to perform some task. The term is normally used to describe mathematical or computer operations.

Algorithms are commonly expressed as a sequence of steps described in:

1. English (or any other human language)
2. Algebraic formulas
3. Pseudocode
4. Flowcharts

You are already familiar with instructions written in English or expressions written as algebraic formulas. Each of these methods is good but too restrictive to be used for all applications. *Pseudocode* is a mix of English, algebra, and computer-language-type instructions that facilitates the development of algorithms. *Flowcharts* represent an alternative to pseudocode. They express an algorithm in a graphical format. We will use only pseudocode for algorithms in this text. The widespread availability of computers with text editors or word processors has made pseudocode a much faster and more convenient method for algorithm development than the use of flowcharts.

Pseudocode language or syntax is not strictly defined. An individual has the freedom to use his or her own style. However, the style that is selected must be well defined, clear, and used consistently throughout.

Top-down Design

A method of designing a program that proceeds from a general description through successively more detailed levels is referred to as *top-down design*. In the top or most general level, the pseudocode will contain English statements that describe each task to be performed in rather nonspecific terminology. The bottom level of pseudocode will contain highly detailed and specific steps. The transition from the bottom level of pseudocode to actual program code should be not much more than a simple language translation.

A characteristic of top-down design is that a program is defined in terms of *modules*. Each module performs a specific task or function. In proceeding toward more refinement of a design, a module is broken down into a series of smaller modules. Each module is a self-contained entity with well-defined inputs and outputs. In designing a program using the top-down approach, we can focus our attention on a particular module, rather than having to consider the program as a whole.

You might well be asking yourself, "What is the difference between a **C** function and a pseudocode module?" The answer is that they are conceptually one and the same. We use the term module as a generic descriptor. In **C**, a module becomes a function. In Pascal, it becomes a Pascal function or procedure, and so on.

Pseudocode Syntax and Structures

The English and algebraic components of pseudocode are straightforward. The only exception is that there must be a clear distinction between the use of equality and assignment operators. The same problem occurs in all high-level languages. We will use the **C** notation of a double equal sign (==) for equality and a single equal sign for assignment. Other notations commonly used include the Pascal convention of the equal sign for equality and the colon/equal sign (:=) combination for assignment. Another uses the equal sign for equality and an arrow to indicate assignment.

The syntax used to indicate input or output operations should be consistent in the pseudocode. We will use **input** and **print** for simplicity.

There must be a clear distinction between a module name and a variable name. We will use the convention that any name terminated by an open parenthesis is a module name. A module is called by any occurrence of the module name that is not the definition of the module. The beginning of a module definition is marked by prefixing the name with the word module. All modules will start with the module name and end with the module name prefixed by **end**. The body of a module will be indented from the name. Parameters passed to a module will be indicated within parentheses following the module name. We will use the **C** convention of indicating the value returned by a function by **return**(*value*).

Since the transition from pseudocode to computer language should be a trivial one, it is convenient to use computer language control structures in our pseudocode language. These are listed in Fig. 6.5. Notice that all the pseudocode included within a control structure is indented to clearly show the extent of that structure.

```
Control structure        Pseudocode format

if                       if (conditions)
                              pseudocode
                         end if

if else                  if (conditions)
                              pseudocode
                         else
                              pseudocode
                         end if

while                    while (conditions)
                              pseudocode
                         end while

for                      for (conditions)
                              pseudocode
                         end for
```

Figure 6.5 Basic pseudocode control structures.

Program Design Procedure

The steps involved in designing a program will be outlined here. We will combine the coding step into the design process, although in a professional environment the two processes are usually kept separate. Examples follow in the next section. Depending on the complexity of the programming project, you may find that certain steps may be omitted or combined. Conversely, you may find that additional levels of pseudocode must be used to arrive at the final solution. Each step should be written and saved as part of the overall program documentation.

The procedure outlined next looks simple. In reality, most programming projects require a lot of thought, some redesign, and a good deal of persistence to arrive at a finished product. Before beginning a project, make sure that you are thoroughly familiar with all the particulars of an application that have an impact on the program itself.

1. *General description:* Write a general description of what the program should do. It may initially be in text form, but you should rewrite it into a series of English statements or instructions to make the next step easier.
2. *Convert to modular format:* Convert the general description into modular format. Remember that a module performs a well-defined task. You

may find it useful to include the basic pseudocode control structures at this point, even if the pseudocode they contain is still English text. Give the modules names and describe what each should do. Identify whatever variables are obviously needed at this point. Some additions or changes will most likely be needed.

3. *Convert to detailed pseudocode:* Look at the contents of each of the modules defined in step 2. If a module appears too complex or vague for coding, break it up into a series of modules, each of which performs a more specific task. Replace English text with specific pseudocode control structures and algebraic formulas. Identify variables needed and their scope. Identify all the parameters that a module needs.
4. *Code in a programming language:* When you are satisfied that each module has been reduced to its simplest form, convert the pseudocode into programming language statements.

6.6 EXAMPLES OF PROGRAM DESIGN

This section contains three examples of program design. The first example, Weighing an Object, is of general interest and does not require any special expertise. The second example, Series/Parallel Circuit Reduction, assumes a knowledge of electric circuit analysis. The third, Decimal to Binary Conversion, assumes a knowledge of the binary number system. You may select from these examples whichever seems most appropriate for your particular interest.

Weighing an Object

Project definition: An object is to be weighed using a balance scale such as the one shown in Fig. 6.6. Design a program that simulates weighing the object. Assume a set of weights ranging from some defined maximum to minimum and that, for any given weight, the next smaller weight will be half its value.

Solution: Before beginning to write any pseudocode, we must be familiar with the particulars of the application that will have an impact on the project itself. In this case, we must know the mechanism by which the balance scale weighs an object. The object whose weight is unknown is placed in one pan, and a combination of standard weights is applied on the other that causes the balance arm to remain horizontal (not tipping either way). The sum of these standard weights will equal the weight of the object. At this point, we can write the general description as in Fig. 6.7. This description corresponds to steps 1 and 2 in the program design procedure. Since the algorithm was relatively simple, we were able to combine the two steps and write the description in modular form.

The pseudocode is still not detailed enough for writing the program. It does not specify how the trial weights will be selected or what happens if all possible weight combinations are exhausted without balancing the scale. We also have to convert vague wording such as ''scale not balanced'' into quantitative test conditions. More information about how to use the scale is needed before proceeding. If you were a student of chemistry, you will recall the procedure used for weighing with a balance scale.

1. Select the largest standard weight as a trial weight and place it on the pan.
2. As long as the scale is not balanced, repeat 2.1 to 2.3.
   2.1. If the scale tips toward the object, keep the trial weight on the pan.
   2.2. If the scale tips toward the trial weight, remove the trial weight.

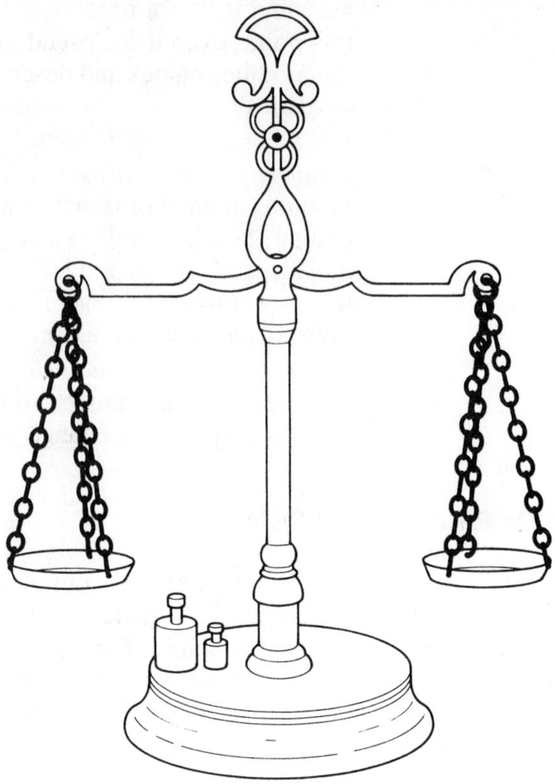

Figure 6.6 Balance scale used for weighing an object.

```
module main()
     place object to be weighed on scale
     while (scale not balanced)
          try standard weight combinations on pan
     end while
     weight of object equals sum of standard weights on pan
end main()
```

Figure 6.7 First-level pseudocode for weighing an object.

2.3. Select the next smaller standard weight as the trial weight and place it on the pan.

3. Add the value of all the standard weights on the pan. Their sum equals the weight of the object.

This procedure is one application of a general algorithm called *successive approximation*. It occurs in other areas such as *analog to digital conversion* and the *binary search* procedure (see Section 7.7). We will incorporate this procedure into our next level of pseudocode along with the variable **trial_weight** (see Fig. 6.8).

```
module main()
     place object to be weighed on scale
     trial_weight = largest weight available

     while (scale not balanced and more standard weights available)
          apply trial_weight
          if (scale tips toward trial_weight)
               remove trial_weight
          else
               keep trial_weight
          end if
          set new trial_weight to half the last trial weight
     end while

     if (scale not balanced and no more trial weights)
          object too heavy to weigh!
     else
          weight of object equals total of applied weights
     end if
end main()
```

Figure 6.8 Second-level pseudocode for weighing an object.

The "scale not balanced" condition occurs when the weight of the object is not equal to the sum of the standard weights applied. To express this condition quantitatively, let's create the variables **weight_applied**, **weight_object**, and **weight_error**. The value of **weight_error** is given by the absolute value of the difference of **weight_object** and **weight_applied**, or

```
weight_error = abs(weight_object - weight_applied)
```

The test condition can now be written as

```
while (weight_error > MAX_ERR)
```

where **MAX_ERR** is the maximum allowable error. It can be defined within our program to yield whatever accuracy is needed. Other constants within the program will include **MAX_WT**, the largest standard weight, and **MIN_WT**, the minimum standard weight.

The statement "if scale tips toward trial weight" can be written as

```
if (weight_applied > weight_object)
```

using the variables we have created; "apply trial weight" can be written as

```
weight_applied = weight_applied + trial_weight
```

Likewise, "remove trial weight" becomes

```
weight_applied = weight_applied - trial_weight
```

The final level of pseudocode is given in Fig. 6.9. Notice that an **input** is used to define **weight_object**. For the purpose of the simulation, **weight_object** will never be assigned to **weight_applied**. Its value will only be compared to **weight_applied** using the inequality operators. This is how the balance scale operates, by comparing quantities.

```
/* pseudocode for simulating the weighing of an object */
module main()
     trial_weight = MAX_WT
     weight_applied = 0

     input weight_object
     weight_error = weight_object

     while ((weight_error > MAX_ERR) and (trial_weight >= MIN_WT))
          weight_applied = weight_applied + trial_weight
          if (weight_applied > weight_object)
               weight_applied = weight_applied - trial_weight
          end if
          trial_weight = trial_weight/2
          weight_error = abs(weight_object - weight_applied)
     end while

     if (weight_error > MAX_ERR)
          print "Object too heavy to weigh!"
     else
          print weight_applied
     end if
end main()
```

Figure 6.9 Third-level pseudocode for simulating the weighing of an object.

The program listing is given in Fig. 6.10. Integer variables were used to represent the various weights. This necessitates using a power of 2 for **MAX_WT** to avoid roundoff errors. If floating-point variables are used, then an arbitrary value of **MAX_WT** can be selected. To see the progression of the weighing process, a routine to print the value of **trial_weight**, its keep/reject status, and the **weight_applied** has been added to the program.

As a point of interest, it is possible to use standard weights that are not powers of 2 if they meet the following criteria: Some combination of the standard weights can be selected to give any weight within the range of the scale to an accuracy equal to **MAX_ERR**.

Series/Parallel Circuit Reduction

Project definition: Develop a program that finds the total resistance of an arbitrary series/parallel circuit such as that shown in Fig. 6.11. Use separate modules to perform series or parallel combinations. Decide whether each variable in the program should be local or global.

Solution: The procedure for finding the total resistance is to begin with the resistor at the point farthest from the voltage source. Call this resistor **r_total**. Determine if the next resistor (**r_next**) to be combined with **r_total** is in series or parallel with it. If it is in series, perform the series combination, calling the result **r_total**. This is done using

```
r_total = r_next + r_total
```

If **r_next** is in parallel with the current value of **r_total**, perform the parallel combination using

```
r_total = r_total*r_next/(r_total+r_next)
```

```
/* Successive approximation applied to weighing an object */

#define MAX_ERR   0
#define MIN_WT    1
#define MAX_WT    1024
#define KEEP      1
#define REJECT  0
#include <stdio.h>
#include <math.h>
main()
      {
      int trial_wt = MAX_WT;
      int wt_appl = 0;
      int wt_obj, wt_err;
      int status;

      puts("Enter weight of object:");
      scanf("%d",&wt_obj);

      wt_err = wt_obj;
      printf("%20s%20s%20s\n","Trial Weight","Status","Total Weight");

      while ((abs(wt_err) > MAX_ERR) && (trial_wt>=MIN_WT))
            {
            /* try a weight */
            wt_appl = wt_appl + trial_wt;
            status = KEEP;
            if (wt_appl > wt_obj)
                  {
                  wt_appl = wt_appl - trial_wt;
                  status = REJECT;
                  }
            /* print line in table */
            printf("%20d",trial_wt);
            if (status == KEEP)
                  printf("%20s","keep");
            else
                  printf("%20s","reject");
            printf("%20d\n",wt_appl);
            /* update parameters */
            trial_wt = trial_wt/2;
            wt_err = wt_appl - wt_obj;
            }

      /* print result */
      if (abs(wt_err)>MAX_ERR)
            puts("Object too heavy to weigh!");
      else
            printf("\n\nSum of applied weights = %d\n",wt_appl);
      }
```

Figure 6.10 Program for simulating the weighing of an object.

```
Enter weight of object:
1200
       Trial Weight            Status          Total Weight
               1024              keep                  1024
                512            reject                  1024
                256            reject                  1024
                128              keep                  1152
                 64            reject                  1152
                 32              keep                  1184
                 16              keep                  1200

Sum of applied weights = 1200


Enter weight of object:
3000
       Trial Weight            Status          Total Weight
               1024          keep                      1024
                512          keep                      1536
                256          keep                      1792
                128          keep                      1920
                 64          keep                      1984
                 32          keep                      2016
                 16          keep                      2032
                  8          keep                      2040
                  4          keep                      2044
                  2          keep                      2046
                  1          keep                      2047
Object too heavy to weigh!
```

Figure 6.10 (continued).

The two resistors have now been replaced by one resistor called **r_total**. Now look at the relationship of the current **r_total** with the next resistor in the circuit, the new value of **r_next**. Perform the appropriate combination. Repeat this procedure until all the resistors have been combined. The final value of **r_total** is the total resistance of the circuit.

The first level of pseudocode can be written as in Fig. 6.12. This pseudocode obviously needs more refinement. How will the program know if there are "more resistors"? How will it decide if the next resistor is in series or parallel? Should **r_total** and **r_next** be local or global variables?

There are two alternatives for determining how many resistors to process. We can count the resistors and supply this number as a program input. The other

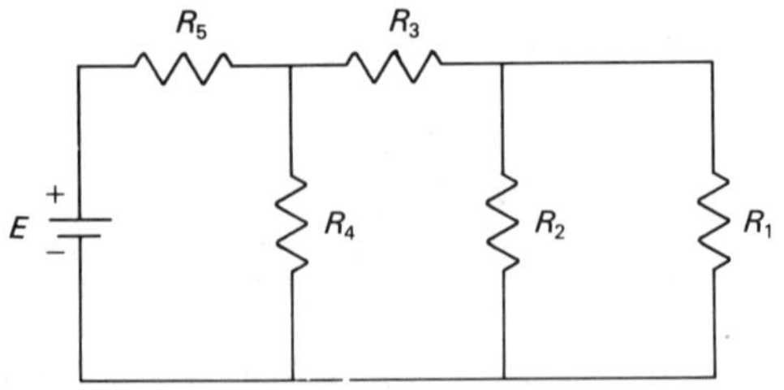

Figure 6.11 Series/parallel circuit.

```
/* series/parallel circuit reduction pseudocode */
module main()
     set r_total equal to the first resistor value
     while (more resistors)
          if (r_next is in series)
               r_total = series()
          else
          if (r_next is in parallel)
               r_total = parallel()
          end if
     end while
     print value of r_total
end main()

module series()
     perform series combination of r_next and r_total
end series()

module parallel()
     perform parallel combination of r_next and r_total
end parallel()
```

Figure 6.12 First-level pseudocode for series/parallel circuit reduction.

method is to input a coded value that tells the program when the last resistor has been encountered. We will use this second method.

Each resistor value will be entered from the keyboard. The program cannot sense the serial/parallel status of each resistor, so we must enter these data as well. This can be done by entering an **s** for series or a **p** for parallel. Since we are using coded characters at this point, an **e** can be used to signify the "end" or "no more resistors."

Main() does not need the value of **r_next**. Therefore, it can be local to the modules **series()** and **parallel()**. Since the value for **r_total** returned from either of these modules will be used to alter the value of **r_total** in **main()**, there is no point to making **r_total** local to **main()**. The final pseudocode is given in Fig. 6.13.

Converting the pseudocode of Fig. 6.13 into **C** is straightforward. In fact, the translation is so simple that an experienced programmer might go directly from the first level of pseudocode to the final **C** program. The variable **r_total** will be declared as external **float** before **main()**. The functions **series()** and **parallel()** must then be declared as **float** within **main()**. We have decided to keep **r_next** local to **series()** and **parallel()**. It will be a **float** type.

The **C** program is listed in Fig. 6.14. If you have a buffered input on your system, you will have to modify the call to **getchar()** to avoid reading a linefeed as an input character. Two possible corrections are as follows:

1. Use the statement **while((s_p = getchar()) == '\n');** in place of **s_p = getchar();** to filter out the linefeed.
2. Use an unbuffered version of **getchar()** if it is available on your system. Some versions of **C** use **getch()** for unbuffered input.

```
/* series/parallel circuit reduction pseudocode */
/* r_total is a global variable */
module main()
     print "Enter first resistor"
     input r_total
     s_p = NULL
     while (s_p not equal to 'e')
          print "Enter s, p, or e"
          input s_p
          if (s_p == s)
               r_total = series()
          else
          if (s_p == p)
               r_total = parallel()
          end if
     end while
     print value of r_total
end main()

module series()
     print "Enter series resistor"
     input r_next
     return(r_total + r_next)
end series()

module parallel()
     print "Enter parallel resistor"
     input r_next
     return(r_total*r_next/(r_total + r_next)
end parallel()
```

Figure 6.13 Second-level pseudocode for series/parallel circuit reduction.

Decimal to Binary Conversion

Project definition: The **C** language provides for number conversions among decimal, octal, and hexadecimal bases. It is sometimes necessary to display numbers in binary form. Develop a program that converts a decimal integer into a binary string.

Solution: To convert a decimal number into any other base, the standard algorithm is to perform repeated divisions by a number that is the base into which the conversion is being made. The remainders from the divisions form the digits of the converted number, starting with the least significant digit (LSD). The quotient becomes the new dividend. When a division yields a zero result, the process is complete.

Let's illustrate this algorithm for decimal to binary conversion. To convert the decimal number 13 into binary,

$13/2 = 6$, remainder $= 1$ LSD (least significant digit)
$6/2 = 3$, remainder $= 0$
$3/2 = 1$, remainder $= 1$
$1/2 = 0$, remainder $= 1$ MSD (most significant digit)

```
/* series/parallel circuit impedance */

float rt;          /* total resistance, rt, is global */
#include <stdio.h>
main()
      {
      float series(), parallel();
      char s_p = '*';

      puts("Enter first resistor: ");
      scanf("%f", &rt);

      while (s_p != 'e')
            {
            puts("Enter 's', 'p', or 'e': ");
            while ((s_p = getchar()) == '\n')
                  ;
            if (s_p == 's')
                  rt = series();
            else if (s_p == 'p')
                  rt = parallel();
            }

      printf("The total resistance = %f ohms\n", rt);
      }

float series()     /* find series combination */
      {
      float r;

      puts("Enter series resistor: ");
      scanf("%f", &r);
      return (rt + r);
      }

float parallel()   /* find parallel combination */
      {
      float r;

      puts("Enter parallel resistor: ");
      scanf("%f", &r);
      return ((rt * r) / (rt + r));
      }
```

```
Enter first resistor:
100
Enter 's', 'p', or 'e':
p
Enter parallel resistor:
100
Enter 's', 'p', or 'e':
s
Enter series resistor:
200
Enter 's', 'p', or 'e':
e
The total resistance = 250.000000 ohms
```

Figure 6.14 Program for series/parallel circuit reduction.

The result is 1101 in binary. Notice that we generated the least significant digit first. If these binary digits, called bits, become characters of our resulting string, the string output would be reversed. Our algorithm for decimal to binary conversion must therefore include a string reversing module. Now we can write the first level of pseudocode as in Fig. 6.15.

```
/* pseudocode for decimal to binary string conversion */

    input decimal number
    convert to binary string
    reverse string
    print binary string
```

Figure 6.15 First-level pseudocode for decimal to binary string conversion.

```
/* pseudocode for decimal to binary string conversion */
module main()
     print "Enter decimal number"
     input dec_num
     dec_bin(dec_num,bin_num)
     print bin_num
end main()

module dec_bin(dec_num,bin_num)
     i = 0
     while (dec_num > 0)
          bin_num[i] = dec_num modulo 2
          dec_num = dec_num/2
          i = i+1
     end while
     str_rev(bin_num)
end dec_bin()

module str_rev(bin_num)
     len = strlen(bin_num)          /* a C library function */
     last = len-1
     for (i = 0 to len/2)
          swap characters bin_num[i] and bin_num[last-i]
     end for
end str_rev()
```

Figure 6.16 Second-level pseudocode for decimal to binary string conversion.

```
/* decimal to binary conversion */
#include <stdio.h>
main()
      {
      int dec_num;
      char bin_num[20];
      void dec_bin();

      puts("Enter decimal number:");
      scanf("%d", &dec_num);
      dec_bin(dec_num, bin_num);
      printf("%s\n", bin_num);
      }

void dec_bin(dec_num, bin_num)          /* converts int dec to char bin */
int dec_num;
char *bin_num;

      {
      int i = 0;

      while (dec_num != 0)
            {
            bin_num[i++] = dec_num % 2 + '0';
            dec_num = dec_num / 2;
            }
      bin_num[i] = '\0';
      str_rev(bin_num);
      }

int str_rev(bin_num)                              /* string reverser */
char *bin_num;

      {
      int i, len, last;
      char temp;

      len = strlen(bin_num);
      last = len - 1;
      for (i = 0;  i < len / 2;  i++)
            {
            temp = bin_num[i];
            bin_num[i] = bin_num[last - i];
            bin_num[last - i] = temp;
            }
      }
```

```
Enter decimal number:
20
10100
```

Figure 6.17 Program for decimal to binary string conversion.

We can define the input number as **dec_num** and the output string as **bin_num[]**. The decimal to binary conversion process will be made a module, called **dec_bin()**, which in turn calls a string reverse module, **str_rev()**. Having **dec_bin()** call **str_rev()** allows it to reverse the **bin_num[]** string before existing **dec_bin()**.

The **dec_bin()** module will consist of a loop that performs repeated divisions of **dec_num** by 2 to form each new dividend. A modulus operation, **dec_num** modulo 2, will provide the remainders that form the digits of the binary number.

To reverse **bin_num[]**, we must know its length. A function called **strlen()** is normally available in **C** to do this job. This function will be called from the **str_rev()** module and the returned length assigned to a variable called **len**. To reverse the characters of **bin_num[]**, we can exchange the first and last characters, the second and second last, and so on, up to the middle of the string. The last character is defined by the variable **last**, which is equal to **len−1**. The middle of the string will occur at **len/2**. Our second level of pseudocode can now be written as in Fig. 6.16.

The module **dec_bin()** receives two parameters. The first is **dec_num**, the number to be converted. The second is **bin_num**, the name of the character array where the result will be stored. Recall that arrays are passed by reference, so **main()** has to tell **dec_bin()** where to find **bin_num[]**. The module **str_rev()** also receives the name **bin_num** to access it for reversing the characters.

Figure 6.17 lists the program for decimal to binary string conversion. The **main()** function is straightforward. **Dec_bin()** requires some explanation. The modulus operation inside the **while** loop appends the integer result of **dec_num%2** to the ASCII character zero ('0'). This produces an ASCII character that is equivalent to the numeric value of the integer number. The result is then assigned to **bin_num[i]**. When the loop is completed, a null character is appended to the end of **bin_num[]** so that it forms a character string.

Str_rev() contains the detailed code for the "swap characters" routine referenced in the pseudocode. It stores a character **bin_num[i]** in the variable **temp**. The corresponding character from the other side of the string **bin_num[last −i]** is then moved into **bin_num[i]**. The original data in **bin_num[i]** are now destroyed. This is why a temporary copy was saved in **temp**. The last step is the swap routine is to move the contents of **temp** into **bin_num[last−i]**. This actually places the original data in **bin_num[i]** into **bin_num[last−i]**.

6.7 RECURSION

A function is said to be *recursive* if it calls itself. The call can be from within the function, referred to as *direct recursion*. In some cases, the function may call another function, which in turn calls the first. This is an example of *indirect recursion*. In either case, the recursive function calls itself to perform a specific task.

A recursive function must include a test for a terminating condition. Each recursive call must simplify its arguments in some way so that the process moves toward the terminating condition.

To illustrate the recursion process, consider the computation of a factorial. The factorial of any number, **n**, can be expressed as the product of **n** and the factorial of **(n−1)**, or

$$\text{factorial}(\mathbf{n}) = \mathbf{n} * \text{factorial}(\mathbf{n} - 1)$$

From this equation, we can see that the factorial of **n** has been expressed in terms of a simpler factorial, that of (**n** − 1). If a function named factorial called itself repeatedly, each call would express a given factorial in terms of a simpler one. The process terminates when factorial 0 is reached. It is defined as having a value of 1.

The recursive function in the following program segment computes the factorial of an integer **n**. Notice that it includes a test for the terminating condition and that each successive call has a reduced value for the argument.

```
factorial(n)       /* recursive computation of a factorial */
int n;
{
 if (n == 0)
      return(1);
 else
      return(n*factorial(n-1))
}
```

Suppose that the function is called with an argument of 3. This will result in **factorial()** calling itself with an argument of 2, which will result in another call to itself with an argument of 1, and again with 0. The factorial of 0 is the first to actually be evaluated. The return from that last call will then permit evaluation of factorial 1. The next return will permit evaluation of factorial 2, and so on. The return from **factorial()** to the function from which it was called will have a return value of the factorial of **n**.

Recursion can simplify programming tasks and produce compact code. However, this is often at the expense of speed. In many cases, it is preferable to use an iterative process (with **for** or **while** loops) instead of the recursive approach.

PROBLEMS

6.1. Find the mistakes in the following function and correct them:

```
sum_of_sq (x,y)          /* function that returns the sum*/
      {                  /* of squares of x and y */
      double x,y;

      return(x*x+y*y);
      }
```

6.2. Find the mistakes in the following function and correct them:

```
hypot(x,y)                  /* function that returns the */
double x,y;                 /* hypotenuse given sides x,y */
      {
      h = sqrt(x*x + y*y);
      return(h);
      }
```

6.3. Write a function that converts radians to degrees. The argument and return value should both be type **double**.

6.4. Name the storage class of all the variables in the following program:

```
double feed = 10.0;
static position = 0.100;
#include <stdio.h>
main()
      {
      double rps;
      static double factor = 200.0;

      rps = feed*position/factor;
      printf("The rps is %f\n";rps);
      }
```

6.5. Write a macro that converts degrees to radians. Call it **TO_RAD(d)**, where **d** is the argument in degrees.

6.6. Write pseudocode for the roots of a quadratic program of Fig. 4.7.

6.7. Write pseudocode for the resultant of vectors program of Fig. 4.12.

6.8. Write a recursive function that computes the value of **x** raised to the **y** power, where **x** is a **double** that can take on any value and **y** is an **int**. The return value should be type **double**. Use the following information in your function:

```
power(x,0)  = 1.0;
power(x,y)  = power  (x,y-1)*y;
```

PROGRAMMING PROJECTS

6.9. Develop pseudocode for a menu-driven program that offers the options of analyzing or designing the bias for the circuit of Fig. 6.18. For analysis, the inputs are V_{CC}, V_{BE}, h_{FE}, R_1, R_2, R_3, and R_4. The outputs are I_c and V_{CE}. For design, the inputs are V_{CC}, h_{FE}, V_{BE}, V_{CE}, and I_C. The outputs are R_1, R_2, R_3, and R_4. Also, you should apply the following design rules:

1. The current flowing through R_4 is to be ten times I_B.
2. The voltage at the emitter is to be one-fourth of V_{CC}.

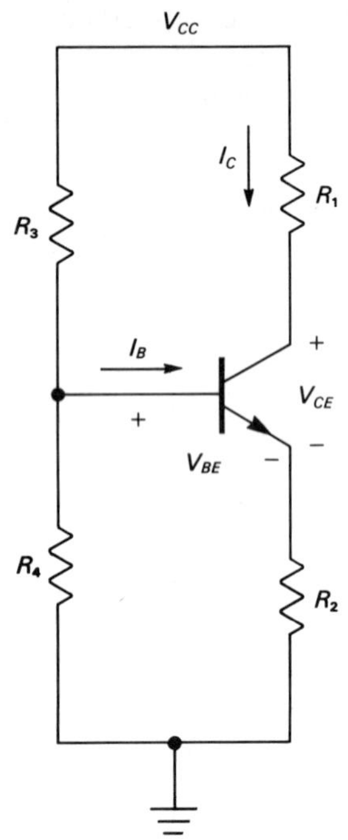

Figure 6.18 Transistor bias circuit of Problem 6.9.

6.10. Convert the pseudocode of Problem 6.9 into a **C** program. Test your program by running the design option first and feeding the results into the analysis option. This should recover your original data.

6.11. Develop the pseudocode for analyzing a common-emitter amplifier given the circuit values and h parameters. The desired outputs are the input and output impedance of the amplifier, the voltage gain, the current gain, and the power gain.

6.12. Convert the pseudocode of Problem 6.11 into a **C** program.

6.13. Develop the pseudocode for analyzing a series resonant circuit. The inputs are the component values of R, L, and C. The desired outputs are the resonant frequency and bandwidth. Also include a printout of circuit impedance over the range of frequencies equal to the resonant frequency $\pm$ five times the bandwidth in increments of one-half the bandwidth.

6.14. Convert the pseudocode of Problem 6.13 into a **C** program.

chapter 7

Pointers and Arrays

7.1 POINTERS

Definition

A *pointer* is a variable or symbolic constant whose value is an address, usually a physical memory location. The value of a pointer is normally the memory location of some variable. We say that a pointer "points to" the variable whose address is given by the value of the pointer.

Pointers are used because they provide a convenient method, and sometimes the only method, of performing an operation. They also tend to produce a final program that runs faster and occupies less memory space.

Figure 7.1 illustrates the relationship of a pointer variable and the variable that it references. This diagram shows the pointer variable **ptr**, located at address **2000** and having a value of **3000**. The value of **ptr** is the address of the variable being "pointed to", in this case **x**. Notice that the value of the variable **x**, assumed to be of type **int**, is 5.

Address of a Variable

The **&** operator is used to find the *address* of a variable. Therefore, the address of **x** is given by **&x**. In this case, the value of **&x** is **3000**. Although **x** is a variable, **&x** is a constant, a *pointer constant* to be specific, since the location of **x** does not change.

A pointer variable must be initialized to some value before it can be used. To initialize **ptr**, we can use the statement

```
ptr = &x;
```

This statement will set the value of **ptr** to **3000**, the location of **x**. Now **ptr** is said to "point to" **x**.

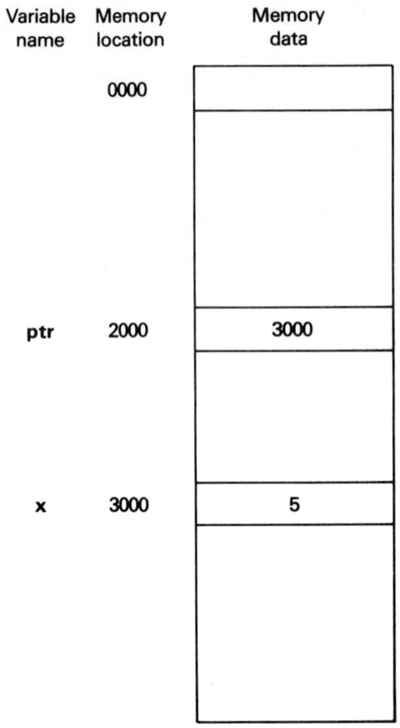

Figure 7.1 Relationship of a pointer and the referenced variable.

Indirection

To find the contents of the location being pointed to by a pointer variable, we can use the *indirection operator* (*). Thus, ***ptr** in our example is **5**, which is the value of **x**. Notice that

```
ptr = &x;
```

and

```
value = *ptr;
```

together assign the same number, **5**, to **value**, as would the statement

```
value = x;
```

This may seem like a roundabout method of accessing the value of **x**, but the utility of pointers will be seen as we proceed.

Declaring Pointers

The declaration of a pointer variable is somewhat different than that of an ordinary variable. With pointers, we must declare the type of what is being "pointed to." Thus, to declare **ptr** as a pointer, assuming that it points to a variable which is of type **int**, we write

```
int *ptr;
```

for the declaration. The indirection operator identifies **ptr** as a pointer, and the **int** declaration says that it points to a type **int**. Pointer variables may point to any of the basic types, including **char**, **int**, **long**, **float**, or **double**, as well as other, more complex, data types.

Other examples of declarations involving pointers are given in Fig. 7.2. The first of these declares **pf** as a pointer to a type **float**. The second declares **fctn()** as a function that returns a pointer to a type **float**. Remember that functions are declared as the type that they return. The last declares **f** as a pointer to a function that returns an **int**. A pointer to a function actually points to the memory location that is the *entry point* or starting memory location for that function. If **f** is a pointer to a function, then a statement such as **(*f)();** would be a call to the function referenced by **f**.

```
float   *pf;        /* pointer to float */
float   *fctn();    /* function returning pointer to float */
int     (*f)();     /* pointer to function returning int */
```

Figure 7.2 Declarations involving pointers.

Pointers as Function Arguments

C permits only one value to be returned by a function. Suppose that a program requires calls to functions that must return more than one value or calls that must alter the value of several variables in the calling function. How can we accomplish this? Instead of passing ''copies'' of the actual parameters as function arguments, we can pass pointers to the variables involved. This permits access to these variables by the called function without having to declare the variables as global.

To illustrate the use of pointers as function arguments, consider a function that exchanges the values of two variables. Such a function might be incorporated into a sorting routine as **swap(&x,&y)**, where **x** and **y** are the variables whose values must be exchanged. The function can be implemented as follows

```
swap(a,b)            /* exchange the values of *a, *b */
int   *a, *b;
{
      int temp;

      temp = *a;
      *a = *b;
      *b = temp;
}
```

Exchanging the values of ***a** and ***b** requires storage of one of these values in a temporary location so that it is not erased in the process. In this case, the variable **temp** provides temporary storage of ***a** by the statement **temp = *a;**. The next statement makes ***a** take on the value of ***b**, and the last makes ***b** take on the value of **temp** or ***a**.

Notice that **swap()** does not return a value. It alters the value of two variables in the calling function by accessing them through the pointers passed to **swap()**, that is, **&x** and **&y**. By exchanging ***a** and ***b**, the function actually exchanges the values of **x** and **y**. If the arguments of **swap()** were not pointers, then the exchange would only have affected its local variables.

7.2 ARRAYS

Definition

In our study of character strings (Chapter 5), we defined an array as a collection of elements of the same data type. In **C**, an array is assigned a name followed by square brackets. When we define an array variable, we indicate the size to be allocated to the array by placing a number within the square brackets that indicates the number of elements in the array. Thus, the declaration

```
int a[100];
```

says that **a[]** is an array variable of type **int** having 100 elements. Since the first element is **a[0]**, the last element in the array is **a[99]**.

Each element of a character array occupies 1 byte of memory. With other data types, the number of bytes occupied by each element is given by

```
sizeof(array type)
```

Array elements are stored *contiguously* in memory. Thus **a[0]** is immediately followed by **a[1]**, which is immediately followed by **a[2]**, and so on.

Initialization

Automatic arrays cannot be initialized. They will contain garbage until some assignment is made to each of the elements. **External** and **static** arrays may be

```
/* Initializing arrays */
#include <stdio.h>
extern int e[5] = {2,4,6,8,10};

main()
     {
     static float s[] = {1.2, 3.14, 6.8, 9.999};
     int i;

     for (i = 0; i < 5; i++)
           printf("e[%d] = %d\n", i, e[i]);
     printf("The size of the array e[] is %d\n", sizeof(e));
     putchar('\n');
     for (i = 0; i < 4; i++)
           printf("s[%d] = %f\n", i, s[i]);
     printf("The size of the array s[] is %d\n", sizeof(s));
     }
```

```
e[0] = 2
e[1] = 4
e[2] = 6
e[3] = 8
e[4] = 10
The size of the array e[] is 10

s[0] = 1.200000
s[1] = 3.140000
s[2] = 6.800000
s[3] = 9.999000
The size of the array s[] is 16
```

Figure 7.3 Initializing an array.

initialized. In the absence of any initialization, external and static arrays will have zero values for all elements. To initialize these arrays, we follow the declaration with an equal sign and a pair of braces containing the element values separated by commas. The program of Fig. 7.3 illustrates the initialization of both external and static arrays. Here, **e[5]** is an **external** array and **s[]** is a **static** array.

Notice that the number of elements in the **s[]** array is not specified by a value within the square brackets. In the absence of this argument in the array name, the compiler will count the number of elements in the initialization and set the array size accordingly.

The program prints the value of each element in the arrays and also the number of bytes occupied by each array. Since the **e[]** array is of type **int** and has five elements, its size is 10 (assuming that the size of **int** is 2 bytes). The **s[]** array has four elements of type **float** for a total size of 16 bytes. Each **float** value occupies 4 bytes.

7.3 POINTERS TO ARRAYS

There is a close interrelationship between pointers and arrays in **C**. We can use either to manipulate a group of elements having a common type. Conceptually, arrays are easier to understand. However, pointers offer several advantages over arrays. They usually make a program run faster, permit dynamic memory allocation, and can reduce the overall memory requirement.

Array Names Are Pointer Constants

An *array name* is actually a symbolic constant whose value is a pointer to the location of the first element in the array. Thus, for an array **data[]**, the name **data** is the same as **&data[0]**. Furthermore, **data+i** is the same as **&data[i]**. The expression **data+i** is actually a pointer to the **i**th element of **data[]**. This can be written as

```
data+i == &data[i]
```

Applying indirection to both sides gives

```
*(data+i) == data[i]
```

As **i** is incremented by 1, the memory location being referenced is incremented by an amount determined by the size of the data type.

Using Pointer Variables with Arrays

We can access any element in the array **data[]** by specifying a subscript within the square brackets. If a pointer variable is initialized to point to the first element of an array, then a pointer expression can also be used to access any element of that array. If the pointer variable **ptr** is initialized by

```
ptr = &data[0]
```

then

```
*ptr == data[0]
```

We can therefore use ***ptr** in place of **data[0]** in any expression. The construction **ptr+i** is used to point to the **i**th element of **data[]**.

Thus

```
ptr+ i == &data[i]
```

and

```
*(ptr+i) == data[i]
```

The expression ***(ptr+i)** can be used in place of **data[i]**. It should now be apparent that any operation on arrays can be performed using pointers instead of the array variable itself. In fact, we will later see that an array can be created and processed without ever using array variables.

From the preceding, it appears that **data** and **ptr** are equivalent. An important distinction, however, is that **data** is a symbolic pointer constant, while **ptr** is a pointer variable. Operations like **ptr++** and **ptr=data** are valid, whereas **data++** and **data = ptr** are not permissible. We cannot increment a constant or assign a value to it. The use of pointers to access array elements is illustrated by the program of Fig. 7.4. Notice that the declaration.

```
int *ptr = data;
```

initializes the pointer variable **ptr** to the value of **data**, which is **&data[0]**.

```
/* Using pointers to access an array */
#include <stdio.h>
main()
      {
      static int data[] = {0, 3, 6, 9, 12, 15};
      int *ptr = data, i;

      for (i = 0; i < 6; i++)
            printf("data[%d] = %d\n", i, *(ptr + i));
      }
```

```
data[0] = 0
data[1] = 3
data[2] = 6
data[3] = 9
data[4] = 12
data[5] = 15
```

Figure 7.4 Accessing an array using pointers.

Array Names as Function Arguments

Arrays are an exception to the "call by value" method of passing parameters used in **C**. When a function is called on to perform an operation on an array, we must tell the function *where* the array is located. This is the alternative method of "call by reference." We can give the location of the beginning of the array to the function by passing the array name. Recall that the array name is a pointer to the location of the first element in the array. We must also tell the function the *size* of the array. This can be done by passing a second parameter whose value is the number of elements in the array.

Thus, if the array **data[]** is to be operated on by the function **transpose()**, the call can be made as

```
transpose(data,n);
```

The first argument, **data**, tells the function where the array is located. The second argument, **n**, tells the function the size of the array. The function **transpose()** must declare the pointer to the array **data** as one of its formal parameters. This can be done in several ways.

Method 1

```
transpose(base,count)      /* base as an array name */
int base[],count;
{
}
```

In this declaration, **base** is treated as the name of the array **base[]**. Notice that the size of **base[]** has not been declared. This is because it really refers to the array **data[]**, whose size has been declared by the calling function.

Method 2

```
transpose(base,count)      /* base as a pointer */
int *base,count;
{
}
```

Here, **base** is treated simply as a pointer and is declared as such. Both methods are valid and fully equivalent.

7.4 POINTER ARITHMETIC AND MANIPULATION

We can perform certain arithmetic and manipulative operations on pointers that enhance their utility. However, care must be taken since not all arithmetic operations are permissible. The common operations performed with pointers are discussed next.

Initialization and Reassignment

A pointer variable must be initialized before it can be used. The initialization takes the form of an assignment such as

```
ptr = &x
```

which assigns the address of **x** to the pointer **ptr**. We may reassign the value given to a pointer variable at any time. A pointer variable may appear on the right side of an assignment. Thus

```
ptr1 = ptr2
```

makes **ptr1** point to the same address as **ptr2**.

Indirection

The indirection operator * is applied to a pointer to give the value contained in the address being referenced. Thus, if **ptr = &x** and **x = 5**, then ***ptr** also equals **5**. Pointers may point to any data type, and indirection may be applied to all these types (except structures).

Address Finding

The **&** operator is used to find the address of its operand. It may be applied to ordinary variables and pointer variables as well. Thus, if the value of **x** is stored at address 3000, the value of **&x** will be 3000. The assignment **ptr = &x** will give **ptr** a value of **3000**. What does **&ptr** give? It will have a value that equals the address where **ptr** itself is stored (see Fig. 7.1). We can say that **&ptr** is a pointer to a pointer variable.

Increment or Decrement

The increment or decrement operations may be applied to pointer *variables*, but not to pointer constants such as array names. If **ptr = &array[0]**, then **ptr++** will point to **array[1]**. We can also add an integer to a pointer. Thus **ptr = ptr + 10** or **ptr += 10** will point to **array[10]**.

Suppose that **ptr_hi = &array[100]**. Then **ptr_hi--** will point to **array[99]**. Also, **ptr_hi = ptr_hi - 10** or **ptr_hi -= 10** will point to **array[90]**.

Returning an Error Condition

Pointers in **C** cannot have a valid value of zero. In other words, a pointer cannot point to something stored at address zero. We can take advantage of this fact in writing functions that return pointers by letting a returned zero or **NULL** indicate an error condition within the function.

Suppose that a function should return a pointer to the location of a substring within a larger string. If the substring is not found, the pointer may return a **NULL** value to indicate this condition.

Offset or Pointer Difference

If two pointers refer to elements of the same array, the difference of the pointers gives the offset or number of array elements between the addresses being referenced. Suppose that **ptr_to_max** is a pointer to the largest element in an array **data[]**. The location of the largest element can be found from the expression **ptr_to_max - data**. Here, **data** is a pointer to the first element, **data[0]**. Thus **ptr_to_max - data** will equal the number of elements from the first to the largest.

Pointing to a Specific Memory Location

A pointer can be set to point to a specific memory location. If we wish a pointer **ptr** to point to location **MEM_LOC**, then **ptr** can be initialized with the cast operation

```
ptr = (data_type*) MEM_LOC;
```

where **data_type** is the type to which **ptr** points.

To illustrate the use of this technique, suppose that we wish to initialize **ptr** to point to the start of video memory in the IBM Personal Computer (decimal 720896 or hexadecimal B0000). This requires a long pointer and may not be realizable on some microcomputer implementations of **C**. The statement

```
ptr = (char *) 720896L;
```

will initialize **ptr** to the desired location. We have cast the location value to a type **char**, which is the type to which **ptr** is assumed to point.

We could have initialized **ptr** within its declaration as

```
char *ptr = (char *) 720896L;
```

In fact, we can initialize **ptr** to one memory location and then assign another value to it at a later point. Also, the memory location may be replaced by a symbolic constant such as **MEM_LOC**. The value of **MEM_LOC** would be established with a preprocessor #**define** directive.

Care must be taken whenever a specific memory location is being accessed. You must be sure of the location of whatever is being addressed and that there is no contention for use of that location by the system. The results may otherwise be catastrophic.

Relational Operations

If two pointers refer to elements of the same array, we can use any of the relational operators (<, <=, >, >=) to compare the pointers. These operations are used to decide the relative positions of the two pointers. We can also test for equality (==) or inequality (!=) of the pointers. This can be used to detect whether or not the pointers are referring to the same element.

The program of Figure 7.5 illustrates using some of the pointer operations discussed. It finds the location and value of the largest element in the integer array **data[]**. The **main()** function initializes the **data[]** array and calls **max(data,10)**. The arguments of **max()** are a pointer to the first element of **data[]** and the length of the array.

The function **max(ptr,n)** receives a pointer to the array, assigned to **ptr**, and the length of the array, assigned to **n**. The process of finding the largest element in the array involves scanning the array and comparing the value at each location to the value at the location identified as holding the current largest value. When a larger value is found, its location is saved as a pointer to the largest element. At the end of this process, the largest-value pointer will point to the largest element in the array.

Refer to the illustration of Fig. 7.6. The pointer **scan** is used to reference consecutive elements of **data[]**, and the current largest value is located by the pointer **loc**. Both **scan** and **loc** are initialized to the value of **ptr**, which points to the start of **data[]**. If the value at the location referenced by **scan** is greater than the value referenced by the largest-value pointer, **loc**, then **loc** will take on the value of **scan** to identify the new location for the current largest value.

The expression **scan − ptr** in Fig. 7.5 is the offset of **scan** from the first element of **data[]**. It is used within the **while** loop to count the number of passes through the loop. The value of **scan − ptr** ranges from **0** to **n − 1** to give **n** passes through the loop. When **scan − ptr = n**, the **while** loop terminates.

On each pass through the loop, the **if** statement compares the value of the element at the pointed to address, ***scan**, to the current largest value, ***loc**. If

```
/* find largest element in an array */
#include <stdio.h>
main()
	{
	static int data[] = {1, 0, 3, 4, 7, 9, 6, 8, 5, 2};
	int x;

	x = max(data, 10);
	printf("The largest element of data[] occurs at position %d\n", x);
	printf("Its value is %d\n", data[x]);
	}

int max(ptr, n)
int *ptr, n;
	{
	int *scan = ptr;
	int *loc = ptr;

	while (scan - ptr < n)
		{
		if (*scan > *loc)
			loc = scan;
		scan++;
		}
	return (loc - ptr);
	}
```

```
The largest element of data[] occurs at position 5
Its value is 9
```

Figure 7.5 Finding the largest element in an array.

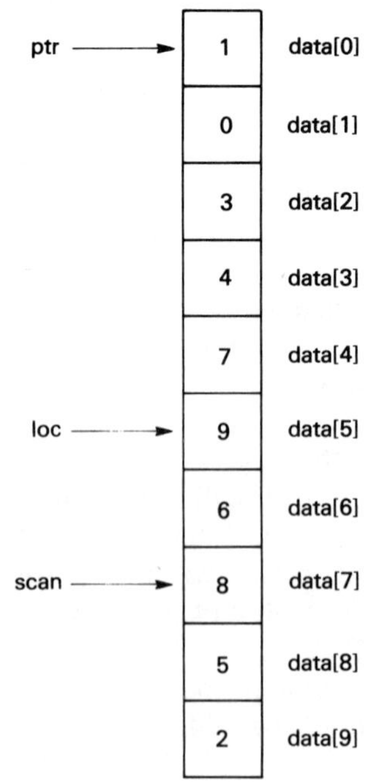

Figure 7.6 Pointers used to find the largest element in the array **data[]**.

***scan** > ***loc**, **loc** is set equal to **scan**. At the completion of the **while** loop, **loc** will store the location where the largest element of the array occurs. The location is returned as **loc – ptr**, an offset from the beginning of the array, which has a type **int**. The **main()** function prints this location, which is assigned to **x**. It then prints the largest value, which is found by **data[x]**.

7.5 MULTIDIMENSIONAL ARRAYS

A two-dimensional array in **C** uses notation of the form **data[i][j]**, where **data** is the array name, **i** is the *row* indicator, and **j** is the *column* indicator. Specifying a value of the subscripts **i** and **j** uniquely identifies one element of the two-dimensional array named **data**. Thus **data[2][0]** is the element of **data** that occupies row two and column zero.

Two-dimensional arrays in **C** actually consist of an array of one-dimensional arrays. Refer to Fig. 7.7, which illustrates a two-dimensional array **data**. Each row of numbers is assigned to a one-dimensional array. The first row is referenced as the one-dimensional array **data[0]** and consists of the four elements 1, 2, 3, 4. The second row is referenced as **data[1]** and consists of the four elements 5, 6, 7, 8. The third row, **data[2]**, consists of 9, 10, 11, 12.

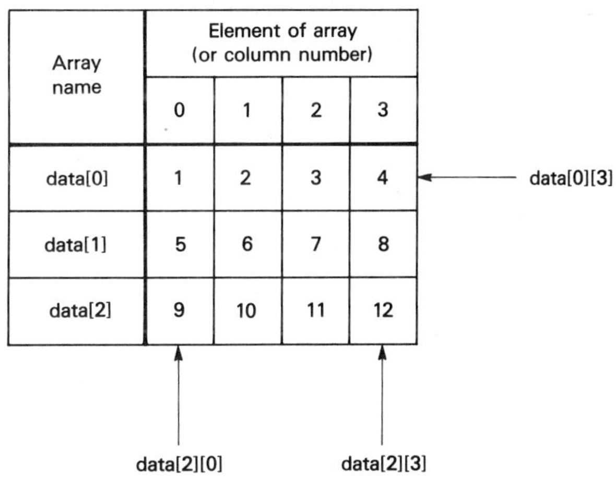

Figure 7.7 Identifying elements of a two-dimensional array.

Since **data[0]** is the name of a one-dimensional array, we can reference its first element as **data[0][0]**. It has a value of 1 in this example. The last element of **data[0]** is **data[0][3]**. It has a value of 4. Notice that **data[i][j]** can be viewed as element **j** of the one-dimensional array **data[i]** and also as the element of row **i** and column **j** of the two-dimensional array **data**.

If the array **data** of Fig. 7.7 is an integer type, the size of any element such as **data[0][0]** is 2 bytes (assuming that **int** has a size of 2 bytes). The size of any row such as **data[0]** is 8 bytes, and the size of the entire array **data** is 24 bytes. The memory space of any array depends on the number of elements it contains and the data type of the array.

Initializing Two-dimensional Arrays

The way in which a two-dimensional array is initialized follows from its definition as being an array of one-dimensional arrays. To initialize a two-dimensional array, we use the initialization structure of a one-dimensional array and replace each element by a one-dimensional array of elements. This is illustrated next for the two-dimensional array of Fig. 7.7.

```
static int data[3][4] = {
                        {1,2,3,4},
                        {5,6,7,8},
                        {9,10,11,12}
                        };
```

The array **data** has three elements: **data[0]**, **data[1]**, and **data[2]**. Thus we have three positions within the outer braces to be filled with the elements of **data**. Since each element is in itself a one-dimensional array of four elements, we include these four elements within braces at each element position of **data**. The entry for the first element of **data** is thus **{1,2,3,4}**. The entry for the second element is **{5,6,7,8}**, and the third is **{9,10,11,12}**.

The program of Fig. 7.8 initializes and prints a two-dimensional array. The print routine outputs both the name of the array element and its value. Notice that, since the array is not **external**, we had to declare it as **static** in order to permit initialization.

```
/* print a two-dimensional array */
#include <stdio.h>
main()
      {
      static int a[3][4] =
                 {
                   {1, 2, 3, 4},
                   {5, 6, 7, 8},
                   {9, 10, 11, 12}
                 };
      int i, j;

      for (i = 0; i < 3; i++)
            {
            for (j = 0;  j < 4;  j++)
                  printf("a[%d][%d]=%2d   ", i, j, a[i][j]);
            putchar('\n');
            }
      }
```

```
a[0][0]= 1   a[0][1]= 2   a[0][2]= 3   a[0][3]= 4
a[1][0]= 5   a[1][1]= 6   a[1][2]= 7   a[1][3]= 8
a[2][0]= 9   a[2][1]=10   a[2][2]=11   a[2][3]=12
```

Figure 7.8 Initializing and printing a two-dimensional array.

Keyboard Input of Two-dimensional Array Data

We can input a two-dimensional array of any size from the keyboard using a simple nested-loop structure. The program of Fig. 7.9 illustrates using nested **for** loops to enter an array whose size is determined by a pair of **#define** directives. The values of **ROW** and **COL** define the maximum number of rows and columns to be used in the array declaration. Once the array is entered, the function **prn_2d()** is called to print the array data.

```
/* input and print a two-dimensional array */
#include <stdio.h>
#define ROW 2
#define COL 3

main()
      {
      static int a[ROW][COL];
      int i,j;
      void prn_2d();

      for (i = 0; i < ROW; i++)
            for (j = 0; j < COL; j++)
                  {
                  printf("Enter a[%d][%d]:", i, j);
                  scanf("%d", &a[i][j]);
                  }
      printf("\n\n");
      prn_2d(a);
      }

void prn_2d(a)
int a[][COL];
      {
      int i, j;

      for (i = 0; i < ROW; i++)
            {
            for (j = 0; j < COL; j++)
                  printf("a[%d][%d]=%2d    ", i, j, a[i][j]);
            putchar('\n');
            }
      }
```

```
Enter a[0][0]:1
Enter a[0][1]:2
Enter a[0][2]:3
Enter a[1][0]:4
Enter a[1][1]:5
Enter a[1][2]:6


a[0][0]= 1    a[0][1]= 2    a[0][2]= 3
a[1][0]= 4    a[1][1]= 5    a[1][2]= 6
```

Figure 7.9 Keyboard input and printing of a two-dimensional array.

The outer **for** loop of the data entry routine increments the row number (**i**) from **0** to **ROW**. The inner **for** loop increments the column number (**j**) from **0** to **COL**. For each value of **i** and **j**, a message is printed prompting the input of the selected array element. A **scanf()** statement is then used to assign the keyboard entry to the proper element of the array.

After completion of the data entry routine, the function **prn_2d()** is called. Notice that the name of the array is passed to the function. This is used as a pointer to the first element of the array. The declaration of the formal parameter of the function must include the number of columns in the two-dimensional array. This is the only way of telling the function how the two-dimensional array is organized. We do not have to specify the number of rows in the declaration. Thus the formal parameter may be declared as

```
int a[ROW][COL];
```

or

```
int a[][COL];
```

or

```
int (*a)[COL];
```

The first two forms should be obvious. The last one says that **a** is a pointer to an array of **COL** integers. This is another way of saying that the array has **COL** elements per row. If the array was originally declared **external** to any function, it would not be necessary to pass any arguments to **prn_2d()** or to declare any formal parameters within that function.

N-dimensional Arrays

We have considered only one- and two-dimensional arrays. These are the most frequently used types. However, it is possible to have an array of any dimension. Just as a two-dimensional array was formed as an array of one-dimensional arrays, so, too, a three-dimensional array can be formed as an array of two-dimensional arrays.

The three-dimensional array **data**, declared as

```
double data[4][10][20];
```

has 800 elements. These can be viewed as four two-dimensional arrays, each of which is 10 by 20 in size.

7.6 COMPUTATIONS INVOLVING COMPLEX NUMBERS

A *complex number* is a number containing both a real and an imaginary component. In this section, we will represent the imaginary component of a complex number by prefixing it with the lowercase letter **j**. Thus, if **z** represents a variable having a real part **r** and an imaginary part **x**, we can express **z** in rectangular form as

$$\mathbf{z = r + jx}$$

An alternative representation of **z** in polar form is given by

$$\mathbf{z = M \angle \phi}$$

where $\mathbf{M = (r^2 + x^2)^{1/2}}$ and $\boldsymbol{\phi} = \mathbf{arctan(x/r)}$. In this form, **M** represents the magnitude of **z** and $\boldsymbol{\phi}$ represents its angle. Both representations are illustrated in Fig. 7.10.

The analysis of certain systems necessitates the use of expressions involving complex numbers to describe their behavior. This is especially true in the case of electrical circuits containing ac (alternating current) signal sources and reactive

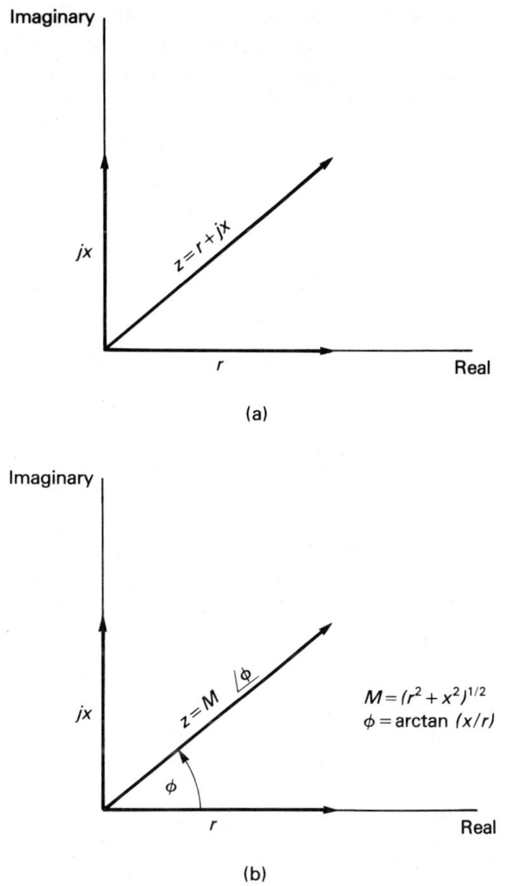

Figure 7.10 A complex number represented in (a) rectangular form and (b) polar form.

components, that is, inductors and/or capacitors. In this section, we describe how to perform computations involving complex numbers in **C**. All the applications will deal with the analysis of ac circuits.

Computations involving complex variables present a problem. Unlike FORTRAN, **C** and almost all other languages do not support the direct use of complex variables in arithmetic expressions. We must create functions that tell **C** how to evaluate complex expressions and where to place the results. Since complex numbers have two components, the function must have access to both parts of the input variables and must give both parts of the result.

A good way of handling this problem is to use arrays or pointers. A complex variable can be defined as an array of two elements. For example, the complex variable **z** can be defined as having a real part **z[0]** and an imaginary part **z[1]**. This variable can be passed to a function simply by passing the array name **z**. The function will then have access to both parts of **z**. If the function must provide a complex result, we can pass the name of the complex variable that will store the result to the function. Thus a function like **vsum(z1,z2,z3)** can be used to find the sum of two complex quantities **z1** and **z2** and place the result in **z3**.

Computation of Impedance from Circuit Values

Consider the circuit of Fig. 7.11. The voltage generator produces a sine-wave signal having an amplitude **v**, a frequency **f**, and a phase angle $\boldsymbol{\phi_1}$. This voltage can be expressed as $\mathbf{V}\angle\boldsymbol{\phi_1}$. The impedance of the circuit is given by **z**, which can be written as $\mathbf{Z}\angle\phi_2$. In rectangular form, the impedance is given by **r + jx**, where **r** is the resistance component of **z** and **jx** represents the reactance component of **z**. The reactance of the capacitor is given by $\mathbf{1/j\omega C}$, where $\boldsymbol{\omega}$ is the radian frequency or $\mathbf{2\pi f}$. The reactance of the inductor is given by $\mathbf{j\omega L}$. The total reactance is the sum of the capacitive and inductive reactance, or

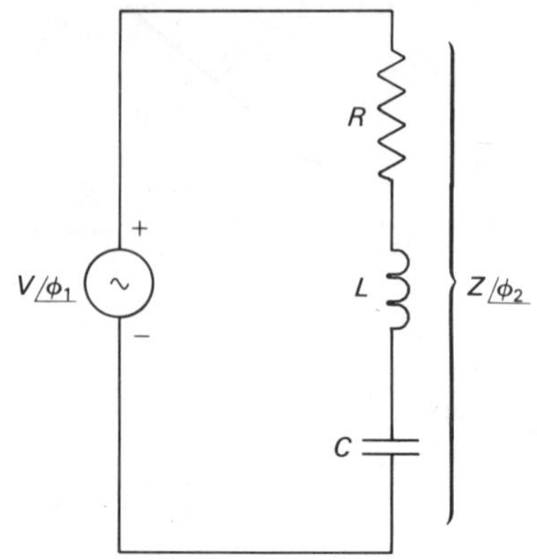

Figure 7.11 AC circuit consisting of a resistor, inductor, capacitor, and sine-wave generator.

$$\mathbf{jx = j\omega L + \frac{1}{j\omega C}}$$

Since $\mathbf{1/j = -j}$, the reactance can be written as

$$\mathbf{jx = j\left(\omega L - \frac{1}{\omega C}\right)}$$

and the value of **z** can be expressed as

$$\mathbf{z = r + j\left(\omega L - \frac{1}{\omega C}\right)}$$

Notice that the impedance is a function of frequency. As the frequency changes, both the magnitude and angle of the impedance will change.

The program of Fig. 7.12 computes the impedance of the circuit in Fig. 7.11 from its component parameters. It includes two functions that are used to print the total impedance in rectangular and polar form. The input parameters are the circuit resistance, **r**, the inductance, **l**, the capacitance, **c**, and the frequency, **f**. The impedance is assigned to the array variable **z**, which is passed to the functions **vprn()** and **pprn()** to print the impedance in rectangular and polar form, respectively.

All the circuit parameters have been defined as type **double**. This is convenient since calls will be made to the **C** standard library math functions, which expect **double** arguments. Notice that the **scanf()** conversion specifiers are **"%lf"** to specify a **long float** or **double**.

The function **pprn()** receives the name of the array (containing a complex number representing an impedance) whose value must be printed in rectangular form. Since the imaginary component of the impedance must be prefixed with the character **j**, its sign must be located before the **j** character. The **if** statement checks the sign of the imaginary component and assigns the corresponding character (+ or −) to the variable **sign**. The following **printf()** statement then prints the real part of the impedance, the value of **sign**, and the magnitude of the imaginary part.

```
/* Computation of impedance from circuit values */
#include <math.h>
#include <stdio.h>
#define PI 3.141592654

main()
      {
      double r, l, c, f, w, z[2];
      char sign;
      void pprn(), vprn();

      printf("Enter resistance: ");
      scanf("%lf", &r);
      printf("Enter inductance: ");
      scanf("%lf", &l);
      printf("Enter capacitance: ");
      scanf("%lf", &c);
      printf("Enter frequency: ");
      scanf("%lf", &f);

      w = 2*PI*f;
      z[0] = r;
      z[1] = w*l - 1.0/(w*c);
      printf("\nThe total impedance at %g hertz is:\n", f);
      printf("z = ");
      vprn(z);
      pprn(z);
      }

void vprn(a)                    /* print impedance in rectangular form */
double a[];
      {
      char sign;

      if (a[1] < 0)
            sign = '-';
      else
            sign = '+';
      printf("%g %cj%g ohms\n", a[0], sign, (a[1] > 0) ? a[1] : -a[1]);
      }

void pprn(a)                    /* print impedance in polar form */
double a[];
      {
      printf("magnitude = %g ohms\n", sqrt(a[0]*a[0] + a[1]*a[1]));
      printf("angle = %f degrees\n", atan2(a[1], a[0])*180.0/PI);
      }
```

```
Enter resistance: 100
Enter inductance: 50e-3
Enter capacitance: 10e-6
Enter frequency: 100

The total impedance at 100 hertz is
z = 100 -j127.739 ohms
magnitude = 162.226 ohms
angle = -51.944519 degrees
```

Figure 7.12 Impedance of an **RLC** circuit.

The function **pprn()** also receives the name of the array containing the complex data to be printed. It calls the standard library functions **sqrt()** and **atan2()**, which are used in computing the magnitude and angle of the impedance. Neither **pprn()** nor **vprn()** returns a value.

Arithmetic Operations with Complex Numbers

An essential set of tools required to analyze ac circuits or other systems involving complex numbers consists of functions that perform complex addition, subtraction, multiplication, and division. These functions will be developed here with applications to circuit analysis. The same functions may be used to perform arithmetic operations with vector quantities. This should not be surprising since complex numbers, also called *phasors,* are actually a special type of vector.

The sum of two or more complex numbers is obtained by summing the real and imaginary components separately. This is similar to the procedure that was used for summing vectors in Chapter 4. If the numbers are in polar form, they must first be converted to rectangular form before they can be added together. To find the difference of two or more complex numbers, the real and imaginary components are subtracted separately.

Functions for adding or subtracting two complex numbers are shown in Fig. 7.13. They receive the names of the arrays storing the two operands (**a** and **b**) and also the name of the array that will store the result (**c**). The result may be stored in one of the two operand arrays as well, although this will destroy the original data stored there. For example, to add **a** and **b** and store the result back in **a**, the call would be **vsum(a,b,a)**. This calling method holds for all the complex arithmetic functions presented here.

```
/*    Vector addition */
/*    Adds a and b and places the result in c */

void vsum(a,b,c)
double a[], b[], c[];
      {
      c[0] = a[0] + b[0];
      c[1] = a[1] + b[1];
      }


/*    Vector subtraction */
/*    Subtracts b from a and places the result in c */

void vdif(a,b,c)
double a[], b[], c[];
      {
      c[0] = a[0] - b[0];
      c[1] = a[1] - b[1];
      }
```

Figure 7.13 Addition or subtraction of complex numbers.

To add or subtract a series of complex numbers, repeated calls can be made to **vsum()** or **vdif()**. Each call would include one new number and the result of the last call as operands.

The product of two complex numbers is easier to compute in polar form. It is given by the product of the magnitudes and the sum of the angles of the two complex numbers. For example,

$$\mathbf{z}_1\underline{/\phi_1} \times \mathbf{z}_2\underline{/\phi_2} = \mathbf{z}_1 \times \mathbf{z}_2\underline{/\phi_1 + \phi_2}$$

If the numbers to be multiplied are in rectangular form, we can convert to polar form and then multiply. However, converting back and forth between polar and rectangular forms will increase program execution time and, if performed repeatedly, can cause an accumulation of roundoff errors. Therefore, it is best to perform the multiplication directly in rectangular form as follows:

$$\begin{aligned}(r_1 + jx_1)(r_2 + jx_2) &= r_1r_2 + r_1jx_2 + r_2jx_1 - x_1x_2 \\ &= (r_1r_2 - x_1x_2) + j(r_1x_2 + r_2x_1)\end{aligned}$$

Figure 7.14 shows a function that performs a multiplication of two complex numbers. The real and imaginary parts of the result are stored in intermediate variables **re** and **im** in order to preserve the ability to store the result in one of the original operands. Otherwise, a call of **vmul(a,b,a)** would have replaced the original **a[0]** with the real part of the result while this quantity is still needed for computation of the imaginary part in the second equation.

```
/*    Vector multiplication */
/*    Multiplies a and b and places the result in c */

void vmul(a,b,c)
double a[], b[],c[];
      {
      double re,im;

      re = a[0]*b[0] - a[1]*b[1];
      im = a[0]*b[1] + b[0]*a[1];
      c[0] = re;
      c[1] = im;
      }
```

Figure 7.14 Multiplication of complex numbers.

The division of two complex numbers is also easier to perform in polar form. It is given by the division of the magnitudes and the difference of the angles. For example,

$$\frac{z_1\angle\phi_1}{z_2\angle\phi_2} = \frac{z_1}{z_2}\angle\phi_1 - \phi_2$$

If the original complex numbers are in rectangular form, we can convert to polar form and then divide. However, it is best to perform the division directly in rectangular form for the same reason as given for the multiplication process. To divide two complex numbers in rectangular form, we multiply the numerator and the denominator by the *conjugate* of the denominator. The conjugate of a complex number is obtained by changing the sign of the imaginary component. This operation will force the denominator to become a real number and leaves only a complex multiplication to be performed in the numerator:

$$\begin{aligned}\frac{r_1 + jx_1}{r_2 + jx_2} &= \frac{r_1 + jx_1}{r_2 + jx_2}\,\frac{r_2 - jx_2}{r_2 - jx_2} \\ &= \frac{r_1r_2 + x_1x_2 - jr_1x_2 + jr_2x_1}{r_2^2 + x_2^2}\end{aligned}$$

The function of Fig. 7.15 performs the division of two complex numbers. The intermediate variables **r** and **x** store the real and imaginary parts of the

```
/*    Vector division */
/*    Divides a by b and places the result in c */

void vdiv(a,b,c)
double a[], b[], c[];
    {
    double r, x, d;

    r = a[0]*b[0] + a[1]*b[1];
    x = a[1]*b[0] - b[1]*a[0];
    d = 1/(b[0]*b[0] + b[1]*b[1]);
    c[0] = d*r;
    c[1] = d*x;
    }
```

Figure 7.15 Division of complex numbers.

```
/* series-parallel circuit reduction pseudocode */
/* zt[] is global and stores the total impedance */
/* z_next[] stores the next impedance to be included */
/* temp[] stores an intermediate result */
/* calls existing modules vsum(), vmul(), vdiv() and vprn()*/
module main()
     print "Enter first impedance"
     input zt
     s_p = NULL
     while (s_p not equal to 'e')
          print "Enter s,p, or e"
          input s_p
          if (s_p == s)
               series()
          else
          if (s_p == p)
               parallel()
          endif
     endwhile
     vprn(zt)
end main()

module series()
     print "Enter series impedance"
     input z_next
           vsum(zt, z_next,zt)
end series()

module parallel()
     print "Enter parallel impedance"
     input z_next
           vmul(zt, z_next,temp)
           vsum(zt, z_next,zt)
           vdiv(temp, zt, zt)
end parallel()
```

Figure 7.16 Pseudocode for combination of series/parallel impedances.

numerator obtained after multiplying the ratio of **a/b** by the conjugate of **b**. The variable **d** stores the real denominator produced by the process. The real part of the result is then **r/d**, and the imaginary part is **x/d**.

To illustrate the use of the complex arithmetic functions presented here, the series/parallel circuit reduction program of Fig. 6.14 will be rewritten for reactive circuits. The concepts presented in the pseudocode of Figs. 6.12 and Fig. 6.13 are valid here. The most significant difference between the resistance circuit reduction program presented in Chapter 6 and the reactive circuit reduction program to be developed here lies in the detail of combining the complex quantities. The pseudocode is repeated in Fig. 7.16 for the ac circuit case.

We need three arrays of two elements each to store the impedances that are being processed by the program at any given point. These are defined in the pseudocode as **zt**, the current total impedance, **z_next**, the next impedance to be included, and **temp**, a variable used for the temporary storage of intermediate results. Notice the pseudocode includes calls to the functions **vsum()**, **vmul()**, **vdiv()** and **vprn()**. The program of Fig. 7.17 implements the pseudocode of Fig. 7.16.

```
/* series-parallel impedance combination program */

double zt[2];
#include <stdio.h>
main()
      {
      char s_p = '*';
      void series(), parallel(), vsum(), vmul(), vdiv(), vprn();

      puts("Enter resistance part of first impedance: ");
      scanf("%lf", &zt[0]);
      puts("Enter reactance part of first impedance: ");
      scanf("%lf", &zt[1]);

      while (s_p != 'e')
            {
            puts("Enter 's', 'p', or 'e':");
            while ((s_p = getchar()) == '\n')
                  ;
            putchar('\n');
            if (s_p == 's')
                  series();
            else if (s_p == 'p')
                  parallel();
            }

      printf("The total impedance = ");
      vprn(zt);
      }

void series()                              /* find series combination */
      {
      double z_next[2];

      puts("Enter resistance part of series impedance: ");
      scanf("%lf", &z_next[0]);
      puts("Enter reactance part of series impedance: ");
      scanf("%lf", &z_next[1]);
      vsum(zt, z_next, zt);
      }
```

Figure 7.17 Program for combination of series/parallel impedances.

```
void parallel()                      /* find parallel combination */
     {
     double z_next[2], temp[2];

     puts("Enter resistance part of parallel impedance: ");
     scanf("%lf", &z_next[0]);
     puts("Enter reactance part of parallel impedance: ");
     scanf("%lf", &z_next[1]);
     vmul(zt, z_next, temp);
     vsum(zt, z_next, zt);
     vdiv(temp, zt, zt);
     }
void vsum(a, b, c)       /* add a to b and place result in c */
double a[], b[], c[];
     {
     c[0] = a[0] + b[0];
     c[1] = a[1] + b[1];
     }

void vmul(a, b, c)       /* multiply a by b and place result in c */
double a[], b[], c[];
     {
     double re, im;

     re = a[0]*b[0] - a[1]*b[1];
     im = a[1]*b[1] + b[0]*a[1];
     c[0] = re;
     c[1] = im;
     }

void vdiv(a, b, c)       /* divide a by b and place result in c */
double a[], b[], c[];
     {
     double r, x, d;

     r = a[0]*b[0] + a[1]*b[1];
     x = a[1]*b[0] - b[1]*a[0];
     d = b[0]*b[0] + b[1]*b[1];
     c[0] = r/d;
     c[1] = x/d;
     }

void vprn(a)             /* print complex number a in rectangular form */
double a[];
     {
     char sign;

     if (a[0] < 0)
          sign = '-';
     else
          sign = '+';
     printf("%f %cj%f ohms\n", a[0], sign, (a[1] > 0) ? a[1] : -a[1]);
     }
```

Figure 7.17 (continued).

```
Enter resistance part of first impedance:
100
Enter reactance part of first impedance:
50
Enter 's', 'p', or 'e':
p

Enter resistance part of parallel impedance:
200
Enter reactance part of parallel impedance:
100
Enter 's', 'p', or 'e':
s

Enter resistance part of series impedance:
75
Enter reactance part of series impedance:
75
Enter 's', 'p', or 'e':
e

The total impedance = 135.000000 +j95.000000 ohms
```

Figure 7.17 (continued).

7.7 APPLICATIONS OF POINTERS AND ARRAYS

This section contains a large number of applications examples. It is not necessary to do all the examples or to cover them in the order in which they are presented. You may select whichever are of particular interest to you.

Transpose of an Array

The transpose of an array is obtained by interchanging all the rows and columns of the array. If the original array has **i** rows and **j** columns, the transposed array will have **j** rows and **i** columns. The program of Fig. 7.18 finds the transpose of the two-dimensional array **a** and assigns it to the array **b**. The relationship of the original elements to the transposed elements is given by **a[i][j] == b[j][i]** for all values of **i** and **j**.

The **a** array is declared as **static int** and initialized within the declaration. It has a size of three rows and four columns. The **b** array must therefore be declared as **b[4][3]**, since it will have four rows and three columns. The program first prints the **a** array, identifying each element that is printed. The second nested **for** structure assigns each element **b[i][j]** the value of **a[j][i]**. Finally, the transposed array is printed.

Summing Array Elements

It is sometimes necessary to find the sum of all the elements in a one-dimensional array (or perhaps the sum of all the elements of a particular row or column in a two-dimensional array). The program of Fig. 7.19 performs the summation for a one-dimensional integer array. The array is declared as **static int** and initialized within the declaration. A function named **sum()** is called to perform the summation. The arguments of **sum()** are the array name and the number of elements it contains. The function returns an integer that represents the value of the sum.

```
/* find transpose of a two-dimensional array */
#include <stdio.h>
main()
     {
     static int a[3][4] =
             {
                 {1, 2, 3, 4},
                 {5, 6, 7, 8},
                 {9, 10, 11, 12}
             };
     static int b[4][3];
     int i, j;

     /* print a[][] array */
     printf("\n\n");
     for (i = 0; i < 3; i++)
           {
           for (j = 0; j < 4; j++)
                 printf("a[%d][%d]=%2d    ", i, j, a[i][j]);
           putchar('\n');
           }

     /* define b[][] equals transpose of a[][] */
     for (i = 0; i < 4; i++)
           for (j = 0; j < 3; j++)
                 b[i][j] = a[j][i];

     /* print b[][] */
     printf("\n\n");
     for (i = 0; i < 4; i++)
           {
           for (j = 0; j < 3; j++)
                 printf("b[%d][%d]=%2d  ", i, j, b[i][j]);
           putchar('\n');
           }
     }
```

```
a[0][0]= 1    a[0][1]= 2    a[0][2]= 3    a[0][3]= 4
a[1][0]= 5    a[1][1]= 6    a[1][2]= 7    a[1][3]= 8
a[2][0]= 9    a[2][1]=10    a[2][2]=11    a[2][3]=12


b[0][0]= 1  b[0][1]= 5  b[0][2]= 9
b[1][0]= 2  b[1][1]= 6  b[1][2]=10
b[2][0]= 3  b[2][1]= 7  b[2][2]=11
b[3][0]= 4  b[3][1]= 8  b[3][2]=12
```

Figure 7.18 Transpose of a two-dimensional array.

Within the function **sum()**, a **for** loop is used to access each element of the array and add its value to the current value of the sum, assigned to **val**. On each pass through the loop, **i** is incremented and **val** is updated to include the value of **array[i]**. After completion of the loop, **val** is returned to the calling function.

The function **sum()** could have been written using a pointer for accessing the elements of the array. Also, if the function sums anything other than **int** data, say **float** or **double**, and it occurs after the calling function, it must be declared within the calling function. (A function is assumed to return **int** unless declared otherwise.)

```
/* Summing array elements */
#include <stdio.h>
main()
	{
	static int data[12] = {31, 28, 31, 30, 31, 30, 31, 31, 30, 31, 30, 31};
	int x;

	x = sum(data, 12);
	printf("The number of days in the year equals = %d\n", x);
	}

int sum(array, count)
int array[], count;
	{
	int i, val = 0;

	for (i = 0; i < count; i++)
		val = val + array[i];
	return (val);
	}
```

```
The number of days in the year equals = 365
```

Figure 7.19 Summing array elements.

Simultaneous Equations Using Cramer's Rule

Arrays may be used to find the solution to a set of simultaneous equations. A generalized method that can be used for any number of equations is called *Gauss–Jordan elimination*. This method yields a fast solution, but the procedure is rather complex. Chapter 14 will consider the Gauss–Jordan method in detail. When only two or three equations are involved, a simpler method, called Cramer's rule, may be used. For the set of equations

$$\mathbf{a_{11}x_1 + a_{12}x_2 = a_{13}}$$

$$\mathbf{a_{21}x_1 + a_{22}x_2 = a_{23}}$$

The solution for $\mathbf{x_1}$ and $\mathbf{x_2}$ is given by Cramer's rule as

$$\mathbf{x_1} = \frac{\begin{vmatrix} \mathbf{a_{13}} & \mathbf{a_{12}} \\ \mathbf{a_{23}} & \mathbf{a_{22}} \end{vmatrix}}{\mathbf{d}} = \frac{\mathbf{a_{13}a_{22} - a_{12}a_{23}}}{\mathbf{a_{11}a_{22} - a_{12}a_{21}}}$$

$$\mathbf{x_2} = \frac{\begin{vmatrix} \mathbf{a_{11}} & \mathbf{a_{13}} \\ \mathbf{a_{21}} & \mathbf{a_{23}} \end{vmatrix}}{\mathbf{d}} = \frac{\mathbf{a_{11}a_{23} - a_{13}a_{21}}}{\mathbf{a_{11}a_{22} - a_{12}a_{21}}}$$

where

$$\mathbf{d} = \begin{vmatrix} \mathbf{a_{11}} & \mathbf{a_{12}} \\ \mathbf{a_{21}} & \mathbf{a_{22}} \end{vmatrix} = \mathbf{a_{11}a_{22} - a_{12}a_{21}}$$

The solution for any number of equations can be found using Cramer's rule, although the solution becomes very cumbersome for anything larger than three equations. In general, the solution for $\mathbf{x_i}$ is given by the ratio of two determinants. The denominator determinant is that of the coefficient matrix of the set of equations. The numerator determinant is that of the coefficient matrix with the **i**th column replaced by the constants.

The program of Fig. 7.20 uses Cramer's rule to find the solution to a set of two equations. The equation coefficients are assigned to the two-dimensional array **a[3][4]**. This array was made larger than necessary in order to have the array subscripts match the equation subscripts. (The zero subscripted elements in the array are not used.)

```
/* Simultaneous equations using Cramer's rule */
#include <stdio.h>
main()
      {
      float a[3][4], d, x1, x2;
      int i, j;

      for (i = 1; i < 3; i++)
            for (j = 1; j < 4; j++)
                  {
                  printf("Enter coefficient a[%d][%d]: ", i, j);
                  scanf("%f", &a[i][j]);
                  }

      d = a[1][1]*a[2][2] - a[1][2]*a[2][1];
      x1 = (a[1][3]*a[2][2] - a[1][2]*a[2][3])/d;
      x2 = (a[1][1]*a[2][3] - a[1][3]*a[2][1])/d;
      printf("x1 = %f\n", x1);
      printf("x2 = %f\n", x2);
      }
```

```
Enter coefficient a[1][1]: 1
Enter coefficient a[1][2]: 5
Enter coefficient a[1][3]: 42
Enter coefficient a[2][1]: -3
Enter coefficient a[2][2]: 8
Enter coefficient a[2][3]: 14
x1 = 11.565217
x2 = 6.086957
```

Figure 7.20 Solution for two simultaneous equations using Cramer's rule.

Our keyboard input routine for entering a two-dimensional array is used here to define the equations to be solved. The value of **d** is calculated first, since it will be used within the equations for $\mathbf{x_1}$ and $\mathbf{x_2}$. After the computation of $\mathbf{x_1}$ and $\mathbf{x_2}$, the solutions are printed and the program terminates.

Sorting Data

A common requirement of applications programs is the sorting of numeric or string data. A variety of sorting algorithms, from simple to very complex, is available. The performance of each is measured by how fast it can sort a given list. Sorting numeric data will be introduced here, with more advanced techniques including the sorting of string data deferred to Chapter 11.

Data that are to be sorted are normally assigned to an array. The array elements are then compared and exchanged where necessary to produce a sorted list. The simpler algorithms are easier to comprehend, but they are much slower in execution than some of the more complex algorithms. If the number of data items to be sorted is small, almost any algorithm will perform satisfactorily. However, for larger lists, sort time varies dramatically with the efficiency of the algorithm.

We all are familiar with manual sorting operations. Consider the list in Fig. 7.21, which is in random alphabetic order. We can generate a new list that is in alphabetic order by repeatedly scanning the original list and selecting the appropriate entry on each scan that must be entered next in the sorted list. The algorithm for this sorting method can be stated simply as follows:

```
while (more data in column 1)
     write lowest alphabetic entry from column 1 in column 2
     cross out this same entry from column 1
end while
```

This algorithm can be readily implemented as a **C** program. However, it is one of the slowest sorting methods available and also requires more than double the memory space of the unsorted list.

	Column 1		*Column 2*
1	Washer	1	
2	Rod	2	
3	Bolt	3	
4	Flange	4	
5	Bracket	5	

Figure 7.21 List to be sorted.

A faster and more efficient method of sorting data is the *bubble sort*, so called because one data element appears to bubble up (or down) to its correct position in the list on each pass. Here, starting at the top of the list, two adjacent elements are compared to see if they are in the correct order. If not, they are exchanged. Next, a comparison is made between the second and third elements in the list. Again, if they are not in the correct order, an exchange of positions is made. This process continues down the list until all the entries have been involved in at least one comparison.

After completion of the first pass through the list, the largest element will appear at the bottom of the list (assuming an ascending order sort). After the second pass, the second-largest element will appear in the second position from the bottom. For each subsequent pass, another element will appear in its correct position. Since the portion of the list that remains unsorted is reduced after each pass, the comparison operation is made over a smaller range from one pass to the next. For the first pass, a list of **N** items will require **N − 1** comparisons. On the last pass, only one comparison is made (unless the sort terminates early).

In the worst case, an array of **N** elements will require **N − 1** passes through the list. This follows from the fact that one element is known to be placed in its correct position after each pass. If the list is partially ordered prior to starting the sort, considerable time can be saved by checking to see if the list is fully sorted after the completion of each pass. If, during the pass, no exchanges are made, the list must be fully sorted and the process can terminate at that point.

To determine if an exchange is made during any pass, a variable, called a *flag*, can be reset to some value indicating *no exchange* prior to the start of the pass. When the first exchange is made, the flag is set to a value indicating an *exchange*. If no exchange is made during a pass, the flag remains reset. The flag value is then tested at the end of each pass. If it is still reset, the sort must be completed.

The pseudocode for the bubble sort is given in Fig. 7.22. It assumes the first element in the array is **a[1]** for simplicity. A call is made to a module **exchange()**. We have already looked at a function that implements the exchange of two elements in an array. Therefore, the pseudocode for this module is not shown.

```
/* pseudocode for the bubble sort */
/* sorts a numeric array a[N] */
/* calls module exchange */
module main()
    for (pass = 1 to N-1)                  /* set the pass number */
        swap = NO                          /* lower the exchange flag */
        for (i = 1 to N-pass)              /* check only the unsorted part */
            if (a[i] > a[i+1])             /* do we need an exchange? */
                exchange (a[i], a[i+1])    /* do it */
                swap = YES                 /* raise the exchange flag */
            endif
        end for
        if (swap == NO)                    /* did we finish early? */
            exit                           /* no exchanges, done */
        end if
    end for
end main()
```

Figure 7.22 Pseudocode for the bubble sort.

The **C** program for the bubble sort is shown in Fig. 7.23. A list of ten integers is assigned to the array **data** within its declaration. The call **sort(data,10)** passes the array name and its length to the bubble sort function. Notice that the zeroth element of the array, **a[0]**, is being utilized here. The limits in the **for** loops must be adjusted accordingly in going from the pseudocode to the **C** program. After completion of the **sort()** function, the list is printed and the program terminates.

Searching an Array

It is frequently necessary to search through the data stored in an array to find a particular value. We may simply be interested in knowing if that value is in the array, or perhaps its location, or we may be looking for other data that are cross-referenced to it through the array subscript. The simplest method for finding an element in an array is called the *linear search*.

To perform a linear search of an array for a match to some data value, we start at one end and compare the selected element to the data value. If they do not match, the array subscript is incremented and a comparison is made between the next element and the data value. This process continues until either a match is found or the end of the list is encountered. If a match is found, the current value of the array subscript indicates the location of the data value in the array. If no match is found after the entire list has been scanned, the data value is not in the array.

```
/* Bubble sort integer data */

#define YES 1
#define NO 0
#include <stdio.h>
main()
      {
      static int data[10] = { 70,13,96,10,18,47,22,81,59,16};
      int i;
      void sort(), exchange();

      sort(data,10);
      for (i = 0; i < 10; i++)
            printf("%d ", data[i]);
      }

void sort(array, count)      /* bubble sort function */
int array[], count;
      {
      int pass, i, swap;

      for (pass = 0; pass < (count - 1); pass++)
            {
            swap = NO;
            for (i = 0; i < (count - pass - 1); i++)
                  if (array[i] > array[i + 1])
                        {
                        exchange(&array[i], &array[i + 1]);
                        swap = YES;
                        }
            if (swap == NO)
                  break;
            }
      }

void exchange(a,b)
int *a, *b;
      {
      int temp;

      temp = *a;
      *a = *b;
      *b = temp;
      }
```

```
10 13 16 18 22 47 59 70 81 96
```

Figure 7.23 Bubble sort program.

A program that implements the linear search is given in Fig. 7.24. An integer array of ten unsorted values is initialized within the declaration of the array **data**. A number entered from the keyboard will be compared to the entries in the list for a match. The **for** loop starts with the first element in the array, selected through the subscript **i**. The value of **i** will be incremented until the last element, **data[9]**, has been examined or a match was found at an earlier position.

The **if** statement following the **for** loop tests the outcome of the search. If **(i == 10)** after completion of the loop, no match was found. If the loop terminated because a match was found, the value of **i** (between 0 and 9) will indicate where the match occurred.

```
/* Linear search */
#include <stdio.h>
main()
      {
      static int data[10] = {33, 42, 18, 29, 53, 88, 91, 70, 67, 3};
      int i, num;

      puts("Enter a number from 0 to 100");
      scanf("%d", &num);
      for (i = 0; i < 10 && (num != data[i]); i++)
            ;
      if (i == 10)
            printf("%d is not in the list\n", num);
      else
            printf("%d is item %d in the list\n", num, i + 1);
      }
```

```
Enter a number from 0 to 100
49
49 is not in the list

Enter a number from 0 to 100
53
53 is item 5 in the list
```

Figure 7.24 Linear search program.

Binary Search

A problem with the linear search is that a list of **N** entries will require, in the worst case, **N** comparisons. A list consisting of thousands of entries may produce an unacceptable delay in the search process. If the list is sorted, a much faster method called the *binary search,* is available. It uses the *successive approximation* technique introduced in Chapter 6. For a list of **N** entries, the worst case will require only **M** comparisons, where **M** is the smallest integer that satisfies the relationship

$$2^{M} > N$$

For a list of 1000 entries, only 10 comparisons will be required in the worst case.

The binary search procedure makes use of the fact that the list is sorted in *ascending* order. The first comparison is made at the midpoint of the list. If the data value for which we are searching is greater than the midpoint element of the array, we can restrict our search to the upper half of the array. If it is smaller than the midpoint element, we can restrict our search to the lower half of the array. (Of course, if a match occurs at the midpoint, then the search is terminated.) With only one comparison, we have ruled out half of the entire array! Now we can search the new shorter list using the same procedure. A new midpoint is selected. Each time a comparison is made, half of the remaining list is eliminated from consideration. The search terminates when a match is found or the list has shrunk to only one element.

The pseudocode for the binary search is given in Fig. 7.25. Inputs to the module include the array name, its length, and the value to find in the array. The variables **high**, **low**, and **mid** contain values for the upper, lower, and midpoint of the array (or segment thereof) to be searched. The value of **high** is initialized to

count-1, the highest element in the array. The value of **low** is initialized to **0**. The value of **mid** is always given by

```
mid = (high+low)/2
```

The **while** loop continues until there is a match or only one element is left. If **array[mid]** > **value**, then the search is restricted to the lower half of the remaining array by setting high to **mid-1**. Since no match occurred, the element at **mid** need not be considered again. This is why **high** is set to **mid-1** instead of **mid**. The **else** case restricts the search to the upper half of the remaining array by setting **low** to **mid+1**. Again, **low** is set above **mid** to **mid+1** since no match occurred at **mid**.

On each pass where there is no match, either **high** or **low** will be reset to a new value. Therefore, **mid** must be recomputed before the start of the next pass. After the **while** loop terminates, the **if** statement detects whether it terminated due to a match condition or exhausting the list. It returns the location of the match (value of **mid**) or a no match indication, depending on the outcome.

```
/*Pseudocode for the binary search */
/* array is sorted in ascending order */
/* and has count elements, starting with 0 */
/* array is searched for value */
module bin_srch(array, count, value)
     high = count -1
     low = 0
     mid = (high + low)/2

     while(no match and high > low)
          if (array[mid] > value)
               new value of high = mid - 1 /* search lower half */
          else
               new value of low = mid + 1  /* search upper half */
          end if
          mid = (high + low)/2             /* reduce size to half */
     end while

     if (match)
          return mid                       /* match occurs at mid */
     else
          return no match indication       /* usually a value of -1 */
     end if
end bin_srch()
```

Figure 7.25 Pseudocode for the binary search.

A program that uses the binary search is given in Fig. 7.26. The **main()** function initializes the array **data**, which is sorted in ascending order. It accepts a keyboard input, assigned to **num**, and calls **bin_srch(data,10,num)** to find **num** in the array. The function **bin_srch()** returns the location of a match, if there is one. Otherwise, it returns a **−1**, which signals that "no match" occurred. The variable **ret** is assigned the returned value. It is tested to determine the outcome of the search. If **ret==−1**, a message indicating "no match" is printed. Otherwise, the location where a match occurred is printed.

```
/* Binary search */
#include <stdio.h>
main()
      {
      static int data[] = {101, 214, 345, 440, 501, 666, 792, 808, 880, 900};
      int ret, num;

      puts("Enter number to find: ");
      scanf("%d", &num);
      ret = bin_srch(data, 10, num);
      if (ret == -1)
            printf("The number %d is not in this list\n", num);
      else
            printf("The number %d is item %d in this list\n", num, ret);
      }

int bin_srch(array, count, val)
int array[], count, val;
      {
      int high = count - 1;
      int low = 0;
      int mid = (high + low) / 2;

      while (array[mid] != val && high > low)
            {
            if (array[mid] > val)
                  high = mid - 1;
            else
                  low = mid + 1;
            mid = (high + low) / 2;
            }
      if (array[mid] == val)
            return (mid);
      else
            return (-1);
      }
```

```
Enter number to find:
501
The number 501 is item 4 in this list

Enter number to find:
880
The number 880 is item 8 in this list

Enter number to find:
33
The number 33 is not in this list
```

Figure 7.26 Binary search program.

Look-up Tables

The computer can be used to look up information in tables that cross-reference one type of data to another. For example, look-up tables can be used to find the description of a part, given the part number. Often, it is faster to look up the value of a math function than it is to calculate it. We can also have tables of nonlinear characteristics that are not available in equation form.

Arrays are frequently used to implement a look-up table. The program of Fig. 7.27 cross-references a decimal digit to the electronics industry color code for that digit. A two-dimensional character array is used to store the colors of the code. The array **col_code[10][7]** consists of ten entries or rows, each of which contains seven characters or columns. A number is cross-referenced to its color through the array name.

The string "black" is assigned to the array named **col_code[0]**. Likewise, "brown" is assigned to **col_code[1]**. We can access the color assigned to any digit **i** by referencing its array name, **col_code[i]**.

```
/* Look-up tables using an array */
#include <stdio.h>
main()
      {
      static char col_code[10][7] =
               {
                  "black",
                  "brown",
                  "red",
                  "orange",
                  "yellow",
                  "green",
                  "blue",
                  "violet",
                  "gray",
                  "white"
               };
      int i;

      puts("Enter a number from 0 to 9");
      scanf("%d", &i);
      printf("The color corresponding to %d is %s\n", i, col_code[i]);
      }
```

```
Enter a number from 0 to 9
9
The color corresponding to 9 is white

Enter a number from 0 to 9
5
The color corresponding to 5 is green
```

Figure 7.27 Color code look-up table.

The program simply inputs a digit, **i**, whose color code is desired. The digit is used as a subscript to obtain the array name for the corresponding color. The **printf()** statement uses the array name **col_code[i]** to print the string assigned to that array.

Accessing Specific Memory Locations with Pointers (or a Peek Function)

A program that prints the contents of successive memory locations is referred to as a *memory dump*. The format of the output is usually in hexadecimal, ASCII text, or both. Such a program is included here to demonstrate how we can access specific memory locations using either pointers or the **peek()** function. **Peek()** is not a part of the standard **C** library, although it is implemented on many microcomputer **C** compilers and interpreters.

The pseudocode for the memory dump is given in Fig. 7.28. The **base_address** for the memory dump is entered along with the **number_of_bytes** to dump. The **last_address** is then computed by adding the **base_address** to the **number_of_bytes** to dump. A **for** loop is then set up to print the contents of 16 consecutive memory locations per line in both hexadecimal and ASCII.

```
/*Pseudocode for memory dump */
module main()
     input base_address for dump
     input number_of_bytes to dump
     last_address = base_address + number_of_bytes
     for (row_base = base_address to last_address,increment 16)
          print row_base address in hex
          print contents of 16 locations from row_base in hex
          print the contents of the same locations in ASCII
          print newline
     end for
end main()
```

Figure 7.28 Pseudocode for memory dump.

The **row_base** is the beginning location for any blocks of 16 bytes to be output. Its address is the first item to be printed on each line. The contents of 16 memory locations starting at **row_base** are then output in hex. The contents of the same 16 locations are then output in ASCII format. A newline character terminates that line, and **row_base** is incremented by 16. Additional rows are printed until **row_base** reaches **last_address**.

The pointer version of the program is shown in Fig. 7.29. All the variables that reference addresses have been declared as **long int**. Whether or not this is necessary on your system depends on the size of **int** or **long int** and the memory capacity of your computer. The pointer **ptr** is initialized to the value of **row_b** (row_base) by the statement

```
ptr = (char *) row_b;
```

To print the contents of the 16 locations starting with the value of **ptr** in hex, a **for** loop is used. As **i** is incremented from **0** to **15**, the value of **ptr** is also incremented. The desired memory contents are accessed by ***ptr** and printed in hexadecimal through the conversion specifier **"%02x"**. Some white space is printed halfway through the row for readability.

To print the contents of the same locations in ACSII, the pointer is reset to the value of **row_b**. The same control structure is used to access each memory location. To output the value of ***ptr** in ASCII, the character conversion specifier, **"%c"**, is used in the **printf** statement. The statement

```
if ((*ptr < 32) || (*ptr > 127))
     printf(".");
```

is used to trap control characters and other garbage and replace them with a period.

```
/* memory dump using pointers */
#include <stdio.h>
main()
      {
      char *ptr;
      int i;
      long row_b, base, last, count;

      printf("Enter base address in hex: ");
      scanf("%lx", &base);
      printf("Enter number of bytes to dump in hex: ");
      scanf("%lx", &count);
      last = base + count;
      for (row_b = base; row_b < last; row_b += 16)
            {
            /* label line base address in hex */
            printf("%05lx:  ", row_b);
            /* print contents of 16 memory locations in hex */
            ptr = (char *) row_b;
            for (i = 0; i < 16; i++, ptr++)
                  {
                  if (i == 8)
                        printf("  ");
                  printf("%02x ", *ptr);
                  }
            /* print contents of same memory locations in ascii */
            printf("    ");
            ptr = (char *) row_b;
            for (i = 0; i < 16; i++, ptr++)
                  {
                  if ((*ptr < 32) || (*ptr > 127))
                        printf(".");
                  else
                        printf("%c", *ptr);
                  }
            printf("\n");
            }
      }
```

```
Enter base address in hex: fe0f0
Enter number of bytes to dump in hex: 60
fe0f0:  eb e8 56 49 44 45 4f 20   52 41 4d 20 54 45 53 54    ..VIDEO RAM TEST
fe100:  20 42 41 44 24 50 72 65   73 73 20 5b 41 6c 74 2d     BAD$Press [Alt-
fe110:  43 74 72 6c 2d 44 65 6c   5d 20 77 69 6c 6c 20 73    Ctrl-Del] will s
fe120:  6b 69 70 20 52 41 4d 20   54 45 53 54 0a 24 52 41    kip RAM TEST.$RA
fe130:  4d 20 54 45 53 54 24 31   38 30 31 24 52 4f 4d 20    M TEST$1801$ROM
fe140:  45 52 52 24 44 69 73 6b   20 6e 6f 74 20 73 65 74    ERR$Disk not set
```

Figure 7.29 Memory dump using pointers.

Some microcomputer implementations of **C** may not permit initializing a pointer to any location in memory. The **peek()** version of the program shown in Fig. 7.30 may work for these systems. If your version of **C** does not include **peek()**, you can refer to Chapter 15. It shows how to write your own **peek()** in assembly language.

In converting the program from using pointers to using **peek()**, the following changes are made: The **long int** variable **addr** is equivalent to **ptr**. Its value is the address to be accessed. The expression **peek(addr)** is equivalent to ***ptr** and gives the contents of **addr**. Some versions of **peek()** require two arguments, a memory

```
/* memory dump using peek() */
#include <stdio.h>
main()
     {
     int  val;
     long addr, row_b, base, last, count;

     printf("Enter base address in hex: ");
     scanf("%lx", &base);
     printf("Enter number of bytes to dump in hex: ");
     scanf("%lx", &count);
     last = base+count;
     for (row_b = base; row_b < last; row_b += 16)
          {
          /* label line base address in hex */
          printf("%05lx:   ", row_b);
          /* print contents of 16 memory locations in hex */
          for (addr = row_b; addr < row_b + 16; addr++)
               {
               if (addr == row_b + 8)
                    printf("  ");
               printf("%02x ", peek(addr));
               }
          /* print contents of same memory locations in ascii */
          printf("   ");
          for (addr = row_b; addr < row_b + 16; addr++)
               {
               val = peek(addr);
               if ((val < 32) || (val > 127))
                    putchar('.');
               else
                    printf("%c",val);
               }
          putchar('\n');
          }
     }
```

```
Enter base address in hex: fe0f0
Enter number of bytes to dump in hex: 60
fe0f0:  eb e8 56 49 44 45 4f 20   52 41 4d 20 54 45 53 54    ..VIDEO RAM TEST
fe100:  20 42 41 44 24 50 72 65   73 73 20 5b 41 6c 74 2d     BAD$Press [Alt-
fe110:  43 74 72 6c 2d 44 65 6c   5d 20 77 69 6c 6c 20 73    Ctrl-Del] will s
fe120:  6b 69 70 20 52 41 4d 20   54 45 53 54 0a 24 52 41    kip RAM TEST.$RA
fe130:  4d 20 54 45 53 54 24 31   38 30 31 24 52 4f 4d 20    M TEST$1801$ROM
fe140:  45 52 52 24 44 69 73 6b   20 6e 6f 74 20 73 65 74    ERR$Disk not set
```

Figure 7.30 Memory dump using **peek()**.

segment address and an offset from that segment. In this case, the segment can be treated as a constant, and the offset can be set to the value of **addr**.

PROBLEMS

7.1. Consider the integer array

```
num[] = {2, 4, 6, 8}
```

Write a declaration for the pointer **ptr**, initializing it to the first element of **num[]**.

7.2. In Problem 7.1, what is the value of **num[2]**? of ***(ptr+2)**? of ***++ptr**?

7.3. Modify the program of Fig. 7.5 so that it finds the minimum value in an array.

7.4. Refer to the program of Fig. 7.18. Write a function that finds the transpose of a two-dimensional array. The function receives four arguments, the name of the array to be transposed, the number of rows and columns of the original array, and the name of the transposed array.

7.5. Refer to the program of Fig. 7.19. Modify the program so that it uses pointers to access the elements for summation.

7.6. Modify the program of Fig. 7.20 to solve three equations in three unknowns using Cramer's rule.

7.7. Modify the bubble sort program of Fig. 7.23 for a descending order.

7.8. Write a function that implements a sine look-up table for angles from 0 to 45 degrees in steps of 5 degrees. It should be called **sine**(*d*), where *d* is the angle in degrees. The table values should be stored in the array **sin_tbl[ ]**.

7.9. Convert the program of Fig. 7.27 to store the look-up table in an array of pointers.

7.10. Run the memory dump program of Fig. 7.29 or Fig. 7.30 on your system. You will need to investigate the limits of pointer addressing with your system and whether or not it includes a **peek()** function.

7.11. Solve for the total impedance of the circuit shown in Fig. 7.31 using the program of Fig. 7.17.

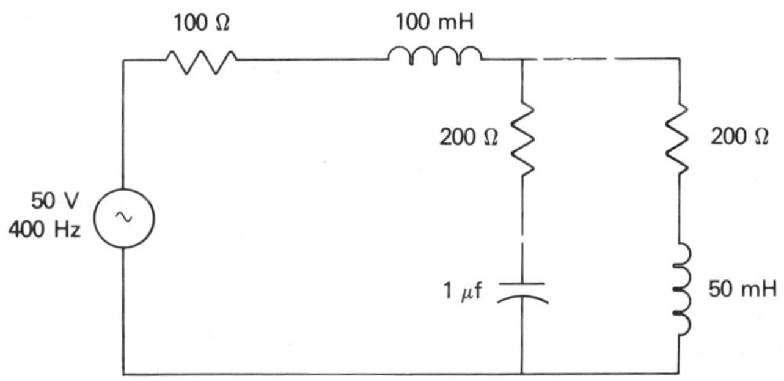

Figure 7.31 AC circuit of Problem 7.11.

PROGRAMMING PROJECTS

7.12. Develop a function for finding the mean value of an array. The arguments of **mean**(*array,size*) are the name of the array and its size. The return value is the mean of all the array elements.

7.13. Modify Problem 7.12 to find the standard deviation. The function **std_dev**(*array, size*) should return the standard deviation of the named array.

7.14. Refer to the programs of Figs. 7.12 and Fig. 7.17. Modify the program of Fig. 7.17 so that the inputs are the circuit element values of **R**, **L**, and **C** and frequency rather than impedances.

chapter 8

Debugging, Testing, and Documentation

8.1 INTRODUCTION

In Chapter 6, we looked at the steps involved in the first phases of developing a program. There, the focus was on defining the problem, designing the program using pseudocode, and actually coding the program in **C**. Here, we will consider *debugging* (eliminating programming errors), testing, and documentation, with special emphasis on debugging.

It is not unusual to see more than 50% of the development time for a program being spent on debug. Therefore, it makes good sense to put some effort into minimizing the time required for debugging. One of the best steps that can be taken is to maintain good programming style within the source code. This helps in identifying and locating problems. A program without sufficient comments or one having too many **goto** statements will undoubtedly add to the debugging time required.

A variety of tools are available to assist in the debugging process. These range from the error messages produced by a compiler or interpreter to professional tools such as symbolic debuggers. We will consider each of these tools in the following sections.

8.2 TYPES OF ERRORS

Syntax Errors

One of the most common types of errors within a program are *syntax errors*. A syntax error occurs when one of the grammatical rules of the language has not been followed or applied correctly. Syntax errors are usually detected by the compiler or interpreter. A good compiler or interpreter will detect and report at least 50 to 100 types of syntax errors. Upon detecting one of these, it will print an *error message* to assist the programmer in identifying or locating the mistake.

Figure 8.1 contains a list of typical error messages produced by common syntax errors. The reference manual for your compiler or interpreter will contain a description of the error messages it prints and may also include suggestions as to possible causes. A beginning programmer will need to refer to this information frequently.

Missing punctuation such as ; , : ( ) [ ] { }
Bad declaration
Missing argument
Expected argument type not provided
Variable not found
Else without if
Do without while
Bad #define
Unmatched parentheses
Unmatched braces
lvalue not found
Negative subscript
Can't initialize auto array
Illegal pointer value
Subscript out of range

Figure 8.1 Typical error messages produced by syntax errors.

Run-time Errors

Run-time errors occur when an executing program attempts to do something that is not possible or not permitted by the compiler or operating system. One of the most frequently encountered run-time errors is an *attempt to divide by zero*. This usually occurs when some variable is not properly initialized or the program fails to detect and avoid a calculated zero divisor. Other run-time errors include *stack overflow* and *out of memory*.

Finding the source of a run-time error is usually more difficult than it is for a syntax error. The error messages may not always suggest what is actually causing the error condition. It is often necessary to trace back through a program to find the cause of these errors.

Logic Errors

A program that compiles, executes, and produces a result is not necessarily error free. In fact, it may produce correct results most of the time and still not be error free. Mistakes in program design will produce *logic errors*. These may result from an incorrect algorithm, errors in the pseudocode, or errors in translating the pseudocode into a computer language. Comprehensive program testing will uncover all or almost all logic errors. More will be said about program testing later in this chapter.

8.3 TEN COMMON MISTAKES NOT CAUGHT BY THE COMPILER

In this section, we will look at ten short programs that contain errors that are not detected by the compiler or interpreter. These errors are the most difficult type to correct since there are no error messages indicating the nature or location of the errors. You will be alerted to the specific errors contained in each program. This should help you to avoid them in your own work. It will also give you insight into the various ways that errors can creep into a program.

Error 1: No Allocation for String Data

The program of Fig. 8.2(a) compiles with no errors but will most likely *crash* at run time. The **scanf()** function requires a pointer for its argument. The variable **str** has been properly declared as a pointer. What is the problem? No space has been allocated for the string data. Where will the compiler store the string? It will most likely overwrite your program with the data.

```
/* error #1: no allocation for string data */

main()
      {
      char *str;

      scanf("%s", str);
      printf("%s", str);
      }
```

(a)

```
/* correction for error #1 */

main()
      {
      char str[100];

      scanf("%s", str);
      printf("%s", str);
      }
```

(b)

Figure 8.2 (a) Error 1: no allocation for string array; (b) corrected program.

To solve the problem, change the declaration to allocate enough space for the string data. Assuming that the string will never exceed 100 characters, you could use

```
char str[100];
```

Then the array name **str**, which is also a pointer, can be used as the argument of the **scanf()** function. The corrected program is shown in Fig. 8.2(b).

Error 2: Wrong Conversion Specifier in scanf

The conversion specifier for a variable must match its declaration type. The program of Fig. 8.3 declares **num** as long, but uses an integer conversion specifier for the **scanf()** argument. The compiler will not simply round off the number to fit into the integer memory space. The overflow will completely destroy the original value and give a garbage result. In this case, entering **123456789** will result in the assignment of an erroneous value to **num**. (This assumes that your compiler uses 2 bytes for **int** and 4 for **long**.)

```
/* error #2: wrong conversion specifier in scanf */
/* for input of 123456789, num = 52501, should be 123456789 */
/* should have "%ld" in scanf */
main()
    {
    long num = 0;

    scanf("%d", &num);
    printf("%ld", num);
    }
```

Figure 8.3 Error 2: Wrong conversion specifier in **scanf**.

How did the compiler convert the original number into the erroneous data value? If you convert the data into hexadecimal format, the answer will be apparent. The value **123456789** in hex is **75BCD15**. Since we told the compiler to store this number in an integer-sized memory space, it kept the digits **CD15** and threw out the rest (overflow). The value of **CD15** in decimal is **52501**. This is the value that will be output provided that **num** was initialized to zero. Otherwise, the output will be unpredictable.

To correct the error, simply use a conversion specifier of "%**ld**" or "%**Ld**". This will provide 4 bytes of storage for the **long int** data. What happens in the case of a variable that is declared **double** or **long float** but is assigned with a float ("%**f**") conversion specifier? You will most likely wind up with a null value for the variable. It is easy to see how such mistakes can have devastating effects on your program.

Error 3: Wrong Conversion Specifier in Printf

A wrong conversion specifier within a **printf** statement may also go undetected by the compiler but produce erroneous results. For example, the program of Fig. 8.4 declares **num** as **long**, but attempts to print its value using an **int** conversion specifier ("%**d**"). The result is that **C** looks at only the lower 2 bytes and interprets the value as an **int**.

```
/* error #3: wrong conversion specifier in printf */
/* for input of 123456789, output is -13035, should be 123456789 */
/* should have "%ld" in printf */
main()
    {
    long num;

    scanf("%ld", &num);
    printf("%d", num);
    }
```

Figure 8.4 Error 3: Wrong conversion specifier in **printf**.

For an input of **123456789**, the lower 2 bytes in hex equal **CD15**. Since the most significant bit of **CD15** is a **1**, **C** will interpret this number as a negative integer whose value is **−13035** in decimal.

Error 4: Illegal Function Calls

Some illegal function calls will not produce compiler error messages during compilation, but merely return a zero value at run time. It is up to the programmer to check arguments passed to the function and returned values. For example, the **sqrt()** function expects a positive argument. If a negative argument is encountered, **C** may simply return a **0** to indicate an error condition. This is illustrated by the example of Fig. 8.5.

```
/* error #4: illegal function call */
/* sqrt(-1) returns 0 */

main()
        {
        printf("%f\n", sqrt(-1.0));
        }
```

Figure 8.5 Error 4: Illegal function call.

If the **0** result returned from a **sqrt()** call is used as a divisor in another arithmetic expression, then a run-time *divide by zero* error will occur. Finding the source of this error may not be so easy.

Error 5: Wrong String Comparison Procedure

Beginners in **C** who learned BASIC as a first language often find themselves trying to compare string variables using the same procedure. In BASIC, the values of the string variables **A$** and **B$** can be compared by

```
IF A$ = B$ THEN statement or line number
```

Figure 8.6 shows the same procedure applied to **C**. It produces an erroneous result. Recall that the name of a character array in **C** is a pointer to its first element. The **if** statement comparing **str1** and **str2** is actually comparing two pointers that point to two separate strings. They will always be different regardless of the values of the strings themselves. The comparison of strings in **C** must be done on a character by character basis. Chapter 10 will look at the library function that performs this operation.

```
/* error #5: attempt to perform string comparison by comparing array names */
/* a typical novice error */
/* must compare on character by character basis or call strcmp() */
main()
        {
        static char str1[] = "hello";
        static char str2[] = "hello";

        if (str1 == str2)
                printf("equal\n");
        else
                printf("not equal");
        }
```

Figure 8.6 Error 5: Wrong string comparison procedure.

Error 6: Comparing Expressions Using = instead of ==

The use of the assignment operator (=) in place of the equality operator (==) is a common mistake made by beginners in the **C** language. The program of Fig. 8.7 does not have the appearance of containing any serious errors. But the **if** statement is not really testing for **num1** equal to **num2**. It is assigning the value of **num2** to **num1** and testing the result. Thus, any nonzero value for **num2** will cause the word **equal** to be printed, regardless of the relationship of **num1** and **num2**. In this case, the program will erroneously conclude that **20** equals **10**.

```
/* error #6: attempt to compare values using = in place of ==  */
/* a typical novice error */
/* result is "equal", should be "not equal" */

main()
      {
      int numl = 10;
      int num2 = 20;

      if (numl = num2)
            printf("equal\n");
      else
            printf("not equal");
      }
```

Figure 8.7 Error 6: Comparing expressions with = instead of ==.

Error 7: Loop Counter off by 1

While it is possible to have program loop counters off by any number of counts, the most common error is to be off by 1. Consider the program of Fig. 8.8. The integer array **data** is initialized to five elements. The **for** loop is used to sum the value of all the elements in the array. A pointer, **ptr**, is initialized to point to the first element in the array. It is then incremented within the **for** loop to reference the other array elements for the summation process.

```
/* error #7: loop counter off by 1 */
/* sum output is wrong, should be 15, for loop should have <=4 or <5 */

main()
      {
      int i, sum;
      static int data[] = {1, 2, 3, 4, 5};
      int *ptr = data;

      sum = 0;
      for (i = 0; i <= 5; i++)
            sum = sum + *(ptr++);
      printf("The sum is %d\n", sum);
      }
```

Figure 8.8 Error 7: Loop counter off by 1.

Sum is initialized to zero before starting the loop. After the first pass through the loop, **sum** will have a value equal to the first element of the array, **data[0]**. On each additional pass through the loop, another element of the array will be added to **sum**. Clearly, the loop statements must be executed five times to pick up all the values in the array.

The loop counter, **i**, starts with a value of **0**. The loop continues to execute until **i<=5**. But this actually causes six passes through the loop. On the last pass, **ptr** is pointing to a location beyond the last element of **data** and will thus reference a garbage value. The problem can be corrected by setting the test condition to **i<5** or **i<=4**.

Error 8: Failure to Initialize a Variable

All **automatic** variables in **C** must be explicitly initialized; otherwise, they will contain garbage values. Figure 8.9 is a corrected version of the program of Fig. 8.8 with some modifications. It references the elements of **data** by using arrays instead of pointers. Also, it uses the variable **sum** without initializing the **auto** variable before the loop begins. The result is that **sum** will contain a garbage value before the first element of **data** is added to it. The final value will be the initial garbage value plus the sum of the five array elements. This, of course, will produce an erroneous answer.

```
/* error #8: failure to initialize a variable */
/* sum is an auto variable that has garbage value unless initialized */

 main()
      {
      int i, sum;
      static int data[] = {1, 2, 3, 4, 5};

      for (i = 0; i < 5; i++)
            sum = sum + data[i];
      printf("The sum is %d\n", sum);
      }
```

Figure 8.9 Error 8: Failure to initialize a variable.

Error 9: Typographical Errors

Most typographical errors will produce a syntax error message and thus are readily detected by the compiler or interpreter. However, some *typos* (informal form of typographical) may escape detection. The program of Fig. 8.10 is a corrected version of Fig. 8.9 with **data[i]** replaced by **data[1]** within the summation. This error will escape detection by the compiler and produce an erroneous result. Instead of summing the five elements of **data**, the result will be the first element multiplied by 5.

```
/* error #9: typographical error */
/* using 1 in place of i for an array subscript */

main()
      {
      int i, sum;
      static int data[] = {1, 2, 3, 4, 5};

      sum = 0;
      for (i = 0; i < 5; i++)
            sum = sum + data[1];
      printf("The sum is %d\n", sum);
      }
```

Figure 8.10 Error 9: Typographical errors.

Error 10: Required Statements Removed by Comment Marks

The next section deals with simple ways of debugging a program. One of the options is to add or remove program lines to facilitate the process. When this is done, care must be taken to be sure that the consequences of the procedure are understood. The program of Fig. 8.11 has a program line effectively removed by placing comment marks around it. This may be useful in determining if the statement is producing a particular error message. However, the absence of the statement **i = v/r;** will produce an erroneous result, since **i** will never be initialized and thus will contain a garbage value.

```
/* error #10: failure to restore statements removed from program by placing */
/* them within comment marks */

main()
    {
    float p, i, v, r;

    puts("Enter voltage");
    scanf("%f", &v);
    puts("Enter resistance");
    scanf("%f", &r);

    /* i = v/r; */
    p = i*v;

    printf("The current is %f amperes\n", i);
    printf("The power is %f watts\n", p);
    }
```

Figure 8.11 Error 10: Required statements removed by comment marks.

8.4 *SIMPLE DEBUGGING TOOLS AND TECHNIQUES*

The choice of tools to aid in the debugging process should be matched to the size and complexity of the project. For short or relatively simple projects, the techniques presented in this section will be adequate. Professional debugging tools are available for more advanced or complex projects. These will be discussed in the next section.

Add Temporary Debug Code

A very simple but powerful debugging tool is to print intermediate results or variable values that are not normally outputs of the program. This allows you to check these intermediate data for possible clues as to the source of an error. For example, if you print the values of variables that were just entered using a **scanf** statement, errors in the **scanf** statement can be identified. Such a technique would uncover error 2 from the previous section.

If some complex computation involves a series of formulas with only the final result as output, it makes sense to print some of the intermediate values to check for the source of an error. Any added code that is intended as temporary debug code should be labeled as such so that it does not mistakenly become part of the final program.

A useful technique for checking to see if a program module was reached during execution is to print a message like "program reached this point" or "module *name* was called." This is a simple method of tracing the flow of a program or how far it had progressed before an error was reached.

Error Handling Built into the Program

One method of minimizing the time it takes to isolate program *bugs* (errors) is to have *error handling* built into the program. This provides for sensing specific error conditions and taking appropriate action. The action may be to:

1. Simply print an error message identifying the error
2. Repeat a program module to seek a correct response
3. Alert the program operator to take some corrective action

C was designed to facilitate the use of error handling. Some illegal function calls in **C** will return a **0** result. For example, the **sqrt()** function call with a negative argument was encountered in error 4 of the previous section. **C** will return a **0** result for such a call. If the result becomes the divisor in an expression, a divide by zero run-time error will occur. To avoid this situation, error handling can be incorporated into the program to either detect negative arguments being passed to the **sqrt()** function or **0** results being returned. The most appropriate action to be taken depends on the application.

Use Automatic Trace

Many compilers and interpreters have an automatic trace feature that can be turned on or off at arbitrary points within the program. When the trace is on, the output indicates the program line in the source code that is currently being executed. This permits tracking the progress and flow of the program. It helps in identifying where the program execution encounters an error. For example, if program execution is trapped in a loop, the trace output would indicate the source lines being repeated and thus identify where the problem lies.

8.5 PROFESSIONAL PROGRAM DEBUGGING TOOLS

Source Code Checking Programs

A variety of *intelligent text editors* is available that will check the syntax of the source code while it is being entered and identify syntax errors before compilation even begins. Syntax-checking editors can save a considerable amount of time in the program development cycle. This feature is not required with interpreters since any syntax errors can be corrected rapidly upon detection.

Some syntax-checking programs, most notably the UNIX **lint** utility, perform extensive checks on the source code. The **lint** utility will check for type mismatches, declared functions that are never called, declared variables that are never used, and so on.

Source Code Formatters

The UNIX utility **cb**, or **C B**eautifier, will format the source code with consistent indentation and line spacing. This feature is available on some **C** interpreters as well. As was mentioned earlier, good style and consistency in the source code will aid the debugging process.

Debuggers: Machine Language Level

Debug programs are used as an aid in the troubleshooting of the final executable code. They come in two basic varieties: machine language level debuggers and symbolic or source code level debuggers. Machine language level debuggers operate on executable code, whether it is the result of an assembly language program or a compiled high-level language program. Machine language level debuggers are more universal in application, but are also more tedious than symbolic debuggers.

Two popular examples of machine language level debuggers are DEBUG, which is included in the MS DOS Operating System, and **adb**, which is part of the UNIX Operating System. The general features provided by debug programs include:

1. Examine and modify CPU (central processing unit) registers
2. Examine and modify contents of memory in hex, ASCII, or some other format
3. Search memory for a data pattern
4. Fill a block of memory with a data pattern
5. Perform arithmetic operations in various base number systems
6. Load and save files
7. Execute a program with a display of the *trace* or execution sequence
8. Step through a program one instruction at a time with a programmed halt after each step
9. Set and clear *breakpoints*, which are user-specified locations at which program execution is to be temporarily halted

Symbolic Debuggers: Source Code Level

Symbolic debuggers provide additional features that permit reference to source code variables and functions during the debug process. They also permit viewing the source code during program execution. The UNIX utility **sdb** is an example of a symbolic debugger for the **C** language. Popular compilers and interpreters that run on microcomputers also provide for symbolic debug.

The general features of symbolic debuggers include:

1. Set breakpoints at addresses, source line numbers, or functions
2. Single step, one source statement at a time
3. Examine variables during program execution
4. View source code
5. Execute a named function
6. Display a trace of called functions

Cross-reference Listers and Profilers

Cross-reference utilities list all the occurrences of variables and functions within a program or module. An example of a cross-reference program is the UNIX **cxref** utility.

Program *profilers* measure the number of calls to specified modules or functions and the amount of time spent within those program segments. They usually present the results in the form of a *histogram*, which is a graphical representation of the profiler's output.

8.6 TESTING, DOCUMENTATION, AND MAINTENANCE

Program Testing

Program testing should be considered during the program design phase of the development cycle. The program design should consider the test data that will be required to verify correct operation of the program for all valid input data. It should also consider detection of invalid input data and the program response to these inputs.

Individual program modules should be tested separately before they are combined to form the entire program. It is generally easier to verify the operation of a module when it is isolated from possible interactions with other modules within the program.

When all the modules of a program have been individually tested, they can then be combined. Integration testing will then be needed to verify that all the modules work together as planned.

The final step in the testing process involves functional testing of the program. This phase of the testing considers all the ranges and types of data to which the program must properly respond. Functional testing verifies that the program performs according to the original specifications from which it was designed.

Documentation

Program documentation falls into two major categories: user documentation and technical documentation. User documentation, usually referred to as a *user's manual*, is of a nontechnical nature. Its primary purpose is to convey to the user the following information:

1. Purpose of the program
2. What it will do
3. How to use it: startup, commands, menus, messages, and so on
4. Required inputs
5. Description of the outputs
6. Limitations of the program

The technical documentation is intended for programmers who will need to know more detail about the program for the purpose of maintenance or redesign. This documentation is normally included in a package called the *technical reference manual*. It usually includes a *commented listing* of the source code. The complete documentation may include any or all of the following:

1. Commented listing of the source code
2. Description of the program
3. Flowcharts
4. Pseudocode
5. Program test procedure and test data
6. List and description of all modules, functions, and important variables
7. *Memory map* that outlines the location of program modules and data areas

Maintenance and Redesign

Even though a program has passed all testing and is ready for use, it may still contain residual bugs that will not show up until it has been in service for some time. Program maintenance involves the continued support of a program after it has been placed in service to correct these residual bugs. It also includes minor modifications to the program that may be requested during its lifetime.

Substantial modifications to a program are referred to as *program redesign*. Both program maintenance and redesign rely heavily on having good original program documentation.

PROBLEMS

8.1. Find the mistakes in the following program and correct them:

```
main()        /* convert from pounds to kilograms */
     {
     double pounds;
     double kilograms;

     scanf("%f",pounds);
     kilograms = pounds/2.2;
     printf("%d pounds equals %d kilograms \n",pounds,kilograms);
     }
```

8.2. Find the mistakes in the following program and correct them:

```
main()
     {
     long big;

     scanf("%d",&big);
     printf("%d\n",big);
     }
```

8.3. Find the mistakes in the following program and correct them:

```
main()
     {
     char data[] = {1,2,3,4,5}
     int i;

     for (i=0;i<= 5;i++)
          if (data[i] = 8)
               printf("Error\n");
          else
               printf("OK\n");
     }
```

8.4. Find the mistakes in the following program and correct them:

```
main()        /* copy message to array */
     {
     static char message[] = "Cherchez les bugs!";
     char *ptr;               /* pointer to array[] */
     char array[30];
     int i;

     for (i=0;i<strlen(message);i++,ptr++)
          *ptr = message[i];
     printf("%s\n",array);
     }
```

chapter 9

Character Graphics

9.1 INTRODUCTION

The term *character graphics* refers to the use of standard ASCII characters or coded graphics shapes to form the graphics output. These characters or shapes are referenced either directly by the characters themselves or through their assigned code values. For example, the asterisk (*) may be used as a graphics element by specifying the actual character '*' or through its ASCII code value '\42' decimal ('\052' octal or '\0×2a' in hex).

The primary advantage of character graphics is that they are very standardized and work on virtually any computer. You can generate character graphics on a video screen or a line printer with very little concern about the hardware itself. It is also very easy to move a program that uses character graphics from one computer to another, especially if it is written in **C**.

The greatest disadvantage of character graphics is the lack of high resolution. The resolution is limited by the number of *characters per inch* and *lines per inch* of the output device. This method of generating graphics is most suitable for plotting functions or data where a resolution of about 1% to 2% is acceptable. In some cases, the resolution can be extended to about 0.1%.

In this chapter, we will develop programs that use character graphics to plot functions or data in both linear and semilogarithmic form. The examples will progress from simple to more complex. Chapter 10 will consider high-resolution video graphics.

9.2 PLOTTING FUNCTIONS

The most conventional method of plotting functions on either the video screen or a line printer is to use *linefeeds* and *tabs* to locate the coordinates at which the graphics character is to be placed. Using this technique, linefeeds represent increments of the **x** coordinate (independent variable) and spaces along a line represent increments of the **y** coordinate (dependent variable). This arrangement produces a graph that is rotated 90 degrees clockwise from the conventional orientation of graphs. The constraints of the hardware make it much easier to produce the graph in this form. If the output is to a line printer, the resulting paper copy can simply be rotated into the conventional orientation for viewing.

In **C**, the newline character ('\n') is printed to perform linefeeds. Unlike BASIC, **C** does not include a **tab** function. Therefore, we must include our own **tab** function within the plotting programs. Let's illustrate this plotting technique with a simple example. The program of Fig. 9.1 plots the equation $\mathbf{y = x^2/2}$ for **x** ranging from **0** to **10**.

```
/* plot of y = x*x/2 */
#include <stdio.h>
main()
     {
     float x, y;
     void tab();

     for (x = 0.0; x <= 10.0; x++)
          {
          y = x*x/2;
          tab((int) (y + 0.5));
          putchar('*');
          putchar('\n');
          }
     }

void tab(n)                   /* tab to column n (first column ==1) */
int n;
     {
     int i;
     for (i = 0; i < (n - 1); i++)
          putchar(' ');
     }
```

```
*
*
 *
    *
       *
            *
                 *
                        *
                               *
                                        *
                                                 *
```

Figure 9.1 Program to plot $\mathbf{y = x^2/2}$.

In this simple program, the independent variable **x** is incremented by 1 for each linefeed. The corresponding value of **y** is computed from the equation that is being plotted; in this case, **y = x*x/2**. The resulting **y** value is rounded off and converted to type **int**. Its value is then passed to the **tab()** function. This function will print a number of spaces along the line that is determined by its argument, the value of **y**. After a return from **tab()**, the cursor is positioned for plotting the asterisk at the proper place for the given function. A linefeed is then generated and the process repeats for the next value of **x**.

Notice that **tab()** assumes the first column is column **1**. Therefore, a **tab(1)** will not print any spaces. A **tab(2)** will print one space, and so on. Some systems assume the first column is **0** and print **1** space for a tab argument of **1**.

The output of Fig. 9.1 shows the shape of the curve but does not facilitate reading any values from the graph. A set of numbered axes will be needed to permit reading values readily from the graph. Also, we selected a function and range for **x** that did not require scaling prior to plotting. In general, we will have to select an appropriate increment of the **x** variable per linefeed and the **y** variable per tab position to properly fit the equation on the graph. The equation will then have to be multiplied by a *scaling factor* to reflect the rate at which values change along the axes.

Scaling an equation so that a plot fits on the video screen or printed page requires knowing the print positions available on the device being used. Figure 9.2 lists some typical video and printer formats. The *columns* figure indicates the number of characters that can be printed per line on the device. The *rows* figure indicates how many lines of characters can be printed on the video screen or printed page. The available print positions for the actual plotting area will be somewhat less than the values shown, since we must include space for the axes, a margin for numbering the axes, and perhaps some extra space for titles.

Columns	*Rows*	*Device*
80	24	Standard video screens (can extend rows by scrolling)
80	66	Printer using standard-sized sheet, 10 pitch, 6 lines/inch
96	88	Printer using standard-sized sheet, 12 pitch, 8 lines/inch
132	66	Wide carriage printer, 10 pitch, 6 lines/inch
158	88	Wide carriage printer, 12 pitch, 8 lines/inch
137	792	Dot matrix printer, 17 pitch, 1/72 line spacing
272	792	Wide carriage dot matrix, 17 pitch, 1/72 line spacing

Figure 9.2 Video and printer formats: character mode.

Most video terminals or microcomputer displays permit moving the cursor to any position on the screen. However, many printers do not support this feature. The plotting program will be compatible with a larger number of devices if all the output occurs in one pass from left to right on a line and from top to bottom of the display or printed page.

Refer to Fig. 9.6 to observe the features of the plot we wish to generate. Remembering the left to right and top to bottom sequence for generating the plot, we can write the first-level pseudocode as shown in Fig. 9.3. Note that the upper-left corner of the graph is nearest to the origin of the axes. It may be helpful to place (or visualize) a sheet of paper over the graph exposing only the top line. Examine the characters on the line, scanning from left to right. The characters must be plotted in the sequence in which they occur. Now slide the paper down one line and scan the new line. These characters must be plotted next. Continue in this fashion down to the bottom of the graph. This will help you to visualize the sequence of events that must occur in plotting the graph.

To determine the graph parameters, we will need to establish the number of print positions on the **x** and **y** axes. We will also need to know the maximum value of the variables on both axes. The **x** axis increment to be used is then given by

$$\mathbf{dx} = \frac{\textbf{maximum x axis value}}{\textbf{print positions on x axis}}$$

```
/* first level pseudocode for function plotting program */
module main()
    determine graph parameters
    number y axis
    draw y axis
    for (each line of graph)
         determine value of x
         if (line is multiple of 10)
              number x axis
              plot axis character for multiple of 10
         else
              plot axis character for line not multiple of 10
         end if
         evaluate y = f(x)
         tab(y)
         plot graph symbol "*"
         print newline
    end for
end main()

module tab(n)
    print n-1 spaces
end tab()
```

Figure 9.3 First-level pseudocode for a function-plotting program.

Also, the **y** axis increment is

$$\mathbf{dy} = \frac{\textbf{maximum y axis value}}{\textbf{print positions on y axis}}$$

To illustrate the use of these equations, suppose that we have 50 print positions on both axes. Assume that the maximum value of the **x** variable is **12**. The value of **dx** is then given by **12/50** or **0.24**. How do we determine the maximum value of the **y** axis variable? This will depend on the nature of the function we are plotting. Assuming an equation of the type $\mathbf{y = x^2}$, the maximum value of **y** will clearly occur at the maximum value of **x**. In this case, it would be $\mathbf{12^2}$ or **144**. Thus **dy** would be given by **144/50** or **2.88**.

If the calculated values of **dx** or **dy** are not increments that you would like to use, they can be adjusted upward. This will have the effect of shrinking the plot size on the graph. We normally select rounded values for axes increments. In the preceding example, it would be desirable to increase the **x** axis increment from **0.24** to **0.5** and the **y** axis increment from **2.88** to **5**.

The scaling factor for the plot is simply the reciprocal of the **y** axis increment or **1/dy**. Thus the maximum distance to be tabbed in plotting the function will be **y_max/dy**. If the calculated axis increment is used, the plot will extend to the extreme end of the **y** axis. An upward adjustment of the axis increment will mean that the plot will not reach the end of the axis.

If we wish to number the **y** axis at every tenth print position, a mechanism will be needed to advance the cursor in increments of 10 and to print the axis value at that point. A formatted print inside a loop will do the job nicely. The format specifier should include a field width of 10. Drawing the **y** axis simply involves printing a string that looks exactly like the axis itself.

The **for** loop in **main()** will number and draw the **x** axis and plot the function on a line by line basis. The value of **x** at any line is simply the line number multiplied by the axis increment, or **x = line*dx**. (This assumes that **x** has a starting value of **0**.) If a line is a multiple of 10, it must be numbered. The special axis symbol marking these multiples must also be printed. Otherwise, the standard axis symbol will be printed. The value of **y** is then determined and the cursor is tabbed by that amount. Finally, an asterisk marking the value of **y** is plotted along with a newline.

The final pseudocode is shown in Fig. 9.4. It shows several refinements. First, it is desirable to define the function being plotted at the top of the program. This makes it easily accessible for modification. It also avoids repeated typing or editing of the equation if it occurs at several places within the program. We have defined **Y** as **f(x)/dy**. Division by **dy** scales the function **f(x)** to fit our graph.

A second important refinement is that we would like to plot on the **x** axis should the value of **Y** be zero. This is not possible if the axis symbol has already been plotted. (We are assuming that the cursor or print head cannot be backspaced.) Thus **Y** is tested prior to printing the axis symbol. If **Y==0**, an asterisk will be plotted in place of the axis symbol. Otherwise, the axis symbol will be plotted, and the asterisk will then be plotted at a distance **tab(Y)**.

The function plotting program is listed in Fig. 9.5. Its output is shown in Fig. 9.6. The **#define** preprocessor directive replaces **Y** with a scaled equation that has been converted to a rounded **int** value. This is necessary since the function **tab()** expects an integer argument. The balance of the program closely follows the pseudocode. To plot another equation, simply change the definition of **Y**. Be sure to preserve the scaling and roundoff within the new definition.

Advanced Function-plotting Program

We can extend the capabilities of the function-plotting program by adding some very desirable features. They include:

1. Plotting in any or all of the four quadrants
2. Program adjustment of the size of the graph for available print positions
3. Arbitrary starting value and range of the **x** or **y** variables
4. Inclusion of a center line or zero axis for functions that have a negative **y** component
5. Adjustment of the intervals at which the **x** axis is numbered
6. Automatic scaling of the function to be plotted

The plot of Figure 9.10 illustrates most of the features that we would like to include in our improved program. To keep the analysis simple, let's consider two special cases. If the function is restricted to **y ≥ 0**, the dashed zero axis or center line will be omitted. (The **x** axis variable may be negative for this case.) If the function has a minimum value of **y** that is less than zero, the center line will then be included.

The first-level pseudocode for this program is shown in Fig. 9.7. As in the previous plotting program, we start by defining the function to be plotted. The graph parameters are entered next. These include the number of print positions for each axis (which we will call **px** and **py**), the starting (**x1**) and ending (**x2**) values for **x**, and the line number multiples to be numbered.

```
/* pseudocode for function plotting program */

define Y as f(x)/dy                                /* Y is defined as scaled f(x) */
module main()
    input dx and dy                                /* get axes increments */
    for (i from 0 to 5)                            /* number y axis */
         print dy*10*i with field width of 10
    end for
    print newline
    print "+---------+---------+---------+---------+---------+"
    /* number and draw x axis and plot function */
    for (line from 1 to 50)
         x = line*dx                               /* determine value of x */
         if (line is multiple of 10)               /* special case */
              print x with field width of 9        /* number x axis */
              if (Y==0)                            /* Y lies on x axis */
                   print "*" and newline           /* plot "*" on x axis */
              else
                   print "+"                       /* plot "+" axis symbol*/
                   tab(Y)
                   print "*" and newline           /* plot "*" at tab(Y) */
              end if
         else
              tab(10)                              /* print 9 spaces */
              if (Y==0)                            /* Y lies on x axis */
                   print "*" and newline           /* plot "*" on x axis */
              else
                   print "|"                       /* plot "|" axis symbol */
                   tab(Y)
                   print "*" and newline           /* plot "*" at tab(Y) */
              end if
         end if
    end for
end main()

module tab(n)
    for (i from 0 to n-1)
         print space
    end for
end tab()
```

Figure 9.4 Pseudocode for a function-plotting program.

The limits for the **y** axis are to be calculated within the program. This can be done by testing the function over the range of the **x** variable to find the minimum (**y_min**) and maximum (**y_max**) values of **y**. Since we have already established the number of print positions to be used, the values of **dx** and **dy** can be calculated from

$$dx = (x2 - x1)/px$$

and

$$dy = (y\_max - y\_min)/py$$

```
#include <stdio.h>
#define Y   (int)(2.0*(x)*(x)/(dy)+0.5)
main()
    {
    float dx, dy, x;
    int i, line;
    void tab();

    puts("Enter x axis increment");
    scanf("%f", &dx);
    puts("Enter y axis increment");
    scanf("%f", &dy);

    /* number and draw y axis */
    tab(5);
    for (i = 0; i <= 5; i++)
        {
        printf("%10.2f", dy*10*i);
        }
    putchar('\n');
    tab(10);
    puts("+---------+---------+---------+---------+---------+");

    /* number and draw x axis and plot function */
    for (line = 1; line <= 50; line++)
        {
        x = dx*line;
        if (line%10 == 0)               /* line is 10 multiple */
            {
            printf("%8.2f ", x);
            if (Y == 0)
                printf("*\n");
            else
                {
                printf("+");
                tab((int) Y);
                printf("*\n");
                }
            }
        else
            {                           /* line is not 10 multiple */
            tab(10);
            if (Y == 0)
                printf("*\n");
            else
                {
                putchar('|');
                tab(Y);
                printf("*\n");
                }
            }
        }
    }

void tab(n)                             /* tab to column n (first column ==1) */
int n;
    {
    int i;

    for (i = 0;  i < (n - 1);  i++)
        putchar(' ');
    }
```

Figure 9.5 Function-plotting program.

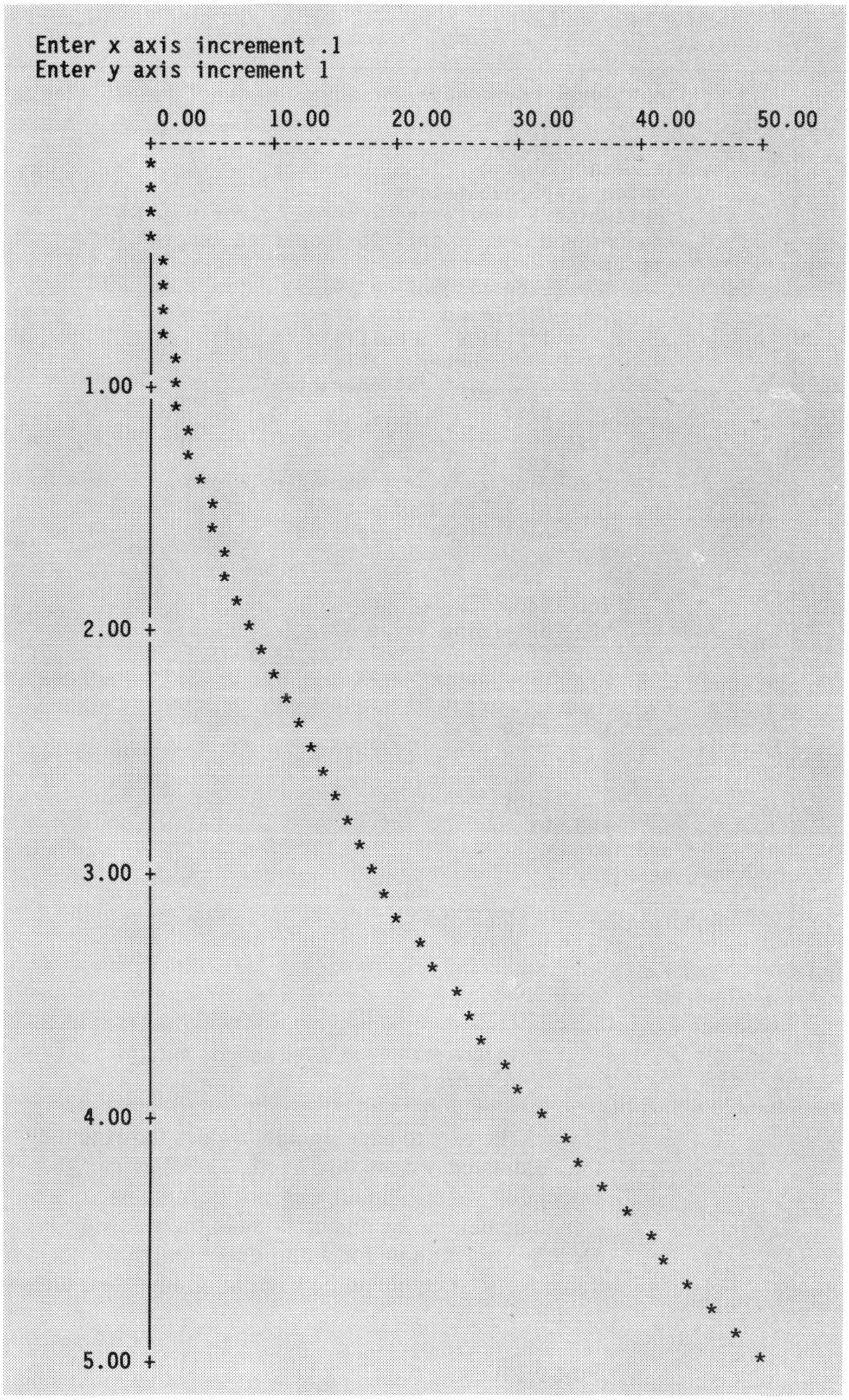

Figure 9.6 Output of the function-plotting program.

```
/* first level pseudocode for advanced function-plotting program */

define Y as f(x)/dy                                  /* Y is scaled f(x) */
module main()
     enter graph parameters
     determine y limits and increments for x and y
     number and draw y axis to specified length
     if (y_min < 0)                                  /* plot with center line */
         for (each line of graph)
              determine value of x
              if (line is multiple of mod)
                   number x axis
                   plot "+" character
              else
                   plot "|" character for line not multiple of mod
              end if
              find zero axis tab value, zero
              plot "*" at Y + zero
              plot "|" at zero axis
         end for
     else                                            /* plot without center line */
         for (each line of graph)
              determine value of x
              if (line is multiple of mod)
                   number x axis
                   plot "+" character
              else
                   plot "|" character for line not multiple of mod
              end if
              plot "*" at Y
         end for
    end if
end main()

module tab(n)
    print n-1 spaces
end tab()
```

Figure 9.7 First-level pseudocode for an advanced function-plotting program.

It would be nice to have rounded values for **dx** and **dy**. This can be done by having the calculated values displayed. The user can then be permitted to adjust the calculated values should they not be suitable.

The numbering and drawing of the **y** axis differs from the previous program. Here we must allow for an arbitrary length for the axis and an arbitrary starting value for **y**. A loop can be used to number and draw the axis to the appropriate length.

Plot with Zero Axis

The value of **y_min** is tested to determine if a zero axis is to be used. The case of using a zero axis is similar to our earlier plotting program with some exceptions. We now have an arbitrary starting point for **x**, and the **x** axis will be numbered at multiples of some specified modulus, assigned to the variable **mod**. Also, we have two items to plot. An asterisk must be plotted to locate the value of **Y**. We must also plot the "¦" symbol for the zero axis. The order in which they are plotted will depend on their relative values. The smaller of the two must be plotted first.

Since **Y** is allowed to be negative and negative tabs cannot be used, we must add a constant to the tab argument that makes the tab distance always positive. The value of the constant is the distance from the **x** axis to the zero axis. This distance must always be greater than the minimum value of **y**.

Plot without Zero Axis

This case is very much like our earlier plotting program with the exception of having an arbitrary starting value for **x** and a variable modulus for numbering the **x** axis. It must also detect a **Y** value of **0** to permit plotting on the **x** axis.

The final pseudocode is shown in Fig. 9.8. Two **defines** are included here. The first defines **Y** as being equal to the original **f(x)**. This makes it easier to enter the equation being plotted. The second defines **YN** as being equal to the normalized (or scaled) value of **Y**. Notice that **YN** is converted to an **integer** type.

After entering the number of **x** and **y** print positions to be used and the values of **x1** and **x2**, **dx** is computed. Its value is displayed and the operator enters an adjusted value for **dx**, or the original value if it is suitable. The line multiples to be numbered is then entered and assigned to **mod**.

Two separate modules are used to determine the minimum and maximum values of **y** over the range **x1** to **x2** using a step of **dx**. These modules receive the values of **x1**, **x2**, and **dx**. They return values for **y_min** and **y_max**. The **y** axis increment can then be computed from

```
dy = (y_max - y_min)/py
```

The computed values of **y_min**, **y_max**, and **dy** are printed to permit operator adjustment of **y_min** and **dy** to some rounded values. The adjusted value of **y_min** must be less than or equal to the original. Also, the adjusted value of **dy** must be greater than or equal to the original. The new value of **y_max** is computed from

```
y_max = y_min +py*dy
```

The value of **y** at any increment of 10 on the axis is given by

```
y = y_min + 10*i*dy
```

where **i** is the number of decades or ten multiples. This equation is used for numbering the **y** axis at every tenth print position. The loop variable **i** goes from **0** to **py/10**. A similar loop is used to draw the **y** axis in increments of **10** print positions.

The test for deciding if a zero or center line is required has been refined by scaling and rounding the value of **y_min** before comparing it to **0**. This is required since a minimum value that is less than zero, but rounds off to zero, should not call for a center line in the plot.

When plotting with a zero axis, we need to know the location of that axis. It is calculated from

```
zero = integer value of (y_min/dy + 0.5)
```

Both the zero axis symbol "¦" and the asterisk for the functional value must be plotted on the same line. The order in which they are plotted depends on their

```
/* pseudocode for advanced function-plotting program */

define Y as f(x)                                /* f(x) is original function */
define YN as the integer value of (Y/dy + 0.5)  /* YN is normalized (scaled) Y */

module main()
/* px, py           print positions on x and y axes */
/* dx, dy           change in x or y per print position */
/* line             line number on graph */
/* xl, x2           lower and upper limit of x */
/* y_min, y_max     min and max values for y */
/* zero             location of zero or center line axis */
/* mod              the modulus used for numbering the x axis */

    /* get graph parameters and determine x axis increment */
    input px, py
    input xl, x2
    dx = (x2-xl)/px
    print dx                            /* display for operator */
    input adjusted dx                   /* option for rounded values */

    input value of mod

    /* determine y axis limits and increment */
    y_min = min(xl,x2,dx)               /* finds min value of y */
    y_max = max(xl,x2,dx)               /* finds max value of y */
    dy = (y_max - y_min)/py             /* finds y axis increment */
    print y_min, y_max, dy              /* display for operator */
    input adjusted y_min and dy         /* option for rounded values */
    y_max = y_min + py*dy

    /* number y axis */
    for (i from 0 to py/10)
         print y_min + 10*i*dy  with field width of 10
    end for
    print newline

    /* label xl and draw y axis */
    print xl and "+" for origin
    for (i from 0 to py/10)
         print "---------+"
    end for
    print newline

    line = 0
    if (integer value of (y_min/dy+0.5) <0 )     /* plot with zero axis */
         for (x from xl to x2 step dx)
              line = line + 1
              if (line is multiple of mod)
                   print x   with field width of 9
              else
                   tab(10)
```

Figure 9.8 Pseudocode for an advanced function-plotting program.

```
                print "|" axis symbol
            end if
            zero = integer value of (y_min/dy +0.5)
            if (YN >0)                         /* plot zero axis first */
                tab(zero)
                print "|" axis symbol
                tab(YN)
                print "*" and newline
            else  if (YN == 0)                 /* plot asterisk only */
                    tab(zero)
                    print "*" and newline
                 end if
            else
                tab(YN+zero)                   /* plot asterisk first */
                print "*"
                tab(-YN)
                print "|" and newline
            end if
        end for
    else                                       /* plot without zero axis */
        for (x from x1 to x2 step dx)
            line = line + 1
            if (line is multiple of mod)
                print x with field width of 9
                if (YN==0)
                    print "*" and newline
                else
                    print "+" axis symbol
                    tab(YN)
                    print "*" and newline
                end if
            else
                if (YN==0)
                    tab(10)
                    print "*" and newline
                else
                    tab(10)
                    print "|" axis symbol
                    tab(YN)
                    print "*" and newline
                end if
            end if
        end for
    end if
end main()

tab(n)                         /* tab to column n (first column == 1) */
    for (i from 0 to n-1)
        print space
    end for
end tab()
```

Figure 9.8 (continued).

```
max(x1,x2,dx)                     /* finds maximum value of Y */
    x = x1
    Y2 = Y
    for (x from x1 to x2, step dx)
         if (Y > y2)
              y2 = Y
         end if
    end for
    return(y2)
end max()

min(x1,x2,dx)                     /* finds minimum value of Y */
    x = x1
    y1 = Y
    for (x from x1 to x2, step dx)
         if (Y < y1 )
              y1 = Y
         end if
    end for
    return(y1)
end min()
```

Figure 9.8 (continued).

relative values. There are three possibilities:

1. If **YN** > **0**, the "¦" is plotted first.
2. If **YN** == **0**, only the "*" is plotted.
3. If **YN** < **0**, the "*" is plotted first.

Notice that the loop variable has been changed from **line** to **x** in going from the first-level pseudocode to the second. Either variable can control the loop. The case of plotting without a center line is straightforward. Notice that a test is included here for **YN == 0** to see if the function must be plotted on the **x** axis.

The **C** program for the advanced function plot is given in Fig. 9.9 and the output in Fig. 9.10. Since the program closely follows the final pseudocode, no additional explanation is required.

9.3 PLOTTING EXPERIMENTAL DATA

We can also plot experimental data using character graphics. The data may initially be entered from the keyboard, read from a disk file, or obtained from some external data-gathering device. Ultimately, the data must be stored in arrays for processing. The first-level pseudocode for the data-plotting program is given in Fig. 9.11. The data are assumed to be stored in two arrays, **x[]** and **y[]**, with the **x[]** array data stored in ascending order. If the **x[]** data are not in ascending order, they would have to be sorted prior to entry into the plotting program.

The key to this program is to scale the **x[i]** so that it equals the line number on which it must be plotted. This is given by **x[i]/dx**. We then take each array

```
/* advanced function-plotting program */
#include <stdio.h>
#include <math.h>
#define Y   (100.0*exp(-0.5*x)*cos(3.0*x))
#define YN  ((int)(Y/dy+0.5))

main()
    {
    double px, py;              /* print positions on x and y axes */
    double dx, dy;              /* change in x or y value per print position */
    double x;                   /* independent variable */
    int line;                   /* line number on graph */
    double x1, x2;              /* lower and upper limits for x */
    double y_min, y_max;        /* min and max values for Y */
    int i;                      /* dummy variable */
    int zero;                   /* location of zero axis */
    int mod;                    /* multiple of x axis increment to be numbered */
    double min(), max();        /* functions returning double */
    void tab();                 /* tab n spaces */

/* input size of graph */
    puts("Enter x axis print positions");
    scanf("%lf", &px);
    puts("Enter y axis print positions");
    scanf("%lf", &py);

/* input range of x variable */
    puts("Enter the starting value for x");
    scanf("%lf", &x1);
    puts("Enter the ending value for x");
    scanf("%lf", &x2);

    puts("Enter multiple of x axis increments to be numbered");
    scanf("%d", &mod);

/* adjust x axis increment */
    dx = (x2 - x1)/px;
    printf("x axis increment = %9.5f\n", dx);
    puts("Enter adjusted x axis increment");
    scanf("%lf", &dx);

/* find y_min, y_max and dy values */
    puts("Please wait for computation");
    y_min = min(x1, x2, dx);
    y_max = max(x1, x2, dx);
    dy = (y_max - y_min)/py;

/* adjust y_min and dy */
    printf("y_min = %f   y_max = %f   dy = %f\n", y_min, y_max, dy);
    printf("Enter adjusted (rounded) y_min and dy values\n");
    printf("The new y_min must be less than or equal to the original value\n");
    printf("The new dy must be greater than or equal to the original value\n");
    scanf("%lf,%lf", &y_min, &dy);
    y_max = y_min + dy*py;
    printf("The new y_max = %f\n", y_max);

/* number y axis */
    printf("\n");
    tab(4);
    for (i = 0; i <= (int)(py/10.0); i++)
        printf("%10.2f", y_min + 10.0*i*dy);
    printf("\n");
```

Figure 9.9 Advanced function-plotting program.

```
/* label x1 and draw y axis */
     printf("%8.3f +", x1);

     for (i = 0; i < (int)(py/10.0); i++)
          printf("---------+");
     printf("\n");

/* number and draw x axis and plot function */
     if ((int)(y_min/dy + 0.5) < 0)
          {
     /* plot with zero axis */
          for (x = x1 + dx, line = 1; x <= x2 + 0.5*dx; x += dx, line++)
               {
               if (line%mod == 0)
                    printf("%8.3f +", x);
               else
                    {
                    tab(10);
                    printf("|");
                    }
               zero = (int) (fabs(y_min) / dy + 0.5);
               if (YN > 0)
                    {
                    tab(zero);
                    printf("|");
                    tab(YN);
                    printf("*\n");
                    }
               else if (YN == 0)
                    {
                    tab(YN + zero);
                    printf("*\n");
                    }
               else
                    {
                    tab(YN + zero);
                    printf("*");
                    tab(-YN);
                    printf("|\n");
                    }

               }
          }
     else
          {
          /* plot without zero axis */
          for (x = x1 + dx,  line = 1;  x <= x2 + 0.5 * dx;  x += dx,  line++)
               if (line % mod == 0)
                    {
                    printf("%8.3f ", x);
                    if (YN == 0)
                         printf("*\n");
                    else
                         {
                         printf("+");
                         tab(YN);
                         printf("*\n");
                         }
                    }
               else
                    {
                    if (YN == 0)
                         {
```

Figure 9.9 (continued).

```
                                tab(10);
                                printf("*\n");
                                }
                          else
                                {
                                tab(10);
                                printf("|");
                                tab(YN);
                                printf("*\n");
                                }
                          }
                }
      }

void tab(n)                              /* tab to column n (first column ==1) */
int n;
      {
      int i;
      for (i = 0;  i < (n - 1);  i++)
            putchar(' ');
      }
double max(x1, x2, dx)        /* find maximum Y from x1 to x2, step dx */
double x1, x2, dx;            /* Y is a #defined function of x and of type int */
      {
      double x, y2;

      x = x1;
      y2 = Y;
      for (x = x1; x <= x2; x += dx)
            if (Y > y2)
                  y2 = Y;
      return (y2);
      }

double min(x1, x2, dx)        /* find minimum Y from x1 to x2, step dx */
double x1, x2, dx;            /* Y is a #defined function of x and of type int */
      {
      double x, y1;

      x = x1;
      y1 = Y;
      for (x = x1; x <= x2; x += dx)
            if (Y < y1)
                  y1 = Y;
      return (y1);
      }
```

```
Enter x axis print positions
50
Enter y axis print positions
100
Enter the starting value for x
0
Enter the ending value for x
5
Enter multiple of x axis increments to be numbered
10
x axis increment =    0.10000
Enter adjusted x axis increment
0.1
Please wait for computation
y_min = -60.046080    y_max = 100.000000    dy = 1.600461
Enter adjusted (rounded) y_min and dy values
The new y_min must be less than or equal to the original value
The new dy must be greater than or equal to the original value
-80,2
The new y_max = 120.000000
```

Figure 9.9 (continued).

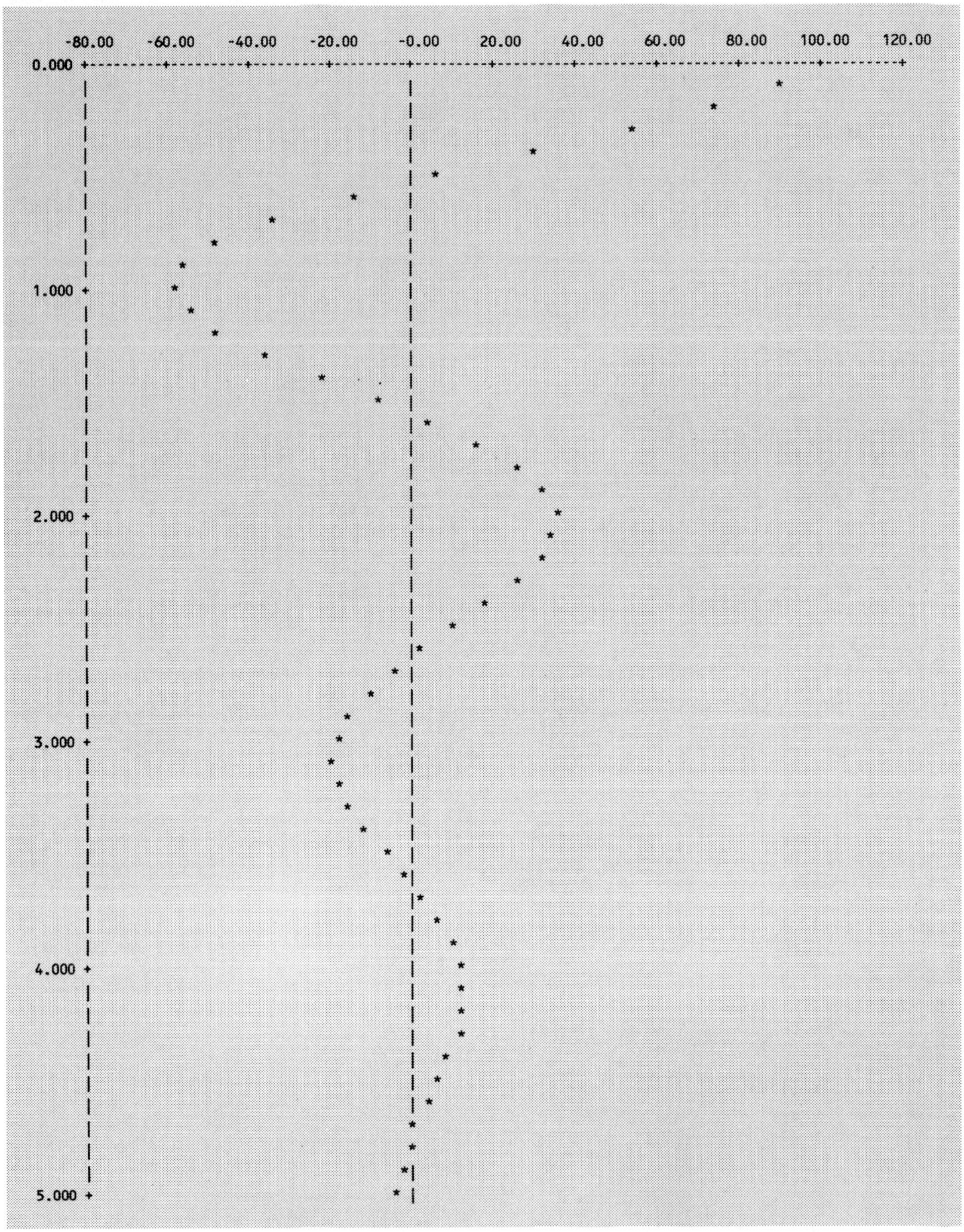

Figure 9.10 Output of the advanced function-plotting program.

element, starting with the lowest, and look for a match between **x[i]/dx** and the current line number. If there is a match, a tab to **y[i]/dy** is performed, and an asterisk is plotted along with the newline character. Otherwise, a linefeed is generated and the line number is incremented. Again, we look for a match between the scaled **x[i]** and the line number. The program terminates when the last line has been reached.

```
/* first level pseudocode for plotting data */
/* data assumed to be in the arrays x[] and y[] */
module main()
     input dx and dy
     number and draw y axis
     i = 0
     for (each line of graph)
         number and plot x axis
         if (x[i]/dx == current line)       /* does x[i] belong here? */
              tab(y[i]/dy)                  /* move to y coordinate */
              plot "*" and newline          /* plot current data value */
         i = i+1                            /* get next data value */
         else
              print newline                 /* no plot on this line */
         end if
     end for
end main()

module tab(n)
    print n-1 spaces
end tab()
```

Figure 9.11 First-level pseudocode for a data-plotting program.

The final pseudocode for the program is given in Fig. 9.12. It refines the first level by allowing data values to fall on the **x** axis. The switch **plotpt** is needed to determine if a data point was plotted either by the routine that plots on the **x** axis or the one that plots at all other points. If **plotpt** is **TRUE**, **i** is incremented to plot the next data item. Otherwise, a newline is generated, and the program looks for a match between the next line and the current data item.

A program listing and run are shown in Figs. 9.13 and 9.14, respectively. The **#define** preprocessor directives are used here to provide a shorthand representation for the scaled array expressions. The arrays are initialized within their declaration.

9.4 LOGARITHMIC PLOTS

In this section, we will develop programs for the semilogarithmic plotting of functions. Semilog scales are used whenever we wish to plot a function over a wide range of the independent variable. They are also used to linearize a plot that would otherwise be curved on a linear scale. Practical applications for these programs include plotting the magnitude and phase response of linear systems. To develop the programs, you will need to understand logarithmic scales and how to work with them.

Logarithmic Scales

On logarithmic scales, the change in value of the variable with respect to distance along the axis is proportional to the logarithm of the variable. However, the axis is numbered using the actual value of the variable, not its logarithm. The log of the

```
/* pseudocode for data plotting program */
/* data are assumed to be stored in the arrays x[] and y[] */

define X as the integer value of (x[i]/dx + 0.5)
define Y as the integer value of (y[i]/dy + 0.5)

module main()
      input dx and dy       /* operator selects values appropriate for data */
      number and draw y axis
      for (line from 0 to 50)
          plotpt = FALSE
          x = line*dx
          if (line is a multiple of 10)          /* number x axis */
               number x axis
          end if
          if (line == X and Y == 0)              /* plot value on axis */
               plot "*" on x axis
               plotpt = TRUE
          else
               if (line is a multiple of 10)     /* plot axis symbol */
                    plot "+" axis symbol
               else
                    plot "|" axis symbol
               end if
          end if
          if (line == X and Y not 0)             /* plot at Y */
               tab(Y)
               plot "*" and newline
               plotpt = TRUE
          end if
          if (plotpt == FALSE)                   /* no match, print newline */
               print newline
          else
               i = i + 1                         /* match, get next data item */
          end if
      end for
end main()

module tab(n)
    print n-1 spaces
end tab()
```

Figure 9.12 Pseudocode for a data-plotting program.

axis variable will increase at a uniform rate with distance, while the axis variable itself will increase exponentially. This can be demonstrated by a relatively simple program that numbers a log scale. The pseudocode for such a program is given in Fig. 9.15.

The starting and ending values of the variable to be used for the axis are entered along with the logarithmic step size to be used. The value of **log_step** will determine the number of lines per decade of the plot. For example, a step size of **0.1** per line of the plot means that there will be **10** lines per decade, since **10** increments of **0.1** give a log value of **1.0**. A log value of **1.0** corresponds to a linear ratio of **10** to **1** or one decade.

```
/* data-plotting program */

#define X    ((int)(x[i]/dx + 0.5))
#define Y    ((int)(y[i]/dy + 0.5))
#define TRUE     1
#define FALSE    0
#include <stdio.h>
main()
      {
      /* initialize arrays of data to be plotted */

      static float x[50] = {0, 2, 4, 6, 8, 10, 12, 14, 16, 18, 20, 22, 24, 26,
            28, 30, 32, 34, 36, 38, 40, 42, 44, 46, 48, 50};

      static float y[50] = {40, 40, 39, 38, 35, 31, 24, 15, 5, 2, 0, 1, 2, 2,
          1, 0, 2, 5, 15, 24, 31, 35, 38, 39, 40, 40};

      float dx, dy;              /* change in x or y value per print position */
      int line;                  /* line counter */
      int i;                     /* dummy variable */
      int plotpt;                /* true if point was plotted on a pass */
      void tab();                /* tab n spaces */

/* input dx,dy */
      puts("Enter change in x per print position");
      scanf("%f", &dx);
      puts("Enter change in y per print position");
      scanf("%f", &dy);

/* number and draw y axis */
      tab(3);
      for (i = 0; i <= 5; i++)
            printf("%10.2f", 10*dy*i);
      putchar('\n');

      tab(10);
      printf("---------+---------+---------+---------+---------+\n");

/* number and draw x axis and plot data */
      for (line = 0, i = 0; line <= 50; line++)
            {
            plotpt = FALSE;
            if (line%10 == 0) /* line is 10 mult */
                  printf("%8.2f ", dx*line);
            else
                  tab(10);
            if (line == X && Y == 0)
                  {
                  printf("*\n");
                  plotpt = TRUE;
                  }
            else
                  {
                  if (line%10 == 0)
                        putchar('+');
                  else
                        putchar('|');
                  }
            if (line == X && Y != 0)
                  {
                  tab(Y);
                  printf("*\n");
                  plotpt = TRUE;
                  }
```

Figure 9.13 Data-plotting program.

```
        if (plotpt == FALSE)
            putchar('\n');
        else
            i++;
        }
    }

void tab(n)            /* tab to column n (first column ==1) */
int n;
    {
    int i;
    for (i = 0; i < (n - 1); i++)
        putchar(' ');
    }
```

Figure 9.13 (continued).

The loop variable to be used for numbering the axis, **logx**, will be logarithmic. This provides us with the uniform log increment per line of the plot. The limits of the loop and the step size will also be logarithmic. Since we wish to number the axis with the actual value of the variable, not its log, the scale value is derived from $\mathbf{10^{logx}}$, which equals **x**.

The program for numbering log scales is shown in Fig. 9.16. Notice that the upper limit of the **for** loop is **logx2 + log_step/2.0**. The added term of **log_step/2.0** is needed to make sure that the last line of the axis is not lost due to **logx** exceeding **logx2** by a very small amount at the last step.

Magnitude Response

The pseudocode of Fig. 9.15 can be easily converted to plot the decibel magnitude response of a complex transfer function. The pseudocode of Fig. 9.17 is obtained by deleting the printing of **logx** and adding the decibel magnitude response for the equation to be plotted, along with a **tab()** function.

A program that implements the pseudocode of Fig. 17 is given in Fig. 9.18. Here, the equation to be plotted is the magnitude response of a low-pass filter, which is

$$|\mathbf{f(x)}| = \frac{\mathbf{1}}{\mathbf{(1 + x^2)^{1/2}}}$$

The decibel value of this equation is

$$\mathbf{y = 20\ log(|f(x)|)}$$

The **tab()** argument will be the integer value of **y − y_min**, where **y_min** is the minimum value of **y**. This difference is used because we are plotting the relative response. The value of **y − y_min** is the difference of the logs of two numbers. This is equal to the log of the ratio of the same numbers. Since the equation is being plotted for **x** from 0.1 to 100, the actual value of **y_min** is −40 dB. A value of −50 dB was used here to avoid plotting at the numbered axis.

The last step in developing our logarithmic plotting program is to add numbered axes. The pseudocode of Fig. 9.19 implements this feature. It also adds centered labels on each axis.

The original magnitude response of the transfer function is assumed to be of the form **f(x)**, where **x** is a linear frequency variable. We have defined **YM** as the magnitude response of **f(z)**, where $\mathbf{z = 10^{logx}}$. **Logx** is our logarithmic variable in

```
Enter change in x per print position 1
Enter change in y per print position 1

        0.00      10.00     20.00     30.00     40.00     50.00
         ----------+---------+---------+---------+---------+
    0.00 +                                       *
         |
         |                                       *
         |
         |                                      *
         |
         |                                     *
         |
         |                                  *
         |
   10.00 +                              *
         |
         |                       *
         |
         |              *
         |
         |    *
         |
         | *
         |
   20.00 *
         |
         |*
         |
         | *
         |
         | *
         |
         |*
         |
   30.00 *
         |
         | *
         |
         |    *
         |
         |              *
         |
         |                       *
         |
   40.00 +                              *
         |
         |                                  *
         |
         |                                     *
         |
         |                                      *
         |
         |                                       *
         |
   50.00 +                                       *
```

Figure 9.14 Output of the data-plotting program.

```
/* pseudocode for numbering logarithmic scales */

input starting and ending values for scale, x1 and x2
input log step size to be used, log_step
logx1 = log10(x1)
logx2 = log10(x2)
for (logx from logx1 to logx2 step log_step)

        x = 10^logx
        print x and logx
end for
```

Figure 9.15 Pseudocode for numbering logarithmic scales.

```
/* numbering log scales */
#include <stdio.h>
#include <math.h>
main()
      {
      double x,x1,x2;
      double logx,logx1,logx2;
      double log_step;

      puts("Enter starting and ending values of x");
      scanf("%lf,%lf", &x1, &x2);
      logx1 = log10(x1);
      logx2 = log10(x2);
      puts("Enter the log step size to use");
      scanf("%lf", &log_step);

      printf("\n%10s\t%10s\t%10s\n","x value","logx","logx-logx1");
      for (logx = logx1; logx <= (logx2 + log_step/2.0); logx += log_step)
            {
            x = pow(10.0, logx);
            printf("%10.4f\t%10.4f\t%10.4f\n", x, logx, logx - logx1);
            }
      }
```

```
Enter starting and ending values of x
0.1, 10.0
Enter the log step size to use
0.2

   x value          logx      logx-logx1
    0.1000       -1.0000          0.0000
    0.1585       -0.8000          0.2000
    0.2512       -0.6000          0.4000
    0.3981       -0.4000          0.6000
    0.6310       -0.2000          0.8000
    1.0000       -0.0000          1.0000
    1.5849        0.2000          1.2000
    2.5119        0.4000          1.4000
    3.9811        0.6000          1.6000
    6.3096        0.8000          1.8000
   10.0000        1.0000          2.0000
```

Figure 9.16 Program for numbering logarithmic scales.

```
/* pseudocode for plotting with logarithmic scales */
module main()
    input starting and ending values for scale, x1 and x2
    input log step size to be used, log_step
    logx1 = log10(x1)
    logx2 = log10(x2)
    for (logx from logx1 to logx2 step log_step)

        x = 10^logx
        print x with fixed field width
        y = 20*log10(magnitude of f(x))
        tab(y-y_min)
        plot "*" and newline
    end for
end main()

module tab(n)
    print n-1 spaces
end tab()
```

Figure 9.17 Pseudocode for plotting with logarithmic scales.

the plotting loop. This transformation makes the independent variable in the transfer function linear. **Y** is defined as the decibel value of **YM**.

Finding the graph parameters is the first part of the **main()** module. Notice that **px**, the total number of lines or print positions on the **x** axis, is given by

px = x_dif/log_step + 1

where **x_dif** is equal to **logx2 − logx1**. In words, the number of print positions equals the range of the log axis over the increment being used to traverse from one end to the other plus 1. If **logx2** equals **logx1**, **px** would equal 1.

The next part of the **main()** module inputs the axes labels and determines their lengths. The starting point for printing the **x** axis label is given by

x_start = (px − x_len)/2

This will center the label on the axis by putting half of the total white space **(px − x_len)** on either side of the label. The same procedure is used for centering the **y** axis label. An added term of **10** is used to center the label on the **y** axis, not including the **x** axis margin.

The **for** loop controls the labeling, numbering, and drawing of the **x** axis. The line counter **i** is used to detect when to start printing the **x** axis label. This will occur when **i = x_start**. One character of the label is printed on each line after **x_start** until the entire label has been printed. On all other lines, a space will be printed as a place holder.

Each line of the graph is numbered by printing **z** with a field width of 9. Remember that **z** is the linear value of the loop variable, **logx**. The balance of the pseudocode should be straightforward.

```
/* plotting with log scales */
#include <stdio.h>
#include <math.h>
main()
      {
      double x, y, xl, x2;
      double logx, logxl, logx2;
      double log_step, y_min;
      void tab();

      puts("Enter starting and ending values of x");
      scanf("%lf,%lf", &xl, &x2);
      logxl = log10(xl);
      logx2 = log10(x2);
      puts("Enter the log step size to use");
      scanf("%lf", &log_step);

      y_min = -50;
      for (logx = logxl; logx <= (logx2 + log_step/2.0); logx += log_step)
            {
            x = pow(10.0, logx);
            printf("%10.4f", x);
            y = 20 * log10(1.0/sqrt(1.0 + x*x));
            tab((int) (y - y_min));                    /* move to y */
            printf("*\n");                             /* plot point */
            }
      }

void tab(n)
int n;
      {
      int i;

      for (i = 0; i < (n - 1); i++)
            putchar(' ');
      }
```

```
Enter starting and ending values of x
0.1, 100.0
Enter the log step size to use
0.2
    0.1000                                                *
    0.1585                                                *
    0.2512                                                *
    0.3981                                                *
    0.6310                                               *
    1.0000                                             *
    1.5849                                           *
    2.5119                                        *
    3.9811                                    *
    6.3096                                *
   10.0000                            *
   15.8489                        *
   25.1189                    *
   39.8107                *
   63.0957            *
  100.0000        *
```

Figure 9.18 Plotting with logarithmic scales.

```
/* pseudocode for logarithmic plot of magnitude response with axis */

define   YM as the magnitude response of the transfer function f(z)
define   Y as the decibel value of YM

module main()
/* find graph parameters */
    input x1 and x2
    input y_min and y_max                    /* dB values */
    logx1 = log10(x1)
    logx2 = log10(x2)
    x_dif = logx2 - logx1
    y_dif = y_max - y_min
    py = 50                                  /* using 50 print positions */
    dy = y_dif/py
    input the log step size, log_step
    px = x_dif/log_step + 1

/* get axes labels, length of strings, and starting positions */
    input x and y axes labels
    find length of strings, x_len and y_len
    x_start = (px - x_len)/2
    y_start = (py - y_len)/2 + 10

print y axis title centered
number and draw y axis
/* label, number, and draw x axis and plot function */
i=1
for (logx from logx1 to logx2 step log_step)
    if (i>=x_start and i < (x_start + x_len))
         print character i of x_label
    else
         print space
    end if
    z = 10logx
    print z with field width of 9
    tab((Y-y_min)/dy)
    plot "*" and newline
    i = i+1
end for
end main()

module tab(n)
    print n-1 spaces
end tab()
```

Figure 9.19 Pseudocode for a logarithmic plot of magnitude response with axes.

```
/* Semilog function plot using character graphics */
/* plotting magnitude response of a low-pass filter */

#define YM  (1.0/sqrt(1.0+z*z))        /* low-pass magnitude response */
#define Y   20.0*log10(YM)             /* dB value */
#include <stdio.h>
#include <math.h>

main()
      {
      double x_min, x_max, y_min, y_max; /* limits of x and y variables */
      double xl_min, xl_max;             /* log of x limits */
      double x_dif, y_dif;               /* difference of limits */
      double dy;                         /* change of y per print position */
      double x_incr;                     /* x axis log step size */
      double px, py = 50;                /* print positions for x or y */
      double x, z;                       /* variables */
      char x_label[50], y_label[50];     /* axes labels */
      int x_len, y_len;                  /* length of x and y axes labels */
      int i;
      int x_start;                       /* start position for x_label */
      void tab();                        /* tab n spaces */

/* get axes labels and find length */
      puts("Enter label for y_axis");
      gets(y_label);
      puts("Enter label for x_axis");
      gets(x_label);
      x_len = strlen(x_label);
      y_len = strlen(y_label);

/* find graph parameters */
      puts("Enter x_min and x_max");
      scanf("%lf,%lf", &x_min, &x_max);
      puts("Enter y_min and y_max");
      scanf("%lf,%lf", &y_min, &y_max);
      xl_min = log10(x_min);
      xl_max = log10(x_max);
      x_dif = xl_max - xl_min;
      y_dif = y_max - y_min;
      dy = y_dif/py;
      puts("Enter log increment for x axis ");
      scanf("%lf", &x_incr);
      px = x_dif/x_incr + 1.0;
      x_start = ((int) px - x_len)/2;

/* print y_axis title at center */
      printf("\n\n\n\n");
      tab((int) ((py - y_len)/2.0 + 10.0));
      printf("%s\n", y_label);

/* number and draw y axis */
      tab(4);
      for (i = 0;  i <= 5;  i++)
            printf("%10.1f", 10.0 * i * dy + y_min);
      putchar('\n');
      tab(10);
      printf("+---------+---------+---------+---------+---------+\n");
/* number and draw x axis and plot function */
      i = 1;
      for (x = xl_min; x <= (xl_max + x_incr/2.0); x += x_incr)
            {
            if ((i >= x_start) && (i < x_start + x_len))
                  printf("%c", x_label[i - x_start]);
            else
                  putchar(' ');
```

Figure 9.20 Logarithmic plot of magnitude response with axes.

```
            z = pow(10.0, x);
            printf("%7.2f +", z);
            if ((Y >= y_min) && (Y <= y_max))
                  {
                  tab((int)((Y - y_min)/dy + 0.5));
                  printf("*\n");
                  }
            else
                  putchar('\n');
            i++;
            }
      }

void tab(n)                             /* tab to column n (first column ==1) */
int n;
      {
      int i;
      for (i = 0;  i < (n - 1);  i++)
            putchar(' ');
      }
```

```
Enter label for y_axis
Response in dB
Enter label for x_axis
Frequency in Hz
Enter x_min and x_max
0.1,100
Enter y_min and y_max
-40,10.0
Enter log increment for x axis
0.1


                            Response in dB
         -40.0     -30.0     -20.0     -10.0       0.0      10.0
          +---------+---------+---------+---------+---------+
     0.10 +                                       *
     0.13 +                                       *
     0.16 +                                       *
     0.20 +                                       *
     0.25 +                                       *
     0.32 +                                       *
F    0.40 +                                      *
r    0.50 +                                      *
e    0.63 +                                      *
q    0.79 +                                     *
u    1.00 +                                    *
e    1.26 +                                   *
n    1.58 +                                  *
c    2.00 +                                *
y    2.51 +                              *
     3.16 +                             *
i    3.98 +                           *
n    5.01 +                         *
     6.31 +                       *
H    7.94 +                     *
z   10.00 +                   *
    12.59 +                 *
    15.85 +               *
    19.95 +             *
    25.12 +           *
    31.62 +         *
    39.81 +       *
    50.12 +     *
    63.10 +   *
    79.43 + *
   100.00 +
```


Figure 9.20 (continued).

```
/* Semilog function plot using character graphics */
/* plotting phase response of a low-pass filter */

#define  Y  (-90.0 + atan(1.0/z)*180.0/pi)    /* low-pass phase response */
#include <stdio.h>
#include <math.h>
main()
      {
      double x_min, x_max, y_min, y_max;  /* limits of x and y variables */
      double xl_min, xl_max;              /* log of x limits */
      double x_dif, y_dif;                /* difference of limits */
      double dy;                          /* change of y per print position */
      double x_incr;                      /* x axis log step size */
      double px, py = 50;                 /* print positions for x or y */
      double x, z;                        /* variables */
      char x_label[50], y_label[50];      /* axes labels */
      int x_len, y_len;                   /* length of x and y axes labels */
      int i;
      int x_start;                        /* start position for x_label */
      double pi = 3.14159265;             /* value of pi */
      void tab();                         /* tab n spaces */

/* get axes labels and find length */
      puts("Enter label for y_axis");
      gets(y_label);
      puts("Enter label for x_axis");
      gets(x_label);
      x_len = strlen(x_label);
      y_len = strlen(y_label);

/* find graph parameters */
      puts("Enter x_min and x_max");
      scanf("%lf,%lf", &x_min, &x_max);
      puts("Enter y_min and y_max");
      scanf("%lf,%lf", &y_min, &y_max);
      xl_min = log10(x_min);
      xl_max = log10(x_max);
      x_dif = xl_max - xl_min;
      y_dif = y_max - y_min;
      dy = y_dif/py;
      puts("Enter log increment for x axis ");
      scanf("%lf", &x_incr);
      px = x_dif/x_incr + 1.0;
      x_start = ((int)px - x_len)/2;

/* print y_axis title at center */
      printf("\n\n\n\n");
      tab((int) ((py - y_len)/2.0 + 10.0));
      printf("%s\n", y_label);

/* number and draw y axis */
      tab(4);
      for (i = 0; i <= 5; i++)
            printf("%10.1f", 10.0 * i * dy + y_min);
      putchar('\n');
      tab(10);
      printf("+---------+---------+---------+---------+---------+\n");

/* number and draw x axis and plot function */
      i = 1;
      for (x = xl_min; x <= (xl_max + x_incr/2.0); x += x_incr)
            {
            if ((i >= x_start) && (i < x_start + x_len))
                  printf("%c", x_label[i - x_start]);
            else
                  putchar(' ');
            z = pow(10.0, x);
            printf("%7.2f +", z);
            if ((Y >= y_min) && (Y <= y_max))
                  {
```

Figure 9.21 Logarithmic plot of phase response with axes.

```
                  tab((int) ((Y - y_min) / dy + 0.5));
                  printf("*\n");
                  }
            else
                  putchar('\n');
            i++;
            }
      }

void tab(n)                               /* tab to column n (first column ==1) */
int n;
      {
      int i;
      for (i = 0;  i < (n - 1);  i++)
            putchar(' ');
      }
```

```
Enter label for y_axis Phase response in degrees
Enter label for x_axis Log frequency in Hz
Enter x_min and x_max 0.01, 100
Enter y_min and y_max -100, 0.0
Enter log increment for x axis 0.1


                     Phase response in degrees
       -100.0     -80.0     -60.0     -40.0     -20.0      0.0
         +---------+---------+---------+---------+---------+
    0.01 +                                                 *
    0.01 +                                                 *
    0.02 +                                                 *
    0.02 +                                                *
    0.03 +                                                *
    0.03 +                                                *
    0.04 +                                                *
    0.05 +                                                *
    0.06 +                                               *
L   0.08 +                                               *
o   0.10 +                                              *
g   0.13 +                                             *
    0.16 +                                            *
f   0.20 +                                           *
r   0.25 +                                          *
e   0.32 +                                        *
q   0.40 +                                      *
u   0.50 +                                    *
e   0.63 +                                 *
n   0.79 +                              *
c   1.00 +                           *
y   1.26 +                       *
    1.58 +                    *
i   2.00 +                 *
n   2.51 +               *
    3.16 +             *
H   3.98 +           *
z   5.01 +          *
    6.31 +         *
    7.94 +        *
   10.00 +       *
   12.59 +      *
   15.85 +      *
   19.95 +     *
   25.12 +     *
   31.62 +     *
   39.81 +     *
   50.12 +     *
   63.10 +    *
   79.43 +    *
  100.00 +    *
```

Figure 9.21 (continued).

The program of Fig. 9.20 closely follows the pseudocode. The declarations include character arrays with a length of 50 for each of the axes labels. The number of print positions for the **y** axis is initialized to 50 within the declaration for **py**. The length of the **x** axis will depend on program inputs.

Phase Response

Converting the magnitude response plotting program for plotting phase response is very simple. This can be done by deleting the definition of **YM** and defining **Y** as the phase response equation, which is a function of **z**. The **y** axis will then represent linear angle response in degrees or radians.

These changes have been incorporated into the program of Fig. 9.21. The equation being plotted is the phase response of the low-pass filter whose magnitude response was plotted earlier. The angles are represented in degrees.

PROBLEMS

9.1. Use the program listing of Fig. 9.5 to plot the following function of **x** over the range $0 < \mathbf{x} < 20$. From the graph determine the minimum value of **y**.

$$\mathbf{y} = \tfrac{3}{4}(\mathbf{x} - 10)^2 + 5$$

9.2. The equation $\mathbf{v(t)} = \mathbf{V}(1 - \mathbf{e}^{-\mathbf{t}/\mathbf{RC}})$ describes the charging of a capacitor. **V**, **R**, and **C** are constants and the instantaneous voltage **v** is a function of **t**. Use the program listing of Fig. 9.5 to plot this equation for the following conditions:

$$\mathbf{R} = 2000 \text{ ohms}$$
$$\mathbf{C} = 0.0001 \text{ farad}$$
$$\mathbf{V} = 100 \text{ volts}$$
$$0 < \mathbf{t} < 1 \text{ second}$$

9.3. The following data are obtained from an experiment. Use the program listing of Fig. 9.13 to plot the data.

X	F
1	52
2	103
3	155
4	206
5	221
6	228
7	204
8	217
9	268
10	320

From the graph, determine the following:

(a) Is the relationship between **F** and **X** linear for any regions on the graph? If so, over what range of **X** is it linear?

(b) Are there any relative maximums or minimums on the graph? If so, determine the values of **X** where they occur.

9.4. Use the program listing of Fig. 9.20 to plot the magnitude response of a parallel resonant circuit whose transfer function is given by

$$\mathbf{TF} = \frac{1}{[1 + \mathbf{Q}^2(\mathbf{f}/\mathbf{f}_0 - 1)^2(\mathbf{f}/\mathbf{f}_0 + 1)^2/(\mathbf{f}/\mathbf{f}_0)^2]^{1/2}}$$

where $\mathbf{f_0}$ is the resonant frequency and **Q** is the *quality factor* of the circuit. Use $\mathbf{f_0}$ = 1 and plot the response for **Q** values of 1 and 10.

9.5. Modify the program of Fig. 9.13 to permit keyboard entry of the data.

PROGRAMMING PROJECTS

9.6. Modify the function-plotting program of Fig. 9.5 to permit an **x** (independent variable) starting value different from zero.

9.7. Modify the function-plotting program of Fig. 9.5 to permit plotting two functions on the same graph.

9.8. Modify the function-plotting program of Fig. 9.5 to automatically set the scaling factor for the **y** axis. (*Hint:* Use functions that find the minimum and maximum **y** values and compute **dy** from

```
dy = (y_max - y_min)/py
```

9.9. Modify the data-plotting program of Fig. 9.13 to plot two sets of data on the same graph. Use a '+' symbol to plot points on one curve and a '*' symbol for the other. Test your program with the following data:

X	Y(X)	Z(X)
10	5	45
20	10	42
30	15	39
40	20	36
50	25	33
60	30	30
70	35	27
80	40	24
90	45	21

chapter 10

High-Resolution Video Graphics

10.1 INTRODUCTION

The most popular hardware scheme of generating images on a computer video screen is referred to as raster, or bit-mapped, graphics. In this technique, the screen is composed of an array of fine dots called *pixels* or picture elements. There may be anywhere from 200 to over 1000 of these pixels going across any row or down any column of the screen. The status of each pixel is controlled by the contents of one or more memory bits. These memory locations are addressable by the programmer. In the case of monochrome (black and white) graphics, a pixel can be turned on or off by setting or clearing one memory bit. For color graphics, the status of each pixel is determined by a larger block of memory.

High-resolution graphics offer more accuracy, detail, flexibility, and visual appeal than character graphics. Unfortunately, there is no single standard in place for the graphics software or hardware. The **C** language does not have graphics functions as part of its standard library. However, we can add a set of graphics functions to meet our needs. The most basic of these functions will be system dependent. They must be tailored to the compiler or interpreter, as well as operating system and/or hardware.

Requirements for Implementing High-resolution Video Graphics

The most fundamental requirement for implementing high-resolution video graphics is to have a system whose hardware includes this graphics capability. In addition, you will need to have four basic functions that are system dependent. A description of these functions and the names assigned to them in this text are given in Fig. 10.1. You may find that these functions are included with your system under slightly different names. If not, then refer to Chapter 15 for information that will help you generate these functions.

Function	Description
1. gmode()	Initialize the graphics mode of operation
2. clr()	Clear the graphics screen
3. locate(row, col)	Locate the text cursor at row and col (column) of the display screen
4. pnt(x, y, c)	Set a pixel at location x, y to the color c

Figure 10.1 System-dependent graphics functions.

In addition to the functions, you must be familiar with the characteristics of your graphics hardware. Specifically, you will need to know:

1. Number of pixels per row and column
2. What colors, if any, are available and the number codes assigned to each color
3. How many rows and columns of characters can be printed on the graphics screen
4. Length and width of a character measured in pixels

Elementary Graphics Examples

All the graphics examples in this text will assume that the pixel in the upper-left-corner of the screen is addressed as **pnt(0,0,c)**. Also, it is assumed that the **x** coordinate is the horizontal coordinate and the **y** coordinate increases downward on the screen. The direction of the **y** axis is determined by the hardware, but can be reversed by software.

Using the four system-dependent functions of Fig. 10.1, we can set pixels on the screen, draw lines, plot functions or data, and add text as needed. For example, the simple program

```
main()      /*set pixel at (100,100) to color 3 */
     {
     gmode();
     clr();
     pnt(100,100,3);
     }
```

will place the system in the graphics mode, clear the graphics screen, and set or turn on the pixel at location **(100,100)** using the color numbered **3**. This pixel appears as a small dot on the screen.

To draw a horizontal line, we can simply set a series of pixels along the same row. The following program draws a line from **(0,100)** to **(300,100)** in color **3**. Notice that the **for** loop is being used to set all the pixels in the row whose **y** coordinate is **100**, starting at **x = 0** up to **x = 300**.

```
main()     /* draw a horizontal line from (0,100) to (300,100)*/
     {
     int x;
     int y = 100;
     int c = 3;

     gmode();
     clr();
     for(x=0;x<=300,x++)
          pnt(x,y,c);
     }
```

Suppose that we wish to plot the equation $\mathbf{y = (x-100)^2}$ from $\mathbf{x = 0}$ to $\mathbf{x = 200}$ in increments of **1**. The program will need to define the **y** coordinate using this equation. For each value of **x**, the corresponding value of **y** will be computed. The maximum value of **y** will occur at $\mathbf{x = 0}$ and $\mathbf{x = 200}$. Since this maximum equals **10,000**, we must scale the **y** values before plotting. Dividing by **100** will give a range of **0** to **100** on the **y** axis.

Most graphics screens have an inverted **y** axis. We can correct the plot to eliminate this inversion by software control. Define the pixel row that is physically the lowest within the plotting area as **GB** (graph bottom). If all **y** values are subtracted from **GB** and the resulting values used for plotting, the inversion will be eliminated. **GB** will become the zero point, and the **y** axis will increase upward. The program of Fig. 10.2 plots our scaled equation without inversion.

```
/* plot of y = (x-100)*(x-100) */

#define Y   ((x-100)*(x-100))         /* original equation */
#define YN  Y/100                     /* scaled equation */
#define GB  199                       /* pixel number at bottom of graph */
#define C   3                         /* default color */

main()
      {
      int x;

      gmode();                        /* initialize graphics mode for display */
      clr();                          /* clear the graphics screen */
      for (x = 0;  x <= 200;  x++)    /* plot the parabola */
            pnt(x, GB - YN, C);
      }
```

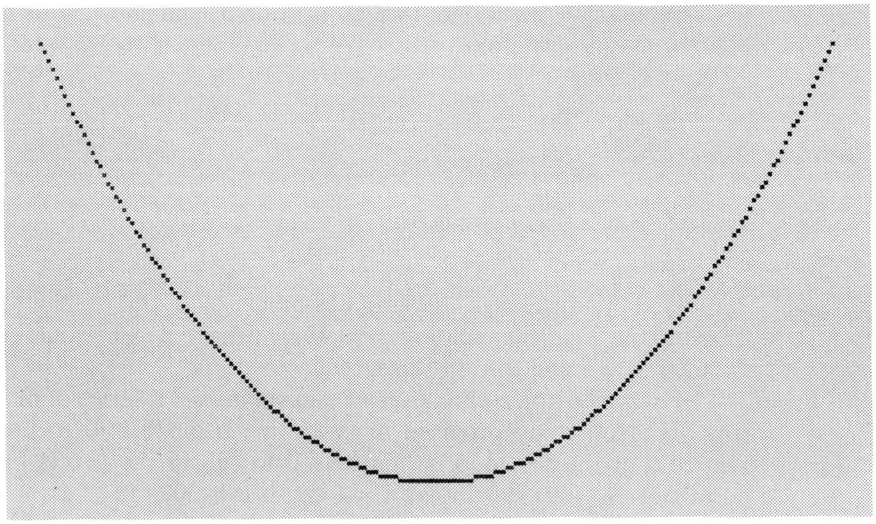

Figure 10.2 Program that plots $\mathbf{(x - 100)^2}$.

10.2 BRESENHAM'S ALGORITHM

We have already looked at a simple program for drawing horizontal lines. It could be converted into a function that draws horizontal lines, which we might call **h_line(x1,x2,y,c)**. Here, the subscript **1** refers to a beginning coordinate of the line and the subscript **2** an end coordinate. The **y** coordinate is constant. A similar function could be written for vertical lines, say, **v_line(x,y1,y2,c)**. But how about drawing lines at any angle or slope? One method of doing this would involve using the equation of a straight line.

Recall that the equation of a straight line is given by

$$y = mx + b$$

where **m** is the slope of the line. Computation of the **y** coordinate of each point would require multiplication of the **x** value by **m**. Because the slope will not normally be an integer value, the multiplication must be done using floating-point numbers. This is a very time consuming operation. Since speed is important in graphics applications, this method of drawing lines is not desirable.

Bresenham's algorithm describes a line-drawing method that does not require any multiplication or division and can be used with integer data. It has become the standard line-drawing method for professional computer graphics. Figure 10.5 illustrates a line that was drawn using this algorithm. We are assuming that the line has a slope between **0** and **45** degrees. For an increment of one pixel in the **x** direction, there are only two choices for **y**. It will either remain the same or be incremented by one.

Bresenham's algorithm uses *decision variables* to determine which course of action to take. In this case, the decision variable is an error term in the straight-line equation. The error term increases if **y** is not incremented and decreases if it is incremented. This error term is compared to a reference value to decide whether or not **y** must be incremented for the next pixel position.

The straight-line equation can be written as

$$y = (delta\_y)/(delta\_x)\ x$$

where **delta_y = y2 − y1** and **delta_x = x2 − x1**. If both sides of the equation are multiplied by **delta_x** and the terms are brought to the same side, we get

$$x\ (delta\_y) - y\ (delta\_x) = 0$$

The left side of this equation would always be zero if each pixel could be plotted exactly where it should be. However, since we are restricted to specific pixel increments, there will usually be an error between where the pixel is placed and where it ideally ought to be. Let's set the left side of the equation equal to **error**. Our equation then becomes

$$x\ (delta\_y) - y\ (delta\_x) = error$$

If **x** is incremented by **1** without incrementing **y**, we get

$$(x+1)\ (delta\_y) - y\ (delta\_x) = error$$

which clearly adds **delta_y** to the value of error. If **x** and **y** are both incremented, the equation becomes

$$(x+1)\ (delta\_y) - (y+1)\ (delta\_x) = error$$

which adds **(delta_y − delta_x)** to **error**. This quantity will be negative for all slopes except 45 degrees, in which case it is zero. To minimize the actual error in pixel settings, we specify that **error** should always be less than or equal to **(delta_x)/2**. This is equivalent to specifying a maximum error of one-half of a pixel above or below the ideal location. The pseudocode for the special case of angles between **0** and **45** degrees can now be written as shown in Fig. 10.3.

```
/* pseudocode for lines using Bresenham's algorithm */
/* for a slope between 0 and 45 degrees */
/* and x1 <= x2 */

module line(x1, y1, x2, y2, c)
      error = 0
      delta_y = y2 - y1
      delta_x = x2 - x1
      sml_err = delta_x/2

      while (x1 <= x2)
            pnt(x1,y1,c)
            x1 = x1 + 1
            error = error + delta_y
            if (error > sml_err)
                  error = error - delta_x
                  y1 = y1 + 1
            end if
      end while
end line()
```

Figure 10.3 Pseudocode for Bresenham's algorithm (special case).

The program of Fig. 10.4 demonstrates line drawing using this technique. Again, it is restricted to angles between **0** and **45** degrees, and **x1** <= **x2**. The function **main()** defines the line to be drawn, and **line()** sets the required pixels.

Let's go through an example using the line of Fig. 10.5. **Delta_x** equals **10** and **delta_y** equals **4**. **Sml_err** equals **delta_x/2** or **5**. Initially, the pixel at **(0,0)** is set and **error** equals **0**. When **x** is incremented by **1**, the value of **error** becomes **delta_y** or **4**. Since this is less than **sml_err**, **y** is not incremented and remains **0**. Therefore, the next pixel is set at **(1,0)**. The value of **error** is incremented by **4** to **8**. Since this is greater than **sml_err**, we subtract **10 (delta_x)** from **error** to bring it down to **−2** and increment **y** to **1**. The next pixel to be set is therefore **(2,1)**. We continue in this fashion until **x1** = **x2**, at which point the line is fully drawn.

Notice that **error** is zero for **x** = **0**, **5**, and **10**. These pixels fall exactly where they should be on the line. Also, there are an equal number of pixels (**4**) below and above the ideal position. All these pixels are within **1/2** pixel distance of the ideal line.

How can we generalize our line drawing program to cover any arbitrary situation? First, if **x1** > **x2**, we can simply decrement **x1**, instead of incrementing it, until it equals **x2**. The balance of the algorithm would remain unchanged. Likewise, if **y1** > **y2**, which would occur for lines having a negative slope, we can simply decrement **y** instead of incrementing it.

What if the angle is greater than 45 degrees or less than −45 degrees? The algorithm works only for slopes whose magnitude is less than or equal to 45 degrees. In this case, we can reverse the roles of **x** and **y**. That is, instead of incrementing **x** and deciding if **y** must be incremented, we will increment **y** and make the decision on **x**. The pseudocode of Fig. 10.6 incorporates all these improvements to permit the drawing of any arbitrary line.

```
/* drawing lines using Bresenham's algorithm (special case) */
#include <stdio.h>
main()
      {
      int x1, y1, x2, y2;
      int c = 3;
      void line();

      puts("Enter x1, y1, x2, y2, c");
      scanf("%d, %d, %d, %d, %d", &x1, &y1, &x2, &y2, &c);
      gmode();
      clr();
      line(x1, y1, x2, y2, c);
      }

void line(x1, y1, x2, y2, c)
int x1, y1, x2, y2, c;
      {
      int error = 0;
      int delta_y = y2 - y1;
      int delta_x = x2 - x1;
      int sml_err = delta_x/2;

      while(x1 <= x2)
            {
            pnt(x1, y1, c);
            x1 = x1 + 1;
            error = error + delta_y;
            if (error > sml_err)
                  {
                  error = error - delta_x;
                  y1 = y1 + 1;
                  }
            }
      }
```

```
Enter x1, y1, x2, y2, c
0, 0, 200, 100
```

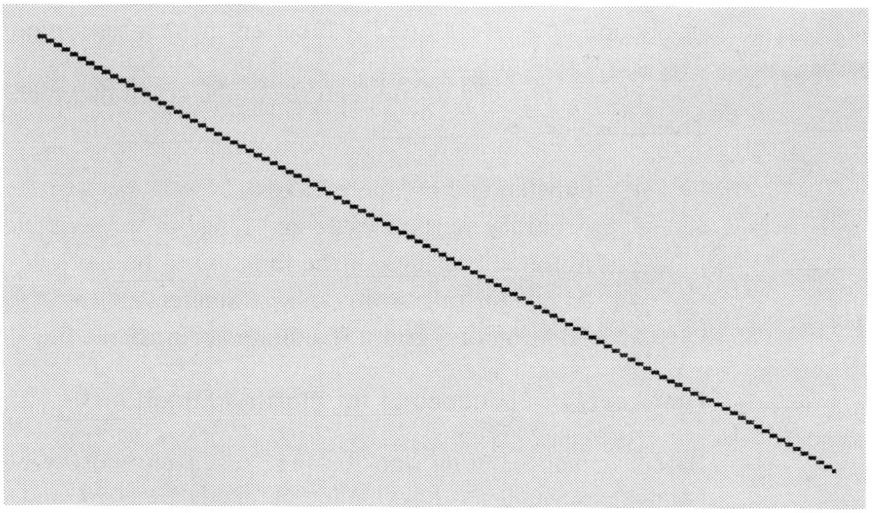

Figure 10.4 Program for Bresenham's algorithm (special case).

X	Y	ideal Y	error term
0	0	0.0	0
1	0	0.4	4
2	1	0.8	−2
3	1	1.2	−4
4	2	1.6	2
5	2	2.0	0
6	2	2.4	4
7	3	2.8	−2
8	3	3.2	2
9	4	3.6	−4
10	4	4.0	0

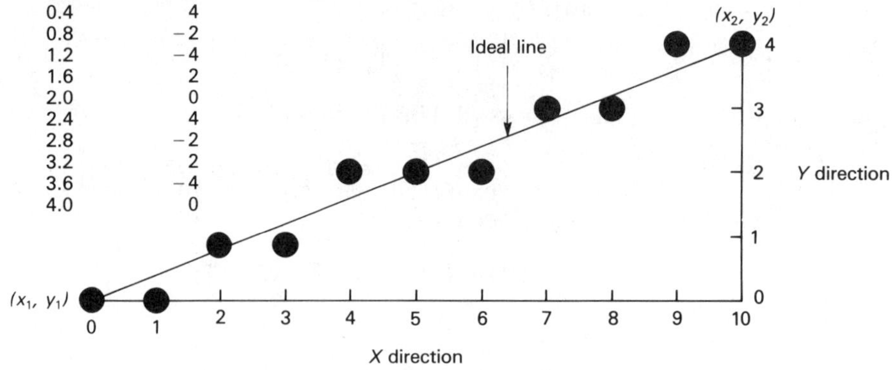

Figure 10.5 Line drawing using Bresenham's algorithm.

The variables **x_step** and **y_step** were introduced to permit easy reversal between increment and decrement operations. If **x2** > **x1**, **x_step** will equal **−1**; otherwise, it will equal **+1**. Likewise, if **y2** > **y1**, **y_step** will equal **−1**; otherwise, it will equal **+1**. Notice that we are working with the absolute values of **delta_x** and **delta_y**.

The **if** statement comparing **delta_x** and **delta_y** is used to determine whether the magnitude of the slope exceeds 45 degrees. If **delta_y** <= **delta_x**, we can increment the value of **x** and test for incrementing **y**. Otherwise, a separate routine will be used to increment **y** and test for incrementing of **x**.

Figure 10.7 lists the final line-drawing function. It closely follows the pseudocode of Fig. 10.6. Observe that the test condition **while (more pixels to set)** in the pseudocode translated into **while (x1 != (x2 + x_step))**. This format was used to set all the pixels from **x1** to **x2** inclusive, regardless of their relative sizes. If **x1 == x2**, the loop will be executed once to set the pixel at **(x1,y1)**. Wherever the function **line()** is used throughout the balance of this text, it will be the version listed in Fig. 10.7.

10.3 PLOTTING FUNCTIONS IN HIGH-RESOLUTION VIDEO

In Section 10.1, we plotted a function in high-resolution video graphics. That example was kept simple to illustrate the concept of plotting on the video screen. Now we can proceed to add features to the graph that make it much more useful. These include:

1. Labeled and numbered axes
2. Arbitrary starting value and range of the variables
3. Automatic scaling of the function to be plotted
4. Easy adjustment of graph parameters
5. Addition of a grid to facilitate accurate reading

First Level of Pseudocode for Plotting Functions

Before actually getting into the process of plotting, we must know the screen parameters, such as the number of pixels per row and column, the available colors, and so on. Then we will have to decide on the size of the graph. Here, consideration must be given to the size of a character measured in pixels. This will

```
/* Pseudocode for Bresenham's algorithm */

module line(x1, y1, x2, y2, c)
      error = 0
      delta_x = x2 - x1
      if (delta_x < 0)
            delta_x = - delta_x
            x_step = -1
      else
            x_step = 1
      end if

      delta_y = y2 - y1
      if (delta_y < 0)
            delta_y = - delta_y
            y_step = -1
      else
            y_step = 1
      end if

      if (delta_y <= delta_x)              /* increment along x */
            sml_err = delta_x/2
            while (more pixels to set)
                  pnt(x1, x2, c)
                  x1 = x1 + x_step
                  error = error + delta_y
                  if (error > sml_err)
                        error = error - delta_x
                        y1 = y1 + y_step
                  end if
            end while
      else                                 /* increment along y */
            sml_err = delta_y/2
            while (more pixels to set)
                  pnt(x1, x2, c)
                  y1 = y1 + y_step
                  error = error + delta_x
                  if (error > sml_err)
                        error = error - delta_y
                        x1 = x1 + x_step
                  end if
            end while
      end if
end line()
```

Figure 10.6 Pseudocode for Bresenham's algorithm.

have an impact on the alignment of text to graphics. (Character size is fixed on most systems, whereas the graphics can be adjusted arbitrarily.)

The next step will be to determine parameters for the function to be plotted. These include the starting value and range of the variables and the scale to be used on each axis. At this point, we can draw and number the axes and plot the function and grid. The first level of pseudocode based on this initial analysis is given in Fig. 10.8.

```
/* line.c */
/* a line-drawing function using Bresenham's algorithm */

int line(x1, y1, x2, y2, c)
int x1, y1, x2, y2, c;
      {
      static int error, sml_err;
      static int delta_x, delta_y;
      static int x_step, y_step;

      error = 0;
      delta_x = x2 - x1;                          /* compute parameters */
      if (delta_x < 0)
            {
            delta_x = -delta_x;
            x_step = -1;
            }
      else
            x_step = 1;

      delta_y = y2 - y1;
      if (delta_y < 0)
            {
            delta_y = -delta_y;
            y_step = -1;
            }
      else
            y_step = 1;

      if (delta_y <= delta_x)                     /* increment along x */
            {
            sml_err = delta_x/2;
            while (x1 != (x2 + x_step))
                  {
                  pnt(x1, y1, c);
                  x1 += x_step;
                  error += delta_y;
                  if (error > sml_err)
                        {
                        error -= delta_x;
                        y1 += y_step;
                        }
                  }
            }
      else
            {                                     /* increment along y */
            sml_err = delta_y/2;
            while (y1 != (y2 + y_step))
                  {
                  pnt(x1, y1, c);
                  y1 += y_step;
                  error += delta_x;
                  if (error > sml_err)
                        {
                        error -= delta_y;
                        x1 += x_step;
                        }
                  }
            }
      }
```

Figure 10.7 C function for Bresenham's algorithm.

```
/* First-level pseudocode for plotting functions */

set up display screen parameters
determine parameters for function to be plotted
draw and number axes
plot the function
plot a grid for accurate reading from the graph
```

Figure 10.8 First-level pseudocode for plotting functions.

Second Level of Pseudocode for Plotting Functions

Now we will add more detail for the next level of pseudocode. Refer to Fig. 10.9 for a listing of this code. Rather than have the equation to be plotted embedded within our program, it would be nice to locate it at the top. The advantage of doing so is that the equation can be located easily for editing. This can be done with a macro (**#define** in **C**) and will be added as the first line in the second level of pseudocode.

The graphics mode must be initialized. We can include this within the setup of the display screen parameters. The axes titles can be entered at any point. We will put them in here.

Establishing the parameters for the function to be plotted must start with entering the range of the **x** axis (independent) variable. We then have to decide on the increments at which the function will be evaluated. This will be related to the number of pixel positions available for the axis. Let's define the variable **dx** as the **x** *axis increment per pixel.* It is related to the starting and ending values of **x** and the number of pixels on the **x** axis by

$$\mathbf{dx} = \frac{\mathbf{x\_max - x\_min}}{\mathbf{pixels\ on\ x\ axis}}$$

where **x_min** and **x_max** are the lower and upper limits of **x** axis values, respectively.

The function will be evaluated at intervals **dx**. It is desirable to take all these function samples and place them into two arrays, which we will call **xd[]** and **yd[]**. Since we will make more than one reference to each sample value, the execution is speeded up by not having to evaluate the function each time we reference its value. Also, the program will be easier to convert into one that plots data instead of equations.

To add automatic scaling of the function, we will need to know the minimum and maximum values of **y** for the selected **x** range. These values will be used to determine the **y** axis range and also **dy**, the increment per pixel for the **y** axis. It is defined as

$$\mathbf{dy} = \frac{\mathbf{y\_max - y\_min}}{\mathbf{pixels\ on\ y\ axis}}$$

where **y_min** and **y_max** are the lower and upper limits of **y** axis values, respectively.

At this point, the screen can be cleared to start drawing the graph. No particular sequence has to be followed, unlike the character graphics plots of

Chapter 9. We can start by drawing, numbering, and labeling the axes. The function is then plotted. For accurate reading of values from the graph, we can add a grid of dots that will simulate real graph paper.

```
/* Second-level pseudocode for function plot */

define the function to be plotted
define display screen parameters
initialize the graphics mode

input axes titles
input range for x
find x axis increment per pixel, dx
sample the function and place samples in arrays xd[] and yd[]
find y_min and y_max
determine y range and increment per pixel, dy

clear the display screen
draw the axes
number the axes
title the axes
plot the function
plot a grid for accurate reading of values
```

Figure 10.9 Second-level pseudocode for plotting functions.

Third Level of Pseudocode for Plotting Functions

The third and final level of pseudocode is given in Fig. 10.10. We have defined **Y** as a macro that stores the definition of the function to be plotted. The display screen parameters have been introduced here. The pixel locations of the left, right, top and bottom of the graph are assigned to **GL**, **GR**, **GT**, and **GB**, respectively. This symbolic representation makes it easier to modify the program for different display screens.

The length of the **x** axis, **PX**, is defined as **GR − GL**. Likewise, the length of the **y** axis, **PY**, is defined as **GB − GT**. The length of a short tick mark is assigned to **TW**. We will use **2*TW** for long tick marks. The grid spacing is defined by **GRIDX** and **GRIDY**.

The first call in **main()** is to **gmode()**, which initializes the graphics display screen. This is a system-specific function assumed to be available. It should be included as an object file during the link portion of compilation. Other object files to be included at this point are **locate()**, **clr()**, and **pnt()**.

The module **get_titles**(x_name,y_name) simply inputs the names to be used for the **x** and **y** axis titles. These names will be stored in the character strings **x_name** and **y_name**.

A call to **get_xparm()** is used to enter the range of the **x** axis variable. It assigns the minimum value to **x_min** and the maximum to **x_max**. The value of **dx** is then computed from **(x_max − x_min)/PX**.

The module **sample_f()** is called to sample **Y** at intervals of **dx**, with the **x** value stored in **xd[]** and the **Y** value stored in **yd[]**. The number of samples is stored in the variable **data_pts**.

Get_yparm() is used to determine the minimum and maximum values of the samples of **Y** stored in **yd[]**. It makes calls to two other functions, **min()** and

max(), to find the subscript of the smallest and largest elements of **yd[]**, respectively. These values are used in the assignments

```
y_min = yd[min()]
y_max = yd[max()]
```

The value of **dy** is then computed from **(y_max − y_min)/PY**. The calculated values of **y_min** and **y_max** will most likely not be rounded numbers suitable for graph limits. Therefore, these values are printed along with **dy**, and the operator will be prompted to adjust the values of **y_min** and **dy**.

At this point, the screen is cleared using **clr()** and the graph generation begins. The module **draw_axes()** will draw the **x** and **y** axes including the tick marks. Drawing the **x** axis line will involve one call to the function **line()**. Adding tick marks is a bit more complicated. We would like to have tick marks at the decade positions longer than those at the units positions. This can be implemented by checking to see if the tick number is a multiple of 10. If so, the tick mark will be drawn to a length of **2*TW**. Otherwise, it will be drawn to a length of **TW**.

The procedure for drawing the **y** axis and its tick marks is similar to that for the **x** axis. Since the vertical resolution is normally less than the horizontal resolution, we have chosen to draw 5 ticks per decade instead of 10.

The module **num_axes()** numbers both axes. Numbering the **x** axis involves locating the cursor below each decade tick mark and printing the value along the axis at that point. For the **y** axis, the cursor is located to the left of the decade tick mark for numbering.

Title(x_name,y_name) is called to print the axis titles. The **x** axis title, **x_name**, is printed centered on line 24. Placing the title on the **y** axis requires printing one character of **y_name** per line in the leftmost column. A loop is used to pick each character from the title string and print it at a position determined by the **locate()** function.

The module **plot()** will plot the digitized values of **Y**. Plotting the function requires converting the array values to integer-type data, since **pnt()** needs integer arguments. The function samples must also be scaled to fit the display size. A call to **pnt()** will be used to actually plot the sample value.

The last portion of the code plots a two-dimensional grid of points at a spacing of **GRIDX** and **GRIDY** points per decade on the axes. This permits easy reading of values and simulates real graph paper. Nested loops are used to select each **x** and **y** position for plotting.

The **C** program implementing our pseudocode is given in Fig. 10.11. Additional symbolic constants have been introduced, and all the constants have been assigned specific values. (These values are based on using the IBM PC color graphics adaptor in high-resolution mode. They are easily adjusted for other display systems.) The color number for drawing, **C**, was given a value of **3**. The graph borders were selected to provide adequate margins for the axes. They provide a value of **500** for **PX** and **160** for **PY**. The tick width was given a value of **2**.

Since many operations reference the decade positions on the graph, the numbers of pixels per decade for each axis were assigned to symbolic constants. **DECX**, the number of pixels per decade on the **x** axis, has a value of **50**. Its equivalent for the **y** axis, **DECY**, has a value of **20**. These values provide **10** decades for the **x** axis and **6** decades for the **y** axis.

The character size in pixels is also assigned to symbolic constants. **PPCX** is the number of pixels per character cell in the **x** direction. **PPCY** is the equivalent for the **y** direction. Both constants have a value of **8**.

We have defined all the variables relating to the data as **external**. The **xd[]** and **yd[]** arrays were declared as **double** and given a size of **PX**. This provides

```
/* Final pseudocode for function plot */

define Y as function of x                          /* function to be plotted */

/* display screen parameters */
define GL   as graph left border
define GR   as graph right border
define GT   as graph top border
define GB   as graph bottom border
define TW   as the tick width for graph
define PX   as (GRX - GLX)
define PY   as (GBY - GTY)
define GRIDX as the number of grid dots per decade along x axis
define GRIDY as the number of grid dots per decade along y axis

module main()
      gmode()                                      /* initialize graphics mode */
      get_titles(x_name,y_name)                    /* input axes titles */
      get_xparm()                                  /* get x_min, x_max, and dx */
      sample_f()                                   /* sample function */
      get_yparm()                                  /* find y_min, y_max, and dy */
      clr()                                        /* clear display screen */
      draw_axes()                                  /* draw the axes */
      num_axes()                                   /* number the axes */
      title(x_name,y_name)                         /* title the axes */
      plot()                                       /* plot the function */
      grid()                                       /* plot the grid */
end main()

module get_titles(x_name, y_name)
      print "Enter title for x axis"
      input x_name
      print "Enter title for y axis"
      input y_name
      return names
end get_titles()

module get_xparm()                                 /* determine x_min, x_max, dx */
      print "Enter range for x"
      input x_min and x_max
      dx = (x_max - x_min)/PX
end get_x_parm()

module sample_f()                   /* place function samples in xd[] and yd[] */
      i = 0
      for (x from x_min to x_max, step dx)
            xd[i] = x
            yd[i] = Y
            i = i + 1
      end for
      data_pts = i
end sample_f()
```

Figure 10.10 Final pseudocode for plotting functions.

```
module get_yparm()             /* determine y_min, y_max, and dy */
      y_min = yd[min()]        /* min() returns subscript for smallest yd[] */
      y_max = yd[max()]        /* max() returns subscript for largest yd[] */
      dy = (y_max - y_min)/PY
      print y_min, y_max, and dy    /* determine y range */
      input operator adjusted y_min, dy
end get_yparm()

module draw_axes()
      draw x axis line              /* draw x axis and ticks */
      for (each tick position)
            if (tick is mod 10)
                  draw tick at width 2*TW
            else
                  draw tick at width TW
            end if
      end for

      draw y axis line              /* draw y axis and ticks */
      for (each tick position)
            if (tick is mod 5)
                  draw tick at width 2*TW
            else
                  draw tick at width TW
            end if
      end for
end draw_axes()

module num_axes()
      for (each decade position)                /* number x axis */
            locate cursor below decade tick
            print x value
      end for
      for (each decade position)                /* number y axis */
            locate cursor left of decade tick
            print y value
      end for
end num_axes()

module title(x_name, y_name)                    /* print titles */
      print x_name centered on line 24
      for (i = 0 to i < length of y_name)       /* print y_name in column 0 */
            locate(i,0)
            print char i of y_name
      end for
end title()

module plot()                                   /* plot the function */
      for (each sample of function)
            yn = integer value of scaled yd[]
            xn = integer value of scaled xd[]
            plot point (xn, yn) on display
      end for
end plot()
```

Figure 10.10 (continued).

```
module grid()                                   /* plot grid */
      for (GRIDX points per x decade)
            for (GRIDY points per y decade)
                  plot point at selected grid position
            end for
      end for
end grid()
```

Figure 10.10 (continued).

storage for one sample of the function at every pixel position on the **x** axis. The variable **data_pts** is an **int** type and stores the number of data points that were sampled. Other **external** variables defined as **double** include **x_min**, **x_max**, **y_min**, **y_max**, **dx**, and **dy**.

Drawing of the line for the **x** axis is straightforward. The loop that generates the **x** axis tick marks uses increments of **DECX/10**, which equals the number of pixels per unit. The tick marks are short line segments drawn at an **x** coordinate of **i + GL**, where **i** is the loop variable. The **y** coordinates for decade ticks are **GB − 2*TW** and **GB**. For unit ticks, the **y** coordinates are **GB − TW** and **GB**. Drawing the **y** axis and its tick marks proceeds in the same fashion.

The **x** axis is numbered at every other decade. This is a constraint of the display system. Numbering every decade would have crowded the numbers too close to one another. The loop variable, **i**, is incremented by **2** to select alternate decades. The cursor is moved to row **23** and column **i*DECX/PPCX + GL/PPCX −5**. **DECX/PPCX** equals the number of characters per decade. **GL/PPCX** is the number of characters to the left border. The constant **5** is used to center the number at the decade tick mark. The value printed at the selected decade is given by **x_min + i*DECX*dx**, where **i*DECX** represents the total number of pixels to that point and **dx** is the increment per pixel. The **y** axis is numbered in the same manner.

Plotting of the function requires scaling the samples and converting to **int** data type. The expression **yd[i] − y_min** gives the value of **yd[i]** relative to **y_min**. Division of this expression by **dy** scales the quantity to fit the **y** axis. The addition of **0.5** is used to round off the number when converting to integer form. The same processing occurs in converting the **xd[i]** values.

The scaled data are plotted at **GL + xn**, **GB − yn**. The offsets **GL** and **GB** are used to reference the plotted point to the origin of the graph. Notice the negative sign preceding **yn**. This is used to invert the **y** axis into the normal positive-up orientation.

The routine that prints a grid on the graph uses **i** and **j** as the **x** and **y** grid dot counters, respectively. The upper limit for each of the loops is given by **PX/DECX*GRIDX** for **i** and **PY/DECY*GRIDY** for **j**. This provides **GRIDX** dots/decade for the **x** axis and **GRIDY** dots/decade for the **y** axis. Points are plotted at **x** coordinates of **GL + i*DECX/GRIDX** and **y** coordinates of **GB − j*DECY/GRIDY**.

The functions **min()** and **max()** return an integer that represents the array subscript at the location of the smallest and largest elements of the array, respectively. The procedure used here was covered in Chapter 7.

A dummy **scanf()** statement is placed at the end of the program to suspend termination until a key is pressed. This provides the operator time to study the

```
/* linear plot of a function in high-resolution video graphics */

#include <stdio.h>
#define Y           -0.1*x*x +x -10.0  /* equation */
#define C           3                 /* default color */
#define GL          112               /* left border for graph */
#define GR          612               /* right border for graph */
#define GT          12                /* top border for graph */
#define GB          172               /* bottom border for graph */
#define TW          2                 /* tick width */
#define DECX        50                /* pixels per decade on x axis */
#define DECY        20                /* pixels per decade on y axis */
#define PPCX        8                 /* pixels per character in x direction */
#define PPCY        8                 /* pixels per character in y direction */
#define PX          (GR-GL)           /* total pixels on x axis */
#define PY          (GB-GT)           /* total pixels on y axis */
#define GRIDX       5                 /* grid dots per decade in x direction */
#define GRIDY       5                 /* grid dots per decade in y direction */

double xd[PX], yd[PX];  /* sampled functional values placed in these arrays */
int data_pts;           /* number of data points in sampled function */
double x_min, x_max;    /* min and max x values of sampled function */
double y_min, y_max;    /* min and max y values of sampled function */
double dx, dy;          /* change in x and y per pixel, respectively  */

main()
      {
      char x_name[50], y_name[50];
      int i;
      void get_titles(), get_xparm(), get_yparm(), sample_f(), draw_axes();
      void num_axes(), title(), plot(), grid();

      gmode();
      get_titles(x_name, y_name);
      get_xparm();
      sample_f();
      get_yparm();
      clr();
      draw_axes();
      num_axes();
      title(x_name, y_name);
      plot();
      grid();
      scanf("%d", &i);                    /* wait for keypress before exit */
      }

void get_titles(x_name, y_name)           /* get titles for axes */
char x_name[], y_name[];
      {
      puts("Enter title for x axis");
      gets(x_name);
      puts("Enter title for y axis");
      gets(y_name);
      }

void get_xparm()                          /* find dx from x_min and x_max */
      {
      puts("Enter range for x");
      scanf("%lf,%lf", &x_min, &x_max);
      dx = (x_max - x_min)/PX;
      }
```

Figure 10.11 Function-plotting program using high-resolution video graphics.

```
void get_yparm()                              /* determine y_min, y_max, dy */
      {
      y_min = yd[min()];
      y_max = yd[max()];
      dy = (y_max - y_min)/PY;
      printf("y_min = %f, y_max = %f, dy = %f\n", y_min, y_max, dy);
      puts("Enter adjusted y_min and dy");
      puts("New y_min must be equal to or less than old value");
      puts("New dy must be equal to or larger than old value");
      scanf("%lf,%lf", &y_min, &dy);
      }

void sample_f()         /* sample function and store in arrays xd[] and yd[] */
      {
      int i;
      double x;

      for (x = x_min, i = 0; (x <= x_max) && (i < PX); x += dx, i++)
            {
            xd[i] = x;
            yd[i] = Y;
            }
      data_pts = i;
      }

void draw_axes()                              /* draw the axes */
      {
      int i;

      /* draw x axis */
      line(GL, GB, GR, GB, C);
      for (i = 0; i <= PX; i += DECX/10)
            if (i%DECX == 0)
                  line(i + GL, GB - 2*TW, i + GL, GB, C);
            else
                  line(i + GL, GB - TW, i + GL, GB, C);

      /* draw y axis */
      line(GL, GB, GL, GT, C);
      for (i = 0; i <= PY; i += DECY/5)
            if (i % DECY == 0)
                  line(GL + 2*TW, GB - i, GL, GB - i, C);
            else
                  line(GL + TW, GB - i, GL, GB - i, C);
      }

void num_axes()                               /* number the axes */
      {
      int i;

      /* number x axis */
      for (i = 0; i <= PX / DECX; i += 2)
            {
            locate(23, i*DECX/PPCX + GL/PPCX - 5);
            printf("%8.3f", x_min + i*dx*DECX);
            }

      /* number y axis */
      for (i = 0; i <= PY/DECY; i += 2)
            {
            locate((GB - DECY * i)/PPCY, GL/PPCX - 10);
            printf("%8.3f", y_min + i*dy*DECY);
            }
      }
```

Figure 10.11 (continued).

```
void title(x_name, y_name)                  /* print titles for axes */
char x_name[], y_name[];
      {
      int i;

      /* title for x axis */
      locate(24, 30);
      printf("%s", x_name);

      /* title for y axis */
      for (i = 0; i < strlen(y_name); i++)
            {
            locate(i, 0);
            putchar(y_name[i]);
            }
      }

void plot()                                 /* plot function */
      {
      int i, yn, xn;

      for (i = 0; i < data_pts; i++)
            {
            yn = (int)((yd[i] - y_min)/dy + 0.5);     /* normalized y */
            xn = (int)((xd[i] - x_min)/dx + 0.5);     /* normalized x */
            pnt(xn + GL, GB - yn, C);
            }
      }

void grid()                                 /* add grid for easy reading */
      {
      int i, j;

      for (i = 0; i <= PX/DECX*GRIDX; i++)
            for (j = 0; j <= PY/DECY*GRIDY; j++)
                  pnt(i*DECX/GRIDX + GL, GB - j*DECY/GRIDY, C);
      }

int min()
      {
      double yl;
      int mn, i;

      mn = 0;
      yl = yd[0];
      for (i = 0; i <= data_pts - 1; i++)
            {
            if (yl > yd[i])
                  {
                  mn = i;
                  yl = yd[i];
                  }
            }
      return (mn);
      }

int max()
      {
      double y2;
      int mx, i;
```

Figure 10.11 (continued).

```
mx = 0;
y2 = yd[0];
for (i = 0; i <= data_pts - 1; i++)
        {
        if (y2 < yd[i])
                {
                mx = i;
                y2 = yd[i];
                }
        }
return (mx);
}
```

```
Enter title for x axis
Frequency in Hz
Enter title for y axis
Voltage in volts
Enter range for x
0, 100
y_min = -902.416000, y_max = -7.500000, dy = 5.593225
```

```
Enter adjusted y_min and dy
New y_min must be equal to or less than old value
New dy must be equal to or larger than old value
-1000, 10
```

Figure 10.11 (continued).

graph before it is corrupted by system messages, scrolling, or some other event at the termination.

Figure 10.12 shows the output from the program of Fig. 10.11 for the equation $\mathbf{y = -0.1x^2 + x - 10.0}$.

10.4 PLOTTING EXPERIMENTAL DATA

The function plot program from the previous section can be modified to plot experimental data with very little effort. In fact, we will not need to write any pseudocode for the conversion. The conversion involves the following steps:

1. Delete the **#define Y** macro from the top of the listing.
2. Delete the **sample_f()** function.
3. Convert the declaration of the arrays **xd[]** and **yd[]** to **static double** and initialize them with the data to be plotted. Set **data_pts** equal to the number of data points in the arrays.
4. Convert plotting of a pixel at the data point to plotting of a symbol, such as a square, cross, or triangle.

Figure 10.13 is a listing of the converted program. The output is shown in Fig. 10.14. Squares were used to identify the data points on the graph. The size of one edge of the square was set to **2*TW**. This can be adjusted to suit the application. Notice that the boxes are centered around the data points.

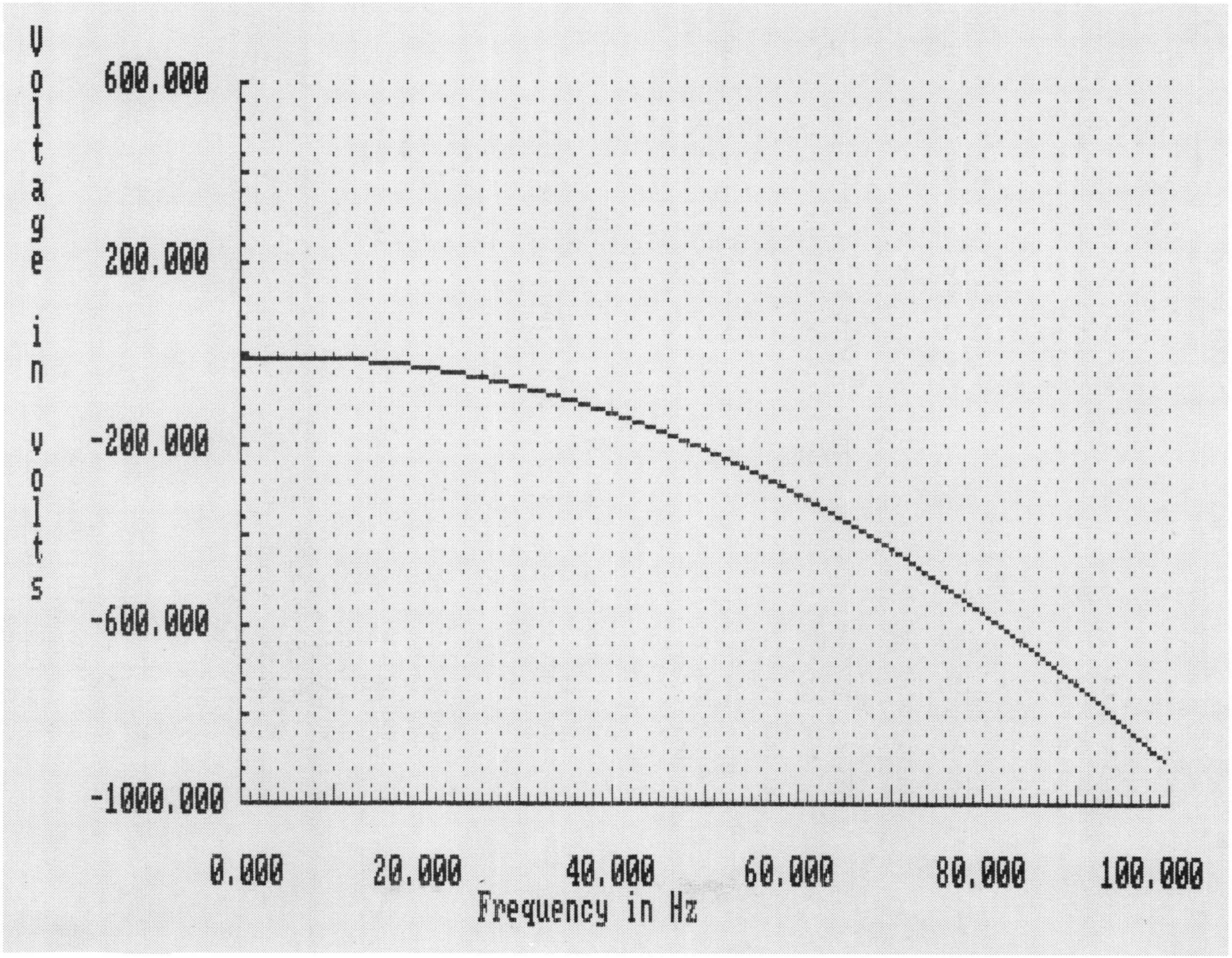

Figure 10.12 Function-plotting program output.

```
/* linear plot of data in high-resolution video graphics */

#include <stdio.h>
#define C         3              /* default color */
#define GL        112            /* left border for graph */
#define GR        612            /* right border for graph */
#define GT        12             /* top border for graph */
#define GB        172            /* bottom border for graph */
#define TW        2              /* tick width */
#define DECX      50             /* pixels per decade on x axis */
#define DECY      20             /* pixels per decade on y axis */
#define PPCX      8              /* pixels per character in x direction */
#define PPCY      8              /* pixels per character in y direction */
#define PX        (GR-GL)        /* total pixels on x axis */
#define PY        (GB-GT)        /* total pixels on y axis */
#define GRIDX     5              /* grid dots per decade in x direction */
#define GRIDY     5              /* grid dots per decade in y direction */

static double xd[100] = {0.0, 0.1, 0.2, 0.3, 0.4, 0.5, 0.6, 0.7, 0.8, 0.9, 1.0,
    1.1, 1.2, 1.3, 1.4, 1.5, 1.6, 1.7, 1.8, 1.9, 2.0};

static double yd[100] = {10.0, 10.1, 10.0, 9.9, 7.1, 4.9, 3.0, 0.9, 0.7, 0.6,
    1.1, 3.3, 5.4, 6.8, 7.9, 9.0, 9.6, 9.9, 10.1, 10.2, 10.1};

int data_pts = 21;

double x_min, x_max;        /* min and max x values of sampled function */
double y_min, y_max;        /* min and max y values of sampled function */
double dx, dy;              /* change in x and y per pixel, respectively  */

main()
      {
      char x_name[50], y_name[50];
      int i;
      void get_titles(), get_xparm(), get_yparm(), draw_axes();
      void num_axes(), title(), plot(), grid();


      gmode();
      get_titles(x_name, y_name);
      get_xparm();
      get_yparm();
      clr();
      draw_axes();
      num_axes();
      title(x_name, y_name);
      plot();
      grid();
      scanf("%d", &i);                    /* wait for keypress before exit */
      clr();
      }

void get_titles(x_name, y_name)           /* get titles for axes */
char x_name[], y_name[];
      {
      puts("Enter title for x axis");
      gets(x_name);
      puts("Enter title for y axis");
      gets(y_name);
      }
```

Figure 10.13 Data-plotting program using high-resolution video graphics.

```
void get_xparm()                          /* find dx from x_min and x_max */
      {
      puts("Enter range for x");
      scanf("%lf,%lf", &x_min, &x_max);
      dx = (x_max - x_min)/PX;
      }

void get_yparm()                          /* determine y_min, y_max, dy */
      {
      y_min = yd[min()];
      y_max = yd[max()];
      dy = (y_max - y_min)/PY;
      printf("y_min = %f, y_max = %f, dy = %f\n", y_min, y_max, dy);
      puts("Enter adjusted y_min and dy");
      puts("New y_min must be equal to or less than old value");
      puts("New dy must be equal to or larger than old value");
      scanf("%lf,%lf", &y_min, &dy);
      }

void draw_axes()                          /* draw the axes */
      {
      int i;

      /* draw x axis */
      line(GL, GB, GR, GB, C);
      for (i = 0; i <= PX; i += DECX/10)
            if (i % DECX == 0)
                  line(i + GL, GB - 2*TW, i + GL, GB, C);
            else
                  line(i + GL, GB - TW, i + GL, GB, C);

      /* draw y axis */
      line(GL, GB, GL, GT, C);
      for (i = 0; i <= PY; i += DECY/5)
            if (i % DECY == 0)
                  line(GL + 2*TW, GB - i, GL, GB - i, C);
            else
                  line(GL + TW, GB - i, GL, GB - i, C);
      }

void num_axes()                           /* number the axes */
      {
      int i;

      /* number x axis */
      for (i = 0; i <= PX/DECX; i += 2)
            {
            locate(23, i * DECX/PPCX + GL/PPCX - 5);
            printf("%8.3f", x_min + i*dx*DECX);
            }

      /* number y axis */
      for (i = 0; i <= PY/DECY; i += 2)
            {
            locate((GB - DECY * i)/PPCY, GL/PPCX - 10);
            printf("%8.3f", y_min + i*dy*DECY);
            }
      }

void title(x_name, y_name)                /* print titles for axes */
char x_name[], y_name[];
      {
      int i;
```

Figure 10.13 (continued).

```
        /* title for x axis */
        locate(24, 30);
        printf("%s", x_name);

        /* title for y axis */
        for (i = 0; i < strlen(y_name); i++)
              {
              locate(i, 0);
              putchar(y_name[i]);
              }
        }

void plot()                                    /* plot data */
        {
        int i, yn, xn;

        for (i = 0; i < data_pts ; i++)
              {
              yn = (int) ((yd[i] - y_min)/dy + 0.5);         /* normalized y */
              xn = (int) ((xd[i] - x_min) / dx + 0.5);       /* normalized x */
              xn = xn + GL;
              yn = GB - yn;
              line(xn - TW, yn + TW, xn + TW, yn + TW, C); /* box at data point */
              line(xn - TW, yn - TW, xn + TW, yn - TW, C);
              line(xn - TW, yn - TW, xn - TW, yn + TW, C);
              line(xn + TW, yn - TW, xn + TW, yn + TW, C);
              }
        }

void grid()                                    /* add grid for easy reading */
        {
        int i, j;

        for (i = 0; i <= PX/DECX*GRIDX; i++)
              for (j = 0; j <= PY/DECY*GRIDY; j++)
                    pnt(i*DECX/GRIDX + GL, GB - j*DECY/GRIDY, C);
        }

int min()
        {
        double y1;
        int mn, i;

        mn = 0;
        y1 = yd[0];
        for (i = 0; i <= data_pts - 1; i++)
              {
              if (y1 > yd[i])
                    {
                    mn = i;
                    y1 = yd[i];
                    }
              }
        return (mn);
        }

int max()
        {
        double y2;
        int mx, i;
```

Figure 10.13 (continued).

```
mx = 0;
y2 = yd[0];
for (i = 0; i <= data_pts - 1; i++)
      {
      if (y2 < yd[i])
            {
            mx = i;
            y2 = yd[i];
            }
      }
return (mx);
}
```

```
Enter title for x axis
Input voltage (rms)
Enter title for y axis
Output voltage rms
Enter range for x
0, 2
y_min = 0.600000, y_max = 10.200000, dy = 0.060000
```

```
Enter adjusted y_min and dy
New y_min must be equal to or less than old value
New dy must be equal to or larger than old value
0, 0.1
```

Figure 10.13 (continued).

10.5 LOGARITHMIC FUNCTION PLOTS

In this section, we will develop programs for the semilogarithmic plotting of functions. Semilog scales are used whenever we wish to plot a function over a wide range of the independent variable. They are also used to linearize a plot that would otherwise be curved on a linear scale. Practical applications for these programs include plotting the magnitude and phase response of a linear system. To develop these programs, you will need to understand logarithmic scales and how to work with them.

Drawing Logarithmic Scales

On logarithmic scales, the change in value of the variable with respect to distance along the axis is proportional to the logarithm of the variable. The log of the axis variable will increase at a uniform rate with distance along the axis, while the variable itself will increase exponentially.

Assume that we wish to draw a logarithmic axis. The length of the axis will be specified by **PX** in pixels. The number of log cycles to be drawn will be specified by **nlc**. Let's develop pseudocode that will draw a tick mark at each tenth of a decade within each log cycle.

The length of each log cycle will be equal. Therefore, since there are **nlc** cycles over **PX** pixels, the length of each log cycle is **PX/nlc**. Let **z** represent any given log cycle. The distance along the axis to the beginning of the **z**th log cycle is given by **(z−1)PX/nlc**. The first log cycle starts at **0**, the second at **PX/nlc**, the third at **2PX/nlc**, and so on. The tick marks at each of these points mark the decade positions.

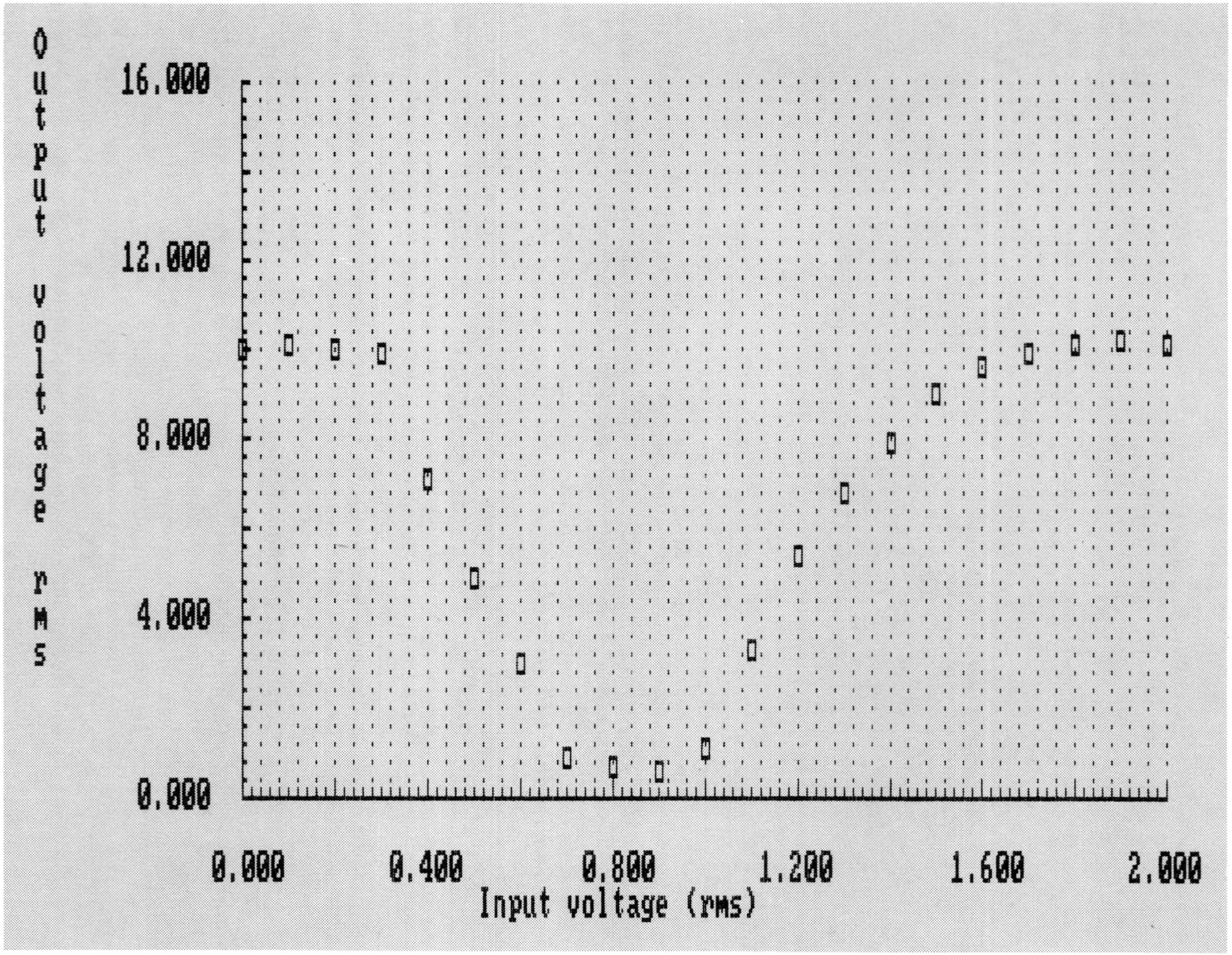

Figure 10.14 Data-plotting program output.

How do we locate points that are tenths of a decade within a log cycle? That distance is directly proportional to the log of the number. Let **x** represent digits from **2** to **10**. The distance to the **x**th tick mark within a log cycle is given by $\mathbf{log_{10}(x)PX/nlc}$. Therefore, the distance to a tick mark within any log cycle will be

$$\texttt{tick\_location} = (z-1)PX/nlc + \log_{10}(x)PX/nlc$$

The pseudocode for drawing a log scale with tick marks can now be written as shown in Fig. 10.15.

```
/* Pseudocode for drawing a horizontal log scale with tick marks */
/* for nlc log cycles over PX pixels in the color c */
/* the graph bottom or y origin is GB */
for (z from 1 to nlc)
      for (x from 2 to 10)
            xb = xe = (z-1)PX/nlc + log10(x)PX/nlc
            yb = GB - TW
            ye = GB
            line (xb, xe, yb, ye, c)
      end for
end for
```

Figure 10.15 Pseudocode for drawing log scales.

Magnitude Response

The first-level pseudocode for the logarithmic plot of magnitude response is given in Fig. 10.16. It is more detailed than the first-level pseudocode for linear plots, since we are building on what has been developed in those earlier programs. For this graph, the **x** axis will be logrithmic, and the independent variable will be frequency. The **y** axis will be linear, representing the decibel response as a function of frequency.

The first step is to define the magnitude response function. We then define the display screen parameters and initialize the graphics mode. It is desirable to display an integer number of log cycles. Therefore, we will input the value of **x_min** and the number of log cycles (**nlc**) to be used. The value of **x_max** can be found from these two parameters. Since the **x** axis will be logarithmic, we need the log of the **x** limits to compute **dx**, the log increment per pixel.

The function is then digitized with the samples stored in arrays. The decibel response range for any given function is generally known. We can therefore enter the decibel lower and upper limits for the **y** axis directly. These will be assigned to **y_min** and **y_max**. The **y** increment per pixel can then be calculated.

At this point, the display screen is cleared, and graph generation begins. We start by drawing the **x** and **y** axes. The axes are then numbered and titled. The function is plotted and a logarithmic grid is added for accurate reading.

The second-level pseudocode is shown in Fig. 10.17. The magnitude response, **YM**, is defined as the magnitude of **f(z)**. The reason for using **z** in place of **x** as the independent variable will be explained later. **Y** is defined as the decibel value of **YM**. All the display screen parameters are defined just as they were for the linear function plots, with the exception of **GRIDX**. It is now defined as the number of grid dots per tenth of a log cycle along the **x** axis.

```
/* First-level pseudocode for logarithmic plot of magnitude response */

define magnitude response function
define display screen parameters
initialize graphics mode

input axis titles
input x_min and number of log cycles
find the log of the x limits
determine log increment per pixel, dx
digitize function and place samples in arrays
input y_min, y_max
determine y increment per pixel, dy

clear display screen
draw the axes
number the axes
plot the function
plot a log grid for accurate reading
```

Figure 10.16 First-level pseudocode for logarithmic plot of magnitude response.

The first module to be called from **main()** is **gmode()**. It will initialize the graphics mode. The next module, **get_titles()**, is identical to that used for the linear plot programs.

The module **get_xparm()** is used to determine the values of parameters for the logarithmic **x** axis. It receives **x_min** and **nlc** as inputs. **X_max** is then computed by **x_max = (10)^{nlc}x_min**. The logs of **x_min** and **x_max** are assigned to **xl_min** and **xl_max**. The value of **dx** is then found from **(xl_max − xl_min)/PX**. Notice that **dx** is the increment of the log of **x** per pixel. Instead of evaluating the function at each pixel position, we will choose a logarithmic increment, **x_incr**, at which to perform the evaluation. These sampled points will then be connected with short line segments. The value of **x_incr** is an input item.

The module **sample_f()** uses a **for** loop to control digitizing the function. The resulting samples are placed in arrays. The loop variable, **x**, is logarithmic and ranges from **xl_min** to **xl_max** in steps of **x_incr**. We transform **x** into its linear equivalent through **z = 10^{x}**. The value of **z** is plugged into **YM** to determine the magnitude of the function. **Y** then gives the decibel value of the magnitude. At each selected **x**, the value of **x** is placed in **xd[]** and **Y** is placed in **yd[]**.

Get_yparm() inputs **y_min** and **y_max**. These are selected to cover an even number of decades. The number of decades is assigned to **y_dec**, which is defined by **(y_max − y_min)/10**. The display will show the number of decades determined by **y_dec**.

At this point, the display screen is cleared by **clr()**, and graph generation begins. We have previously developed the pseudocode for drawing the log axis tick marks. It can be included here without description. Numbering and labeling the **x** axis are similar to our linear plotting programs. So, too, are the drawing, numbering, and labeling of the **y** axis.

To plot the function using line segments, the module **plot()** initializes **xb** and **yb** to the first sample value. Within a loop, it draws a line to the next sample value, whose coordinates are assigned to **xe,ye**. The value of **xe,ye** are then assigned to **xb,yb** before repeating the loop. Notice that the sample values are scaled and

```
/* Second-level pseudocode for logarithmic plot of magnitude response */

define YM         as magnitude of f(z)    /* function to be plotted */
define Y          as decibel value of YM

/* display screen parameters */
define GL         as graph left border
define GR         as graph right border
define GT         as graph top border
define GB         as graph bottom border
define TW         as the tick width for graph
define PX         as (GR - GL)
define PY         as (GB - GT)
define GRIDX      as the grid dots per tenth of a log cycle along x axis
define GRIDY      as the grid dots per decade along y axis

module main()
      gmode()                     /* initialize graphics mode */
      get_titles()                /* input axis titles */
      get_xparm()                 /* determine xl_min, xl_max, x_incr, dx */
      sample_f()                  /* sample function and place in arrays */
      get_yparm()                 /* find y_min, y_max, dy, y_dec */
      clr()                       /* clear the display screen */
      draw_axes()                 /* draw the axes */
      num_axes()                  /* number the axes */
      title()                     /* title the axes */
      plot()                      /* plot the function samples */
      grid()                      /* plot log grid */
end main()

module get_titles()
      print "Enter title for x axis"
      input x_name
      print "Enter title for y axis"
      input y_name
end get_titles()

module get_xparm()
      input x_min and nlc         /* get starting x and log cycles */
      x_max = x_min*10^nlc        /* compute x_max */
      xl_min = log10(x_min)       /* find the log of the x limits */
      xl_max = log10(x_max)
      dx = (xl_max - xl_min)/PX   /* find dx */
      print "Enter log step size for x"
      input x_incr
end get_xparm()

module sample_f()
      i = 0
      for (x from xl_min to xl_max, step x_incr)

            z = 10^x
            xd[i] = x
```

Figure 10.17 Second-level pseudocode for logarithmic plot of magnitude response.

```
            yd[i] = Y
            i = i + 1
        end for
        data points = i
end sample_f()

module get_yparm()
        print "Enter y_min and y_max"
        input y_min and y_max
        dy = (y_max - y_min)/PY              /* find dy */
        y_dec = (y_max - y_min)/10           /* y_dec is the number of y decades*/
end get_yparm()

module draw_axes()
        draw x axis line                     /* draw x axis and ticks */
        for (z from 1 to nlc)
            for (x from 2 to 10)
                xb = xe = (z-1)PX/nlc + log10(x)PX/nlc
                yb = GB - TW
                ye = GB
                line (xb,xe,yb,ye,c)
            end for
        end for
        draw y axis line                     /* draw y axis and ticks */
        for (each decade position)
            draw tick mark at width TW
        end for
end draw_axes()

module num_axes()
        for (each decade position)               /* number x axis */
            locate cursor below decade tick
            print x value
        end for
        for (each decade position)               /* number y axis */
            locate cursor left of decade tick
            print y value
        end for
end num_axes()

module title()
        print x_name centered on line 24
        for (i = 0 to i < length of y_name)      /* print y title in column 0 */
            locate(i,0)
            print char i of y_name
        end for
end title()

module plot()
        intialize xb and yb              /* plot function using line segments */
        for (each sample of function)
            ye = GB - integer value of scaled yd[]
            xe = integer value of scaled xd[]
```

Figure 10.17 (continued).

```
            line (xb,yb,xe,ye,C)
            xb = xe
            yb = ye
        end for
end plot()

module grid()                              /* add log grid for accurate reading */
        for (z from 1 to nlc)
            for (x from 1+1/GRIDX to 10, step 1/GRIDX)
                i = (z-1)PX/nlc + log10(x)*PX/nlc + GL
                for (y from 0 to PY in steps of PY/y_dec/GRIDY)
                    j = GB - y
                    pnt(i,j,C)
                end for
            end for
        end for
end grid()
```

Figure 10.17 (continued).

converted to integer form before plotting. Also, the **x** coordinate receives an offset of **GL** to plot relative to the graph left border. The **y** coordinate is subtracted from **GB** to remove the inversion and plot relative to the graph origin.

The code for adding a logarithmic grid combines the concepts presented for adding a linear grid with the pseudocode for drawing a logarithmic scale. We plot **GRIDX** points in the **x** direction for each tenth of a log cycle and **GRIDY** points per decade along the **y** direction. If the number of decades being displayed on the **y** axis is small, the grid can be plotted more densely by increasing the value of **GRIDY**.

The **C** program for logarithmic plot of magnitude response is given in Fig. 10.18. The output of this program is shown in Fig. 10.19. As with the linear plotting programs, we have made all the variables that directly relate to the data **external**. These include the arrays **xd[]** and **yd[]**, the minimum and maximum values **x_min**, **x_max**, **y_min**, **y_max**, **xl_min**, and **xl_max**, and the increments per pixel **dx** and **dy**.

The variables **x_name**, **y_name**, **x_incr**, **y_dec**, and **nlc** have all been declared in **main()**. Functions that assign values to these variables receive pointers to them. These include **get_titles**(x_name, y_name), **get_xparm**(&nlc, &x_incr), and **get_yparm**(&y_dec). The variables are passed by value to functions that need to know that information. These include **sample_f**(x_incr), **draw_axes**(nlc, y_dec), **num_axes**(nlc, y_dec), **title**(x_name, y_name), and **grid**(nlc, y_dec).

Phase Response

Converting the magnitude response plotting program for plotting phase response is very simple. This can be done by deleting the definition of **YM** and defining **Y** as the phase response equation. (The independent variable must be **z** for this equation.) The **y** axis will then represent linear angle response in degrees or radians. We have selected degrees here and included the definition of **PI** for conversion from radians to degrees.

```
/* log plot of magnitude response in high-resolution video graphics */

#include <stdio.h>
#include <math.h>
#define YM     (1.0/sqrt(1.0 + z*z)) /* low-pass magnitude response */
#define Y      20.0*log10(YM)        /* dB value */

#define C      3                   /* default color */
#define GL     80                  /* left border for graph */
#define GR     580                 /* right border for graph */
#define GT     12                  /* top border for graph */
#define GB     172                 /* bottom border for graph */
#define TW     3                   /* tick width */
#define PPCX   8                   /* pixels per character in x direction */
#define PPCY   8                   /* pixels per character in y direction */
#define PX     (GR-GL)             /* total pixels on x axis */
#define PY     (GB-GT)             /* total pixels on y axis */
#define GRIDX  1                   /* grid dots per tenth log cycle in x direction */
#define GRIDY  2                   /* grid dots per decade in y direction */

/* declare global variables */
double xd[PX], yd[PX];                /* sampled values placed in arrays */
int data_pts;                         /* number of samples */
double x_min, x_max, y_min, y_max;    /* x and y limits */
double xl_min, xl_max;                /* log of x limits */
double dx, dy;                        /* change in x or y per pixel */

main()
      {
      char x_name[50], y_name[50];
      double x_incr;                  /* log step size for x */
      double y_dec;                   /* number of decades for y axes */
      double nlc;                     /* number of log cycles for x axis */
      int i;
      void get_titles(), get_xparm(), get_yparm(), sample_f(), draw_axes();
      void num_axes(), title(), plot(), grid();

      gmode();
      get_titles(x_name, y_name);
      get_xparm(&nlc, &x_incr);
      sample_f(x_incr);
      get_yparm(&y_dec);
      clr();
      draw_axes(nlc, y_dec);
      num_axes(nlc, y_dec);
      title(x_name, y_name);
      plot();
      grid(nlc, y_dec);
      scanf("%d", &i);                /* wait for keypress before exit */
      clr();
      }

void get_titles(x_name, y_name)       /* get titles for axes */
char x_name[], y_name[];
      {
      puts("Enter title for x axis ");
      gets(x_name);
      puts("Enter title for y axis");
      gets(y_name);
      }
```

Figure 10.18 Logarithmic plot of magnitude response.

```
void get_xparm(pnlc, px_incr)       /* determine x axis parameters */
double *pnlc, *px_incr;
      {
      double x_dif;                 /* difference of limits */

      puts("Enter x_min and number of log cycles");
      scanf("%lf,%lf", &x_min, pnlc);
      x_max = x_min * pow(10.0, *pnlc);
      xl_min = log10(x_min);
      xl_max = log10(x_max);
      x_dif = (xl_max - xl_min);
      dx = x_dif/(double) PX;
      puts("Enter the log step size for x");
      scanf("%lf", px_incr);
      }

void sample_f(x_incr)    /* sample function and store in arrays xd[], yd[] */
double x_incr;
      {
      int i;
      double z, x;

      for (x = xl_min, i = 0; (x <= xl_max) && (i < PX); x += x_incr, i++)
            {
            z = pow(10.0, x);
            xd[i] = x;
            yd[i] = Y;
            }
      data_pts = i;
      }

void get_yparm(py_dec)              /* determine y_min, y_max, dy, and y_dec */
double *py_dec;
      {
      puts("Enter y_min and y_max");
      scanf("%lf,%lf", &y_min, &y_max);
      dy = (y_max - y_min)/PY;
      *py_dec = (y_max - y_min)/10.0;
      }

void draw_axes(nlc, y_dec)          /* draw x and y axes */
double nlc, y_dec;
      {
      double ctp;                   /* tick position within a log cycle */
      double x, z;
      int xb, xe, yb, ye;           /* line drawing arguments */

      /* draw x axis */
      line(GL, GB, GR, GB, C);
      /* draw x axis tick marks */
      for (z = 1.0; z <= (nlc + 0.1); z++)
            for (x = 2.0; x <= 10.0; x++)
                  {
                  ctp = log10(x)*PX/nlc;
                  xb = xe = (int)(ctp + (z - 1.0)*PX/nlc + GL);
                  yb = GB - TW;
                  ye = GB;
                  line(xb, yb, xe, ye, C);
                  }
      /* draw y axis */
      line(GL, GB, GL, GT, C);
      /* draw db tick marks */
      for (x = 0.0; x <= (y_dec + 0.1); x++)
```

Figure 10.18 (continued).

```
            {
            xb = GL;
            xe = GL + TW;
            yb = ye = GB - (int)(x*PY/y_dec);
            line(xb, yb, xe, ye, C);
            }
      }

void num_axes(nlc, y_dec)           /* number x and y axes */
double nlc, y_dec;
      {
      int yi, i;

      locate(23, 0);
      for (i = 0; i <= (int) (nlc + 0.1); i++)
            {
            locate(23, PX/PPCX/(int)(nlc + 0.5)*i + GL/PPCX - 3);
            printf("%8.3f", x_min*pow(10.0, (double)i));
            }
      /* number y axis */
      for (i = 0; i <= (int)(y_dec + 0.5); i++)
            {
            locate(GB/PPCY - i*PY/PPCY/(int)(y_dec + 0.5), 2);
            yi = (y_min < 0.0) ? (int)(y_min - 0.5) : (int)(y_min + 0.5);
            printf("%4d", yi + 10*i);
            }
      }

void title(x_name, y_name)          /* title x and y axes */
char x_name[], y_name[];
      {
      int i;

      /* title x axis */
      locate(24, 30);
      printf("%s", x_name);

      /* title y axis */
      for (i = 0; i < strlen(y_name); i++)
            {
            locate(i, 0);
            putchar(y_name[i]);
            }
      }

void plot()                         /* plot the function */
      {
      int xb, yb, xe, ye;           /* line arguments */
      int i;


      yb = GB - (int) ((yd[0] - y_min) / dy + 0.5);
      xb = (int) ((xd[0] - xl_min) / dx + 0.5) + GL;

      for (i = 1; i < data_pts; i++)
            {
            ye = GB - (int)((yd[i] - y_min)/dy + 0.5);
            xe = (int)((xd[i] - xl_min)/dx + 0.5) + GL;
            line(xb, yb, xe, ye, C);
            xb = xe;
            yb = ye;
            }
      }
```

Figure 10.18 (continued).

```
void grid(nlc, y_dec)                    /* add grid for easy reading */
double nlc, y_dec;
      {
      double x, y, z;
      double ctp;
      int i, j;

      for (z = 1.0; z <= (nlc + 0.1); z++)
            for (x = 1.0 + 1.0/GRIDX; x <= 10.0; x += 1.0/GRIDX)
                  {
                  ctp = log10(x)*PX/nlc;
                  i = (int)(ctp + (z - 1.0)*PX/nlc + GL);
                  for (y = 0; y <= PY; y += PY/y_dec/GRIDY)
                        {
                        j = GB - (int)y;
                        pnt(i, j, C);
                        }
                  }
      }
```

```
Enter title for x axis
Log frequency in Hz
Enter title for y axis
Response in dB
Enter x_min and number of log cycles
0.1, 4
Enter the log step size for x
0.1
Enter y_min and y_max
-60, 0
```

Figure 10.18 (continued).

These changes have been incorporated into the program of Fig. 10.20. The equation being plotted is the phase response of the low-pass filter whose magnitude response was plotted earlier. Figure 10.21 shows the output of this program.

10.6 LOGARITHMIC DATA PLOTS

We can convert the logarithmic function plotting program into one that plots experimental data with very few changes. In fact, we will not need to write any pseudocode for the conversion. The conversion involves the following steps:

1. Delete the function definition (**#define Y**) from the top of the listing.
2. Delete the module that digitizes the function **sample_f()** and also the variable **x_incr**.
3. Convert the declaration of the arrays **xd[]** and **yd[]** to **static double** and initialize them with the data to be plotted. Set **data_pts** equal to the number of data points in the arrays.
4. Use **log10(xd[i])** in place of **xd[i]** in the plotting routine.
5. Optionally, you can convert the drawing of line segments connecting the data points to the plotting of a symbol such as a square, cross, or triangle at each data point.

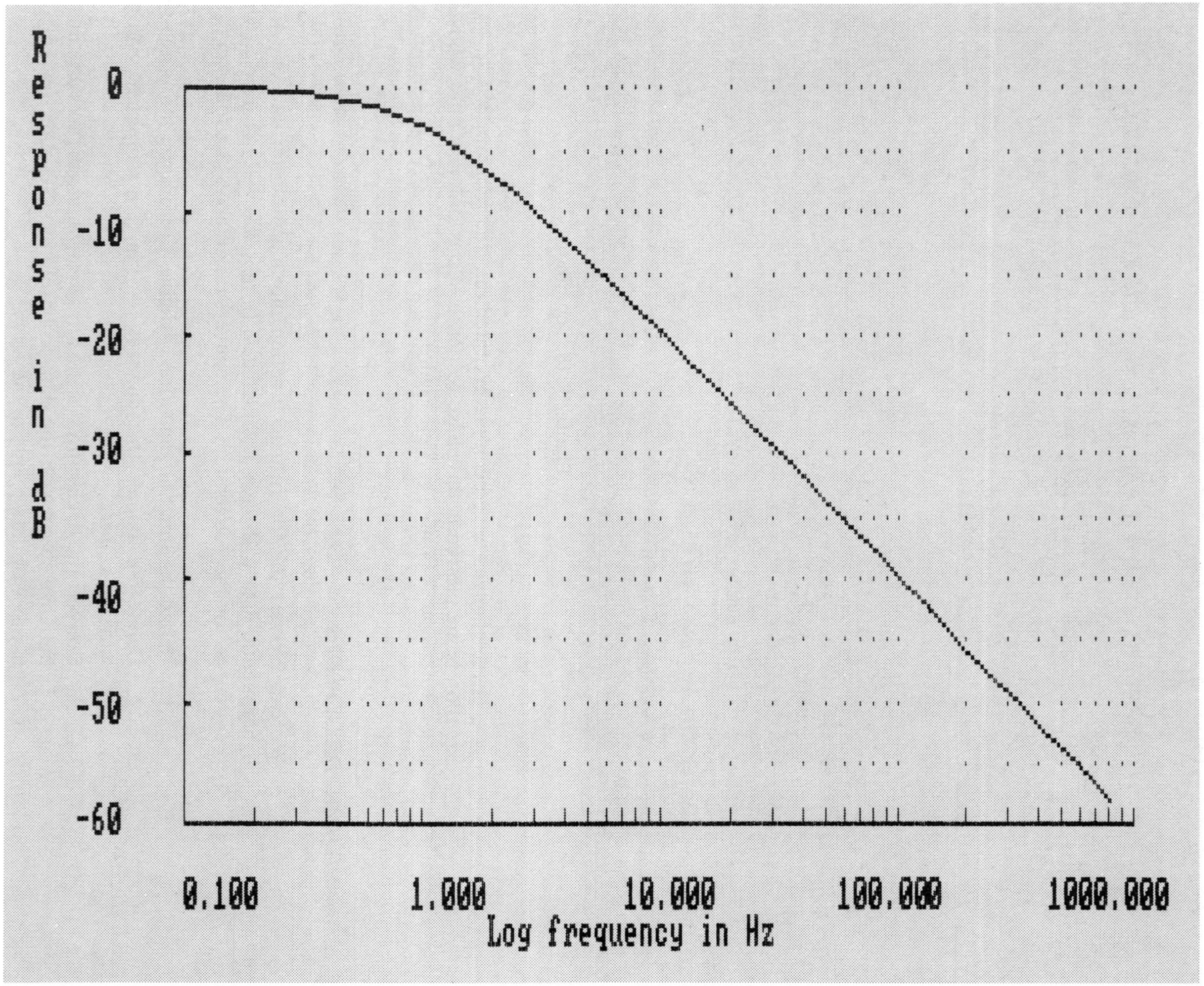

Figure 10.19 Log magnitude response program output.

```
/* log plot of phase response in high-resolution video graphics */

#include <stdio.h>
#include <math.h>
#define Y      (-90.0 + atan(1.0/z)*180.0/PI)    /* low-pass phase response */

#define C      3                /* default color */
#define GL     80               /* left border for graph */
#define GR     580              /* right border for graph */
#define GT     12               /* top border for graph */
#define GB     172              /* bottom border for graph */
#define TW     3                /* tick width */
#define PPCX   8                /* pixels per character in x direction */
#define PPCY   8                /* pixels per character in y direction */
#define PX     (GR-GL)          /* total pixels on x axis */
#define PY     (GB-GT)          /* total pixels on y axis */
#define GRIDX  1                /* grid dots per tenth log cycle in x direction */
#define GRIDY  2                /* grid dots per decade in y direction */
#define PI     3.14159265       /* value of pi */

/* declare global variables */
double xd[PX], yd[PX];                      /* sampled values placed in arrays */
int data_pts;                               /* number of samples */
double x_min, x_max, y_min, y_max;          /* x and y limits */
double xl_min, xl_max;                      /* log of x limits */
double dx, dy;                              /* change in x or y per pixel */

main()
      {
      char x_name[50], y_name[50];
      double x_incr;                        /* log step size for x */
      double y_dec;                         /* number of decades for y axes */
      double nlc;                           /* number of log cycles for x axis */
      int i;
      void get_titles(), get_xparm(), get_yparm(), sample_f(), draw_axes();
      void num_axes(), title(), plot(), grid();

      gmode();
      get_titles(x_name, y_name);
      get_xparm(&nlc, &x_incr);
      sample_f(x_incr);
      get_yparm(&y_dec);
      clr();
      draw_axes(nlc, y_dec);
      num_axes(nlc, y_dec);
      title(x_name, y_name);
      plot();
      grid(nlc, y_dec);
      scanf("%d", &i);                      /* wait for keypress before exit */
      clr();
      }

void get_titles(x_name, y_name)             /* get titles for axes */
char x_name[], y_name[];
      {
      puts("Enter title for x axis ");
      gets(x_name);
      puts("Enter title for y axis");
      gets(y_name);
      }
```

Figure 10.20 Logarithmic plot of phase response.

```
int get_xparm(pnlc, px_incr)              /* determine x axis parameters */
double *pnlc, *px_incr;
      {
      double x_dif;                       /* difference of limits */

      puts("Enter x_min and number of log cycles");
      scanf("%lf,%lf", &x_min, pnlc);
      x_max = x_min * pow(10.0, *pnlc);
      xl_min = log10(x_min);
      xl_max = log10(x_max);
      x_dif = (xl_max - xl_min);
      dx = x_dif/(double) PX;
      puts("Enter the log step size for x");
      scanf("%lf", px_incr);
      }

void sample_f(x_incr)   /* sample function and store in arrays xd[], yd[] */
double x_incr;
      {
      int i;
      double z, x;

      for (x = xl_min, i = 0; (x <= xl_max) && (i < PX); x += x_incr, i++)
            {
            z = pow(10.0, x);
            xd[i] = x;
            yd[i] = Y;
            }
      data_pts = i;
      }

void get_yparm(py_dec)              /* determine y_min, y_max, dy, and y_dec */
double *py_dec;
      {
      puts("Enter y_min and y_max");
      scanf("%lf,%lf", &y_min, &y_max);
      dy = (y_max - y_min)/PY;
      *py_dec = (y_max - y_min)/10.0;
      }

void draw_axes(nlc, y_dec)          /* draw x and y axes */
double nlc, y_dec;
      {
      double ctp;                   /* tick position within a log cycle */
      double x, z;
      int xb, xe, yb, ye;           /* line drawing arguments */

      /* draw x axis */
      line(GL, GB, GR, GB, C);
      /* draw x axis tick marks */
      for (z = 1.0; z <= (nlc + 0.1); z++)
            for (x = 2.0; x <= 10.0; x++)
                  {
                  ctp = log10(x)*PX/nlc;
                  xb = xe = (int)(ctp + (z - 1.0)*PX/nlc + GL);
                  yb = GB - TW;
                  ye = GB;
                  line(xb, yb, xe, ye, C);
                  }
      /* draw y axis */
      line(GL, GB, GL, GT, C);
      /* draw dB tick marks */
      for (x = 0.0; x <= (y_dec + 0.1); x++)
            {
```

Figure 10.20 (continued).

```
          xb = GL;
          xe = GL + TW;
          yb = ye = GB - (int)(x*PY/y_dec);
          line(xb, yb, xe, ye, C);
          }
     }

void num_axes(nlc, y_dec)           /* number x and y axes */
double nlc, y_dec;
     {
     int yi, i;

     locate(23, 0);
     for (i = 0; i <= (int)nlc + 0.1); i += 3)
          {
          locate(23, PX/PPCX/(int)(nlc + 0.5)*i + GL/PPCX - 3);
          printf("%8.3f", x_min*pow(10.0, (double)i));
          }
     /* number y axis */
     for (i = 0; i <= (int)(y_dec + 0.5); i += 3)
          {
          locate(GB/PPCY - i*PY/PPCY/(int)(y_dec + 0.5), 2);
          yi = (y_min < 0.0) ? (int)(y_min - 0.5) : (int)(y_min + 0.5);
          printf("%4d", yi + 10*i);
          }
     }

void title(x_name, y_name)          /* title x and y axes */
char x_name[], y_name[];
     {
     int i;

     /* title x axis */
     locate(24, 30);
     printf("%s", x_name);
     /* title y axis */
     for (i = 0; i < strlen(y_name); i++)
          {
          locate(i, 0);
          putchar(y_name[i]);
          }
     }

void plot()                         /* plot the function */
     {
     int xb, yb, xe, ye;            /* line arguments */
     int i;


     yb = GB - (int)((yd[0] - y_min)/dy + 0.5);
     xb = (int)((xd[0] - xl_min)/dx + 0.5) + GL;

     for (i = 1; i < data_pts; i++)
          {
          ye = GB - (int)((yd[i] - y_min)/dy + 0.5);
          xe = (int)((xd[i] - xl_min)/dx + 0.5) + GL;
          line(xb, yb, xe, ye, C);
          xb = xe;
          yb = ye;
          }
     }
```

Figure 10.20 (continued).

```
void grid(nlc, y_dec)                /* add grid for easy reading */
double nlc, y_dec;
      {
      double x, y, z;
      double ctp;
      int i, j;

      for (z = 1.0; z <= (nlc + 0.1); z++)
            for (x = 1.0 + 1.0/GRIDX; x <= 10.0; x += 1.0/GRIDX)
                  {
                  ctp = log10(x)*PX/nlc;
                  i = (int)(ctp + (z - 1.0)*PX/nlc + GL);
                  for (y = 0; y <= PY; y += PY/y_dec/GRIDY)
                        {
                        j = GB - (int)y;
                        pnt(i, j, C);
                        }
                  }
      }
```

```
Enter title for x axis
Log frequency in Hz
Enter title for y axis
Phase response in degrees
```

```
Enter x_min and number of log cycles
0.01, 4
Enter the log step size for x
0.1
Enter y_min and y_max
-90, 0
```

Figure 10.20 (continued).

Figure 10.22 lists a version of the data-plotting program that connects the data points with line segments. The output of this program is shown in Fig. 10.23. The plotting routine in Fig. 10.24 converts the program into one that plots an **X** symbol at each data point. The output of the program using this routine is shown in Fig. 10.25.

10.7 MORE GRAPHICS PRIMITIVES

Thus far we have looked at graphics primitives for points and straight lines. As you see from the previous sections, it is possible to generate very useful professional graphics using only these primitives. Another fundamental primitive whose development is somewhat similar to Breshenham's algorithm is one that generates fast circles. It can be extended to do ellipses and arcs as well.

Circles

Decision variables were used to generate straight lines in Section 10.2. We can utilize the same concept here to generate circles. The equation of a circle centered at the origin is

$$x^2 + y^2 = r^2$$

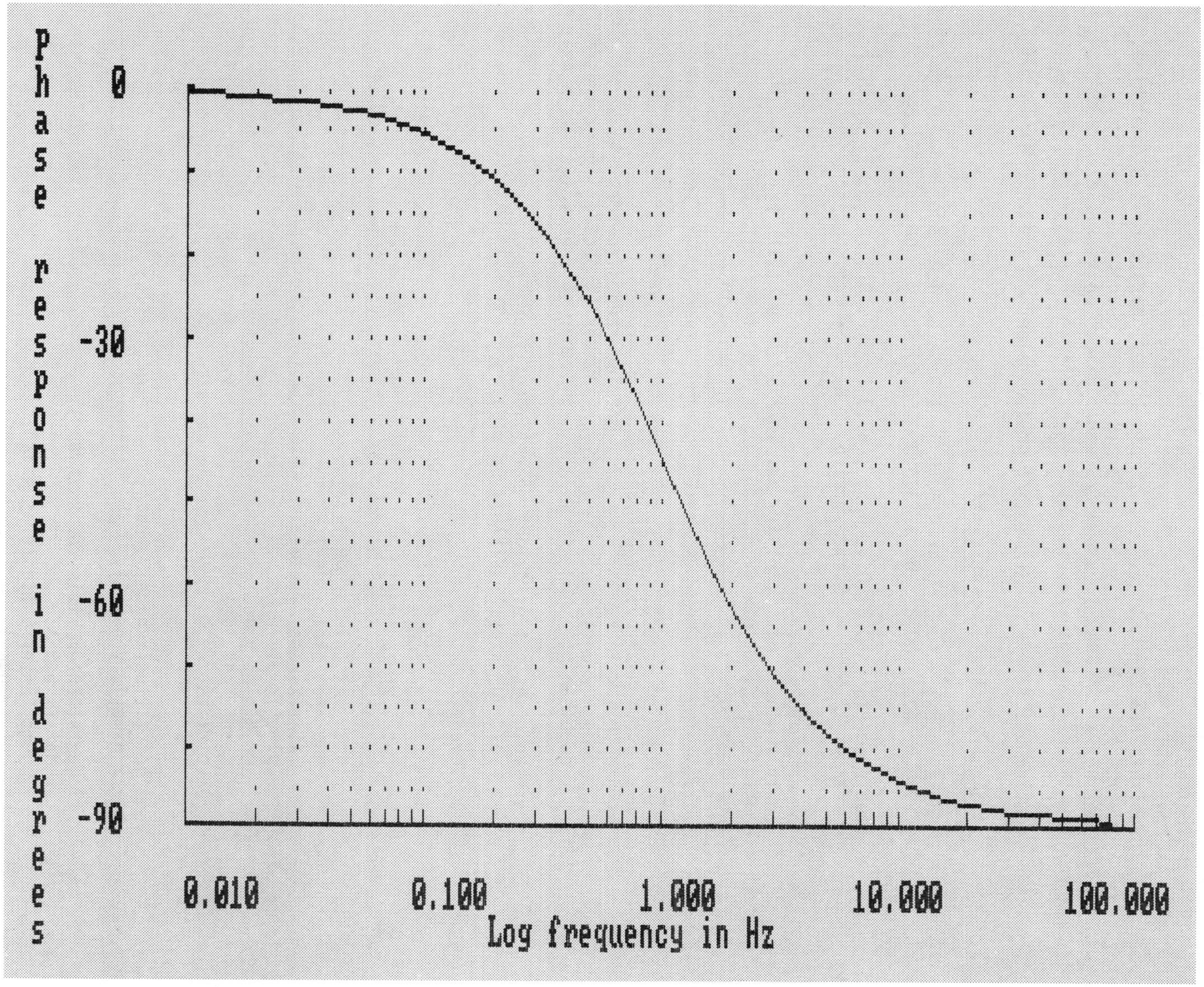

Figure 10.21 Log phase response program output.

```
/* log plot of data in high-resolution video graphics */

#include <stdio.h>
#include <math.h>
#define C     3               /* default color */
#define GL    80              /* left border for graph */
#define GR    580             /* right border for graph */
#define GT    12              /* top border for graph */
#define GB    172             /* bottom border for graph */
#define TW    3               /* tick width */
#define PPCX  8               /* pixels per character in x direction */
#define PPCY  8               /* pixels per character in y direction */
#define PX    (GR-GL)         /* total pixels on x axis */
#define PY    (GB-GT)         /* total pixels on y axis */
#define GRIDX 1               /* grid dots per tenth log cycle in x direction */
#define GRIDY 5               /* grid dots per decade in y direction */

/* declare global variables */

double xd[PX] = {0.2, 0.4, 0.6, 0.8, 1.0, 2.0, 4.0, 6.0, 8.0, 10.0, 20.0,
    40.0, 60.0, 80.0, 100.0, 200.0, 400.0, 600.0, 800.0, 1000.0};

double yd[PY] = {0.0, 0.4, 0.9, 1.6, 3.1, 5.0, 8.4, 11.6, 13.3, 13.1, 13.0,
    13.2, 11.6, 8.4, 5.1, 3.2, 1.5, 0.8, 0.5, 0.3, 0.2};

int data_pts = 20;
double x_min, x_max, y_min, y_max;  /* x and y limits */
double xl_min, xl_max;              /* log of x limits */
double dx, dy;                      /* change in x or y per pixel */

main()
      {
      char x_name[50], y_name[50];
      double x_incr;                /* log step size for x */
      double y_dec;                 /* number of decades for y axes */
      double nlc;                   /* number of log cycles for x axis */
      int i;
      void get_titles(), get_xparm(), get_yparm(), draw_axes();
      void num_axes(), title(), plot(), grid();

      gmode();
      get_titles(x_name, y_name);
      get_xparm(&nlc);
      get_yparm(&y_dec);
      clr();
      draw_axes(nlc, y_dec);
      num_axes(nlc, y_dec);
      title(x_name, y_name);
      plot();
      grid(nlc, y_dec);
      scanf("%d", &i);              /* wait for keypress before exit */
      clr();
      }

void get_titles(x_name, y_name)     /* get titles for axes */
char x_name[], y_name[];
      {
      puts("Enter title for x axis ");
      gets(x_name);
      puts("Enter title for y axis");
      gets(y_name);
      }

int get_xparm(pnlc)                 /* determine x axis parameters */
double *pnlc;
      {
      double x_dif;                 /* difference of limits */
```

Figure 10.22 Log data plot program using line segments.

```
	puts("Enter x_min and number of log cycles");
	scanf("%lf,%lf", &x_min, pnlc);
	x_max = x_min*pow(10.0, *pnlc);
	xl_min = log10(x_min);
	xl_max = log10(x_max);
	x_dif = (xl_max - xl_min);
	dx = x_dif/(double)PX;
	}

void get_yparm(py_dec)             /* determine y_min, y_max, dy, and y_dec */
double *py_dec;
	{
	puts("Enter y_min and y_max");
	scanf("%lf,%lf", &y_min, &y_max);
	dy = (y_max - y_min)/PY;
	*py_dec = (y_max - y_min)/10.0;
	}

void draw_axes(nlc, y_dec)         /* draw x and y axes */
double nlc, y_dec;
	{
	double ctp;                /* tick position within a log cycle */
	double x, z;
	int xb, xe, yb, ye;        /* line drawing arguments */

	/* draw x axis */
	line(GL, GB, GR, GB, C);
	/* draw x axis tick marks */
	for (z = 1.0; z <= (nlc + 0.1); z++)
		for (x = 2.0; x <= 10.0; x++)
			{
			ctp = log10(x)*PX/nlc;
			xb = xe = (int)(ctp + (z - 1.0)*PX/nlc + GL);
			yb = GB - TW;
			ye = GB;

			line(xb, yb, xe, ye, C);
			}
	/* draw y axis */
	line(GL, GB, GL, GT, C);
	/* draw dB tick marks */
	for (x = 0.0; x <= (y_dec + 0.1); x++)
		{
		xb = GL;
		xe = GL + TW;
		yb = ye = GB - (int)(x*PY/y_dec);
		line(xb, yb, xe, ye, C);
		}
	}

void num_axes(nlc, y_dec)          /* number x and y axes */
double nlc, y_dec;
	{
	int yi, i;

	locate(23, 0);
	for (i = 0; i <= (int)(nlc + 0.1); i++)
		{
		locate(23, PX/PPCX/(int)(nlc + 0.5)*i + GL/PPCX - 3);
		printf("%8.3f", x_min*pow(10.0, (double)i));
		}
	/* number y axis */
	for (i = 0; i <= (int)(y_dec + 0.5); i++)
		{
		locate(GB/PPCY - i*PY/PPCY/(int)(y_dec + 0.5), 2);
		yi = (y_min < 0.0) ? (int)(y_min - 0.5) : (int)(y_min + 0.5);
		printf("%4d", yi + 10*i);
		}
	}
```

Figure 10.22 (continued).

```
void title(x_name, y_name)          /* title x and y axes */
char x_name[], y_name[];
    {
    int i;

    /* title x axis */
    locate(24, 30);
    printf("%s", x_name);

    /* title y axis */
    for (i = 0; i < strlen(y_name); i++)
        {
        locate(i, 0);
        putchar(y_name[i]);
        }
    }

void plot()                         /* plot the function */
    {
    int xb, yb, xe, ye;             /* line arguments */
    int i;
    yb = GB - (int)((yd[0] - y_min)/dy + 0.5);
    xb = (int)((log10(xd[0]) - xl_min)/dx + 0.5) + GL;

    for (i = 1; i < data_pts; i++)
        {
        ye = GB - (int)((yd[i] - y_min)/dy + 0.5);
        xe = (int)((log10(xd[i]) - xl_min)/dx + 0.5) + GL;
        line(xb, yb, xe, ye, C);
        xb = xe;
        yb = ye;
        }
    }

void grid(nlc, y_dec)               /* add grid for easy reading */
double nlc, y_dec;
    {
    double x, y, z;
    double ctp;
    int i, j;

    for (z = 1.0; z <= (nlc + 0.1); z++)
        for (x = 1.0 + 1.0/GRIDX; x <= 10.0; x += 1.0/GRIDX)
            {
            ctp = log10(x)*PX/nlc;
            i = (int)(ctp + (z - 1.0)*PX/nlc + GL);
            for (y = 0; y <= PY; y += PY/y_dec/GRIDY)
                {
                j = GB - (int)y;
                pnt(i, j, C);
                }
            }
    }
```

```
Enter title for x axis
Frequency in Hz
Enter title for y axis
Output voltage in volts
Enter x_min and number of log cycles
0.1, 4
Enter y_min and y_max
0, 20
```

Figure 10.22 (continued).

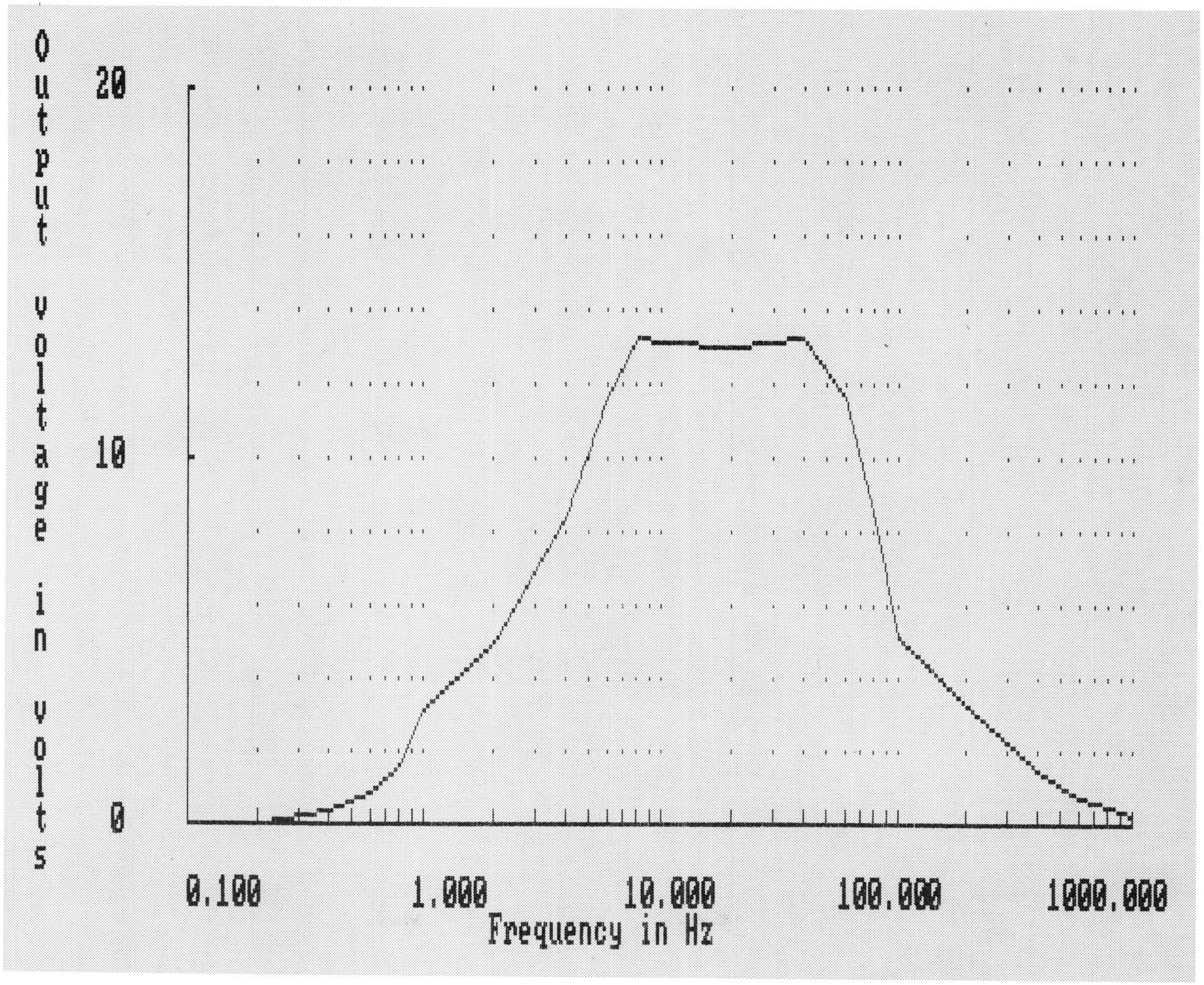

Figure 10.23 Log data plot output using line segments.

```
/* log plot of data in high-resolution video graphics */
/* using 'x' as the plot symbol */

#include <stdio.h>
#include <math.h>
#define C      3                /* default color */
#define GL     80               /* left border for graph */
#define GR     580              /* right border for graph */
#define GT     12               /* top border for graph */
#define GB     172              /* bottom border for graph */
#define TW     3                /* tick width */
#define PPCX   8                /* pixels per character in x direction */
#define PPCY   8                /* pixels per character in y direction */
#define PX     (GR-GL)          /* total pixels on x axis */
#define PY     (GB-GT)          /* total pixels on y axis */
#define GRIDX  1                /* grid dots per tenth log cycle in x direction */
#define GRIDY  5                /* grid dots per decade in y direction */

/* declare global variables */

double xd[PX] = {0.2, 0.4, 0.6, 0.8, 1.0, 2.0, 4.0, 6.0, 8.0, 10.0, 20.0,
    40.0, 60.0, 80.0, 100.0, 200.0, 400.0, 600.0, 800.0, 1000.0};

double yd[PY] = {0.0, 0.4, 0.9, 1.6, 3.1, 5.0, 8.4, 11.6, 13.3, 13.1, 13.0,
    13.2, 11.6, 8.4, 5.1, 3.2, 1.5, 0.8, 0.5, 0.3, 0.2};

int data_pts = 20;
double x_min, x_max, y_min, y_max;  /* x and y limits */
double xl_min, xl_max;              /* log of x limits */
double dx, dy;                      /* change in x or y per pixel */

main()
      {
      char x_name[50], y_name[50];
      double x_incr;                /* log step size for x */
      double y_dec;                 /* number of decades for y axes */
      double nlc;                   /* number of log cycles for x axis */
      int i;

      gmode();
      get_titles(x_name, y_name);
      get_xparm(&nlc);
      get_yparm(&y_dec);
      clr();
      draw_axes(nlc, y_dec);
      num_axes(nlc, y_dec);
      title(x_name, y_name);
      plot();
      grid(nlc, y_dec);
      scanf("%d", &i);              /* wait for keypress before exit */
      clr();
      }

void get_titles(x_name, y_name)     /* get titles for axes */
char x_name[], y_name[];
      {
      puts("Enter title for x axis ");
      gets(x_name);
      puts("Enter title for y axis");
      gets(y_name);
      }

int get_xparm(pnlc)                 /* determine x axis parameters */
double *pnlc;
      {
      double x_dif;                 /* difference of limits */
```

Figure 10.24 Log data-plotting routine using **X** as the data point symbol.

```
        puts("Enter x_min and number of log cycles");
        scanf("%lf,%lf", &x_min, pnlc);
        x_max = x_min*pow(10.0, *pnlc);
        xl_min = log10(x_min);
        xl_max = log10(x_max);
        x_dif = (xl_max - xl_min);
        dx = x_dif/(double)PX;
        }

void get_yparm(py_dec)              /* determine y_min, y_max, dy, and y_dec */
double *py_dec;
        {
        puts("Enter y_min and y_max");
        scanf("%lf,%lf", &y_min, &y_max);
        dy = (y_max - y_min)/PY;
        *py_dec = (y_max - y_min)/10.0;
        }

void draw_axes(nlc, y_dec)          /* draw x and y axes */
double nlc, y_dec;
        {
        double ctp;                 /* tick position within a log cycle */
        double x, z;
        int xb, xe, yb, ye;         /* line drawing arguments */

        /* draw x axis */
        line(GL, GB, GR, GB, C);
        /* draw x axis tick marks */
        for (z = 1.0; z <= (nlc + 0.1); z++)
                for (x = 2.0; x <= 10.0; x++)
                        {
                        ctp = log10(x)*PX/nlc;
                        xb = xe = (int)(ctp + (z - 1.0)*PX/nlc + GL);
                        yb = GB - TW;
                        ye = GB;

                        line(xb, yb, xe, ye, C);
                        }
        /* draw y axis */
        line(GL, GB, GL, GT, C);
        /* draw db tick marks */
        for (x = 0.0; x <= (y_dec + 0.1); x++)
                {
                xb = GL;
                xe = GL + TW;
                yb = ye = GB - (int)(x*PY/y_dec);
                line(xb, yb, xe, ye, C);
                }
        }

void num_axes(nlc, y_dec)           /* number x and y axes */
double nlc, y_dec;
        {
        int yi, i;

        locate(23, 0);
        for (i = 0; i <= (int)(nlc + 0.1); i++)
                {
                locate(23, PX/PPCX/(int)(nlc + 0.5)*i + GL/PPCX - 3);
                printf("%8.3f", x_min*pow(10.0, (double)i));
                }
        /* number y axis */
        for (i = 0; i <= (int)(y_dec + 0.5); i++)
                {
                locate(GB/PPCY - i*PY/PPCY/(int)(y_dec + 0.5), 2);
                yi = (y_min < 0.0) ? (int)(y_min - 0.5) : (int)(y_min + 0.5);
                printf("%4d", yi + 10*i);
                }
        }
```

Figure 10.24 (continued).

```
void title(x_name, y_name)          /* title x and y axes */
char x_name[], y_name[];
      {
      int i;

      /* title x axis */
      locate(24, 30);
      printf("%s", x_name);

      /* title y axis */
      for (i = 0; i < strlen(y_name); i++)
            {
            locate(i, 0);
            putchar(y_name[i]);
            }
      }

void plot()                         /* plot the function */
      {
      int xb, yb, xe, ye;           /* line arguments */
      int i;
      for (i = 0; i < data_pts; i++)
            {
            yb = GB - (int)((yd[i] - y_min)/dy + 0.5);
            xb = (int)((log10(xd[i]) - xl_min)/dx + 0.5) + GL;
            line(xb - TW, yb + TW, xb + TW, yb - TW, C);
            line(xb + TW, yb + TW, xb - TW, yb - TW, C);
            }
      }

void grid(nlc, y_dec)               /* add grid for easy reading */
double nlc, y_dec;
      {
      double x, y, z;
      double ctp;
      int i, j;

      for (z = 1.0; z <= (nlc + 0.1); z++)
            for (x = 1.0 + 1.0/GRIDX; x <= 10.0; x += 1.0/GRIDX)
                  {
                  ctp = log10(x)*PX/nlc;
                  i = (int)(ctp + (z - 1.0)*PX/nlc + GL);
                  for (y = 0; y <= PY; y += PY/y_dec/GRIDY)
                        {
                        j = GB - (int)y;
                        pnt(i, j, C);
                        }
                  }
      }
```

```
Enter title for x axis
Frequency in Hz
Enter title for y axis
Output voltage in volts
Enter x_min and number of log cycles
0.1, 4
Enter y_min and y_max
0, 20
```

Figure 10.24 (continued).

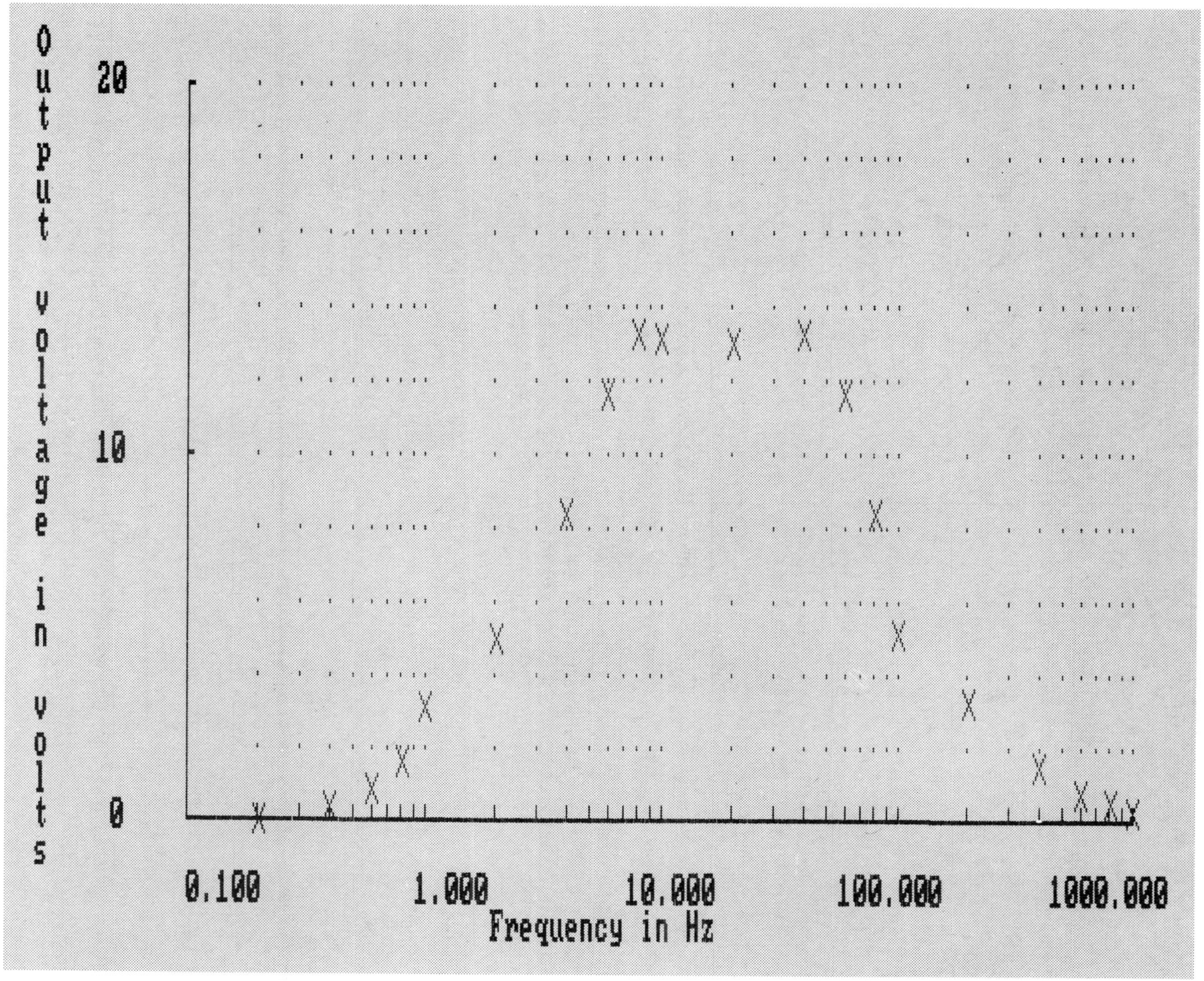

Figure 10.25 Log data plot output using **X** as the plotting symbol.

where **r** is the radius of the circle. Using decision variables, we will set pixels along a circle octant as shown in Fig. 10.26. The value of **y** will be incremented in unit pixel steps from **0** to a point where **y** = **x**. The only possible choices for **x** over this range are that it will remain the same or be decremented by 1.

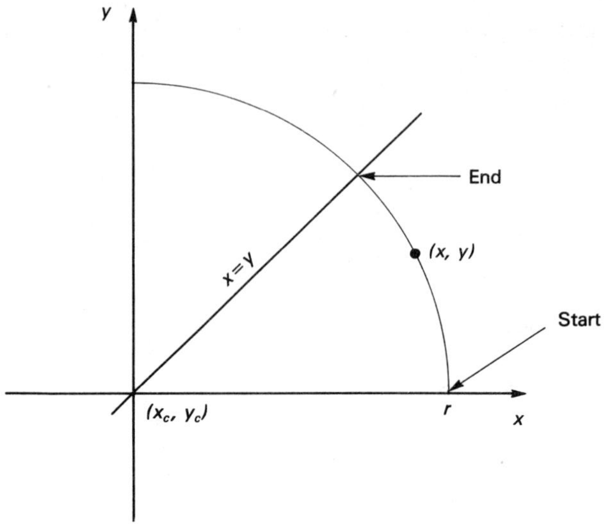

Figure 10.26 Setting pixels on a circle octant.

Whether or not **x** will be decremented when **y** is incremented will be based on an error term, which will be our decision variable. The circle equation including the error term is written as

$$\mathbf{x^2 + y^2 - r^2 = error}$$

If **y** is incremented by **1** without decrementing **x**, the error term increases in proportion to the square of the change in **y**. We would like to avoid any multiplication in computing the error term. To do this, we make use of a property associated with the square of integer numbers, which is illustrated in Fig. 10.27.

y	y^2	*First difference*	*Second difference*
0	0	—	—
1	1	1	—
2	4	3	2
3	9	5	2
4	16	7	2

Figure 10.27 First and second differences for squared integers.

The first difference in the value of $\mathbf{y^2}$ for any value of **y** is given by **2y − 1**. Thus, when **y** = **3**, the first difference is **2(3) − 1** or **5**. This says that when **y** goes from **2** to **3** its square will increase by **5**, from **4** to **9**. Also, the second difference is always equal to **2**. In other words, the change in the first difference is a constant. Thus, the first difference always increases by **2** from **1** to **3** to **5**, and so on.

When **y** is incremented to **1**, the first difference, which we will call **sqry_incr**, can be initialized to **1**. Thus the value of $\mathbf{y^2}$ increases from **0** to **1**. When **y** is incremented to **2**, we simply add **2** to **sqry_incr**, which makes it **3**. The value of $\mathbf{y^2}$ then goes from **1** to **1 + 3** or **4**. Adding **2** to the value of **sqry_incr** will always give us the change in the value of $\mathbf{y^2}$ as **y** is incremented by **1**. We will use this property to adjust the error term for each increment of **y**. The same procedure will be used to compute the value of $\mathbf{x}^2$ when **x** is decremented by 1 and to adjust the error term accordingly.

Our circle-drawing procedure will compute the **(x,y)** coordinates for pixels on the arc from 0 to 45 degrees, as shown in Fig. 10.26. To complete the circle, we will make use of the symmetry about the **x** and **y** axes, as well as the symmetry about the 45 degree line. For any given **(x,y)** coordinate pair, one pixel can be set in each of the eight circle octants. Setting eight pixels per computed coordinate pair speeds up the procedure considerably. The pseudocode for drawing circles is shown in Fig. 10.28.

```
/* Pseudocode for drawing circles */
module circle(xc,yc,r,c)
      x = r
      y = 0
      sqrx_incr = 2*r-1
      sqry_incr = 1
      error = 0
      while (y < = x)
            set pixels in each octant as defined by (x,y)
            y = y + 1
            error = error + sqry_incr
            sqry_incr = sqry_incr + 2
            if (error > r)
                  x = x -1
                  error = error - sqrx_incr
                  sqrx_incr = sqrx_incr - 2
            end if
      end while
end circle()
```

Figure 10.28 Pseudocode for drawing a circle.

The arguments **xc** and **yc** identify the coordinates of the center of the circle. The radius of the circle is given by **r**, and the color to be used for drawing is **c**. The variables **x** and **y** within the module are distances relative to **xc** and **yc**. Thus **x** is initialized to **r** and **y** to **0**. **sqrx_incr** is initialized to **2r−1** and **sqry_incr** to **1** in accordance with our previous analysis.

The **error** term is initialized to **0**. The **while** loop continues while **(y <= x)** is true. This specifies a **0** to **45** degree range for the loop. Pixels are set in each of the eight octants defined by the **(x,y)** coordinate pair (for **xc,yc** and radius **r**). The **y** variable is then incremented by **1** and **sqry_incr** is added to **error**. The value of **sqry_incr** is increased by **2**.

The decision as to whether or not **x** should be decremented is based on comparing **error** to **r**. If **error** > **r**, then **x** will be decremented. Comparing the decision variable **error** to **r** keeps the actual error within a half of one pixel. If **x** is decremented, **error** will be reduced by **sqrx_incr**. The value of **sqrx_incr** will then be decremented by **2**. A **circle()** function implementing our pseudocode is shown in Fig. 10.29.

Arcs

The **circle()** function just presented could be extended to draw arcs as well, with an added degree of complexity. We will consider a simpler, although considerably slower, procedure for generating arcs. It is based on dividing the arc into equal

```
/* a fast circle-drawing function */
void circle(xc, yc, r, c)
int xc, yc, r, c;
      {
      int x, y, error, sqrx_incr, sqry_incr;

      x = r;
      y = 0;
      sqrx_incr = 2*r - 1;
      sqry_incr = 1;
      error = 0;
      while (y <= x)
            {
            pnt(x + xc, y + yc, c);
            pnt(y + xc, x + yc, c);
            pnt(-y + xc, x + yc, c);
            pnt(-x + xc, y + yc, c);
            pnt(-x + xc, -y + yc, c);
            pnt(-y + xc, -x + yc, c);
            pnt(y + xc, -x + yc, c);
            pnt(x + xc, -y + yc, c);
            y += 1;
            error += sqry_incr;
            sqry_incr += 2;
            if (error > r)
                  {
                  x -= 1;
                  error -= sqrx_incr;
                  sqrx_incr -= 2;
                  }
            }
      }
```

Figure 10.29 Circle function.

small segments and connecting them with straight lines. If the segments are small enough, they will appear to form a smooth arc.

The procedure will be relatively slow, since it uses calls to the **sin()** and **cos()** functions and performs floating-point multiplication. However, it is very simple and can be extended to draw ellipses with little effort.

The arguments passed to the module will include the coordinates of the center of the arc, **(xc,yc)**, its radius, **r**, the starting and ending angles for the arc, **a1** and **a1**, and the color of the arc, **c**. The starting point on the arc is identified by

```
x1 = rcos(rad) + xc
y1 = rsin(rad) + yc
```

where **rad** equals **a1*PI/180**. We divide the arc into equal small segments defined by a small increment in angle, which we will call **A_STEP**. Thus the end point of the first line segment is given by

```
x2 = rcos(rad) + xc
y2 = rsin(rad) + yc
```

where **rad** equals **(a1 + A_STEP)*PI/180**. We can draw the first line segment from **(x1,y1)** to **(x2,y2)**. The coordinates **(x2,y2)** are then assigned to **(x1,y1)**. New values for **(x2,y2)** are calculated based on the end point of the second line segment, and so on. The pseudocode for this procedure is given in Fig. 10.30, and the corresponding **C** function is given in Fig. 10.31.

```
/* Pseudocode for drawing an arc */

define PI          as 3.14159265
define A_STEP      as 5 degrees
define TO_RAD      as PI/*180

module arc(xc,yc,r,a1,a2,c)
      rad = a1*TO_RAD
      x1 = r*cos(rad) + xc
      y1 = r*sin(rad) + yc
      for (a from a1 to a2 using step A_STEP)
            rad = a*TO_RAD
            x2 = r*cos(rad) + xc
            y2 = r*sin(rad) + yc
            line(x1, y1, x2, y2, c)
            x1 = x2
            y1 = y2
      end for
end arc()
```

Figure 10.30 Pseudocode for drawing an arc.

```
/* a function that draws an arc */
void arc(xc, yc, r, a1, a2, c)
double xc, yc, r, a1, a2;
int c;
      {
      int x1, y1, x2, y2;
      double a, pi = 3.14159;
      double a_step = 3.0;

      x1 = (int)(r * cos(a1*pi/180) + xc);
      y1 = (int)(r/2.0*sin(a1*pi/180) + yc);
      pnt(x1, y1, 0);

      for (a = a1 + a_step; a <= a2; a += a_step)
            {
            x2 = (int)(r*cos(a*pi/180.0) + xc);
            y2 = (int)(r/2.0*sin(a*pi/180.0) + yc);
            line(x1, y1, x2, y2, c);
            x1 = x2;
            y1 = y2;
            }

      }
```

Figure 10.31 Arc function.

10.8 DRAWING

A convenient way of drawing complex images under program control is to define a series of commands, each of which executes a specific graphics primitive. These commands can consist of unique characters stored in a character string. For example, **L** may represent a **line()** command, **B** a **box()** command, and so on. A command interpreter reads the character representing a command and decides which primitive is to be used. Arguments for each primitive, which are stored in a data array, are passed to the function that implements a particular primitive.

Pseudocode for drawing the control system diagram of Fig. 10.32 is given in Fig. 10.33. From the diagram, we can see that the primitives required are those for connecting lines, boxes, and the adder symbol. The command string **cmd[]** is initialized to contain the series of characters representing the graphics primitives that will be called. A primitive may be called more than once. The **data[]** array contains the arguments for each of the commands. They must be listed in the sequence prescribed by **cmd[]**.

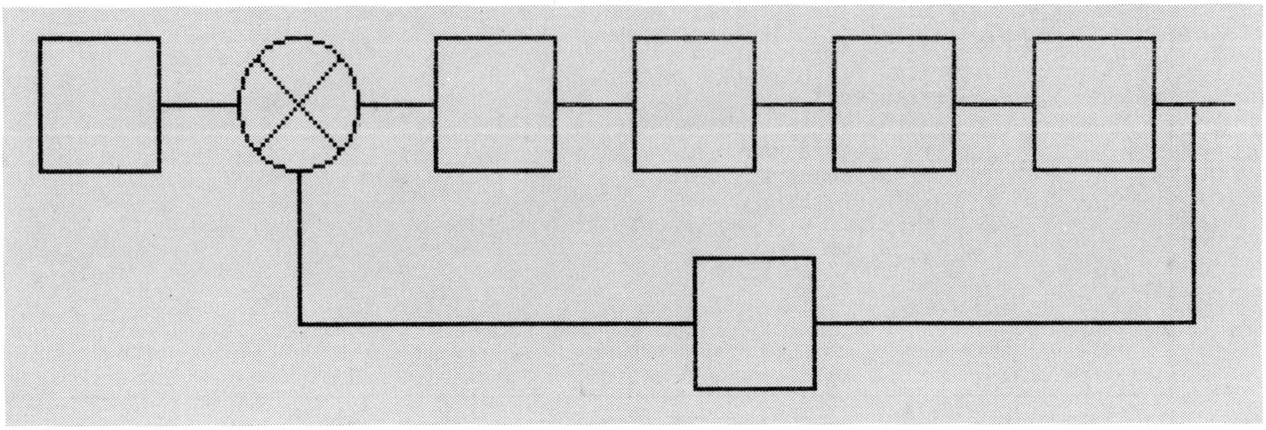

Figure 10.32 Control system diagram.

```
/* Pseudocode for drawing a control system diagram */

initialize cmd[] array to contain drawing command characters
initialize data[] array to contain arguments for each command in cmd[]

module main()
      initialize graphics mode
      clear display screen
      for (each command in cmd[])
            interpret command and extract arguments from data[]
            call module that draws primitive, passing arguments
            increment pointer to data[] by number of arguments used
      end for
end main()

module line(x1, y1, x2, y2, c)
      draw line
end line()

module box(x, y, c)
      draw four lines of fixed size box centered around x,y
end box()

module adder(xc, yc, c)
      draw fixed size circle at xc,yc
      draw an X inside of circle
end adder()
```

Figure 10.33 Pseudocode for drawing control system diagram.

The module **main()** reads each common in **cmd[]** and decides which primitive must be called. The required arguments are extracted from the **data[]** array. A call is then made to the appropriate module to draw the primitive. Upon a return from the module, a pointer to the **data[]** array is incremented by the number of arguments used. It will then point to the arguments for the next command in **cmd[]**.

The **box()** module receives the coordinates of the center of the box and the color to be used. The box is assumed to be of a fixed size. Drawing the box simply involves calling the **line()** module four times, once for each side of the box.

Likewise, the **adder()** module receives the coordinates of the center of the adder and its color. It, too, is assumed to be of fixed size. A circle is drawn at **(xc,yc)**, and an **X** is drawn inside the circle to complete the adder symbol.

A **C** program implementing this pseudocode is listed in Fig. 10.34. The **cmd[]** array lists 17 commands consisting of **L** for **line()**, **B** for **box()**, and **A** for **adder()**. The corresponding arguments are listed in the **data[]** array. Notice that **line()** requires four arguments in addition to color, whereas **box()** and **adder()** require two. The color argument is constant and thus not stored in the array.

```
/* control system block diagram */
#include <stdio.h>
#include <math.h>
#define PI  3.14159265
#define R 15
#define SZ 30

char cmd[] = {"BLALBLBLBLBLLLBLL"};

int data[] =
   {10, 115,                /* B */
    40, 100, 60, 100,       /* L */
    75, 100,                /* A */
    90, 100, 110, 100,      /* L */
    110, 115,               /* B */
    140, 100, 160, 100,     /* L */
    160, 115,               /* B */
    190, 100, 210, 100,     /* L */
    210, 115,               /* B */
    240, 100, 260, 100,     /* L */
    260, 115,               /* B */
    290, 100, 310, 100,     /* L */
    300, 100, 300, 150,     /* L */
    300, 150, 205, 150,     /* L */
    175, 165,               /* B */
    175, 150, 75, 150,      /* L */
    75, 150, 75, 115};      /* L */


main()
      {
      int i, *v, len, c = 2;
      void box(), adder();

      gmode();
      clr();
      v = &data[0];
      len = strlen(cmd);
      for (i = 0; i < len; i++)
            {
            if (cmd[i] == 'L')
                  {
```

Figure 10.34 Program that draws a control system diagram.

```
                line(*v, *(v + 1), *(v + 2), *(v + 3), c);
                v += 4;
                }
            else if (cmd[i] == 'B')
                {
                box(*v, *(v + 1), c);
                v += 2;
                }
            else if (cmd[i] == 'A')
                {
                adder(*v, *(v + 1), c);
                v += 2;
                }
            else
                puts("ERROR!");
            }
        }

void box(x, y, c)
int x, y, c;
        {
        line(x, y, x + SZ, y, c);
        line(x + SZ, y, x + SZ, y - SZ, c);
        line(x + SZ, y - SZ, x, y - SZ, c);
        line(x, y - SZ, x, y, c);
        }

void adder(xc, yc, c)               /* function to draw an adder symbol */
int xc, yc, c;
        {
        int xp, yp;                 /* draw circle */
        int x, y, error, a, b;

        x = R;
        y = 0;
        a = -2*R + 1;
        b = 1, error = 0;
        while (y <= x)
            {
            pnt(x + xc, y + yc, c);
            pnt(y + xc, x + yc, c);
            pnt(-y + xc, x + yc, c);
            pnt(-x + xc, y + yc, c);
            pnt(-x + xc, -y + yc, c);
            pnt(-y + xc, -x + yc, c);
            pnt(y + xc, -x + yc, c);
            pnt(x + xc, -y + yc, c);
            y += 1;
            error += b;
            if (error > R)
                {
                error += a;
                a += 2;
                x -= 1;
                }
            b += 2;
            }

        xp = (int)(R*cos(PI/4.0));     /* draw an X */
        yp = (int)(R*sin(PI/4.0));
        line(xc - xp, yc - yp, xc + xp, yc + yp, c);
        line(xc - xp, yc + yp, xc + xp, yc - yp, c);
        }
```

Figure 10.34 (continued).

PROBLEMS

10.1. Write a function called **h_line**(x1,x2,y,c) that draws a horizontal line from **x1** to **x2** at a **y** coordinate of **y** using the color **c**.

10.2. Write a function called **v_line**(x,y1,y2,c) that draws a vertical line from **y1** to **y2** at an **x** coordinate of **x** using the color **c**.

10.3. Modify the program of Fig. 10.2 to plot the function

```
y = fabs(sin(x))
```

for **x** from 0 to 180 degrees. This is the absolute value of the sine function. You will need to convert the sine argument to radians and scale the value of **y**.

10.4. Use the program listing of Fig. 10.11 to plot the function

$$x(t) = 100e^{-0.5t} \cos 3t$$

for $0 < t < 5$ seconds.

10.5. Use the program listing of Fig. 10.13 to plot the data of Problem 9.3.

10.6. Modify the data-plotting program of Fig. 10.13 to permit keyboard input of data.

10.7. Use the program listing of Fig. 10.18 to plot the response of the parallel resonant circuit described in Problem 9.4

PROGRAMMING PROJECTS

10.8. Modify the function-plotting program of Fig. 10.11 to permit plotting two functions on the same graph. Test your program with an appropriate set of equations.

10.9. Modify the data-plotting program of Fig. 10.13 to permit plotting two sets of data on the same graph. Use an **X** symbol for one set of data and an **O** for the other. Test your program with an appropriate set of data.

10.10. Develop a program to draw the amplifier circuit shown in Fig. 10.35. Your program should be similar to that of Fig. 10.33. Use line, resistor, and operational amplifier (triangle) symbols as graphics primitives.

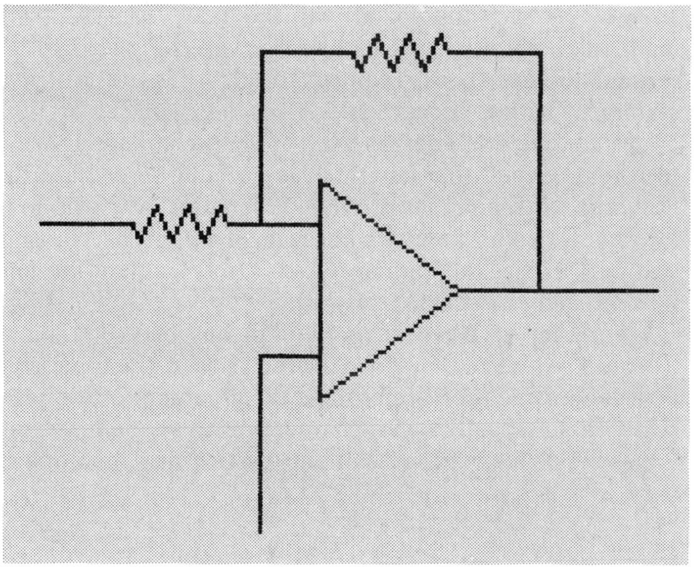

Figure 10.35 Amplifier drawing of Problem 10.10.

chapter 11

Pointer Arrays, Character, and String Functions

11.1 POINTER ARRAYS

In Chapter 7, we made use of pointers to reference elements of a numeric array. Pointers can be used to reference a character within a string or a string within an array of strings as well. In the latter case, an array of pointers is used.

Advantage of Pointers

Consider the programs listed in Fig. 11.1. In Fig. 11.1(a), the character array **name[]** has been initialized with the data ''chassis''. The length of that array is eight characters. It consists of the seven characters in the word ''chassis'' plus a terminating null that is required for all strings. The string is printed using a **printf** statement with a **%s** conversion specifier and the argument **name**.

The size of **name[]** is fixed at eight characters. We cannot reassign any data to it that exceed that length. It is possible to declare the character array with a numeric argument that provides a length that is the maximum expected length. However, that assumes we know in advance what the maximum length of the data will be. Also, if the data are always shorter than the length of the array, we are wasting memory space.

In Fig. 11.1(b), the pointer **id** has been initialized to point to the string ''chassis''. Notice that it is declared as **char**, the type to which it points. The string is printed using the pointer **id** as the argument of the **printf** statement. Unlike the restriction associated with character arrays, pointers can be reassigned to point to larger or smaller strings without wasting any memory space. Thus, a statement such as

```
id = "cover plate";
```

```
/* initializing a character array */
#include <stdio.h>
main()
      {
      static char name[] = "chassis";

      printf("%s\n", name);
      }
```

```
chassis
```

(a)

```
/* initializing a pointer to type char */
#include <stdio.h>
main()
      {
      static char *id = "chassis";

      printf("%s\n", id);
      }
```

```
chassis
```

(b)

Figure 11.1 Initialization with a single string: (a) for a character array; (b) for a pointer to type **char**.

will cause **id** to point to the longer string ''cover plate''. If this statement occurs before the **printf**, then ''cover plate'' will be printed in place of ''chassis''.

Another advantage of pointers is that we can use increment or decrement operators to reference characters within the pointed to string. Since array names are pointer constants, they cannot be incremented or decremented. Thus **name++** is an invalid operation.

Pointer Arrays

Suppose that we wish to work with an array of strings. This can be implemented with a two-dimensional character array as shown in the program of Fig. 11.2(a). A better arrangement uses an array of pointers as shown in the program of Fig. 11.2(b). Notice that the initialization of the pointer array is the same as that for the two-dimensional character array.

The pointer **id[0]** points to the first character of the first string in the initialization data. Likewise, **id[1]** points to the first character of the second string, and so on. An operation such as **id[0]++** will cause that pointer to reference the second character of the first string.

The number of pointers in the array **id[]** is determined by the number of strings in the initialization (in this case, three). As an alternative, we can specify the number of pointers explicitly with a numeric argument. Thus, **char *id[20]** declares the pointer array to consist of 20 pointers to type **char**.

```
/* Initializing a two-dimensional character array */
#include <stdio.h>
main()
      {
      static char name[][] =
               {
                "chassis",
                "bracket",
                "plate"
               };

      printf("%s %s %s\n", name[0], name[1], name[2]);
      }
```

```
chassis bracket plate
```

(a)

```
/* Initializing an array of pointers */
#include <stdio.h>
main()
      {
      static char *id[] =
               {
                "chassis",
                "bracket",
                "plate"
               };

      printf("%s %s %s\n", id[0], id[1], id[2]);
      }
```

```
chassis bracket plate
```

(b)

Figure 11.2 Initialization with an array of strings: (a) for a two-dimensional character array; (b) for an array of pointers.

Using Pointer Arrays

Pointer arrays are especially useful for processing strings. Consider an array of pointers to strings such as that listed in the program of Fig. 11.3. Let's say that it is necessary to interchange the order in which two strings are printed. We can do this simply by exchanging the pointers to those strings. This procedure avoids having to move the strings themselves, a time-consuming operation. It also precludes the need to manage the storage of strings that must be moved around.

In Fig. 11.3, the pointer variables are always printed in the same order. The value assigned to these variables is what changes. A swap routine is used to exchange the values of the pointer variables **id[0]** and **id[1]**. This forces ''bracket'' to be printed before ''chassis''.

Pointer arrays are also convenient for performing other operations on strings. These include string copying, *concatenation* (joining two strings to form a

```
/* Swapping pointers */
#include <stdio.h>
main()
     {
     char *temp;
     static char *id[] =
              {
               "chassis",
               "bracket",
               "plate"
              };

     temp = id[0];
     id[0] = id[1];
     id[1] = temp;

     printf("%s %s %s\n", id[0], id[1], id[2]);
     }
```

```
bracket chassis plate
```

Figure 11.3 Swapping pointers to strings.

larger one), comparison, and so on. In each case, we can reference a string of arbitrary length through a pointer to the beginning of the string. Since each string is conveniently tagged by an element in the pointer array, we have a means to quickly reference the strings for processing.

11.2 COMMAND-LINE ARGUMENTS

When a **C** program is invoked, we can pass arguments, to the **main()** function. These are called *command-line arguments*. For example, suppose that a **C** program called **convert** will convert a number from decimal to hexadecimal. The number to be converted can be supplied as a command-line argument. It would appear as follows (assuming $ is the system prompt):

```
$ convert 237
```

The program **convert** would receive the argument **237**, perform the conversion, and print the result. You might be thinking that this does not offer any advantage over entering the argument within the program. We will see in later examples where command-line arguments are advantageous.

Multiple arguments can be passed to **main()**. In our previous example, perhaps we might want the number **237** converted to octal. An additional argument, **−o** could be used as a flag that tells **main()** we want the output in octal. It would appear as follows:

```
$ convert -o 237
```

It is a convention of the **UNIX** operating system that all optional parameters begin with the minus character. Also, notice that the arguments of **convert** are separated by a space. These arguments will be read by **main()** as strings. We use the space as a separator to tell **main()** where one argument ends and the next begins.

To incorporate command-line arguments into a program, **C** provides for two arguments to the function **main()**. The first is the number of arguments (strings) being passed to **main()**, and the second is an array of pointers to these strings. By convention, the argument count is called **argc** and the pointer array **argv[]**. Also, **argv[0]** is the name by which the program is invoked. This mean that **argc** will always be greater than or equal to 1.

```
/* command line arguments */
#include <stdio.h>
main(argc, argv)
int argc;
char *argv[];
      {
      int i;

      printf("%20s %20s %20s\n\n", "pointer location", "pointer contents",
      "target string");
      for (i = 1; i < argc; i++)
            {
            printf("%20u %20u %20s\n", &argv[i], argv[i], argv[i]);
            }
      }
```

```
this information will help you understand pointer arrays

    pointer location     pointer contents        target string

                3964                  133                 this
                3966                  138          information
                3968                  150                 will
                3970                  155                 help
                3972                  160                  you
                3974                  164           understand
                3976                  175              pointer
                3978                  183               arrays
```

Figure 11.4 Echo program using command line arguments.

The program of Fig. 11.4 illustrates the use of command-line arguments. The program echoes all the arguments except **argv[0]**. It identifies the location of the pointer to the argument through **&argv[i]**. Notice that all the pointers form a contiguous array. Since the example program ran on a system using 2-byte pointers, their beginning locations are separated by two counts.

The contents of each pointer (the location to which it is pointing) are also printed. It is obtained by using the conversion specifier **%u** to print the value of **argv[i]**. The values given here will most likely be different than those on your system, but the offsets will be the same. The first pointer value is **133**. It points to the beginning of the string "This". Since the string consists of five characters (four plus a null), the next pointer value will be five higher, or **138**. Likewise, the string "information" consists of 12 characters. Therefore, the next pointer will have a value of **138** plus **12**, or **150**.

The pointer locations remain fixed. However, it is possible to change the contents of the pointers. Thus, if we wished the entire printed message to read "will this information help you understand pointer arrays", an exchange of the values of **argv[1]** and **argv[3]** and then **argv[2]** and **argv[3]** would be performed. Notice that the strings themselves are not moved. We only change the pointer values.

```
/* echo command line arguments, second form */
#include <stdio.h>
main(argc, argv)
int argc;
char **argv;
      {
      int i;

      printf("%20s %20s %20s\n\n", "pointer location", pointer contents",
      target string");
      for (i = 1; i < argc; i++)
            {
            argv++;
            printf("%20u %20u %20s\n", argv, *argv, *argv);
            }
      }
```

```
this information will help you understand pointer arrays

    pointer location      pointer contents          target string

                3964                   133                   this
                3966                   138            information
                3968                   150                   will
                3970                   155                   help
                3972                   160                    you
                3974                   164             understand
                3976                   175                pointer
                3978                   183                 arrays
```

Figure 11.5 Another version of the echo program.

Figure 11.5 gives an alternative version of the program of Fig. 11.4. The declaration **char **argv** says that **argv** is a pointer to a pointer. Thus **argv** in Fig. 11.5 has an initial value identical to **&argv[0]** in Fig. 11.4, since **argv** gives the location of the first pointer in the array. Both forms are in common use and are fully equivalent.

11.3 USING THE STANDARD LIBRARY CHARACTER FUNCTIONS

C provides a number of functions (usually implemented as macros) that test characters or convert them from one form to another. Figure 11.6(a) lists the character tests and Fig. 11.6(b) lists the character conversion functions. Some typical entries are:

```
#define isdigit(c)  ((c) - '0' < 10)
#define toupper(c)  ((c) - 'a' + 'A')
```

The function **isdigit(c)** tests whether or not the character **c** is a digit from **0** to **9**. If **c** is a digit, **isdigit(c)** will be true. Otherwise, it will be false or **0**. The function **toupper(c)** will convert the character **c** from lowercase to uppercase.

Function	*Converts* **c** *from:*
isalpha(c)	Alphabetic
isdigit(c)	A digit
isspace(c)	A blank, tab, or newline
islower(c)	lowercase
isupper(c)	uppercase
isalnum(c)	Aphabetic or a digit
iscntrl(c)	A control character
isgraph(c)	A graphics character
isprint(c)	A printable character
ispunct(c)	A punctuation mark
isxdigit(c)	A hexadecimal digit

(a)

Function	*Converts* **c** *from:*
tolower(c)	Uppercase to lowercase
toupper(c)	Lowercase to uppercase

(b)

Figure 11.6 (a) Character test and (b) conversion functions.

```
/* test hex number input */
#include <stdio.h>
main()
      {
      char c, hex[10];
      int i;

      puts("Enter a hex number");
      i = 0;
      while ((c = getchar()) != '\n')
            if (isxdigit(c))
                  {
                  hex[i] = c;
                  i++;
                  }
            else
                  {
                  printf("\nSorry, %c is not a hex digit. Please try again.\n", c);
                  exit();
                  }
      printf("Your hex number is %s\n", hex);
      }
```

```
Enter a hex number
4bc2
Your hex number is 4bc2


Enter a hex number
az5

Sorry, z is not a hex digit. Please try again.
```

Figure 11.7 Testing for hex digits with **isxdigit()**.

To illustrate the use of the character test functions, consider the program of Fig. 11.7. It requests the entry of a hex number and tests each character using **isxdigit(c)**. If the character is a digit from **0** to **9** or a letter from **a** to **f** (either case), the character will be accepted and added to **hex[]**. Otherwise, an error message is printed and the program terminates. Characters are accepted until a newline is entered. At that point, the completely assembled hex number is printed.

11.4 USING THE STANDARD LIBRARY STRING FUNCTIONS

The string functions provided in the standard library are listed in Fig. 11.8 along with a brief description of their use. These string functions are the ones that occur most frequently. Your compiler or interpreter may have fewer or more entries. If a function you need is missing from this list, don't be concerned. You can build the string function library to suit your own application. That is a nice feature of **C**.

The entries in Fig. 11.8 fall into two categories. The first group (having names starting with **str**) performs basic operations on strings. The second group converts strings of digits into a numeric data format. The variable names are defined in the figure.

```
char *str,*str1,*str2;
int n;
char c;
```

strcat (*str1, str2*)	Appends *str2* to *str1*
strchr (*str, c*)	Returns pointer to first occurrence of *c* in *str*
strcmp (*str1, str2*)	Compares *str1* and *str2*; returns 0 if equal
strcpy (*str1, str2*)	Copies *str2* to *str1*
strlen (*str*)	Returns number of characters in *str*
strncat (*str1, str2, n*)	Appends *n* characters from *str2* to *str1*
strncmp (*str1, str2, n*)	Compares first *n* characters of *str1* and *str2*
strncpy (*str1, str2, n*)	Copies first *n* characters from *str2* to *str1*
strpbrk (*str1, str2*)	Returns first occurrence in *str1* of any character in *str2*
strrchr (*str, c*)	Returns pointer to last occurrence of *c* in *str*
atof (*str*)	Convert *str* to **double**
atoi (*str*)	Convert *str* to **int**
atol (*str*)	Convert *str* to **long**

Figure 11.8 Standard library string functions.

Let's look inside some of these functions to become better acquainted with them. We will start with **strlen()**, a function that was introduced earlier. This function returns the length of a string. To implement **strlen()**, all we need do is count the characters in the argument string up to but not including the terminating **NULL**. The function receives a pointer to the beginning of the string and returns an integer number for the count.

Figure 11.9 gives a listing for **strlen()**. The pointer **ptr** is initialized to the beginning of the target string. We then increment **ptr** while the character to which it points is different from the terminating **NULL** ('\0'). The difference between **ptr** and the string pointer **str** is then the length of the string.

Another string function that you will find very useful is **strcmp(str1,str2)**. It compares two strings and returns an integer whose value indicates their relationship. If the returned value is **0**, the strings are equal. If the string referenced by **str1** is greater than that referenced by **str2**, a positive number will be returned. Otherwise, a negative number will be returned.

```
/* strlen(str) returns the length of the string referenced by str */

int strlen(str)
char *str;
      {
      char *ptr;

      ptr = str;
      while (*ptr)
            ++ptr;
      return (ptr - str);
      }
```

Figure 11.9 Strlen() function.

The program of Fig. 11.10 implements **strcmp()** using pointers. The two strings are compared at successive character positions until a difference is detected. While equality exits and ***str1** is not a **NULL**, both pointers are incremented. If a **NULL** is reached on ***str1** while the two strings still match, they are equal and a **0** is returned. Should a difference be detected, the while loop terminates. Returning ***str – *str2** gives the difference of the characters at the position where a mismatch occurred. If ***str1** has a higher **ascii** value than ***str2**, a positive number is returned; otherwise, the returned value will be negative.

```
/* strcmp(str1,str2) compares the strings referenced by str1 and str2 */

int strcmp(str1, str2)
char *str1, *str2;
      {
      while (*str1 == *str2)
            if (*str1++)
                  ++str2;
            else
                  return (0);
      return (*str1 - *str2);
      }
```

Figure 11.10 Strcmp() function.

Now that we have seen what is inside some of the string functions, let's look at some typical applications. In Chapter 7, we used a table look-up to convert a number into its corresponding color code. Let's do the reverse procedure here. We will enter a color name and look up its number. This necessitates having a string array containing our standard colors for reference.

Figure 11.11 lists a color-to-number conversion program. The pointer array **color[]** is used to reference the color table. It is declared as a pointer to type **char**. The **strcmp()** function is used to compare the input color to each entry in the table. Both of its arguments are pointers to strings. If a match is found, the pointer subscript equals the color number. This number is printed, and an **exit()** is executed. If no match is found after reaching the bottom of the list, a message indicating this condition is printed.

Notice that the comparison of **color[i]** and **band** starts at the top of the table and works toward the bottom, considering each entry in succession. This is referred to as a **linear search**. In a sorted list, a much faster technique called the *binary search* can be used. It is presented in the next section.

The program of Fig. 11.12 makes use of the **atoi()** function to convert a string of decimal digits from type **char** to type **int**. This integer number is printed in hexadecimal, or optionally in octal format using the **%x** or **%o** conversion specifi-

```
/* linear search table look-up */
#include <stdio.h>
main()
      {
      char band[10];
      int i;
      static char *color[10] =
          {
          "black",
          "brown",
          "red",
          "orange",
          "yellow",
          "green",
          "blue",
          "violet",
          "gray",
          "white"
          };

      puts("Enter color of band");
      scanf("%s", band);
      for (i = 0;  i < 9;  i++)
            {
            if (strcmp(color[i], band) == 0)
                  {
                  printf("The number corresponding to  %s is %d\n", band, i);
                  exit();
                  }
            }
      printf("The color %s is not on this list\n", band);
      }
```

```
Enter color of band
red
The number corresponding to red is 2


Enter color of band
violet
The number corresponding to violet is 7
```

Figure 11.11 Linear search using **strcmp()**.

ers. The string is entered as a command-line argument. If an octal output is desired, a **−o** is typed at the command line as an optional parameter.

The program is named **convert**. If it is invoked without any arguments, **argc** will equal **1**. This condition is detected, and a message is printed indicating that the function requires an integer argument.

If **argc == 2**, the decimal string contained in **argv[1]** is converted into **int** using **atoi()**, and the number is printed in hexadecimal format. Otherwise, a test is performed to see if the **−o** option was entered as the first argument of **convert**. If so, the second argument, **argv[2]**, is converted to **int** and printed in octal format. Should two arguments be present where the first is not **−o**, a message indicating proper use of the program is printed.

```
/* convert to hex or octal */
#include <stdio.h>
main(argc, argv)
int argc;
char *argv[];
      {
      if (argc == 1)
            {
            printf("Convert requires an integer argument\n");
            exit();
            }
      if (argc == 2)
            printf("%x\n", atoi(argv[1]));
      else
            if ((*argv[1] == '-') && (*++argv[1] == 'o'))
                  printf("%o\n", atoi(argv[2]));
            else
                  printf("Usage: convert -o integer\n");
      }
```

```
-o 255
377


255
FF


8000
1F40
```

Figure 11.12 Data conversion using **atoi()**.

11.5 SEARCHING AND SORTING STRING ARRAYS

In Chapter 7, we developed programs that perform linear and binary searches of one-dimensional numeric arrays. Also considered was the bubble sort procedure. The same algorithms can be applied to arrays of strings with some slight changes. This was demonstrated in the previous section with the linear search program.

In this section, we will look at the binary search procedure applied to string arrays. We will also consider popular sorting algorithms, including the bubble, Shell, and quick sort, applied to string arrays.

Binary Search

The binary search pseudocode of Fig. 7.25 can be applied to the searching of strings. All we need change in the actual program are the declaration and comparison code. The data array being referenced will now contain a series of strings. The program of Fig. 11.13 performs a binary search of the strings referenced by the pointer array **data**. Compare this program to that of Fig. 7.26.

```
/* binary search of a string array */
#include <stdio.h>
main()
      {
      static char *data[] =
          {
          "cable",
          "capacitor",
          "chassis",
          "chip",
          "harness",
          "header",
          "inductor",
          "microprocessor",
          "plug",
          "resistor",
          "socket",
          "transistor"
          };

      char str[50];
      int ret;

      puts("Enter string to find: ");
      scanf("%s", str);
      ret = bin_srch(data, 12, str);
      if (ret == -1)
            printf("The string %s is not in this list\n", str);
      else
            printf("The string %s is item %d in this list\n", str, ret + 1);
      }

int bin_srch(array, count, str)
char *array[], *str;
int count;
      {
      int high = count - 1;
      int low = 0;
      int mid = (high + low)/2;

      while (strcmp(array[mid], str) != 0 && high > low)
            {
            if (strcmp(array[mid], str) > 0)
                  high = mid - 1;
            else
                  low = mid + 1;
            mid = (high + low)/2;
            }
      if (strcmp(array[mid], str) == 0)
            return (mid);
      else
            return (-1);
      }
```

```
Enter string to find:
socket
The string socket is item 11 in this list
```

Figure 11.13 Binary search program.

```
/* Bubble sort a string array */
#include <stdio.h>
#define YES 1
#define NO 0
main()
	{
	static char *data[] =
		{
		"transistor",
		"cable",
		"harness",
		"plug",
		"capacitor",
		"socket",
		"chip",
		"chassis",
		"resistor",
		"microprocessor",
		"header",
		"inductor"
		};
	int i;
	void sort();

	sort(data, 12);
	for (i = 0; i < 12; i++)
		printf("%s\n", data[i]);
	}

void sort(array, count)
char *array[], count;
	{
	int pass, i, swap;
	char *temp;

	for (pass = 0; pass < (count - 1); pass++)
		{
		swap = NO;
		for (i = 0; i < (count - pass - 1); i++)
			if (strcmp(array[i], array[i + 1]) > 0)
				{
				temp = array[i];
				array[i] = array[i + 1];
				array[i + 1] = temp;
				swap = YES;
				}
		if (swap == NO)
			break;
		}
	}
```

```
cable
capacitor
chassis
chip
harness
header
inductor
microprocessor
plug
resistor
socket
transistor
```

Figure 11.14 Bubble sort program.

Bubble Sort

The bubble sort pseudocode of Fig. 7.22 can also be applied to string data. This has been done in the program of Fig. 11.14. Again, the only changes in going from integer to string data are the declaration and comparison code. Compare this program to that of Fig. 7.23.

Shell Sort

The Shell sort, named after Donald Shell, has a speed advantage over the bubble sort for larger arrays. In the bubble sort, data items far away from their correct positions require many exchanges before being properly located in the list. This is due to the fact that only adjacent items are compared for exchange. In the Shell sort, items separated by a gap are compared and swapped if needed. This quickly places all the items somewhere near their final positions. The net result is that fewer comparisons and exchanges are needed.

The Shell sort actually consists of a series of bubble sorts. For a list of **n** items, the first bubble sort is made for elements separated by a **gap** equal to **n/2**, where **n** is a type **int**. After each bubble sort is completed, the **gap** is reduced by a factor of 2. The value of **n** on the last pass will equal 1. Each time the gap is changed, a new sort begins. As the **gap** distance gets smaller, the number of comparisons for each pass gets larger.

The Shell sort pseudocode is given in Fig. 11.15. The inner loop performs one complete pass of comparisons, with exchanges where needed. Comparisons are made on **data[i]** and **data[i+gap]** for **i** ranging from **0** to **count – gap**. If an exchange is made on any given pass, **swap** is set to **YES**. The center loop initiates additional passes until no exchanges are made (**swap == NO**). The outer loop controls the **gap** value and terminates when **gap** equals zero. Figure 11.16 is a listing of the Shell sort program.

```
/* pseudocode for Shell sort */
/* sorts array data[] consisting of n items */

set gap to integer value of n/2
while (gap >0)
      do
            swap = NO
            for (i=0 to i < (count - gap))
                  if (data[i] and data[i+gap] not in order)
                        exchange  values
                        swap = YES
                  end if
            end for
       while (swap == YES)
      gap = gap/2
end while
```

Figure 11.15 Shell sort pseudocode.

```
/* Shell sort a string array */
#include <stdio.h>
#define YES 1
#define NO  0
main()
      {
      static char *data[] =
            {
            "transistor",
            "cable",
            "harness",
            "plug",
            "capacitor",
            "socket",
            "chip",
            "chassis",
            "resistor",
            "microprocessor",
            "header",
            "inductor"
            };
      int i;
      void sort();

      sort(data, 12);
      for (i = 0; i < 12; i++)
            printf("%s\n", data[i]);
      }

void sort(array, count)                    /* Shell sort routine */
char *array[];
int count;
      {
      int i, gap, swap;
      char *temp;

      gap = count;
      while ((gap /= 2) > 0)
            {
            do
                  {
                  swap = NO;
                  for (i = 0; i < count - gap; i++)
                        if (strcmp(array[i], array[i + gap]) > 0)
                              {
                              temp = array[i];
                              array[i] = array[i + gap];
                              array[i + gap] = temp;
                              swap = YES;
                              }
                  }
            while (swap);
            }
      }
```

Figure 11.16 Shell sort program.

Quick Sort

The quick sort is one of the fastest sorting algorithms. It divides the list to be sorted into two sublists. The left sublist contains all the elements whose value is less than or equal to some selected element. The right sublist contains all the remaining elements. Using recursion, each sublist is then submitted to quick sort to form two smaller sublists. The process continues until each sublist consists of only one element. At this point, the list is sorted.

To illustrate the quick sort, we will use the list of numbers given in Fig. 11.17(a). The list consists of ten elements. We select an element whose value will be a dividing point for the two sublists using

```
lst_div = (first + last)/2;
```

where **lst_div** is the *list divider*. If the array name is **data**, the value of the list divider element will be **data[lst_div]**. **First** and **last** are the subscripts or positions of the first and last elements. In this case, **first** and **last** and **0** and **9**, respectively, making **lst_div** equal to **4**. The value referenced by **lst_div** is **6**.

```
first                 last
{  2 0 9 4 6 1 3 8 7 5  }
   ^       ^         ^

   i     lst_div     j
```

(a) Original list

```
{  2 0 9 4 6 1 3 8 7 5  }
       ^             ^

       i             j
```

(b) **i** and **j** at first swap

```
{  2 0 5 4 6 1 3 8 7 9  }
           ^   ^

           i   j
```

(c) **i** and **j** at second swap

```
{  2 0 5 4 3 1 6 8 7 9  }
             ^

            i,j
```

(d) **i** and **j** after second swap

```
{  2 0 5 4 3 1 6 8 7 9  }
             ^ ^

             j i
```

(e) Final locations of **i** and **j**

```
{ 2 0 5 4 3 1 }    { 6 8 7 9 }
      ^                ^

{ 2 0 1 4 3 }      { 6 7 } { 8 9 }
      ^              ^       ^

{ 1 0 }  { 2 4 3 }
  ^          ^

       { 2 3 }
         ^
```

(f) Sublists submitted to quick sort

Figure 11.17 Quick sort: (a) original list; (b) **i** and **j** at first swap; (c) **i** and **j** at second swap; (d) **i** and **j** after second swap; (e) final locations of **i** and **j**; (f) sublists submitted to quick sort.

To order the list, we will use the indexes **i** and **j** to reference particular elements. The values being referenced are identified by arrows in Fig. 11.17. We begin with **i = first** and **j = last**. Assuming that the list is to be sorted in ascending order, the value of **i** is incremented while it points to an element whose value is less than that of the list divider, or

```
while (data[i] < data[lst_div])
     ++i;
```

Likewise, **j** will be decremented under the condition

```
while (data[j] > data[lst_div])
     --j;
```

At this point, **i** and **j** point to two elements that must be interchanged. This condition is illustrated in Fig. 11.17(b). After swapping these elements, we continue incrementing **i** and decrementing **j** using the preceding criteria. The next swap will occur at the locations shown in Fig. 11.17(c). The procedure continues **while i <= j**. If the values of **i** and **j** should coincide, as is shown in Fig. 11.17(d), **i** is incremented by 1 to satisfy the terminating condition as shown in Fig. 11.17(e).

The two sublists have now been formed. The left sublist extends from **first** to **j** and the right sublist from **i** to **last**. Each sublist will be submitted to the quick sort procedure provided they have a length greater than 1. Figure 11.17(f) gives all the sublists that will be submitted to quick sort for this example. The pseudocode describing the quick sort is given in Fig. 11.18.

```
/* pseudocode for quick sort */
module q_sort(array, first, last)
      i = first
      j = last
      lst_div = (first + last)/2

      while (i <= j)
            while (array[i] < array[lst_div])
                  i = i + 1
            end while

            while (array[j] > array[lst_div])
                  j = j + 1
            end while

            if (i < j)
                  swap array[i] and array[j]
                  i = i + 1
                  j = j - 1
            else if (i == j)
                  i = i + 1
            end if

            if (left sublist longer than 1)
                  q_sort(array,first,j)
            if (right sublist longer than 1)
                  q_sort(array,i,last)
      end q_sort()
```

Figure 11.18 Pseudocode for the quick sort.

```
/* quick_sort a string array */
#include <stdio.h>
main()
     {
     static char *data[] =
          {
          "transistor",
          "cable",
          "harness",
          "plug",
          "capacitor",
          "socket",
          "chip",
          "chassis",
          "resistor",
          "microprocessor",
          "header",
          "inductor"
          };
     int i, first = 0, last = 11;

     q_sort(data, first, last);
     for (i = 0;  i < 12;  i++)
          printf("%s\n", data[i]);
     }

int q_sort(array, first, last)
char *array[];
int first, last;
     {
     int i = first;
     int j = last;
     char *lst_div = array[(first + last)/2];
     char *temp;

     while (i <= j)
          {
          while (strcmp(lst_div, array[i]) > 0)
                i++;
          while (strcmp(array[j], lst_div) > 0)
                j--;
          if (i < j)
                {
                temp = array[i];
                array[i] = array[j];
                array[j] = temp;
                i++;
                j--;
                }
          else if (i == j)
                i++;
          }

     if (first < j)
          q_sort(array, first, j);
     if (i < last)
          q_sort(array, i, last);
     }
```

Figure 11.19 Quick sort program.

Q_sort() receives the name of the array and the subscripts of the first and last elements of the array to be included within the sort procedure. The values of **i** and **j** are initialized to **first** and **last**, and **lst_div** is initialized to **(first + last)/2**. The value of **i** is incremented while (**array[i]** < **array[lst_div]**) is true. Likewise, **j** is decremented while (**array[j]** > **array[lst_div]**). If **i** is still less than **j** at this point, the pointers they reference are swapped.

After swapping **array[i]** and **array[j]**, **i** is incremented and **j** is decremented. This can be done since the elements currently being referenced are known to be in order. The pseudocode was written for a numeric array. As was the case with previous sorting routines, it can be converted for string arrays with some minor changes.

The program of Fig. 11.19 implements the quick sort on an array of strings. The pointer array **data[]** references the start of each string. In this program, the test for the left sublist being longer than 1 is written as (**first** < **j**). Likewise, (**i** < **last**) tests for the right sublist being longer than 1.

Several changes can be made to speed up the quick sort. First, for sublists that have only two elements, we can easily compare and order the elements without calling **q_sort()**. Second, the quick sort algorithm can be implemented without recursion. This saves time, since there is a considerable overhead involved in the large number of recursive calls made to **q_sort()**.

11.6 MEMORY MANAGEMENT

Memory Allocation Functions

Whenever arrays are used within a program, the **C** compiler or interpreter knows exactly how much memory space to allocate for each array. This information is extracted from the array declaration. Once the size of an array has been established, it cannot be changed.

For some applications, we do not know in advance the required size for arrays. How do we resolve this problem? The most effective method is to reference our data using pointers instead of arrays. This will permit *dynamic memory allocation*, wherein blocks of memory are allocated as needed while a program is executing. When the memory is no longer needed for storage, it can be released or deallocated. Figure 11.20 lists the standard library memory allocation functions.

Function	*Description*
malloc(*size*)	Allocates memory block of *size* bytes
calloc(*n, size*)	Allocates memory for *n* elements of *size* bytes
realloc(*ptr, size*)	Changes size of previously allocated memory
free(*ptr*)	Deallocates memory block referenced by *ptr*

Figure 11.20 Standard library memory allocation functions.

Memory Allocation Using Malloc()

The function **malloc**(*size*) allocates size bytes for storage. It returns a pointer to the beginning of the storage area. If the requested memory space is not available, it will return a **NULL**. The **malloc()** function returns a pointer to type **char**. If the storage is to be used for some other data type, a cast operation can be performed.

To illustrate the use of **malloc()**, let's set up a storage area for **10000** characters. We must define a pointer that will hold the beginning address of the storage area. This pointer will be initialized with the value returned by **malloc()**. Thus

```
char *base_ptr;
base_ptr = malloc(10000);
```

will result in **base_ptr** pointing to the beginning of our storage area. The value of **base_ptr** should be preserved, since it will be needed to free the storage area or change its size.

A character that is offset by **n** bytes from **base_ptr** can be referenced by **base_ptr + n**. Alternatively, we can define another pointer, **char *offset**, and initialize it to **base_ptr**. The increment and decrement operators can then be applied to **offset** to reference any character in the storage area.

Releasing or Changing the Size of Allocated Memory

If a particular storage area is no longer needed within a program, we can release the memory space and make it available to other program segments. Thus we can deallocate the **10000** character memory space pointed to by **base_ptr** with

```
free(base_ptr);
```

The value of **base_ptr** must be the same as that returned by **malloc()** when the space was originally allocated.

Suppose that the **10000** character space is not sufficient for existing conditions within the program. We now need **20000** characters. This space can be adjusted by **realloc(base_ptr,20000)**. The function **realloc()** will return a pointer that may be different in value from **base_ptr**. This happens if there is not sufficient memory space in the original storage area. Whenever the returned pointer is different, the contents of the original storage area are moved to the new storage area. The **realloc()** function may also be used to reduce the size of an allocated memory block.

The program of Fig. 11.21 illustrates the use of **malloc()** and **free()**. The output of the program is the number of kilobytes of free memory. **KB** is defined as **1024**, which equals 1 kilobyte. A kilobyte of pointers to type **char** is also defined within the declarations. Memory is allocated in kilobyte increments until a full kilobyte is no longer available. The pointer returned from the allocation of each block is assigned to one of the elements of the pointer array **block[i]**. The value of **i** at the point where no more kilobyte blocks are available equals the number of blocks that were allocated. This value is assigned to **k**.

The next loop releases each block that was allocated using **free(block[i])**; **block[i]** is a pointer to an allocated block **i** that is being released. The last statement prints the value of **k**, which is the number of kilobytes of free memory.

Memory Allocation Using Calloc()

The **calloc()** function is a variation of **malloc()**. It allocates memory as **n** multiples of some *size*. Unlike **malloc()**, which does not alter the allocated memory, **calloc()** initializes all this memory to a value of **0**. By default, it returns a pointer to type **char**. The cast operator is used when **calloc()** is allocating memory for other data types. For example, to allocate storage for **200** integers, we could use the following:

```
int *stor_int;
stor_int = (int*)calloc(200,2);
```

```
/* check free memory space */
#include <stdio.h>
#include <malloc.h>
#define KB  1024
main()
    {
    char *block[KB];
    int i, k;

    /* allocate free memory */
    i = 0;
    block[i] = malloc(KB);
    while (block[i++] != 0)
        block[i] = malloc(KB);
    k = i;

    /* release allocated memory */
    for (i = 0; i < k; i++)
        free(block[i]);

    printf("Total free memory = %d kilobytes\n", k);
    }
```

```
Total free memory = 60 kilobytes
```

Figure 11.21 Program to check free memory space.

The size of each integer is **2** bytes. We are allocating storage for **200** of these 2-byte elements. A cast is used to convert the pointer returned by **calloc()** into a pointer to type **int**. This value, which points to the base address of our storage area, is assigned to **stor_int**.

Memory Buffer Functions

The standard library memory buffer functions are listed in Fig. 11.22. They perform operations on blocks of memory that are equivalent to their string function counterparts. That is, **memchr()** is analogous to **strchr()**, **memcmp()** to **strcmp()**, and so on.

Why do we need separate functions to operate on memory blocks? With strings, a pointer to the first character defines the entire entity on which an operation will be performed. The string extends up to the first **NULL**. A memory block may contain any collection or mix of data types. Therefore, a pointer to the beginning of a block does not define its extent. We need to specify its size. Notice that all the memory buffer functions have an argument **n** that specifies the length of the buffer.

memchr (*buf*, *c*, *n*)	Returns pointer to first occurrence of *c* in first *n* characters of *buf*
memcmp (*buf1*, *buf2*, *n*)	Compares first *n* characters of *buf1* and *buf2*
memcpy (*buf1*, *buf2*, *n*)	Copies *n* characters from *buf2* to *buf1*
memset (*buf*, *c*, *n*)	Sets first *n* characters of *buf* to *c*

Figure 11.22 Standard library memory buffer functions.

The arguments used in the memory buffer functions are defined as follows:

```
char *buf, *buf1, *buf2;
char c;
int n;
```

where **buf**, **buf1**, and **buf2** are pointers to the beginning of a buffer. Figure 11.23 lists a program that illustrates using the **memcpy()** function to move memory blocks. This program is used for fast display of video screen data.

SCREEN_BASE is a symbolic constant equal to the base address of the video screen display. **SCRN_LENGTH** is the length of the screen memory in bytes. **NEW_SCRN_DATA** equals the address of the beginning of a memory region containing the information to be displayed next. The pointers **video** and **buffer** are initialized to **SCREEN_BASE** and **NEW_SCRN_DATA**, respectively. A call to **memcpy(video, buffer, SCRN_LENGTH)** then moves **SCRN_LENGTH** bytes from **buffer** to **video**. This transfer will take place at a very fast rate, producing instant screen display changes.

```
/* fast screen displays */
#include <memory.h>
main()
    {
    char *video, *buffer;

    video = (char *)SCREEN_BASE;
    buffer = (char *)NEW_SCRN_DATA;
    memcpy(video, buffer, SCRN_LENGTH);
    }
```

Figure 11.23 Fast screen displays using **memcpy()**.

PROBLEMS

11.1. What is the output of the following program?

```
main()
    {
    static char *ptr[] =
            {
            "pointing",
            "to",
            "strings"
            };

    while (*ptr[2] != '\0')
        putchar(*ptr[2]++);
    }
```

11.2. What is output from the following program?

```
main()
    {
    static char *ptr[] =
        {
        "pointing",
        "to",
        "strings"
        };
```

```
ptr[2] = ptr[0];
printf("%s\n",ptr[2]);
}
```

11.3. Indicate if the following character tests are true or false:

```
(a) isalpha('z')
(b) isdigit('a')
(c) isspace('\t')
(d) islower('b')
(e) isalnum('?')
(f) iscntrl('\13')
(g) isxdigit('f')
```

11.4. What is output from the following program?

```
main()
     {
     static char one[20] = "first";
     static char two[20] = "second";

     printf("%s\n",strcat(two,one));
     }
```

11.5. Modify the bubble sort program of Fig. 11.14 to sort in reverse alphabetic order (z to a).

PROGRAMMING PROJECTS

11.6. Modify the data-conversion program of Fig. 11.12 to include conversion to binary output. Use the program of Fig. 6.17 for a reference.

11.7. Write a function that duplicates the standard library string copy function **strcpy**(*str1*,*str2*).

11.8. Write a function that duplicates the standard library string concatenate function **strcat**(*str1*,*str2*).

11.9. Prepare a file of 1000 random words and sort the file using the bubble, Shell, and the quick sort programs. Compare execution speeds.

11.10. Use the sorted file from Problem 11.9 and search for an entry near the middle of the list using the linear and binary search programs. Compare execution speeds.

11.11. Implement the fast screen display program of Fig. 11.23 on your system. Compare the screen generation time to printing the new screen line by line.

chapter 12

Structures

12.1. INTRODUCTION

A *structure* is a collection of related variables. Any number or type of variables may be included within its definition. The use of structures permits us to work with related data items as single entities. Structures are treated as unique data types. Variables may be declared as having a type defined by a particular structure.

For example, we can define a structure for long-distance dialing information as containing the variables **area_code**, **city**, **state**, and **time_zone**. These variables are referred to as the structure *members*. A name, such as **long_dist**, can be assigned to this structure. It is referred to as the structure *tag*. Any variable may then be declared as having the structure **long_dist**. An array variable called **my_list[]** is declared as being of type **long_dist** by

```
struct long_dist mylist[]
```

where the keyword **struct** indicates that we are declaring a complex data structure and not a simple data type.

Structures are conceptually related to arrays. An array is a collection of variables of the same type. A structure allows you to include any mix of variables.

12.2 DEFINING AND USING STRUCTURES

Structure Templates

The declaration of a structure defines its composition in terms of its member variables. This is referred to as the structure *template*. For example, **long_dist** is declared as

```
struct long_dist
     {
     unsigned area_code;
     char     city[MAX_CTY];
     char     state[MAX_ST];
     char     time_zone
     };
```

This declaration does not allocate any memory for storage since it does not define any variables having the structure **long_dist**.

We can declare variables of type **long_dist** in one of two ways. If the structure has already been defined, a declaration of the type

```
struct long_dist my_list[1000];
```

would define an array **my_list** consisting of 1000 elements of type **struct long_dist**. As an alternative, **my_list** or any number of variables may be defined by listing them immediately after the right brace of the structure declaration as

```
struct long_dist
     {
     unsigned area_code;
     char     city[MAX_CTY];
     char     state[MAX_ST];
     char     time_zone
     } my_list[1000];
```

If no more structures with the same form will be allocated, the structure tag may be omitted. In the case of the preceding structure, the tag **long_dist** could be deleted.

Structure Initialization

The initialization of structures is similar to that of arrays. External or static structure variables can be initialized by following their declaration by a list of items separated by commas and enclosed within braces. For example,

```
struct complex
     { double real;
       double imag;
     };
```

defines a structure for complex variables. The variables **z** and **y** can be declared as type **complex** and initialized by

```
static struct complex z = {10.0, 20.0},
                      y = {5.0, 7.07};
```

Accessing Structure Members with the Member Operator

A member of a structure can be accessed by using an expression of the form

structure-name.member-name

where "." is called the member operator. For example, to add the **real** members of **z** and **y** defined previously, we write

```
z.real + y.real
```

where **z.real** has a value of **10.0** and **y.real** has a value of **5.0**. Member variables are treated the same as any ordinary variable in expressions. To change the value of the imaginary member of **z**, we can make an assignment such as

```
z.imag = 14.14;
```

Accessing Structure Members with Pointers

As you might have expected, structure members can also be accessed using pointers. The declaration

```
struct complex *p_complex;
```

declares **p_complex** as a pointer to a structure of type **complex**. If we initialize **p_complex** with

```
p_complex = &z;
```

then

```
*p_complex == z
```

The notation

pointer-to-structure -> structure-member

is used to access a structure member from a pointer to the structure. The "->" operator is formed with a hyphen (minus sign), followed by a right-angle bracket (greater than symbol). The two expressions

```
p_complex -> real
```

and

```
z.real
```

are fully equivalent and refer to the same structure member.

Nested Structures

One structure may be nested within another. For example,

```
struct load
     {double          power_rating;
      struct complex  impedance;
     } motor = {250.0, 0.63, 0.2};
```

defines the structure **load** as consisting of two members. The first is a type **double** defining the member **power_rating**. The second is of type **struct complex**, defining the member impedance. The **imag** member of **impedance** for the variable **motor** is accessed as

```
motor.impedance.imag
```

12.3 STRUCTURES AND FUNCTIONS

The original K&R (Kernighan and Ritchie) version of **C** does not permit assigning structures or passing them to functions as a whole. It forces assignments to be made on a member by member basis. Individual members can be passed as arguments to functions. However, a pointer to a structure may be passed to a function. Working with pointers to structures is much less restrictive.

The ANSI **C** standard permits assigning one structure to another or passing an entire structure as a function argument. Functions are able to return structures. UNIX System V supports these features. Since many existing implementations of **C** do not, we will use only the features of the K&R version.

Structure Members as Function Arguments

Structure members can be passed by value to a function. They are treated the same as any variable that is not a structure member. Figure 12.1 lists a program that defines **struct complex** as consisting of the **double** members **real** and **imag**. The complex variable **z** is declared as being of type **static struct complex** and initialized. The function **to_polar()** is called to convert **z** from rectangular to polar form and print the resulting quantity.

```
/* passing structure members to a function */
#include <stdio.h>
#include <math.h>
#define PI 3.14159265
main()
      {
      struct complex
            {
            double real;
            double imag;
            } ;
      static struct complex z = {10.0, 10.0};
      void to_polar();

      to_polar(z.real, z.imag);
      }

void to_polar(re, im)
double re, im;
      {
      double mag, angle;

      mag = sqrt(re*re + im*im);
      angle = atan2(im, re)*180.0/PI;
      printf("magnitude = %f, angle = %6.2f degrees\n", mag, angle);
      }
```

```
magnitude = 14.142136, angle =  45.00 degrees
```

Figure 12.1 Passing structure members to a function.

To_polar() accepts the real and imaginary components of **z** as function arguments. These are included in the call as

```
to_polar(z.real, z.imag);
```

The function receiving these arguments cannot distinguish them as being structure members. They are treated as ordinary type **double**. The magnitude and angle of the **struct complex** quantity are calculated and printed.

Pointers to Structures as Function Arguments

An alternative method of communicating structure content to a function is to pass a pointer to the structure. The program of Fig. 12.2 repeats the rectangular to polar conversion for complex quantities that was performed in Fig. 12.1. However, in this case we pass a pointer to a structure instead of the structure members.

The template for the rectangular form is defined by **struct rectangular** and that for the polar form by **struct polar**. The variable **zr** is declared as being of type **static struct rectangular** and initialized. The function **to_polar()** accepts a pointer to the variable **zr** as its argument. This is assigned to the formal parameter **z**,

```
/* passing structure pointers to a function */
#include <stdio.h>
#include <math.h>
#define PI 3.14159265
struct rectangular
      {
      double real;
      double imag;
      } ;

struct polar
      {
      double mag;
      double angle;
      } ;

main()
      {
      static struct rectangular zr = {10.0, 10.0};
      void  to_polar();

      to_polar(&zr);
      }

void to_polar(z)
struct rectangular *z;
      {
      struct polar zp;

      zp.mag = sqrt(z->real*z->real + z->imag*z->imag);
      zp.angle = atan2(z->imag, z->real)*180.0/PI;
      printf("magnitude = %f, angle = %6.2f degrees\n", zp.mag, zp.angle);
      }
```

```
magnitude = 14.142136, angle = 45.00 degrees
```

Figure 12.2 Passing structure pointers to a function.

which is a pointer to **struct rectangular**. The real part of the argument is accessed as **z->real** and the imaginary part as **z->imag**.

The variable **zp** is declared in **to_polar()** as being type **struct polar**. It will hold the polar form of **zr**. The polar form of **zr** is calculated with its magnitude assigned to **zp.mag** and its angle assigned to **zp.angle**. The resulting quantity is then printed.

To_polar() could have been written to return a pointer to **zp** to the calling function instead of printing the results. In such a case, the function would have to be declared as returning a pointer to **struct polar** both in the function header and in **main()**. The function header would appear as

```
struct polar *to_polar(z)
struct rectangular *z;
```

where **z** is a pointer to **struct rectangular**. This variation is included as a problem at the end of the chapter.

12.4 ARRAYS OF STRUCTURES

Working with an Array of Structures

Whenever we are dealing with arrays of data that are related but have different type, a structure is the logical method of organizing the data. For example, in Section 10.8, two arrays were needed to specify the drawing of objects. The first was a string array (**cmd[]**) that stored characters indicating the type of drawing operation. The second was an integer array (**data[]**) giving the argument values for the drawing operation. Although maintaining two arrays is workable, it does not permit grouping logically associated data.

The two arrays **cmd[]** and **data[]** can be replaced by a structure such as:

```
struct primitives
      {
      char cmd;
      int data[MAX_ARG];
      } graphics[];
```

which permits grouping the command with its associated arguments. For example, an entry in the **graphics[]** array for a circle might look like **{'c', 200, 100, 50, 3}**. Here, **'c'** is the value of **cmd** indicating a circle command. The values for **data[]** could represent the center of the circle, its radius, and the color to be used in drawing the circle.

To access **cmd** from the first element of **graphics[]**, the notation is

```
graphics[0].cmd
```

Likewise, to access the first data value in the same element, we would write

```
graphics[0].data[0]
```

Let's consider a simple but complete example. Say that we wish to store information on **ascii** control characters within an array of structures and be able to print the data. The structure should contain the decimal value of the control character, a hexadecimal equivalent, the abbreviated name, and the key sequence used to generate the control character.

The program of Fig. 12.3 lists an implementation using structures. **Struct table** is defined as

```
struct table
     {
     int dec;
     char hex[3];
     char ascii[4];
     char *key;
     };
```

where **dec** is an **int** that stores the decimal value of a control key. (A type **char** could have been used to store this number.) **Hex[3]** stores a two-digit character string containing the hexadecimal equivalent of **dec**. The third character position

```
/* arrays of structures */
/* program that prints a complex table */
struct table
      {
      int dec;
      char hex[3];
      char ascii[4];
      char *key;
      } ;
#include <stdio.h>
#define TABL_LEN    7

main()
      {
      static struct table ctrl_keys[] =
                 {
                   {0, "00", "NUL", "CTRL/1"},
                   {7, "07", "BEL", "CTRL/G"},
                   {8, "08", "BS", "CTRL/H,BACKSPACE"},
                   {9, "09", "HT", "CTRL/I,TAB"},
                   {10, "0A", "LF", "CTRL/J,LINEFEED"},
                   {13, "0D", "CR", "CTRL/M,RETURN"},
                   {27, "1B", "ESC", "ESCAPE"}
                 };
      int i;

      for (i = 0; i < TABL_LEN; i++)
            {
            printf("%3d  ", ctrl_keys[i].dec);
            printf("%-4s", ctrl_keys[i].hex);
            printf("%-5s", ctrl_keys[i].ascii);
            printf("%-22s\n", ctrl_keys[i].key);
            }
      }
```

```
  0  00  NUL  CTRL/1
  7  07  BEL  CTRL/G
  8  08  BS   CTRL/H,BACKSPACE
  9  09  HT   CTRL/I,TAB
 10  0A  LF   CTRL/J,LINEFEED
 13  0D  CR   CTRL/M,RETURN
 27  1B  ESC  ESCAPE
```

Figure 12.3 Arrays of structures.

is needed for the **NULL** string terminator. Likewise, **ascii[4]** stores a three-character abbreviation for the control key. Finally, **key** is a pointer to type **char**. It points to the variable length string that contains a description of the key sequence for the control character. The size of **struct table** is 11 bytes (assuming **int** and pointers are 2 bytes each).

The array **ctrl_keys[]** is declared as being of type **static struct table** and initialized. Notice that the format for initialization is similar to ordinary arrays of data, except that here we are mixing data types. Also observe that **key** is initialized with the actual string constant.

A **for** loop is used to print the table. Each structure of **ctrl_keys[]** is referenced through the array subscript. Each member of a structure is accessed using the member operator and variable name.

Using Pointers to Access Elements of a Structure Array

An alternative method for printing our control keys table is to make use of pointers to structures. The program of Fig. 12.4 calls the function **prn_tbl()** to print the structure array. The arguments for this function are the array name and its size. The array name is used as a pointer to the first element of the structure.

The function **prn_tbl()** uses the variable **array** to receive a pointer to the first element of **ctrl_keys[]**; **array** is declared as a pointer to type **struct table**. Each structure is accessed by incrementing **array**. When **array** is incremented, it points to the beginning of the next structure within **ctrl_keys[]**.

12.5 BIT FIELD STRUCTURES

Definition

A *bit field* is a set of contiguous bits within an **int** or **unsigned int**. A structure is used to define bit fields. The definition of each member in a bit field structure follows the member name (if there is one) by a colon and the number of bits for that member. For example,

```
struct nibbles
     {
     unsigned low :4;
     unsigned mid :4;
     unsigned hi  :4;
     } sub_char;
```

defines a bit field structure with the tag name **nibbles** that consists of three members. Each member has a size of 4 bits and is of type **unsigned**. The variable **sub_char** is declared as being of type **struct nibbles**.

If several bit fields are of the same type, we can group their definitions on the same line using commas for separators. This is the same procedure that we have been using for all our variable declarations. For example, the preceding declaration could be written as

```
struct nibbles
     {
     unsigned low :4, mid:4, hi:4;
     } sub_char;
```

```
/* arrays of structures */
/* accessing elements of an array of structures using pointers */
struct table
      {
      int dec;
      char hex[3];
      char ascii[4];
      char *key;
      } ;
#include <stdio.h>
#define TABL_LEN  7

main()
      {
      static struct table ctrl_keys[] = {
          {0, "00", "NUL", "CTRL/1"},
          {7, "07", "BEL", "CTRL/G"},
          {8, "08", "BS", "CTRL/H,BACKSPACE"},
          {9, "09", "HT", "CTRL/I,TAB"},
          {10, "0A", "LF", "CTRL/J,LINEFEED"},
          {13, "0D", "CR", "CTRL/M,RETURN"},
          {27, "1B", "ESC", "ESCAPE"}
            };
      void prn_tbl();

      prn_tbl(ctrl_keys, TABL_LEN);
      }

void prn_tbl(array, count)
struct table *array;
int count;
      {
      int i;

      for (i = 0; i < count; i++, array++)
            {
            printf("%3d  ", array->dec);
            printf("%-4s", array->hex);
            printf("%-5s", array->ascii);
            printf("%-22s\n", array->key);
            }
      }
```

```
  0 00 NUL CTRL/1
  7 07 BEL CTRL/G
  8 08 BS  CTRL/H,BACKSPACE
  9 09 HT  CTRL/I,TAB
 10 0A LF  CTRL/J,LINEFEED
 13 0D CR  CTRL/M,RETURN
 27 1B ESC ESCAPE
```

Figure 12.4 Using pointers to access a structure array.

Bit fields can be used to pack data items that are smaller than **int** into a compact format. This saves memory space. They are also useful for accessing the registers of peripheral devices such as UARTS or CRT controllers. Bitwise operations are simplified when using bit fields.

Accessing Bit Fields

The method for access to a bit field member is identical to that of other structures. For example, to assign values to the members of **sub_char**, we write

```
sub_char.low = 0;
sub_char.mid = 15;
sub_char.hi  =  6;
```

Notice that none of the values exceeds **15**. This is the largest unsigned number (4 bits long) that fits into our **struct nibbles** members. Each member of the structure is treated as an ordinary variable and may be used in expressions such as

```
sub_char.mid += 2;
```

or

```
if ((sub_char.hi >> 2) > 0)
```

Restrictions and Caveats

A member of a bit field structure may not be larger than the size of an **int**. It may not cross an **int** boundary. If a field definition does not fit in the current **int** space, it will be aligned at the start of the next adjacent **int**. A gap is then left in the bit field definition.

We can force gaps or **pad** a field structure by inserting unnamed field widths. An unnamed width of **0** forces alignment of the next field to the beginning of the next **int** boundary. For example,

```
struct wide_1
      { unsigned b0:1, b1:2, :4, b2:2, :0, b3:4;};
```

uses the first 3 bits for **b0** and **b1**. Four padding bits are inserted between **b1** and **b2** (which is 2 bits wide). The remaining bits in the current **int** are skipped over by the **:0** specification, with **b3** aligning to the start of the next **int**.

Fields are assigned left to right on some systems and right to left on others. This is a hardware dependency that must be considered when accessing externally defined data.

All the members of a bit field structure must be of type **int** or **unsigned**. Bit fields do not have assigned addresses. Therefore, attempting to take the address of a bit field with the **&** operator is meaningless. We cannot form an array of bit fields, but we can form an array of bit field structures. Therefore, the bit field structure

```
struct illegal
      {
      unsigned b[MAX] :1;
      }
```

is illegal, whereas

```
struct bit_array
     {
     unsigned b0:1, b1:1, b2:1, b3:1;
     } bit_map[MAX];
```

is permissible.

The program of Fig. 12.5 defines an array of bit field structures, **n[SIZE]**. Each structure consists of four nibbles, **n0** through **n3**. There are five structures within the array, each occupying one **int**. The total size of the array is therefore **5 ints** or 10 bytes. In essence we are storing 20 numbers in the space of 10 bytes.

The unsigned variable **val** is initialized to **0**. The first **for** loop assigns the value of **val** to the first nibble in the first structure of the array. **Val** is incremented and its value assigned to the next nibble. One structure is initialized on each pass through the loop. This process continues until each structure has been initialized. The second **for** loop prints out the contents of the entire array.

The largest value of **val** assigned to a nibble is 19. From the printout, we can see that the largest number stored in a nibble is **15**. Why the difference? Remember that each nibble consists of only 4 bits. If **val** exceeds **15**, only the lower 4 bits will be copied into a bit field. The actual value stored in such a case is given by **val%16**.

```
/* an array of bit field structures */
#define SIZE    5
#include <stdio.h>
struct nibbles
      {
      unsigned n0: 4, nl: 4, n2: 4, n3: 4;
      } n[SIZE];

main()
      {
      int i, val;

      val = 0;
      for (i = 0;  i < SIZE;  i++)
            {
            n[i].n0 = val++;
            n[i].nl = val++;
            n[i].n2 = val++;
            n[i].n3 = val++;
            }
      for (i = 0; i < SIZE; i++)
            printf("%2d  %2d  %2d  %2d\n", n[i].n0, n[i].nl, n[i].n2, n[i].n3);
      }
```

```
 0  1  2  3
 4  5  6  7
 8  9 10 11
12 13 14 15
 0  1  2  3
```

Figure 12.5 Arrays of bit field structures.

Applying Bit Field Definitions at Arbitrary Memory Locations

It is possible to define a particular bit field structure and to apply this structure definition to a variable or memory location. This is a very useful aspect of bit fields. It can be used for convenient access to bits within a variable or to flags within a peripheral device register.

Let's define the structure

```
struct bit
     {
     unsigned b0:1, b1:1, b2:1, b3:1, b4:1, b5:1, b6:1, b7:1;
     } *sp;
```

The variable **sp** is a pointer to type **struct bit**. Suppose that we wish to examine the bits of a character **c**. By pointing **sp** at **c**, we can access the bits of **c** using the **struct bit** field definitions.

To point **sp** at **c**, we cast a pointer to **c** as a pointer to type **struct bit** and assign the value to **sp**. This is written as

```
sp = (struct bit *) &c;
```

The low-order bit of **c** is then accessed by **sp->b0**, the next higher bit by **sp->b1**, and so on.

A program that uses this technique to compute the parity of each character in a string is listed in Fig. 12.6. The output of the program consists of each character followed by its binary representation. The parity bit is inserted in the most significant bit position.

The target string **"abcdefg"** is assigned to the character array **data[]**. A **char** pointer, **dp**, is initialized to the beginning of **data[]**. The bit field structure is applied to the first character in the string by

```
sp = (struct bit *)dp;
```

Bits **0** through **7** of this character are accessed and added together. The sum is assigned to **bit_sum**. **Bit_sum** will equal the total number of "1" bits in the character. Even parity is formed by taking **bit_sum%2**. After printing the character and its binary representation, including the added parity bit, **dp** is incremented by 1 and the loop repeats. When ***dp == '\0'**, the end of the string has been reached, and the **while** loop terminates.

12.6 TYPE DEFINITION

The **C** language **typedef** keyword is used to rename existing data types. This permits simpler, easier to read type names to be substituted for more complex type definitions. For example,

```
typedef char *STRING;
```

can be used to define **STRING** as a pointer to type **char**. We can then use **STRING** as a synonym for **char *** in declarations such as

```
STRING message, table[];
```

```
/* check sum using bit fields */
#include <stdio.h>
struct bit
      {
      unsigned b0: 1, b1: 1, b2: 1, b3: 1, b4: 1, b5: 1, b6: 1, b7: 1;
      } *sp;

main()
      {
      int bit_sum, parity;
      static char data[] = "abcdefg";
      char *dp;

      dp = data;
      while (*dp != '\0')
            {
            sp = (struct bit *) dp;
            bit_sum = sp->b0 + sp->b1 + sp->b2 + sp->b3 + sp->b4 + sp->b5
            + sp->b6;
            parity = bit_sum % 2;
            printf("%c ", *dp);
            printf("%d%d%d%d%d%d%d%d\n", parity, sp->b6, sp->b5, sp->b4, sp->b3,
            sp->b2, sp->b1, sp->b0);
            dp++;
            }
      }
```

```
a 11100001
b 11100010
c 01100011
d 11100100
e 01100101
f 01100110
g 11100111
```

Figure 12.6 Using bit fields to generate parity.

Complicated declarations can be simplified by using **typedef**. For example,

```
typedef struct bitfield
     {
     unsigned b0:1,
              b1:1,
              b2:1,
              b3:1,
              hi_nib 4;
     } BITS, *BFP;
```

creates the type names **BITS** and ***BFP**. A variable named **status_reg** can be declared as being of type **struct bitfield** with the declaration

```
BITS status_reg;
```

Likewise, **stat_reg_ptr** can be declared as a pointer to type **struct bitfield** with

```
BFP stat_reg_ptr;
```

The most important use of **typedef** is to ensure program portability. For example, the size of the types **short**, **int**, and **long** is machine dependent. If a specific-sized integer is needed for an application, it can be defined in terms of the known sizes on a given machine.

Typedef is analogous to **#define**. Some important differences are that **typedef** is processed by the compiler, not the preprocessor. Also, it is restricted to renaming data types.

12.7 UNIONS

A **union** is a specially defined variable that can be used to store different types and sizes of data. It permits different data types to share a common memory space. **Unions** are defined in the same way that we define structures.

Suppose that we wish to have a variable named **value** store at various times a character pointer, an integer, and a long integer. The following **union** definition could be used.

```
union multi
     {
     char *chr;
     int num;
     long l_num;
     } value;
```

Union definitions must start with the keyword **union**. The word **multi** is the tag name for this particular **union**. The union members are defined within the body of the declaration. Any variables to be declared of type **multi** are listed after the closing brace. In this case, we have declared **value** to be of type **union multi**.

To declare additional variables as being of type **union multi**, we write

```
union multi mix, *match;
```

In this case, the variable **mix** has been declared as being of type **union multi**, whereas **match** has been declared as a pointer to type **union multi**.

To access a member of a **union**, we use the member operator just as we did for structures. The syntax is

union-name.member-name

or, if we are working with a pointer to a **union**,

union-pointer -> member-name

The programmer must know what type is stored within a **union** at all times. If data of one type are written into a union, they cannot be accessed as another type, even if the second type is defined within the union. The program of Fig. 12.7 illustrates the errors that occur when the type being stored is different from the type being extracted.

The assignment

```
value.num = 2000;
```

stores an **int** in **union multi**. When it is extracted as an **int**, the correct value is obtained. When it is extracted as a **long**, an incorrect value is obtained. Likewise, the assignment

```
value.l_num = 200000L;
```

```
/* unions */
#include <stdio.h>
main()
      {
      union
            {
            char *chr;
            int num;
            long l_num;
            } value;

      value.num = 2000;
      printf("%d\n", value.num);                  /* right */
      printf("%ld\n", value.l_num);               /* wrong */

      value.l_num = 200000L;
      printf("%ld\n", value.l_num);               /* right */
      printf("%d\n", value.num);                  /* wrong */

      value.chr = "Join the union!";              /* right */
      printf("%s\n", value.chr);
      printf("The size of value is %d bytes\n", sizeof (value));
      }
```

```
2000
-1676015664
200000
3392
Join the union!
The size of value is 4 bytes
```

Figure 12.7 Working with unions.

stores a **long int** in **union multi**. Again, if it is not extracted as the same type, an error occurs.

Finally, the assignment

```
value.chr = "Join the union!";
```

places a pointer to a character string in **union multi**. The size of a **union** is the size of the largest type that it stores. On most systems, **union multi** will have a size of 4 bytes.

PROBLEMS

12.1. Complete the **printf()** statement in the following program to output the data stored in the structure **responses**.

```
main()
    {
    struct quiz
        {
        char ans;
        int multi;
        char essay[100];
        };
    static struct quiz responses = {'T',3,"hole-electron pair"};

    printf("
    }
```

12.2. Refer to Problem 12.1. The pointer definition

```
struct quiz *ptr = &responses;
```

is added to the program. Rewrite the **printf()** statement to output the data by access through the pointer **ptr**.

12.3. Modify the program of Fig. 12.2 to return a pointer to **struct polar** as a means of conveying the converted data to **main()**.

12.4. Write a program that uses the following structure template to store the resistor color code in an array of structures. Your program should print the entire array.

```
struct color_table
    {
    int num;           /* color code number */
    char color[10];    /* color name */
    };
```

12.5. A bit field structure template is given by

```
struct bits
    {
    unsigned b0: 1, b1: 1, b2: 1, b3: 1, n:4;
    };
```

Write a program that declares **modem** to be of type **struct bits** and initializes the **b0** bit to 0, the **b1** bit to 1, the **b2** bit to 1, the **b3** bit to 0, and **n** to 13. The program should output the value of each bit field in **modem**.

PROGRAMMING PROJECTS

12.6. Rewrite the program of Fig. 10.33 to store all the commands and data in a structure defined by

```
struct primitives
      {
      char cmd;
      int data[4];
      };
```

12.7. Rewrite the program of Fig. 7.17 to store all the impedances in a structure defined by

```
struct complex
      {
      double real;
      double imag;
      };
```

chapter 13

Files

13.1 INTRODUCTION

The term *files* normally refers to a permanent data storage arrangement on a magnetic media. The most popular devices for file storage are *disks*, which come in *hard* and *floppy* varieties. A hard disk is based on a rotating rigid platter that stores tens or hundreds of millions of bytes (megabytes). The floppy disk, usually found on microcomputers, is flexible and removable. Its storage capability is on the order of 1 megabyte. Besides offering a larger storage capacity, the hard disk also provides faster data access.

The details of storage management on the disk are rather complicated. Software called the *operating system* (OS) or *disk operating system* (DOS) takes care of the difficult aspects of this storage. We are provided with a set of simple functions or commands that permit storing and retrieving data in files. Popular operating systems include UNIX and MSDOS.

The **C** language does not have a predefined file structure. All file data are considered to consist of a series of bytes. There are two basic file access methods. The first is a standardized interface referred to as *stream* or *buffered* input/output (I/O). The second is referred to as *low-level* or *unbuffered* I/O. Low-level I/O is system dependent but provides a more direct channel of communication with the files. We will consider only stream or buffered I/O in this text.

Buffered I/O refers to the accumulation of I/O data in a temporary storage location called a buffer. During a *write* operation (data storage), when the buffer is full, its contents are transferred to the disk. During a read operation (data retrieval), when the buffer is empty, a new block is read from the disk. The advantage of buffered I/O is that data are transferred to and from the disk in large blocks. This improves the efficiency by limiting the number of times the disk must be accessed.

A file is assigned a name by the user when it is created. To access a file, it must first be *opened*. For stream files, a *file pointer* replaces the file name for all references to the file after it has been opened. The file pointer points to a structure definition contained in **stdio.h** called **FILE**. The details of the structure **FILE** are important to the system, but can be ignored by the user.

13.2 STREAM INPUT/OUTPUT

To use stream files within a program, you must include the header file **stdio.h**. Although it is not necessary to become familiar with the contents of **stdio.h**, a programmer will find some of its definitions useful. These include the following constants:

```
#define EOF     -1
#define NULL     0
#define BUFSIZ  512
```

The **EOF** constant is the value returned during a read when the *end of file* has been reached. The **NULL** value for a pointer is returned if an error has occurred. **BUFSIZ** sets the size of the buffer to be used for stream I/O. It can be adjusted by the programmer, although the default setting is usually optimum.

A large number of standard library functions are available for processing stream files. The most commonly used functions are listed in Fig. 13.1. The arguments used by these functions are defined as follows:

```
FILE *stream;
char c, *filename, *type, *string, *format;
char *pathname, *buffer, *old, *new;
int n, size, origin;
long offset;
```

The argument **stream** is a pointer to an opened file. Another commonly used name for this pointer if **fp**, which stands for *file pointer*. You may use any valid name for this pointer provided that it is declared as being of type **FILE**.

Opening a File

The first step in creating a new file or accessing an existing one is to open the file with **fopen()**. This function accepts a *filename* and *type* as arguments and returns a pointer to the file. The *filename* is assigned by the user. The *type* defines the access mode and is one of the following:

"r" Read an existing file.
"w" Create a new file for writing or write over an existing file, destroying its contents.
"a" Write to the named file, appending to its end.

The **"r"** *type* is used to read from a file that was previously created. It cannot creat a file. The **"w"** *type* is used to write to a new file. It can also be used to write to an existing file, but will destroy the old contents of that file. If you wish to add information to an existing file, then the **"a"** *type* is used. This permits appending to the end of an existing file.

Fopen() returns a pointer to the file that it opened. If the file was not successfully opened, it returns a **NULL** pointer. The returned value should always be tested for a **NULL**, with appropriate action taken if the file was not successfully opened. The file pointer replaces the *filename* for all references to the opened file.

Function	*Description*
fopen (*filename, type*)	Opens *filename* for access *type* "*r*", "*w*", or "*a*"
getc (*stream*)	Reads a character from file pointed to by *stream*
fgetc (stream)	Reads a character from file pointed to by *stream*
putc (*c, stream*)	Writes character *c* to file pointed to by *stream*
fputc (*c, stream*)	Writes character *c* to file pointed to by *stream*
ungetc (*c, stream*)	Pushes character *c* back onto input *stream*
fclose (*stream*)	Closes file pointed to by *stream*
fgets (*string, n, stream*)	Reads a string of up to *n* − *1* characters from *stream* and places them into *string*
fputs (*string, stream*)	Writes *string* into file pointed to by *stream*
fscanf (*stream, format, arg, . . .*)	Reads data from *stream* using *format* conversion specifier into address specified by *arg*
fprintf (*stream, format, arg, . . .*)	Writes *arg* into *stream* using *format* conversion specifier
fread (*buffer, size, n, stream*)	Reads *n* items of length *size* from *stream* into *buffer*
fwrite (*buffer, size, n, stream*)	Writes *n* items of length *size* into *stream* from *buffer*
fseek (*stream, offset, origin*)	Locates file pointer for *stream* at *offset* bytes from *origin*
rename (*old, new*)	Renames file specified by *old* to that given by *new*
rewind (*stream*)	Sets file pointer for *stream* to beginning of file
remove (*pathname*)	Deletes file specified by *pathname*
clearerr (*stream*)	Clears error and end of file conditions on *stream*
freopen (*filename, type, stream*)	Closes current file and reassigns *stream* to *filename*
setbuf (*stream, buffer*)	Assigns user specified *buffer* to *stream*
fflush (*stream*)	Writes buffer contents to file pointed to by *stream*
ftell (*stream*)	Returns current position of file pointer for *stream*
feof (*stream*)	Detects end of file on file pointed to by *stream*
ferror (*stream*)	Detects a read/write error on *stream*
perror (*string*)	Prints *string* error message to **stderr**

Figure 13.1 Stream I/O functions.

A standard format for opening files with built-in checking for a possible **NULL** pointer is given in the program segment below.

```
/* program segment demonstrating how to properly open a file for writing */
FILE *fp;
char myfile[20];

printf("Enter the file name :");
scanf("%s",myfile);
```

```
If ((fp=fopen(myfile,"w"))==NULL);
     {
     printf("Can't open %s\n",myfile);
     exit();
     }
/* balance of program goes here */
```

The file pointer **fp** is declared as being of type **FILE**. The name of the file is assigned to the character array **myfile[20]**. The name of this array is a pointer to its starting location. It is used as the *filename* argument in **fopen()**. If the **fopen()** statement returns a **NULL** pointer, a message indicating this condition is printed and the program is terminated. Otherwise, the program continues normally.

Closing a File

The **fclose()** function is used to close a file. The argument of **fclose()** is a pointer to the file being closed. If the file is successfully closed, a **0** or **NULL** is returned. Otherwise, a **−1** is returned. The statement

```
fclose(fp);
```

closes the file pointed to by **fp**. It does not perform any error checking. A better way of closing a file is

```
if ((fclose(fp))!=NULL)
     printf("Error: can't close file\n");
```

It is important to close all open files before terminating a program; otherwise, data may be lost. Remember that data to be written into a file are stored in a buffer until the buffer is filled. The **fclose()** function will *flush* a partially filled buffer of any remaining data and write it to the file.

Character-level Input/Output

The functions **fgetc()** and **fputc()** are used, respectively, for reading and writing a character from/to a file. They are related to the now familiar functions **getchar()** and **putchar()**. The **stdio.h** header includes the definitions

```
#define getchar()   getc(stdin)
#define putchar(c)  putc((c),stdout)
```

From these definitions, we can see that **getchar()** is a special case of **getc()**. The source for the character is predefined as the standard input by the file pointer **stdin**. Likewise, **putchar(c)** is a special case of **putc(c)**, where the destination is directed to the standard output by the file pointer **stdout**.

To read a character from any specified file, the format is

```
fgetc(fp);
```

where **fp** is a pointer to the opened file. To write a character **c** to the same file, the format is

```
fputc(c,fp);
```

The program of Fig. 13.2 illustrates the use of **fgetc()** and **fputc()**. It is stored under the name **listfile** and accepts a command line argument for the file to be listed. Thus, to list a program named *filename*, the command-line syntax is

```
listfile filename
```

The program checks for the correct number of command-line arguments. If **argc == 1**, no argument was supplied and an appropriate error message is printed. If **argc > 2**, another error message is printed indicating too many arguments were supplied. The **fopen()** statement uses **argv[1]** as a pointer to the *filename* for the file to be opened. (Recall that **argv[0]** points to the name by which the program was invoked.) An alternative form would be to use ***++argv** to reference the *filename*.

If the file is successfully opened, the **while** loop reads characters from the file using **fgetc(fp)** until the end of file (**EOF**) is reached. Each character is printed to **stdout** using **fputc(c,stdout)**. We could have used **putchar(c)** in place of **fputc(c,stdout)**. Why is this possible?

Notice that **fgetc()**, **getc()**, and **getchar()** all return an **int**. This is necessary since the **EOF** value is **−1** and type **char** stores only unsigned byte-sized data. When performing file access, we must assign the value returned from these functions to a type **int**. If an application does not test for **EOF**, then the returned value may be assigned to a type **char**. Observe that **fputc()** will output a character value of size **int** or **char**.

```
/* listfile */
#include <stdio.h>

main(argc, argv)
int argc;
char *argv[];
      {
      FILE *fp;
      int c;

      if (argc == 1)
            printf("Usage: listfile file_name\n");
      else if (argc > 2)
            printf("Too many arguments to listfile\n");
      else if ((fp = fopen(argv[1], "r")) == NULL)
            {
            printf("Can't open %s\n", argv[1]);
            exit();
            }
      else
            {
            while ((c = fgetc(fp)) != EOF)
                  fputc(c, stdout);
            fclose(fp);
            }
      }
```

Figure 13.2 Listing a file using character I/O.

The functions **getc()** and **putc()** are nearly identical to **fgetc()** and **fputc()**. They are defined as macros and behave in the same manner as their functional counterparts. The function **ungetc(c,stream)** ''ungets'' the character **c** by pushing it back into the input buffer specified by **stream**.

Line Input/Output

The functions **fgets()** and **fputs()** are similar to **gets()** and **puts()** with some very important exceptions. **Fgets()** requires three arguments to read a string from a file. Its syntax is

```
fgets(string, n, stream)
```

where *string* is a pointer to the location where the string will be stored in memory. Characters are read from the file until a newline or **EOF** character is encountered or a maximum of $n - 1$ characters have been read. Why $n - 1$? Because **fgets()**, unlike **gets()**, retains the newline character and appends a **NULL** (**'\0'**) at the end. Therefore, the *n*th character in the string array becomes the **NULL**. The third argument to **fgets()** is a pointer to the stream from which the string will be read.

Fgets() returns a pointer to the string if it performed a successful read. If a **NULL** is returned, the function either encountered the **EOF** or a read error occurred. These two conditions can be distinguished by calling **feof()** or **ferror()**.

Figure 13.3 lists a program that illustrates the use of **fgets()**. This program uses command-line arguments just like the previous example. It also performs error checking on the number of command-line arguments. The program adds line numbers to any **ascii** file. It is stored under the name **linenum**. To number a file named *filename*, the command line syntax is

```
linenum filename
```

The string read by **fgets()** is assigned to the character array **line[MAX_LN]**. With **MAX_LN** set to **80**, the maximum number of characters that can be read by **fgets()** is **79**. The variable **ln** stores the line number. It is incremented after each string that is read and is printed at the start of each line.

The **fputs()** function has the syntax

```
fputs(string, stream)
```

where *string* is a pointer to the string being written into the file pointed to by *stream*. **Fputs()** does not copy the terminating **NULL** of the string into the file, nor does it append a newline character. The function returns a **NULL** if the write was successful and an **EOF** if an error occurred.

To write the string ''test'' into the file pointed to by **fp**, the **fputs()** statement would appear as follows:

```
fputs("test",fp);
```

Formatted Input/Output

The functions **fscanf()** and **fprintf()** are used for formatted input/output to a file. They are used just like the functions **scanf()** and **printf()**. The syntax for **fscanf()** and **fprintf()** is

```
fscanf(stream,format, arg,...)
fprintf(stream,format, arg,...)
```

where *stream* is a pointer to the target file. The *format* argument is a control string identical to those used for **scanf()** and **printf()**. It is followed by a list of arguments to be read or written.

```
/* linenum.c */
#include <stdio.h>
#define MAX_LN  80

main(argc, argv)
int argc;
char *argv[];
      {
      FILE *fp;
      char line[MAX_LN];
      int ln;

      if (argc == 1)
            printf("Usage: linenum file_name\n");
      else if (argc > 2)
            printf("Too many arguments to linenum\n");
      else if ((fp = fopen(*++argv, "r")) == NULL)
            {
            printf("Can't open %s\n", *argv);
            exit();
            }
      else
            {
            ln = 0;
            while (fgets(line, MAX_LN, fp))
                  printf("%3d : %s", ++ln, line);
            fclose(fp);
            }
      }
```

```
  1 : /* linenum.c */
  2 : #include <stdio.h>
  3 : #define MAX_LN  80
  4 :
  5 : main(argc, argv)
  6 : int argc;
  7 : char *argv[];
  8 :       {
  9 :       FILE *fp;
 10 :       char line[MAX_LN];
 11 :       int ln;
 12 :
 13 :       if (argc == 1)
 14 :             printf("Usage: linenum file_name\n");
 15 :       else if (argc > 2)
 16 :             printf("Too many arguments to linenum\n");
 17 :       else if ((fp = fopen(*++argv, "r")) == NULL)
 18 :             {
 19 :             printf("Can't open %s\n", *argv);
 20 :             exit();
 21 :             }
 22 :       else
 23 :             {
 24 :             ln = 0;
 25 :             while (fgets(line, MAX_LN, fp))
 26 :                   printf("%3d : %s", ++ln, line);
 27 :             fclose(fp);
 28 :             }
 29 :       }
```

Figure 13.3 Line numbering a file using line I/O.

Like **scanf()**, **fscanf()** returns the number of fields that were successfully read and assigned. If an end of file is encountered, an **EOF** is returned. Should no values be assigned, a **NULL** is returned.

The program of Fig. 13.4 uses **fprintf()** to write formatted floating-point data into a file in tabular form. It is stored under the name **writdata** and accepts a command-line argument for the name of the file where the data will be stored.

After checking for proper invocation of the program, the function **writdata()** is called. A pointer to the opened file is passed to **writdata()**. This function accepts column headings for the data table and writes them into the file. The column headings may be up to **20** characters long. The array size of **xtitle[]** and **ytitle[]** is set to **21** to accommodate the **NULL** that is appended to the end. Notice that **fprintf()**, just like **printf()**, does not output the terminating **NULL**. Therefore, the format specifier for writing the column headings into the file provides for only **20** characters.

Double type values are then read from the standard input for **x** and **y** and written into the file. The data entry loop continues while **data** are **TRUE**. This condition lasts until the **x** value is **0.0**. After a **return** from **writdata()**, the file is closed and the program terminates.

The program of Fig. 13.5 reads back the data written by the program of Fig. 13.4. The **main()** function is the same as that in the previous program with two exceptions. The file is opened as type **"r"**, and all references to **writdata** are replaced by **readdata**.

Readdata() receives a pointer to the opened file. The column headings are read from the file using **fscanf()**. A length of **21** characters is provided by the format specifier to account for the **NULL** that is appended to the strings being read.

The **fscanf()** function is used within a **while** loop to read the file data. The data are printed to the standard output aligned with the column headings. The loop continues until the function returns an **EOF**. At this point, a **return** from **readdata()** is made, the file is closed, and the program terminates.

Storing and Retrieving Data Using Fwrite() and Fread()

Data that are written into a file using **fprintf()** are stored in **ascii** form. This is not a very efficient format. Storing data in binary form saves on disk space and also speeds up access. Two standard library functions are available to facilitate the storage of data arrays in binary form. These are **fwrite()** and **fread()**.

The **fwrite()** function has the syntax

```
fwrite(buffer, size, n, stream)
```

where *buffer* is a pointer to the start of the buffer to be written into *stream*. There are *n* items in the buffer of length *size* in bytes. The arguments for the **fread()** function are identical to those for **fwrite()**. It reads *n* items of *size* length from *stream* into *buffer*. The syntax for **fread()** is

```
fread(buffer, size, n, stream)
```

Both **fwrite()** and **fread()** return the number of items actually written or read from stream. The returned number will differ from *n* only if an error occurs or the end of file is reached. This information can be used for error trapping.

A program that writes an array of integers into a file is given in Fig. 13.6. The array **buffer[]** consists of **14 int** sized numbers. Notice that the **fwrite()** statement casts **buffer** into a type **char**. The length of each item to be written is 2 bytes and

```
/* writdata */
#include <stdio.h>
#define TRUE     1
#define FALSE   0

main(argc, argv)
int argc;
char *argv[];
      {
      FILE *fp;
      void writdata();

      if (argc == 1)
            printf("Usage: writdata file_name\n");
      else if (argc > 2)
            printf("Too many arguments to writdata\n");
      else if ((fp = fopen(*++argv, "w")) == NULL)
            {
            printf("Can't open %s\n", *argv);
            exit();
            }
      else
            {
            writdata(fp);
            fclose(fp);
            }
      }

void writdata(dfp)
FILE *dfp;
      {
      double x, y;
      char xtitle[21], ytitle[21];
      int i, data;

      puts("Enter X column heading");
      gets(xtitle);
      puts("Enter Y column heading");
      gets(ytitle);

      fprintf(dfp, "%20s%20s\n", xtitle, ytitle);

      i = 0;
      data = TRUE;
      while (data)
            {
            printf("Enter x%d, y%d : ", i, i);
            scanf("%lf,%lf", &x, &y);
            if (x == 0)
                  data = FALSE;
            else
                  fprintf(dfp, "%lf %lf\n", x, y);
            i++;
            }
      }
```

```
writdata labdatal
Enter X column heading
Voltage
Enter Y column heading
Current
Enter x0, y0 : 0.1, 5.5
Enter x1, y1 : 0.2, 6.8
Enter x2, y2 : 0.3, 7.9
Enter x3, y3 : 0.4, 10.1
Enter x4, y4 : 0.5, 11.8
Enter x5, y5 : 0.0, 0.0
```

Figure 13.4 Writing numeric data using formatted I/O.

```
/* readdata */
#include <stdio.h>

main(argc, argv)
int argc;
char *argv[];
      {
      FILE *fp;
      void readdata();

      if (argc == 1)
            printf("Usage: readdata file_name\n");
      else if (argc > 2)
            printf("Too many arguments to readdata\n");
      else if ((fp = fopen(*++argv, "r")) == NULL)
            {
            printf("Can't open %s\n", *argv);
            exit();
            }
      else
            {
            readdata(fp);
            fclose(fp);
            }
      }

void readdata(dfp)
FILE *dfp;
      {
      double x, y;
      char xtitle[21], ytitle[21];

      fscanf(dfp, "%21s%21s", xtitle, ytitle);
      printf("%20s%20s\n\n", xtitle, ytitle);
      while ((fscanf(dfp, "%lf %lf", &x, &y)) != EOF)
            printf("%20.6lf%20.6lf\n", x, y);
      }
```

```
readdata labdata1
             Voltage             Current

            0.100000            5.500000
            0.200000            6.800000
            0.300000            7.900000
            0.400000           10.100000
            0.500000           11.800000
```

Figure 13.5 Reading numeric data using formatted I/O.

there are a total of **14** items. If you can view the file image of the data that are written, you will observe that it consists of binary data, not **ascii** coded numbers.

Figure 13.7 lists a program that reads the data written by the program in Fig. 13.6. The data are read into the array **buffer[]**. A **for** loop is used to print the array members to the standard output.

Fseek() and Ftell()

The **fseek()** function allows setting the file pointer to any position within the file. This permits random access to any file entry. Its syntax is

fseek (*stream, offset, origin*)

```
/* fwrite */
#include <stdio.h>
main()
	{
	static int buffer[] =
		{
		70, 71, 72, 73, 74, 75, 76, 77, 78, 79, 80, 81, 82, 83
		};
	FILE *fp;
	int i;

	fp = fopen("testdata", "w");
	fwrite((char *) buffer, 2, 14, fp);
	fclose(fp);
	}
```

Figure 13.6 Writing an array of data using **fwrite()**.

```
/* fread*/
#include <stdio.h>

main()
	{
	FILE *fp;
	static int buffer[14];
	int i;

	fp = fopen("testdata", "r");
	fread((char *) buffer, 2, 14, fp);
	fclose(fp);
	for (i = 0; i < 14; i++)
		printf("%d\n", buffer[i]);
	}
```

```
70
71
72
73
74
75
76
77
78
79
80
81
82
83
```

Figure 13.7 Reading an array of data using **fread()**.

where *origin* is an **int** that defines a reference position according to the following scheme:

0 Beginning of file
1 Current position of file pointer
2 End of file

The argument *offset* is a **long** type and indicates the location relative to the *origin* to which the file pointer will be moved. **Fseek()** returns a zero if the pointer was reset without error.

The **ftell**(*stream*) function returns the current position of the file pointer associated with *stream*. The returned value is **long**. If a **−1L** is returned, an error has occurred.

A short program that illustrates the use of **fseek()** and **ftell()** is given in Fig. 13.8. The contents of **buffer[]** are written into the file **testdata** using **fwrite()**. The data consist of the first seven letters of the alphabet. The file is then reopened for reading.

```
/* fseek and ftell*/
#include <stdio.h>

main()
        {
        static char buffer[] = "abcdefg";
        FILE *fp;
        long pick;
        long offset;
        char c;

        fp = fopen("testdata", "w");
        fwrite(buffer, 1, 7, fp);
        fclose(fp);

        fp = fopen("testdata", "r");
        for (pick = 3;  pick < 7;  pick++)
                {
                fseek(fp, pick, 0);
                offset = ftell(fp);
                fscanf(fp, "%c", &c);
                printf("data item at offset %ld is %c\n", offset, c);
                }
        fclose(fp);
        }
```

```
data item at offset 3 is d
data item at offset 4 is e
data item at offset 5 is f
data item at offset 6 is g
```

Figure 13.8 Using **fseek()** and **ftell()**.

The reference point for reading is set to the beginning of the file by the *origin* value of **0**. The variable **pick** is the *offset* relative to the *origin*. After the file pointer is positioned by **fseek()**, its location is read by **ftell()** and assigned to the variable **offset**. The value of **offset** is printed to verify correct setting of the file pointer. **Pick** ranges from **3** to **6**. For each location, a character is read from the file and printed to the standard output. The output of the program consists of the **offset** values determined by **pick** and the contents of the file at those locations.

Other File Operations

Let's look briefly at the other stream I/O functions listed in Fig. 13.1. **Rename**(*old*,*new*) renames a file from *old* name to *new* name. The arguments *old* and *new* are pointers to the type **char**. If **rename()** is successful, a **0** is returned.

The **rewind**(*stream*) function relocates the file pointer associated with *stream* to the beginning of the file. This is equivalent to using **fseek**(*stream, 0L, 0*). Rewind returns a **0** if the *stream* is successfully rewound.

Remove(*pathname*) is used to delete a file specified by *pathname* from the system directory. The original **C** function that is equivalent to **remove()** is **unlink**(*pathname*). If **remove()** is successful, a **0** is returned.

Freopen(*filename, type, stream*) closes the file associated with *stream* and assigns *stream* to *filename*. The *type* argument takes on the same values that it would with the **fopen()** function, that is, **"r"**, **"w"**, and **"a"**. A typical application of **freopen()** is to redirect I/O from **stdin**, **stdout**, or **stderr**. **Freopen()** returns a pointer to the new *filename* or a **0** should an error occur.

The **setbuf**(*stream, buffer*) function is used to control buffering on the file specified by *stream*. If the *buffer* argument is **NULL**, the stream will be unbuffered. Otherwise, *buffer* must point to an array of type **char**. The size of the array is **BUFSIZ** as defined in **stdio.h. Setbuf()** permits a user-allocated buffer to be substituted for the default system buffer. It also permits selecting buffered or unbuffered I/O on a particular *stream*.

The following program fragment opens a file named **my_data** and provides a user-specified buffer called **my_buf**.

```
#include <stdio.h>
FILE *fp;
char *my_buf, my_data[20];

fp = fopen("my_data","r");
my_buf = malloc(BUFSIZ);
setbuf(fp,my_buf);
```

To eliminate buffering on this *stream*, **setbuf()** is called with a **NULL** argument for *buffer*. The allocated memory should then be freed with **free(my_buf)**.

The **fflush**(*stream*) function is used to write the contents of a buffer to the file specified by *stream*. It is used to clear any remaining data from the buffer and transfer them into the file. The **fclose()** function automatically flushes a buffer before closing the *stream*. A **0** value is returned by **fflush()** if the buffer was successfully flushed.

The **feof**(*stream*) function is used to detect end of file on *stream*. It returns a nonzero value when the location of the file pointer is beyond the end of file and a **0** when **EOF** is not detected.

A pair of functions are available to detect and clear read or write errors on any stream. **Ferror**(*stream*) returns a nonzero value if a read/write error has occurred on *stream*. If no error has occurred, a **0** is returned. All error indications on a stream remain until the stream is closed or rewound or the **clearerr()** function is called. **Clearerr**(*stream*) resets the error indications on *stream* and also clears a detected **EOF** condition.

The **perror**(*string*) function prints error messages to **stderr**. It prints the user-supplied *string* followed by a colon, the system error message, and a newline. The output stream for **perror()** is not affected by redirection of the **stdout** to another stream.

13.3 REDIRECTION, PIPES, AND FILTERS

Operating systems such as UNIX and MSDOS provide convenient features for file manipulation. These include:

1. *Redirection* of a program *input* from **stdin** to a file or other device.
2. *Redirection* of a program *output* from **stdout** to a file or other device.
3. *Piping* (connecting) programs together so that the output of one is automatically directed into the input of another.
4. *Filter* programs. Filters are utility programs that take data from **stdin**, perform some operation on the data, and write the data to **stdout**.

The preceding features are invoked under software control using standard operators. These are listed in Fig. 13.9 with a description of their function. *Infile* refers to a file that is to be used in place of **stdin** as the source of input. *Outfile* refers to a file that is to be used in place of **stdout** as the destination for output.

Indevice and *outdevice* refer to I/O device names that are recognized by the operating system. These include I/O devices that have standard names assigned by the operating system and any others that are assigned names when the software for these devices (called *device drivers*) is installed. Standard device names for UNIX and MSDOS are listed in Fig. 13.10.

Operator	*Usage*	*Description*
>	*program* > *outfile* or *program* > *outdevice*	Redirects output of *program* to *outfile* or *outdevice*. If *outfile* did not exist, it is created. Otherwise, the previous content of outfile is destroyed.
>>	*program* >> outfile	Redirects output of *program* to *outfile* appending to the end of existing file data.
<	*program* < infile	Redirects the input of *program* from **stdin** to *infile*.
	or *program* < indevice	Redirects the input of *program* from **stdin** to *indevice*, which may be any input device that is recognized by the operating system.
¦	*program1* ¦ program2	Pipes (connects) the output of *program1* to the input of *program2*.

Figure 13.9 Symbols used for redirection and piping.

Device	*UNIX name*	*MSDOS name*
Line printer	LP:	LPT1:, LPT2:, or LPT3:
Console	CONSOLE:	CON:
Floppy drive	RDFO:	
Serial terminal	TTY1:, TTY2:, etc.	COM1:, COM2:

Figure 13.10 Standard device names under UNIX and MSDOS.

Redirection

To illustrate the use of redirection, suppose that a program called **helper** generates output that is normally printed on the standard output (console). Let's say that we want the output saved in a file called **gooddata**. When the program name is typed at the command line, simply add the redirection operator > followed by the destination file name as follows:

```
helper > gooddata
```

Care must be taken in using the redirection operation. *All* the output is redirected, including any messages or prompts generated by the program.

Let's assume that **helper** normally gets its input from the standard input (console), and we wish to redirect the input to come from a file called **rawdata**. This is implemented by invoking **helper** as follows:

```
helper < rawdata
```

We can go one step further and tell **helper** to get its input from **rawdata** and sent its output to **gooddata**. This uses combined input and output redirection.

```
helper < rawdata > gooddata
```

Both UNIX and MSDOS treat devices as files. We can therefore redirect output to a particular device conveniently. To send the output of **helper** to the line printer in a UNIX system, we type at the command line

```
helper > /dev/lp
```

where the notation /**dev**/ is used to specify that the device **lp** is found in a subdirectory called **dev** (devices). In an MSDOS system, we accomplish the same result with

```
helper > lpt1:
```

Piping

We can connect two or more programs together and have them act as one by *piping*. The output of the first program automatically becomes the input of the second, and so on. For example, suppose that we wish to print a sorted directory of files. The command to print a directory is *ls* for UNIX and **dir** for MSDOS. Both operating systems have a **sort** *filter* that sorts data from the standard input and prints to the standard output. To obtain a sorted directory, all we need do is pipe the output of **ls** (**dir**) into the **sort** filter as follows:

For UNIX `ls ¦ sort`
For MSDOS `dir ¦ sort`

Filters

As mentioned earlier, filters are utility programs that take data from the standard input (or a specified file), perform some operation on the data, and write the result to the standard output. Filters are supplied with the operating system. Figure 13.11 lists some common filters provided by UNIX and MSDOS.

UNIX name	*MSDOS name*	*Description*
sort	**sort**	Sorts data from **stdin**
grep	**find**	Finds pattern in a given file
more	**more**	Views files one screen at a time with pauses for reading

Figure 13.11 Common filters under UNIX and MSDOS.

A filter may be used in conjunction with redirection or piping operators. For example, we can redirect the input to the **sort** filter so that it comes from the file **rawdata** and have its output redirected into the file **sortdata** with

```
sort < rawdata > sortdata
```

To illustrate piping with filters, consider the following:

For MSDOS `dir | sort | more`
For UNIX `ls | sort | more`

The directory command (**dir** or **ls**) output is piped into the **sort** filter. The sort filter output is then piped into the **more** filter. The final output to the console will be a sorted directory printed one screen at a time.

PROBLEMS

13.1. Modify the program of Fig. 13.2 to count the characters in a file instead of printing the file to the standard output. The only output will be the total number of characters in the file (or the length of the file in bytes).

13.2. Refer to the **listfile.c** program of Fig. 13.2. Modify this program to copy one file to another. It should be invoked at the command line as

copy *sourcefile newfile*

13.3. Modify the program in Problem 13.2 to convert the *sourcefile* to uppercase in the *newfile*.

13.4. Modify the **linenum.c** program of Fig. 13.3 to list a number of lines from a file as specified at the command line (with a default count of 10). It should be invoked as

view *filename -linecount*

13.5. Use I/O redirection to convert **listfile.c** into a file copy utility.

13.6. Use I/O redirection with **linenum.c** to store a line-numbered version of the specified *filename*.

PROGRAMMING PROJECTS

13.7. Modify the function-plotting program of Fig. 10.11 to receive the function samples from a file. This will require a separate program that digitizes a function and stores the samples in a file.

13.8. Modify the data-plotting program of Fig. 10.13 to receive the data samples from a file. This will require a separate program that places the data to be plotted in a file.

13.9. Use **fwrite()** and **fread()** to save a video screen to a file and recall it from the file. You will need to know the base address of video memory for your system.

13.10. Binary data that are to be transmitted between computers are often converted into what is called a hex ASCII format. Each binary byte is converted into a two-digit ASCII representation. Thus the binary value A5 would be converted into an ASCII A (41), followed by an ASCII 5 (35). One standard protocol for data transmission utilizing this conversion scheme is the Motorola S-record format:

```
¦ type ¦ byte count ¦ address ¦ data bytes ¦ checksum ¦
```

The type always starts with the ASCII character 'S' followed by an ASCII 0, 1, 2, 8, or 9. The byte count (two ASCII characters) equals the number of bytes in the balance of the record, including address, data, and checksum bytes. The address is the memory location where the first byte of the record will be loaded. The data bytes are the data to be transmitted in hex ASCII format. Finally, the checksum (two ASCII characters) is the complement of the sum of the byte count, address bytes, and data bytes. At the receiving end, a calculated checksum is compared to the received checksum to detect transmission errors.

The first record to be transmitted is called the header record. It is a type S0 and does not contain any data, but may include some file description in the data field. An S1 type record is a data record with a 2-byte address field. It is used with an S9 termination record. An S2 type record is a data record with a 3-byte address field. It is used with an S8 termination record. Neither termination record contains any data. The number of data bytes in an S1 or S2 data record is not standardized. You may use 25 bytes or 50 hex ASCII characters for convenience.

The following pseudocode describes how to convert an S record file into a binary file. Refine the pseudocode and write a **C** program to implement the S record to binary file conversion.

```
/* pseudocode for S record to binary file conversion */
open S record input file
open binary output file
get the record type from input file
while (record type not termination)
     get hex ASCII count and convert to integer
     get address and convert to integer
     add address to checksum
     for (each data byte)
          get data byte from input and convert to integer
          add data to checksum
          put data in output file
     end for
     get (rcv_checksum and convert to integer
     if (rcv_checksum != checksum)
          process error
     end if
     get the record type from the input file
end while
close input file
close output file
/* end of pseudocode */
```

13.11. Refer to Problem 13.10. Develop pseudocode for converting a binary file into an S record file. Write a **C** program for the conversion. You should be able to convert in both directions and recover the original binary file.

chapter 14

Numerical Methods and Applications

14.1 GAUSS–JORDAN SOLUTION FOR SIMULTANEOUS EQUATIONS

The most frequently used manual method for the solution of simultaneous equations is *Cramer's rule*. This method of determinants is perfectly acceptable when dealing with two or three equations in as many unknowns. However, as the number of equations increases, the computations required by Cramer's rule increase at a very rapid rate. (The evaluation of an $\mathbf{N} \times \mathbf{N}$ determinant requires in excess of $\mathbf{N!}$ multiplications.) This can increase the computation time to an unacceptable level and also reduce the accuracy of the results.

For larger systems of equations, especially when implementing a computer solution, other methods are preferred. The Gauss–Jordan elimination method will yield a fast and accurate solution for up to ten or more equations. The Gauss–Seidel method, which uses an iterative or successive approximation technique, allows the user to specify the required accuracy of the solution. The computation time of the Gauss–Seidel method depends on the required accuracy and the equations themselves.

The Gauss–Jordan algorithm is based on the elimination of variables method used in algebra courses. However, rather than relying on an arbitrary or intuitive method of selecting which variables to eliminate, the procedure utilizes a systematic method of elimination. Let's review the elimination process prior to formalizing the algorithm. Consider the set of simultaneous equations shown in Fig. 14.1.

$$\begin{aligned} 2X_1 + 3X_2 + 5X_3 &= 10 \qquad (1) \\ X_1 + 2X_2 + 4X_3 &= 5 \qquad (2) \\ 4X_1 + 7X_2 + 3X_3 &= 15 \qquad (3) \end{aligned}$$

Figure 14.1 Set of simultaneous equations.

To eliminate X_1 from the second equation, we can multiply the first equation by ½ and then subtract equation (1) from (2). Similarly, to eliminate X_1 from the third equation, we can multiply the first equation by 2 and subtract equation (1) from (3). This yields the equations of Fig. 14.2.

$$
\begin{aligned}
2X_1 + 3X_2 + 5X_3 &= 10 \quad (1)\\
0.5X_2 + 1.5X_3 &= 0 \quad (2)\\
X_2 - 7X_3 &= -5 \quad (3)
\end{aligned}
$$

Figure 14.2 Equations after eliminating **x1** from (2) and (3).

Notice that the first equation was used to eliminate the first variable (X_1) from equations (2) and (3). Following the same procedure, we can eliminate the second variable from equations (1) and (3) by using the second equation. If we multiply (2) by 6 and subtract from (1), the second variable will be eliminated from (1). Similarly, multiplying (2) by 2 and subtracting from (3) will eliminate the second variable from (3). The resulting equations are shown in Fig. 14.3.

$$
\begin{aligned}
2X_1 - 4X_3 &= 10 \quad (1)\\
0.5X_2 + 1.5X_3 &= 0 \quad (2)\\
-10X_3 &= -5 \quad (3)
\end{aligned}
$$

Figure 14.3 Equations after eliminating **x2** from (1) and (3).

The last step is to use the third equation to eliminate the third variable from equations (1) and (2). This leaves only one variable in each of the three equations, as shown in Fig. 14.4. At this point, the solutions for X_1, X_2, and X_3 can be obtained simply by dividing both sides of each equation by the coefficients of the variables. Carrying out the division yields.

$$
\begin{aligned}
2X_1 &= 12 \quad (1)\\
0.5X_2 &= -0.75 \quad (2)\\
-10X_3 &= -5 \quad (3)
\end{aligned}
$$

Figure 14.4 Equations after eliminating **x3** from (1) and (2).

$$
\begin{aligned}
X_1 &= 6\\
X_2 &= -1.5\\
X_3 &= 0.5
\end{aligned}
$$

We can generalize the procedure discussed for **N** equations in **N** unknowns. Consider the set of equations

$$
\begin{aligned}
&a_{11}x_1 + a_{12}x_2 + a_{13}x_3 + \cdots + a_{1N}x_N = a_{1(N+1)}\\
&a_{21}x_2 + a_{22}x_2 + \cdots\\
&\cdot\\
&\cdot\\
&\cdot\\
&a_{N1}x_1 + a_{N2}x_2 + a_{N3}x_3 + \cdots + a_{NN}x_N = a_{N(N+1)}
\end{aligned}
$$

Suppose that we wish to use equation **i** to eliminate variable **i** from equation **j**. Equation **i** would be multiplied by some factor such that, when subtracting the resulting equation from equation **j**, it will cause the **i**th coefficient in **j** to become zero. Based on the preceding example, the multiplying factor to be used in equation **i** would be given by

$$\mathbf{m} = \frac{\mathbf{a_{ji}}}{\mathbf{a_{ii}}}$$

When equation **i** is then subtracted from equation **j**, the resulting coefficients of **j** become

$$(\mathbf{a_{j1}} - \mathbf{ma_{i1}})\mathbf{x_1} + (\mathbf{a_{j2}} - \mathbf{ma_{i2}})\mathbf{x_2} + \cdots + (\mathbf{a_{jN}} - \mathbf{ma_{iN}})\mathbf{x_N} = \mathbf{a_{j(N+1)}} - \mathbf{ma_{i(N+1)}}$$

with $\mathbf{a_{ji}} - \mathbf{ma_{ii}} = \mathbf{0}$.

If this procedure is repeated for all values of **j** from **1** to **N** except for **j** = **i**, variable **i** will have been eliminated from all equations except equation **i**. The entire procedure may then be repeated for all values of **i** from **1** to **N**. This will produce a set of equations with all coefficients $\mathbf{a_{ij}} = \mathbf{0}$ except for the main diagonal elements $\mathbf{a_{ii}}$. At this point, the unknowns may be solved for simply by dividing each equation by the coefficient of the only remaining variable. The solution for each $\mathbf{x_i}$ is then given by

$$\mathbf{x_i} = \frac{\mathbf{a_{i(N+1)}}}{\mathbf{a_{ii}}}$$

The pseudocode for the Gauss–Jordan elimination method is given in Fig. 14.5. It is derived from the preceding analysis. A **C** program to solve a set of simultaneous equations based this pseudocode is given in Fig. 14.6. The **main()** function reads in the number of equations, assigning the value to **n**. The function **getdata**(*a,n*) reads in the coefficients of the **n** equations and assigns them to the array **a**. Notice that the name of the array and the number of equations are passed to **getdata()**. The declaration of **a** in **getdata** includes the number of columns in the array. This is needed by the function so that it knows how the array is organized.

The function **prtdata**(*a,n*) merely prints the coefficients that were just entered to the standard output. It can be used to verify data entry. **Gauss_jordan**(*a,n*) performs the elimination routine. It forces all the coefficients off the main diagonal to zero. A call to **prtx**(*a,n*) then divides the remaining variable in each equation by its coefficient to solve for the **x** value and print the result.

```
/* pseudocode for Gauss-Jordan elimination */
     for (i from 1 to N)
          for (j from 1 to N)
               if (j!= i)
                    m = a(j,i)/a(i,i)
                    for (k from 1 to N+1)
                           a(j,k) = a(j,k) - m*a(i,k)
                    end for
               end if
          end for
     end for
```

Figure 14.5 Pseudocode for Gauss–Jordan elimination.

```
/* Gauss-Jordan Solution for Simultaneous Equations */
#include <stdio.h>
#define MAX_ROWS    10
#define MAX_COLS    11

main()
      {
      int i, j, k, n;
      double m;
      static double a[MAX_ROWS][MAX_COLS];
      void getdata(), prtdata(), gauss_jordan(), prtx();

      puts("Enter the number of equations");
      scanf("%d", &n);
      getdata(a, n);
      prtdata(a, n);
      gauss_jordan(a, n);
      prtx(a, n);
      }

void getdata(a, n)
int n;
double a[][MAX_COLS];
      {
      int i, j;

      for (i = 1; i <= n; i++)
            for (j = 1; j <= n + 1; j++)
                  {
                  printf("\nEnter coefficient A(%d,%d)  ", i, j);
                  scanf("%lf", &a[i][j]);
                  }
      }

void prtdata(a, n)
int n;
double a[][MAX_COLS];
      {
      int i, j;

      for (i = 1; i <= n; i++)
            {
            for (j = 1; j <= n + 1; j++)
                  printf("\t%f", a[i][j]);
            putchar('\n');
            }
      }

void gauss_jordan(a, n)
int n;
double a[][MAX_COLS];
      {
      int i, j, k;
      double m;
      for (i = 1; i <= n; i++)
            for (j = 1; j <= n; j++)
                  if (j != i)
                        {
                        m = a[j][i]/a[i][i];
                        for (k = 1; k <= n + 1; k++)
                              a[j][k] = a[j][k] - m*a[i][k];
                        }
      }
```

Figure 14.6 Gauss–Jordan solution for simultaneous equations.

```
void prtx(a, n)
int n;
double a[][MAX_COLS];
        {
        int i, j;
        double x[MAX_ROWS];

        for (i = 1; i <= n; i++)
                {
                x[i] = a[i][n + 1]/a[i][i];
                printf("\nX(%d)= %f", i, x[i]);
                }
        }
```

Figure 14.6 (continued).

Although the program is useful in its present form, some desirable improvements can be made. In computing the multiplication factor **m**, division by $\mathbf{a_{ii}}$ was performed. $\mathbf{a_{ii}}$ is called the *pivot element*. What if $\mathbf{a_{ii}} = \mathbf{0}$? This condition would cause our program to become useless, since the computer cannot handle division by zero. Even if $\mathbf{a_{ii}}$ is not zero but merely small in comparison to other terms, excessive roundoff errors may occur. To avoid each of these pitfalls, a technique called *partial pivoting* is used.

Partial pivoting involves exchanging equations to place the largest coefficient on or below the main diagonal point of any column at the main diagonal position. This process is performed prior to computing the multiplication factor **m** and effectively eliminates the problem of zero or small pivot elements.

Another improvement to the algorithm involves eliminating unnecessary computations. When the **i**th equation is used in the elimination process, all off-diagonal terms in columns between **1** and $\mathbf{i - 1}$ will have been set to zero. Therefore, it is not necessary to compute new values for these coefficients. Also, the **i**th coefficient is excluded from the computation ($\mathbf{i = j}$). This leaves only the coefficients in the range $\mathbf{i + 1}$ to **N** that must be computed in subtracting the **i**th equation from the **j**th equation.

The pseudocode for Gauss–Jordan elimination with partial pivoting is given in Fig. 14.7. A **C** program to solve simultaneous equations based on this pseudocode is given in Fig. 14.8. The only differences between this program and the last occurs within the elimination function, which is called **gj_pp()** here. A routine is added to find the equation with the largest coefficient on or below the main diagonal in column **i**. It assigns to the variable **r** the row number of the equation with the largest coefficient. The equation at row **r** is then swapped with that at row **i**. The only other change is made to the lower limit of the **for** loop in the elimination routine. It becomes $\mathbf{i + 1}$, thus eliminating unnecessary computations.

To apply the Gauss–Jordan method for solving a set of equations, let's analyze the circuit of Fig. 14.9. It represents an R-2R ladder used to convert digital input signals into an analog output. Assume that we wish to solve for the output voltage, $\mathbf{v_o}$, when the input voltages are specified as

$$\mathbf{v_1} = \mathbf{v_3} = \mathbf{v_5} = \mathbf{0} \text{ volts}$$

$$\mathbf{v_2} = \mathbf{v_4} = \mathbf{v_6} = \mathbf{5} \text{ volts}$$

and the resistance values are

$$\mathbf{R} = \mathbf{10{,}000} \text{ ohms}$$

$$\mathbf{2R} = \mathbf{20{,}000} \text{ ohms}$$

```
/* pseudocode for Gauss-Jordan elimination with partial pivoting */
for (i from 1 to N)
    find equation with largest coefficient in column i on or below main diagonal
    swap equations to place largest coefficient in column i on main diagonal
    for (j from 1 to N)
       if (j!= i)
            m = a(j,i)/a(i,i)
            for (k from i+1 to N+1)
               a(j,k) = a(j,k) - m*a(i,k)
            end for
       end if
    end for
end for
```

Figure 14.7 Pseudocode for Gauss–Jordan solution to simultaneous equations with partial pivoting.

```
/* Gauss-Jordan Solution for Simultaneous Equations */
/* with partial pivoting */
#include <stdio.h>
#include <math.h>
#define MAX_ROWS    10
#define MAX_COLS    11

main()
      {
      int i, j, k, n, r;
      double m, t, max;
      static double a[MAX_ROWS][MAX_COLS];
      void getdata(), prtdata(), gj_pp(), prtx();

      puts("Enter the number of equations");
      scanf("%d", &n);
      getdata(a, n);
      prtdata(a, n);
      gj_pp(a, n);
      prtx(a, n);
      }

void getdata(a, n)
int n;
double a[][MAX_COLS];
      {
      int i, j;

      for (i = 1; i <= n; i++)
            for (j = 1; j <= n + 1; j++)
                  {
                  printf("\nEnter coefficient A(%d,%d)  ", i, j);
                  scanf("%lf", &a[i][j]);
                  }
      }

void prtdata(a, n)
int n;
double a[][MAX_COLS];
      {
      int i, j;
```

Figure 14.8 Gauss–Jordan solution for simultaneous equations with partial pivoting.

```
        for (i = 1; i <= n; i++)
              {
              for (j = 1; j <= n + 1; j++)
                    printf("\t%f", a[i][j]);
              putchar('\n');
              }
        }

void gj_pp(a, n)
int n;
double a[][MAX_COLS];
        {
        int i, j, k, r;
        double max, temp, m;

        for (i = 1; i <= n; i++)
              {
              /* find equation with max coefficient on or below main diagonal */
              max = -1.0;
              for (k = i; k <= n; k++)
                    if (abs(a[k][i]) > max)
                          {
                          max = abs(a[k][i]);
                          r = k;
                          }
              /* swap equation at row r with that at the ith row */
              for (k = i; k <= n + 1; k++)
                    {
                    temp = a[i][k];
                    a[i][k] = a[r][k];
                    a[r][k] = temp;
                    }
              /* Perform elimination */
              for (j = 1; j <= n; j++)
                    if (j != i)
                          {
                          m = a[j][i]/a[i][i];
                          for (k = i + 1; k <= n + 1; k++)
                                a[j][k] = a[j][k] - m*a[i][k];
                          }
              }
        }

void prtx(a, n)
int n;
double a[][MAX_COLS];
        {
        int i, j;
        double x[MAX_ROWS];

        for (i = 1; i <= n; i++)
              {
              x[i] = a[i][n + 1]/a[i][i];
              printf("\nX(%d)= %e", i, x[i]);

              }
        }
```

Figure 14.8 (continued).

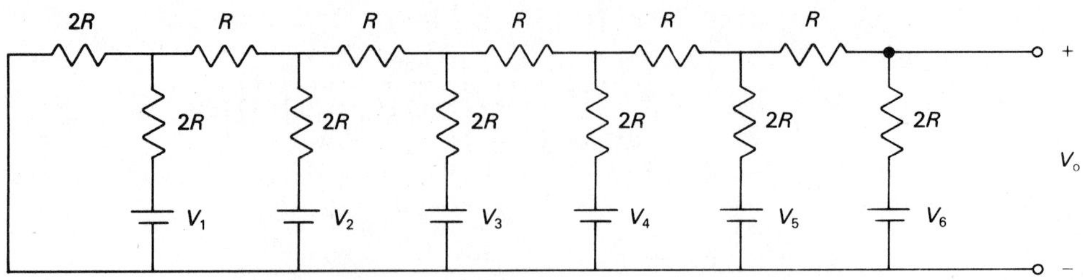

Figure 14.9 R-2R ladder used in D/A conversion.

The loop equations for the network are

$$
\begin{aligned}
40000i_1 - 20000i_2 &= 0\\
-20000i_1 + 50000i_2 - 20000i_3 &= 5\\
-20000i_2 + 50000i_3 - 20000i_4 &= -5\\
-20000i_3 + 50000i_4 - 20000i_5 &= 5\\
-20000i_4 + 50000i_5 - 20000i_6 &= -5\\
-20000i_5 + 50000i_6 &= 5
\end{aligned}
$$

These equations are entered into the program of Fig. 14.8 as follows:

```
Enter the number of equations 6
Enter coefficient A(1,1) 40000
Enter coefficient A(1,2) -20000
Enter coefficient A(1,3) 0
Enter coefficient A(1,4) 0
Enter coefficient A(1,5) 0
Enter coefficient A(1,6) 0
Enter coefficient A(1,7) 0
Enter coefficient A(2,1) -20000
Enter coefficient A(2,2) 50000
Enter coefficient A(2,3) -20000
Enter coefficient A(2,4) 0
Enter coefficient A(2,5) 0
Enter coefficient A(2,6) 0
Enter coefficient A(2,7) 5
Enter coefficient A(3,1) 0
Enter coefficient A(3,2) -20000
Enter coefficient A(3,3) 50000
Enter coefficient A(3,4) -20000
Enter coefficient A(3,5) 0
Enter coefficient A(3,6) 0
Enter coefficient A(3,7) -5
Enter coefficient A(4,1) 0
Enter coefficient A(4,2) 0
Enter coefficient A(4,3) -20000
Enter coefficient A(4,4) 50000
Enter coefficient A(4,5) -20000
Enter coefficient A(4,6) 0
Enter coefficient A(4,7) 5
Enter coefficient A(5,1) 0
Enter coefficient A(5,2) 0
Enter coefficient A(5,3) 0
Enter coefficient A(5,4) -20000
Enter coefficient A(5,5) 50000
Enter coefficient A(5,6) -20000
Enter coefficient A(5,7) -5
```

```
Enter coefficient A(6,1) 0
Enter coefficient A(6,2) 0
Enter coefficient A(6,3) 0
Enter coefficient A(6,4) 0
Enter coefficient A(6,5) -20000
Enter coefficient A(6,6) 50000
Enter coefficient A(6,7) 5

X(1)= 5.639648e-05
X(2)= 1.127930e-04
X(3)= -2.441406e-05
X(4)= 7.617187e-05
X(5)= -3.515625e-05
X(6)= 8.593750e-05
```

From the output, it can be seen that loop current $\mathbf{i}_6$ is equal to 85.9375 microamperes (85.9375×10^{-6} ampere). Thus $\mathbf{v}_0$ can be found from a loop equation written at the output as

$$\mathbf{v}_0 = \mathbf{v}_6 - \mathbf{20000i}_6$$

or

$$\mathbf{V}_0 = 5 - 20000(85.9375 \times 10^{-6}) = 3.28125 \text{ volts}$$

The theoretical value of output can be calculated for this 6-bit digital to analog converter as

$$\mathbf{v}_{\text{theo}} = \frac{(\text{input count})5 \text{ V}}{2^6} = \frac{42(5)}{64} = 3.28125 \text{ volts}$$

showing that the circuit analysis was very accurate.

14.2 SIMULTANEOUS EQUATIONS WITH COMPLEX NUMBERS

To solve a set of simultaneous equations involving complex numbers, some method must be devised for handling the complex arithmetic. One scheme involves performing complex addition and subtraction in rectangular form, while performing multiplication and division in polar form. This requires functions that convert data between the two forms, a time-consuming process that can also produce significant roundoff errors. Some improvement can be made by performing all computations in rectangular form using the methods presented in Section 7.6. But here, too, the computations become involved.

A more efficient method of solution is based on converting each complex equation into two scalar equations. Consider the complex equation

$$\mathbf{V} = \mathbf{Z} \times \mathbf{I}$$

where **V**, **Z**, and **I** represent complex quantities. When these quantities are expressed in terms of their real and imaginary components, the equation becomes

$$\mathbf{V}_r + \mathbf{jV}_i = (\mathbf{R} + \mathbf{jX}) \times (\mathbf{I}_r + \mathbf{jI}_i)$$

where $\mathbf{R}$ and $\mathbf{X}$ represent the real and imaginary terms of $\mathbf{Z}$. If the indicated multiplication is carried out, we get

$$\mathbf{V_r + jV_i = RI_r + jRI_i + jXI_r - XI_i}$$

In this form, it is clear that $\mathbf{V_r}$ must equal the sum of all the real terms on the right side of the equation and $\mathbf{V_i}$ must equal the sum of all the imaginary terms. Thus the complex equation can be expressed as two scalar equations, as shown in Fig. 14.10. These equations can be solved for $\mathbf{I_r}$ and $\mathbf{I_i}$ by any of the methods used to solve scalar equations.

$$\mathbf{V_r = RI_r - XI_i}$$
$$\mathbf{V_i = XI_r + RI_i}$$

Figure 14.10 Two scalar equations formed from a complex equation.

Now consider the set of complex equations shown in Fig. 14.11. They represent the loop voltage equations for a two-loop network with complex impedances. Replacing each of the complex quantities by their real and imaginary components yields

$$\mathbf{V_{1r} + jV_{1i} = (R_1 + jX_1)\,(I_{1r} + jI_{1i}) + (R_3 + jX_3)\,(I_{2r} + jI_{2i})}$$
$$\mathbf{V_{2r} + jV_{2i} = (R_3 + jX_3)\,(I_{1r} + jI_{1i}) + (R_2 + jX_2)\,(I_{2r} + jI_{2i})}$$

If the indicated operations are carried out, the resulting complex equations can be converted into a set of four scalar equations by the same procedure that was used in the preceding example. These scalar equations are shown in Fig. 14.12.

$$\mathbf{V_1 = Z_1I_1 + Z_3I_2}$$
$$\mathbf{V_2 = Z_3I_1 + Z_2I_2}$$

Figure 14.11 Set of two complex equations.

$$\mathbf{V_{1r} = R_1I_{1r} - X_1I_{1i} + R_3I_{2r} - X_3I_{2i}}$$
$$\mathbf{V_{1i} = X_1I_{1r} + R_1I_{1i} + X_3I_{2r} + R_3I_{2i}}$$
$$\mathbf{V_{2r} = R_3I_{1r} - X_3I_{1i} + R_2I_{2r} - X_2I_{2i}}$$
$$\mathbf{V_{2i} = X_3I_{1r} + R_3I_{1i} + X_2I_{2r} + R_2I_{2i}}$$

Figure 14.12 Four scalar equations formed from two complex equations.

Comparing the equations of Fig. 14.10 with those of Fig. 14.12, one can observe a pattern emerging. The pattern will be described here without attempting to prove that it holds for any number of complex equations.

1. The equations for the real components of the $\mathbf{V}$'s have pairs of terms of the form $\mathbf{RI_r - XI_i}$ that relate to a $\mathbf{Z \times I}$ product having corresponding subscripts in the original equations.
2. The equations for the imaginary components of the $\mathbf{V}$'s have pairs of terms of the form $\mathbf{XI_r + RI_i}$ that relate to a $\mathbf{Z \times I}$ product having corresponding subscripts in the original equations.

From these observations, we can develop an algorithm for generating the scalar equations from any number of complex equations. This allows for the solution of complex equations by using efficient methods such as Gauss–Jordan elimination.

Let's say that we wish to solve a set of **e** complex equations. An array of **e** rows by **2e + 2** columns will be needed to store the complex coefficients of the original equations. We will store the real part of any coefficient adjacent to and below the corresponding imaginary part. Thus, if **a[1][1]** = $\mathbf{R_1}$, then **a[1][2]** = $\mathbf{X_1}$, and so on. For the equations of Fig. 14.11, we would have the input array shown in Fig. 14.13.

$$\begin{matrix} R_1 & X_1 & R_3 & X_3 & V_{1r} & V_{1i} \\ R_3 & X_3 & R_2 & X_2 & V_{2r} & V_{2i} \end{matrix}$$

Figure 14.13 Input array for the equations of Fig. 14.11.

The scalar equations to be formed will occupy an array of size **2e** rows and **2e + 1** columns. Comparing the input array elements in Fig. 14.13 with those of the scalar array elements of Fig. 14.14, we can write the pseudocode for generation of the scalar array elements as shown in Fig. 14.15. Since each pair of scalar equations derives from a corresponding input equation, we fill in the array elements two rows at a time, on a column by column basis. Thus elements in rows **i − 1** and **i** in the scalar array are derived from elements in row **i/2** in the input array. Even columns are processed differently from odd columns.

$$\begin{matrix} R_1 & -X_1 & R_3 & -X_3 & V_{1r} \\ X_1 & R_1 & X_3 & R_3 & V_{1i} \\ R_3 & -X_3 & R_2 & -X_2 & V_{2r} \\ X_3 & R_3 & X_2 & R_2 & V_{2i} \end{matrix}$$

Figure 14.14 Scalar array for the equations of Fig. 14.11.

```
/* pseudocode for generating a scalar array from the input array */
/* for complex equations */
/* input array is a[][], scalar array is b[][] */
/* the zeroth element of each array is not being used */

for (i from 2 to 2e, step 2)
      for (j from 1 to 2e+1)
            if (j is even)
                  b[i-1][j] = -a[i/2][j]
                  b[i][j] = a[i/2][j-1]
            else
                  b[i-1][j] = a[1/2][j]
                  b[i][j] = a[i/2][j+1]
            end if
      end for
end for
```

Figure 14.15 Pseudocode for defining the scalar equations array from the input equations array.

A **C** program for solving simultaneous equations with complex numbers is given in Fig. 14.16. There are only two unique features to this program as compared to our earlier version. First is the conversion of the input array into a scalar array, for which we have already developed the pseudocode.

The second unique feature relates to recovering the complex solutions from the scalar solutions. For an original set of **e** complex equations, we will generate **2e** scalar solutions. Looking at the scalar equations of Fig. 14.12, we can see that the four scalar variables whose values are to be solved include $\mathbf{I_{1r}}$, $\mathbf{I_{1i}}$, $\mathbf{I_{2r}}$, and $\mathbf{I_{2i}}$. To convert these values into the corresponding solutions for the complex equations, we simply take the solution to the first variable in the scalar equation ($\mathbf{I_{1r}}$) as the real part of the solution for the first variable in the complex equations. Likewise, the solution for the second variable in the scalar equations becomes the imaginary part of the solution for the first complex variable. Thus pairs of variables solved for in the scalar equations form a solution for one variable in the complex equations. The **prtx()** function in Fig. 14.16 converts the scalar solutions into complex solutions according to the preceding scheme.

```
/* Gauss-Jordan Solution for Simultaneous Equations with Complex Coefficents */
#include <stdio.h>
#include <math.h>
#define MAX_ROWS    10
#define MAX_COLS    22

main()
      {
      int i, j, k, n, r, e;
      double m, t, max;
      static double a[MAX_ROWS][MAX_COLS], b[2*MAX_ROWS][2*MAX_ROWS + 1];
      void getdata(), prtx();

      puts("Enter the number of equations");
      scanf("%d", &e);
      getdata(a, e);
      n = 2*e;
      /* define scalar equations */
      for (i = 2; i <= n; i += 2)
            for (j = 1; j <= (n + 1); j++)
                  if (j % 2 == 0)
                        {
                        b[i - 1][j] = -a[i/2][j];
                        b[i][j] = a[i/2][j - 1];
                        }
                  else
                        {
                        b[i - 1][j] = a[i/2][j];
                        b[i][j] = a[i/2][j + 1];
                        }
      /* perform elimination */
      for (i = 1; i <= n; i++)
            {
            /* find largest coefficient on or below main diagonal */
            max = -1.0;
            for (k = i; k <= n; k++)
                  if (abs(b[k][i]) > max)
                        {
                        max = abs(b[k][i]);
                        r = k;
                        }
```

Figure 14.16 Solution to simultaneous equations with complex numbers.

```
            /* swap equation at row r with that at the ith row */
            for (k = i; k <= n + 1; k++)
                  {
                  t = b[i][k];
                  b[i][k] = b[r][k];
                  b[r][k] = t;
                  }
            /* Perform elimination */
            for (j = 1; j <= n; j++)
                  if (j != i)
                        {
                        m = b[j][i]/b[i][i];
                              for (k = i + 1; k <= n + 1; k++)
                                    b[j][k] = b[j][k] - m*b[i][k];
                              }
            }
      prtx(b, n);
      }

void getdata(a, n)
int n;
double a[][MAX_COLS];
      {
      int i, j;

      for (i = 1; i <= n; i++)
            for (j = 2; j <= 2*n + 2; j += 2)
                  {
                  printf("\nEnter coefficient A(%d,%d) as real,imaginary", i, j/2);
                  scanf("%lf,%lf", &a[i][j - 1], &a[i][j]);
                  }
      }
void prtx(b, n)
int n;
double b[][2*MAX_ROWS + 1];
      {
      int i, j;
      double x[2*MAX_ROWS];
      char sign;

      for (i = 1; i <= n; i++)
            x[i] = b[i][n + 1]/b[i][i];
      for (i = 2; i <= n; i += 2)
            {
            if (x[i] < 0)
                  sign = '-';
            else
                  sign = '+';
            printf("x(%d) = %f %cj%f\n", i/2, x[i - 1], sign, fabs(x[i]));
            }
      }
```

Figure 14.16 (continued).

Let's use the program just developed to analyze the Butterworth low-pass filter circuit shown in Fig. 14.17. The cutoff frequency of this circuit is 1 radian/second. Assume that we wish to calculate the output voltage of the circuit at 2 radians/second. The equations that describe the circuit are

$$\mathbf{V_s = j(X_{L1} - X_{c1})I_1 + jX_{c2}I_2}$$

$$\mathbf{0 = jX_{c1}I_1 + (1 + j(X_{L2} - X_{c1}))I_2}$$

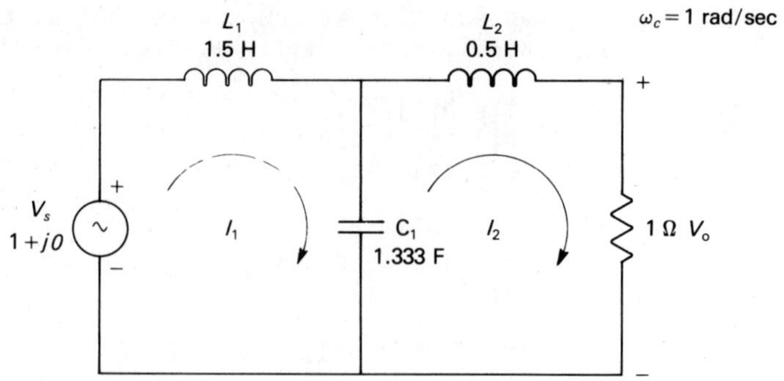

Figure 14.17 Butterworth low-pass filter.

Based on the given component values and the specified frequency of 2 radians/second, the following table of impedances can be calculated.

	Ohms
X_{L1}	3.000000
X_{L2}	1.000000
X_{C1}	0.3750000
$X_{L1} - X_{c1}$	2.625000
$X_{L2} - X_{c1}$	0.6250000

Since the load resistor is equal to 1 ohm, the load voltage will be numerically equal to the load current $\mathbf{I}_2$. The value of $\mathbf{I}_2$ will be obtained directly from the solution of the set of equations describing the circuit. A run of the program is given next. It shows the input values and the result obtained for $\mathbf{I}_2$ (labeled as $\mathbf{X}_2$). The magnitude of $\mathbf{I}_2$ is equal to 0.124034 ampere and represents the magnitude of the voltage output from the circuit at 2 radians/second. This indicates that, at twice the cutoff frequency, the filter output drops from the passband value of 1 volt to a value of about 0.124 volt.

```
Enter the number of equations
2
Enter coefficient A(1,1) as real, imaginary 0, 2.625000
Enter coefficient A(1,2) as real, imaginary 0, 0.375000
Enter coefficient A(1,3) as real, imaginary 1, 0
Enter coefficient A(2,1) as real, imaginary 0, 0.375000
Enter coefficient A(2,2) as real, imaginary 1, 0.625000
Enter coefficient A(2,3) as real, imaginary 0, 0

X(1) = 0.015384 -j0.389743
X(2) = -0.107692 +j0.061538
```

The beauty of this approach in analyzing complex circuits is that it is not necessary to manipulate the circuit equations to obtain a transfer function, a task that can prove to be very formidable in many cases. We simply provide the complex coefficients of each equation. If it is desired to compute the output of the circuit for a series of frequencies, the circuit impedances can be redefined in terms of the frequency variable. A solution is then computed at each of the frequencies of interest.

14.3 INTEGRATION

The computer extends the analytical capabilities of anyone who masters its usage. In the previous section, we saw how the response of a complex filter could be obtained without having to derive its transfer function. In this section, we will see that the computer simplifies problems dealing with integral calculus. Without any reference to handbooks of integral calculus or laboring through complex integration problems, we can find the area under a curve to whatever accuracy is desired by performing summations of small areas using the computer.

Figure 14.18 shows a quarter-circle divided into rectangular slices. As the width of these rectangles is made smaller, the sum of their areas more closely approximates the area of the quarter circle. Let's represent the width of each rectangle by **w**. The height **h** is then given by

$$\mathbf{h} = (\mathbf{R}^2 - \mathbf{x}^2)^{1/2}$$

where **R** is the radius of the circle and **x** is the distance along the **x** axis to the center of the rectangle. The width should be chosen such that the sum of the widths for all the rectangles equals the radius of the circle.

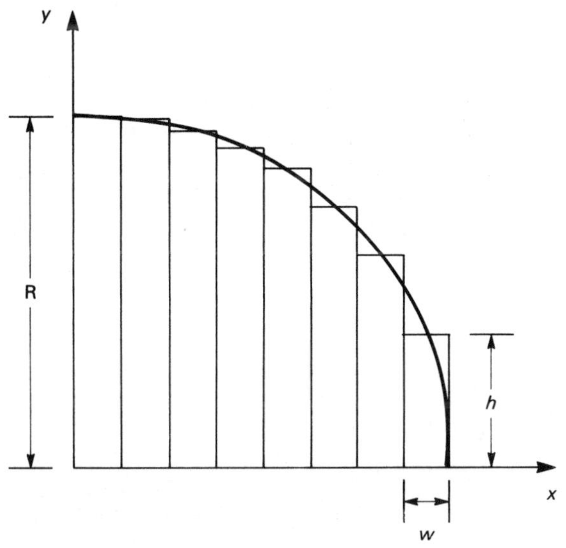

Figure 14.18 Finding the area under a curve.

The program of Fig. 14.19 finds the area of a circle having a radius of **1**. The **WIDTH** of each rectangle is chosen as **0.01*RADIUS** to provide **100** rectangles for the approximation. The summation of areas occurs for **x** values ranging from **WIDTH/2** to **RADIUS − WIDTH/2** in increments of **WIDTH**. These **x** values locate the center of each rectangle being included in the summation. The area of each rectangle is given simply by its width multiplied by its height. Notice that using **100** rectangles provided four digits of accuracy in the computation of the area of the entire circle.

```
/* using integration to find the area of a circle */
#include <stdio.h>
#include <math.h>
#define RADIUS          1.0
#define WIDTH           0.01*RADIUS

main()
      {
      double area, height, x;

      for (x = WIDTH/2; x <= RADIUS - WIDTH/2; x += WIDTH)
            {
            height = pow(1.0 - x*x, 0.5);
            area = area + WIDTH*height;
            }
      printf("The area of a circle with radius %f is %f\n", RADIUS, 4.0*area);
      printf("Using a rectangle width of %f\n",WIDTH);
      }
```

```
The area of a circle with radius 1.000000 is 3.141937
Using a rectangle width of 0.010000
```

Figure 14.19 Program to find the area of a circle.

14.4 DIFFERENTIATION

The derivative of a function **F(x)** is defined by

$$\mathbf{F'(x)} = \lim_{\Delta x \to 0} \frac{\mathbf{F[x + (\Delta x/2)] - F[x - (\Delta x/2)]}}{\Delta \mathbf{x}}$$

This relationship defines the slope of a straight line that is tangent to the original curve at a given value of **x**. If we wish to approximate the derivative of a function, finite values must be used for computation of the slope. In this case, the derivative can be expressed as

$$\mathbf{F'(x)} = \frac{\mathbf{F[x + (w/2)] - F[x - (w/2)]}}{\mathbf{w}}$$

where **w** is a small increment of **x** that is used for computation of the slope. This method of approximating the derivative of a function is illustrated in Fig. 14.20.

The program of Fig. 14.21 computes the derivative of the sine function using the approximation presented previously. Note that the degree of accuracy is dependent only on the size of **w**. Using $\pi/1000$ for **w** yields six digits of accuracy for the derivative.

14.5 SPECTRAL ANALYSIS

Continuous Fourier Transform

Any time-domain function may be converted into its equivalent frequency-domain representation by use of the continuous Fourier transform (CFT). The frequency-

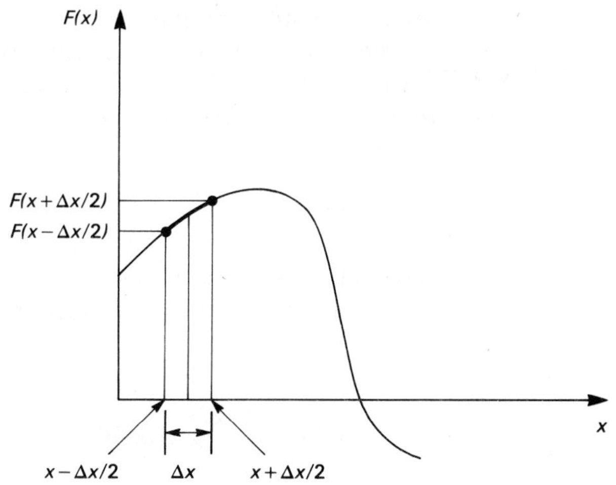

Figure 14.20 Approximation of a derivative.

```
/* derivative of sin(x) */
#define PI          3.14159265
#define DX          (PI/10000.0)
#include <math.h>
#include <stdio.h>
main()
      {
      double x, deriv_sin;

      printf("%8s\t%8s\n", "sin(x)", "derivative");
      for (x = 0; x <= PI/2.0; x += PI/6.0)
            {
            deriv_sin = (sin(x + DX/2.0) - sin(x - DX/2.0))/DX;
            printf("%8.6f\t%8.6f\n", sin(x), deriv_sin);
            }
      }
```

```
  sin(x)          derivative
0.000000          1.000000
0.500000          0.866025
0.866025          0.500000
1.000000          -0.000000
```

Figure 14.21 Finding the derivative of a sine function.

domain representation consists of a series of sine functions having values of amplitude, frequency, and phase such that the sum of these components equals the time-domain signal. The CFT is defined by

$$\mathbf{X(jw)} = \int_{-\infty}^{\infty} \mathbf{x(t)e^{-jwt}\,dt}$$

where **x(t)** is a function of time and **X(jw)** is its equivalent function of frequency.

The inverse of the Fourier transform can be used to express **x(t)** in terms of **X(jw)**. It is given by

$$\mathbf{x(t)} = \frac{1}{2\pi}\int_{-\infty}^{\infty} \mathbf{X(jw)e^{-jwt}\,dw}$$

Periodic signals exhibit the relationship **x(t) = x(t + T)**, where **T** is called the period of the signal. Such signals will have a frequency-domain representation that consists of a series of *discrete* frequencies. Nonperiodic signals will possess a *continuous* frequency spectrum. These waveforms can be viewed as having an infinite period.

Discrete Fourier Transform

An approximation to the continuous Fourier transform that is suitable for implementation on a digital computer is called the discrete Fourier transform (DFT) and is defined by

$$X(k) = \frac{1}{N}\sum_{m=o}^{N-1} x(m)W^{mk}, \qquad k = 0, 1, 2, 3, \ldots, N-1$$

where

$$W = e^{-j2\pi/N}$$

The **x(m)** values represent **N** samples of the time-domain signal or function that are separated by equal time intervals **T**. The value of **NT** is the total time interval for sampling, called a *window*. The frequency spacing between the **X(k)** values is given by **1/(NT)**. This identifies the frequency at **X(k)** as **kF** or **k/(NT)**.

If **x(m)** is a real function, then only **N/2** of the **X(k)** values will be unique. In such cases, the computation of **X(k)** is carried out for **k** values for **0** to **N/2 − 1**.

By using Euler's identity

$$e^{-j\theta} = \cos(\theta) - j\sin(\theta)$$

X(k) can be written in a more convenient form as

$$X(k) = \frac{1}{N}\sum_{m=o}^{N-1} x(m)\left[\cos\left(\frac{2\pi mk}{N}\right) - j\sin\left(\frac{2\pi mk}{N}\right)\right]$$

DFT of a Rectangular Pulse Train

A program that makes use of the preceding equation for computation of the DFT is given in Fig. 14.22. Using this program, the pulse train shown in Fig. 14.23(a) yields the spectral plot of Fig. 14.23(b). The program output is in the form of a bar graph. It makes use of the **gmode()** and **line()** functions defined in Chapter 10. A simple modification will provide a tabulated output instead.

The time-domain samples of the function are stored in the array **xt[]**. The real and imaginary components of the transformed signal are stored in **fx[]** and **fy[]**, respectively. The magnitude of the frequency-domain output is given by the square root of the sum of the squares of **fx[]** and **fy[]**. These values are stored in **xf[]** and plotted using the **line()** function. Scaling of the output provides a maximum spectral line length of 100 pixels.

The first spectral line in the output, **xf[0]**, represents the dc component of the frequency-domain signal. Each of the other lines represents the amplitude of the corresponding harmonic. The eighth, sixteenth, twenty-fourth, and so on, harmonics have zero amplitude. They appear as dots in the display.

For this run, 128 sample points were used. Since the period of the input signal is given as 1 second, the sampling interval is 1/128 second. The product of **NT** thus equals 1, and the frequency spacing of the spectral lines is 1 hertz.

```
/* Discrete Fourier Transform with graphics output */
#include <stdio.h>
#include <math.h>
#define TWO_PI    6.283185307
#define MAX_PTS   256
#define F_SPC     8
#define BASE      180

main()
      {
      static double xt[MAX_PTS], fx[MAX_PTS], fy[MAX_PTS], xf[MAX_PTS];
      double a, q, z;
      int k, m, n;

      printf("Enter the number of sample points: ");
      scanf("%d", &n);

      gmode();
      clr();
      /* define the function here */
      /* rectangular pulse waveform */
      for (m = 0; m < n/8; m++)
            xt[m] = 1.0;
      for (m = n/8; m < n; m++)
            xt[m] = 0.0;

      /* compute DFT */
      for (k = 0; k < n/2; k++)
            {
            a = TWO_PI/n;
            fx[k] = 0.0;
            fy[k] = 0.0;
            z = 1.0/n;
            q = a*k;
            for (m = 0; m < n; m++)
                  {
                  fx[k] = fx[k] + xt[m]*cos(m*q);
                  fy[k] = fy[k] + xt[m]*sin(m*q);
                  }
            xf[k] = sqrt(fx[k]*fx[k] + fy[k]*fy[k])*z;
            line(F_SPC*k, BASE, F_SPC*k, BASE - (int)(100.0/xf[0]*xf[k]), 1);
            }
      scanf("%d", &k);          /* wait for keypress before exit */
      }
```

Figure 14.22 Program for computation of discrete Fourier transform of a pulse train.

DFT of an Amplitude-Modulated Sine Wave

An equation of the form

$$\mathbf{f(t) = [1 + \cos(2\pi f_m t)]\sin(2\pi f_c t)}$$

describes a 100% amplitude-modulated sine wave such as that shown in Fig. 14.24(a). Here, $\mathbf{f_c}$ represents the frequency of the *carrier* and $\mathbf{f_m}$ the frequency of the *modulating signal* or waveform envelope. The spectral components of this waveform can be found by using the DFT.

If we use 128 sampling points, the following code will define a carrier that has 16 cycles within the sampling window and a modulating signal that has 2

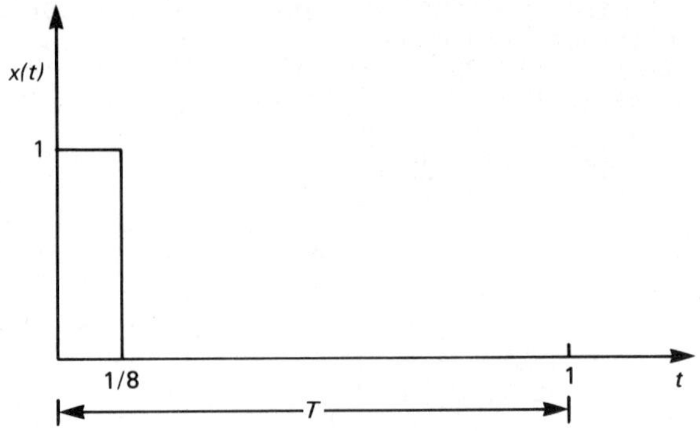

(a)

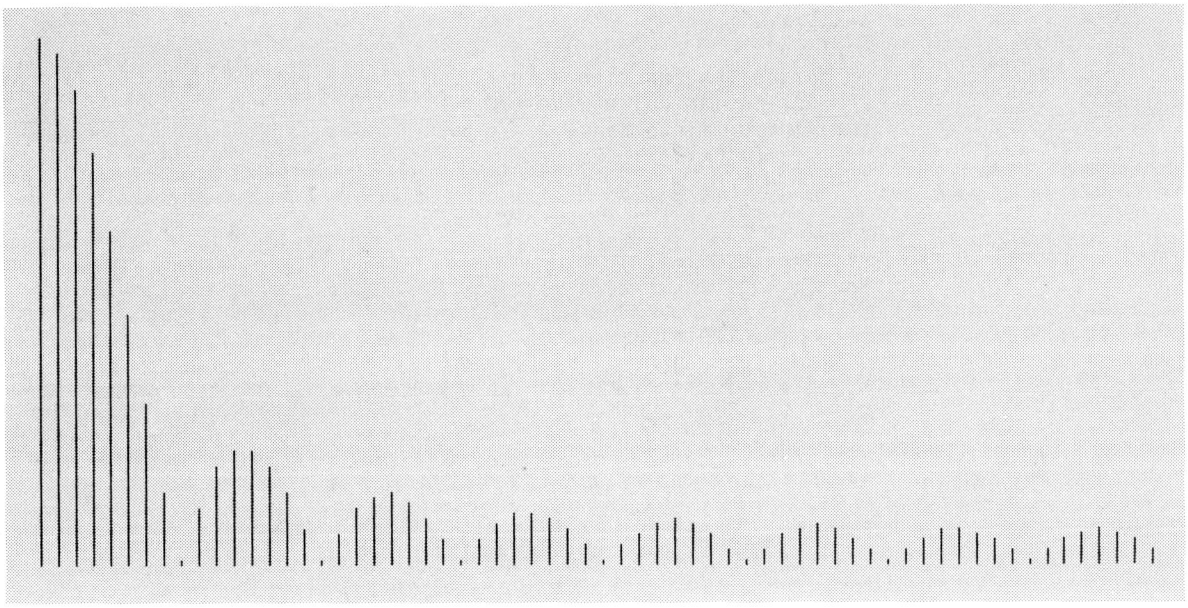

(b)

Figure 14.23 (a) A pulse train with a 1/8 duty cycle; (b) plot of DFT of pulse train.

cycles within the window. An integral number of cycles is essential to avoid discontinuities at the edge of the window.

```
/* AM waveform with 100% modulation */
/* Use 128 sampling points for 16 cycles of the carrier */
/* and 2 cycles of the modulating signal within the window */
for (m=0;m<n;m++)
    xt[m] = (1.0 + cos(TWO_PI*m/64))*sin(TWO_PI*m/8);
```

The output scaling must be handled differently here since the **xf[0]** component is not the largest. The **line()** statement is modified as follows.

```
line(F_SPC*k,BASE,F_SPC*k,BASE-(int)(BASE*xf[k]),1);
```

To avoid having to consider the output scaling for each waveform, a function can be added to find the largest spectral component, which we use to set the scaling factor for the display.

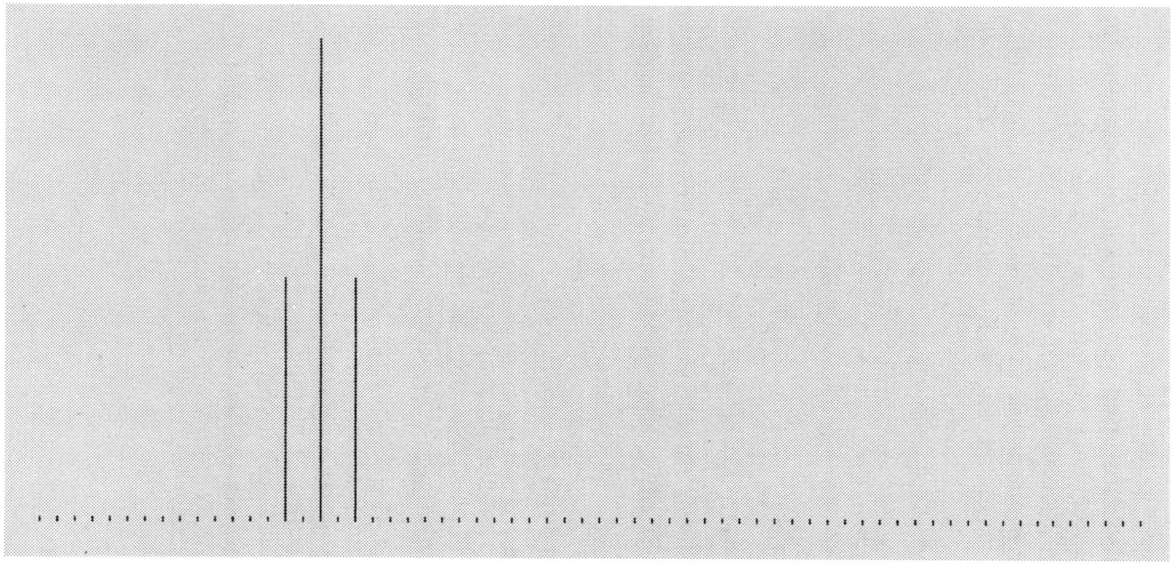

(a)

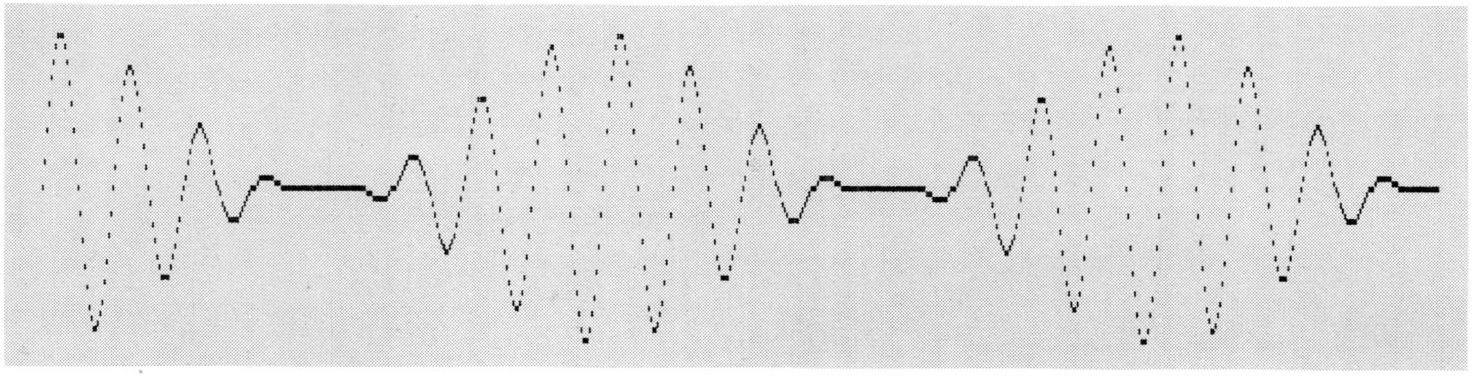

(b)

Figure 14.24 (a) A 100% amplitude-modulated (AM) sine wave; (b) plot of DFT of AM wave.

Figure 14.24(b) shows the resulting spectra. If the window is assumed to be 1 second, we then have three spectral components at 14, 16, and 18 hertz. The amplitude of the 16-hertz component is twice that of the other two. This component is at the carrier frequency. The other two are referred to a *sidebands*. The frequencies of the sidebands are equal to the sum and difference of the carrier and the modulating frequency.

DFT of an FSK Signal

A frequency shift keying (FSK) signal is used as a modulation technique for the transmission of digital data. One frequency represents a binary 1 and the other a binary 0. Figure 14.25(a) illustrates an FSK waveform. The higher frequency has been arbitrarily set to three times the lower frequency. For this example, the output frequency will toggle between the two at a uniform rate. The code for defining the FSK signal is

```
/* FSK waveform, use 128 sampling points */
for (m=0;m<n/2;m++)
     xt[m] = sin((double)(m*16*TWO_PI/n));
for (m=n/2;m<n;m++)
     xt[m] = sin((double)(m*48*TWO_PI/n));
```

The output spectrum is shown in Fig. 14.25(b). Assuming a sampling window of 1 second, we can see that there are two peaks in the output spectra, one at 16 hertz and another at 48 hertz. There is a significant amount of energy in the harmonics on either side of these two peaks.

Speeding up the Fourier Transform

The DFT requires a considerable amount of computation. If executed in an interpreted high-level language, a 256-point DFT can take tens of minutes for completion. Speed-up techniques for software-based Fourier transforms include using an efficient compiled language such as **C**, coding directly in assembly language, and/or adding a hardware *numeric coprocessor*.

The computation time for the DFT increases at a rate proportional to the square of the number of sample points. A method of speeding up execution based on reducing the number of computations involved was developed by Cooley and Tukey in 1965. Their algorithm is called the fast Fourier transform (FFT). It provides a substantial speed improvement when the number of sample points is large.

14.6 ADDRESS DECODER ANALYSIS AND DESIGN

Address Decoder Analysis

A variety of addressable devices can be attached to a computer through the address, data, and control buses. Each of these devices occupies a specific address range within the total *address space* of the computer. Figure 14.26(a) illustrates how these devices are interfaced to the address bus.

The lower-order address bus lines feed directly into the device. The number of these lines depends on the total address space of the device. For example, a memory chip with 1024 addresses will require the ten lowest-order address lines entering the chip directly, since 2^{10} equals 1024. The balance of the address lines

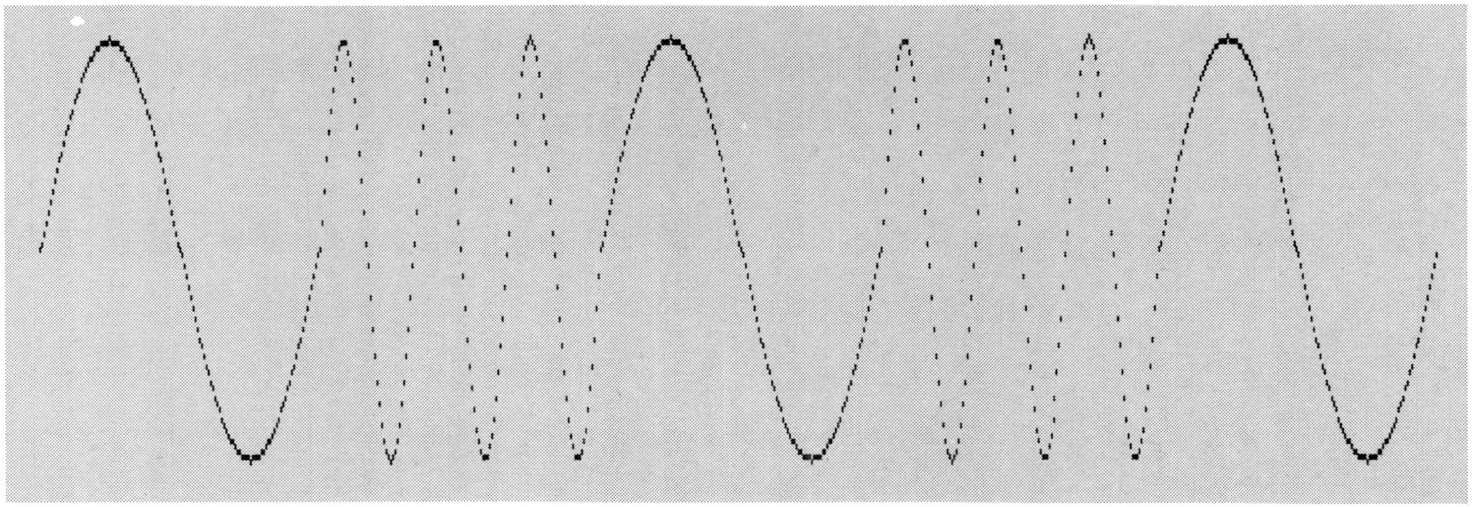

(a)

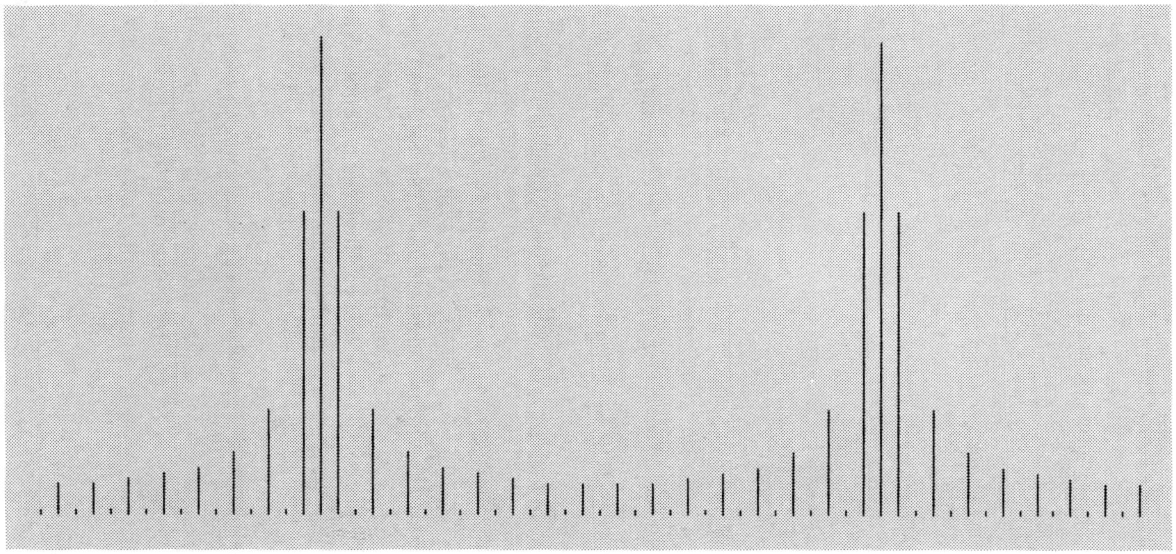

(b)

Figure 14.25 (a) FSK signal; (b) plot of DFT of FSK signal.

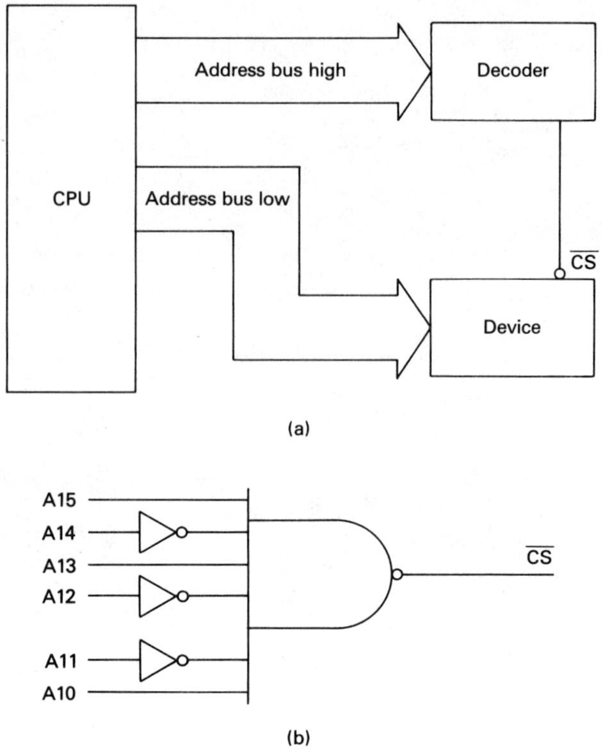

Figure 14.26 Computer address decoder.

will go into a decoder circuit to establish where in the computer address space the device will be mapped.

Figure 14.26(b) illustrates a typical address decoder. The inputs A10 through A15 represent address bus lines. Some of these lines are inverted to establish the desired address location for the device within the system's memory map. The output of the NAND gate will be active low (a binary 0) for the selected address space. The lowest decoded address is called the *base address* for the device. Let's go through the manual procedure used to find the base address for the device and also its address space based on analysis of the decoder circuit. We can then write a relatively simple **C** program to automate the process.

The highest address line input is A15. (The lowest is A0.) This means that the address bus is 16 bits wide. Since there are six inputs into the decoder itself, the balance of the inputs must be going into the device. In this case 16 − 6 or 10 inputs into the device gives an address space of 2^{10} or 1024. In general, the address space will be:

$$\textbf{device address space} = 2^{(\text{bus\_width}-\text{decoder\_inputs})}$$

The base address of the device can be calculated from the formula

$$\textbf{base address} = \sum_{n=N1}^{N2} A_n 2^n$$

where $\mathbf{A_n}$ is 1 for address inputs that are not inverted and 0 for those that are. In this particular case, the base address is calculated as:

$$
\begin{aligned}
1 \times 2^{15} &= 32768 \\
0 \times 2^{14} &= 0 \\
1 \times 2^{13} &= 8192 \\
0 \times 2^{12} &= 0 \\
0 \times 2^{11} &= 0 \\
1 \times 2^{10} &= \underline{1024} \\
 & \ 41984 \quad (\text{or } A400_{16})
\end{aligned}
$$

The program of Fig. 14.27 computes the address space of a device and its base address based on the preceding analysis. Notice that the variables **base** and **addr_sp** were declared as **long** to accommodate a large base address for the decoder or large address space for the device.

```
/* address decoder analysis */
#include <stdio.h>
#include <math.h>

main()
      {
      int bus_w, decod_in, bit, i, a;
      long base, addr_sp;

      printf("Enter the width of the address bus:");
      scanf("%d", &bus_w);
      printf("Enter the number of inputs into the decoder:");
      scanf("%d", &decod_in);
      printf("Enter a '1' for direct address inputs and a '0' for inverted
      inputs\n");
      base = 0;
      for (i = 1; i <= decod_in; i++)
            {
            bit = bus_w - i;
            printf("A%d:", bit);
            scanf("%d", &a);
            if ((a != 0) && (a != 1))
                  {
                  printf("Input error\n");
                  exit();
                  }
            if (a == 1)
                  base = base + (long)pow(2.0, (double)bit);
            }
      printf("The base address of the decoder is %ld decimal or %lx hex\n", base,
      base);
      addr_sp = (long)pow(2.0, (double)(bus_w - decod_in));
      printf("The address space of the decoder is %ld decimal or %lx hex\n",
      addr_sp, addr_sp);
      }
```

```
Enter the width of the address bus:16
Enter the number of inputs into the decoder:6
Enter a '1' for direct address inputs and a '0' for inverted inputs
A15:1
A14:0
A13:1
A12:0
A11:0
A10:1
The base address of the decoder is 41984 decimal or a400 hex
The address space of the decoder is 1024 decimal or 400 hex
```

Figure 14.27 Address decoder analysis.

The **for** loop is used to enter the state of each address decoder input and calculate the base address. The address bit position is assigned to the variable **bit**. The value of any bit position is entered and assigned to **a**. If **a == 1,** 2^{bit} will be added to **base**. If **a** is neither 0 nor 1, an input error occurred.

The computation of address space is independent of the computation of base address. Both of these quantities are printed in decimal and hexadecimal format for convenience. Notice that the conversion specifiers are **"%ld"** and **"%lx"** to handle the **long** types.

Address Decoder Design

The design of address decoders is conceptually the reverse of the analysis procedure. Our inputs will be the width of the address bus, the required address space for the device, and the desired base address of the device. From this information, we will need to determine the required number of inputs for the decoder and whether each input is inverted or not inverted.

The required address space is restricted to being a power of 2. The number of inputs into the decoder can be calculated from

```
decoder_inputs = bus_width - log(address_space)/log(2)
```

The **log(address_space)/log(2)** term is actually the number of inputs into the device to provide **address_space** addresses. Subtracting this number from **bus_width** gives the number of inputs into the decoder. For example, using a 16-bit address bus with a device having an address space of 1024, we get $16 - \log(1024)/\log(2) = 16 - 10 = 6$.

To determine the state of each address line input into the decoder, the entered base address is converted into a binary string. The length of the string is set to the width of the address bus by padding leading bits with zeros wherever needed. (Actually, the length could be set to the number of inputs to the decoder.) This preserves the position value of the bits in the converted base address. Each bit in the string is then examined. If it equals 1, the corresponding address line input to the decoder is direct; otherwise, the line is inverted.

For example, a base address of A400 converts to a binary value of 1010010000000000. The first six most significant bits represent inputs into the decoder. The most significant bit of 1 represents the required state for A15. In this case, it is not inverted and thus goes directly into the decoder. We can list the state of the other address bus inputs as follows:

Base address bit	*Decoder input*
1 (MSB)	A15 direct
0	A14 inverted
1	A13 direct
0	A12 inverted
0	A11 inverted
1	A10 direct

A program implementing the preceding procedure is given in Fig. 14.28. The program inputs are the bus width, assigned to **bus_w**, device address space, assigned to **addr_sp**, and the base address, assigned to **base**. The user is given the choice of entering the base address as a decimal or hexadecimal number. This value is passed to **dec_bin()** for conversion to binary string form. Other arguments passed to **dec_bin()** include the name of the array, **b**, where the string will be stored, and the desired length of the string, either **bus_w** or **decod_in**.

Once the base address has been converted into a binary string, **decod_in** bits from the MSB side are analyzed within the **for** loop to determine the state of the associated address bus inputs. A prime symbol, the apostrophe, is printed after each line that must be inverted before input to the decoder.

```
/* address decoder design */
#include <stdio.h>
#include <math.h>
#define SIZE 33

main()
      {
      int bus_w, decod_in, bit, i;
      char mode, b[SIZE];
      long base, addr_sp;
      void dec_bin(), str_rev();

      printf("Enter the width of the address bus:");
      scanf("%d", &bus_w);
      printf("Enter the address space of the device: ");
      scanf("%ld", &addr_sp);
      printf("Enter 'd' or 'h' to enter the base address of device in decimal or
      hex:");
      scanf("\n%c", &mode);
      if (mode == 'd')
            {
            printf("Enter decimal base address:");
            scanf("%ld", &base);
            }
      else if (mode == 'h')
            {
            printf("Enter hex base address:");
            scanf("%lx", &base);
            }
      else
            {
            printf("\nInput error\n");
            exit();
            }
      decod_in = bus_w - (int)(log((double)addr_sp)/log(2.0));
      dec_bin(base, b, bus_w);
      printf("\nThe following unprimed address lines go directly into the
      decoder\n");
      printf("The primed address lines must go through inverters into the
      decoder\n");
      for (i = 0; i < decod_in; i++)
            {
            bit = bus_w - i - 1;
            printf("A%d", bit);
            if (b[i] == '0')
                  printf("'\n");
            else
                  printf("\n");
            }
      }

void dec_bin(dec, s, len)             /* converts int dec to char bin */
long dec;
int len;
```

Figure 14.28 Address decoder design.

```
char *s;
    {
    int i = 0, j;

    while (dec != 0)
        {
        s[i++] = dec%2 + '0';
        dec = dec/2;
        }
    for (j = i; j < (int)(len - (long) i); j++)
        s[j] = '0';
    s[j] = '\0';
    str_rev(s);
    }

void str_rev(s)                     /* string reverser */
char *s;
    {
    int i, len, last;
    char temp;

    len = strlen(s);
    last = len - 1;
    for (i = 0; i < len/2; i++)
        {
        temp = s[i];
        s[i] = s[last - i];
        s[last - i] = temp;
        }
    }
```

```
Enter the width of the address bus:16
Enter the address space of the device: 1024
Enter 'd' or 'h' to enter the base address of device in decimal or hex:h
Enter hex base address:a400

The following unprimed address lines go directly into the decoder
The primed address lines must go through inverters into the decoder
A15
A14'
A13
A12'
A11'
A10
```

Figure 14.28 (continued).

14.7 CONVERTING BOOLEAN EXPRESSIONS TO MINTERM FORM

A Boolean expression that is in sum-of-products form may occur in either *minterm* or simplified form. For example, the equation

$$f(a, b, c) = a'bc + ab'c + abc' + abc$$

is in minterm form since all the variables are present in each of the terms. A simplified form of this equation is

$$f(a, b, c) = ab + ac + bc$$

The two equations are fully equivalent and have identical truth tables.

Another way of expressing the minterm form is to replace each unprimed variable by a 1 and each primed variable by a 0. The binary number that results can be converted to decimal form. This number identifies one of the minterms of the expression. For example, the binary form of the preceding minterm equation is

f(a, b, c) = Σ (011, 101, 110, 111)

which can be written in decimal form as

f(a, b, c) = Σ (3, 5, 6, 7)

The minterms as thus 3, 5, 6, and 7.

Finding the minterms from a simplified equation is not quite as simple. Notice that one or more variables will be missing from one or more terms in a simplified equation. These variables must be restored in order to identify each minterm of the equation. The procedure for restoring the variables starts by inserting a dash for each missing variable in each term. Thus, for the simplified equation, we get

f(a, b, c) = ab− + a−c + −bc

Next, each term with a dash is replaced by two terms, one with the missing variable primed and another with the missing variable unprimed. This gives the equation

f(a, b, c) = abc' + abc + ab'c + abc + a'bc + abc

The last step is to eliminate any duplicate entries. Notice that the term **abc** occurs three times in the expanded equation. When the duplicates are eliminated, the original minterm form results.

If a term has two missing variables, it expands into four minterms. For three missing variables, it would expand into eight minterms, and so on. To illustrate this, consider a term of **f(w, x, y, z)**, which is **wx**. Adding the dashes gives **wx−−**. The first expansion yields **wxy'−** and **wxy−**. Each of these terms must then be expanded to eliminate the remaining dash. This will give a total of four minterms.

The first-level pseudocode for converting any expression into minterm form is given in Fig. 14.29. It is based on the preceding analysis. The inputs are the number of terms in the expression, the variables used (single character names only), and the actual terms of the expression.

Dashes are inserted for missing variables. The terms are then converted into binary form and stored in a table. For computer solution, it is easier to expand the binary form into minterms than to work with the variable form of the terms. Each table entry is expanded into minterm form. The resulting minterms, which will be binary strings in our program, are converted into decimal form and stored in a minterm table. Duplicates will convert into the same decimal number. The decimal minterms are then printed.

The second-level pseudocode for finding minterms is given in Fig. 14.30. The module **restore**(*term*) inserts dashes for missing variables in *term* to restore positional value. The key to the operation of this module is that the characters of **term[]** are compared to those of **var_list[]**, the list of variables being used. One of three conditions must be detected. First, if a given character from **term[]** is a variable from the list, it is copied to **m_term[]** and the next variable from **var_list[]**

```
/* pseudocode for noncanonical to canonical transformation */
/* converts terms to minterms */

enter number of terms in boolean expression
enter variable names to be used in left to right order
calculate number of variables from input list
for (each term)
      input term
      add '-' for missing variables
      convert to binary form
      store in table
end for
expand binary terms into minterm form
convert binary terms into decimal representation
print decimal minterms
```

Figure 14.29 Pseudocode for Boolean expression to minterm conversion.

is considered. If **term[]** contains a prime (′) at the current position, it is also copied to **m_term[]** without advancing the current character of **var_list[]**. (There still may be a match at the next position of **term[]**.) Last, if neither of the preceding two conditions holds, then the current variable of **var_list[]** is missing from **term[]**. A dash (-) is inserted into **m_term[]** to indicate a missing variable position and the next character of **var_list[]** is considered.

The **while** loop will not detect a prime that is the last character of **term[]**. Some method must be used for detecting a trailing prime and copying it to **m_term[]**. One method is to check the final value of the subscript **j** to the length of **term[]**. If **j** is less than the length of the term, then a trailing prime must be present.

The module **restore()** uses three unique subscripts to reference characters of **var_list[]**, **term[]**, and **m_term[]**. This is necessary because the three arrays are of different lengths, with any variable being likely to occur at different positions within these arrays. The next module, **convert_to_binary()**, associates each variable with a specific position within a term. This makes it easier to convert the terms into minterm form.

The module **convert_to_binary()** converts **m_term[]** into a binary form by replacing all unprimed variables with a 1 and all primed variables with a 0. Dashes are preserved. The resulting binary array is stored in a table called **left_table**, which must be a two-dimensional array. Another two-dimensional array called **right_table** will be used by the module **to_minterms()** for expansion of the terms of the input expression into minterm form. (Two tables are used because the list of terms gets larger with each pass.)

The module **to_minterms()** expands the input terms into minterms by making a number of passes equal to the number of variables in **var_list[]**. Each pass looks at a specific character position, starting with position zero. Every term in **left_table** is examined for the presence of a dash at the selected position. If a dash is detected, the term is expanded into two terms, which are copied to **right_table**. Otherwise, the term is copied without modification to **right_table**. When all terms

```
/* level 2 pseudocode for noncanonical to canonical transformation */
/* converts terms to minterms */
module main()
      input number of terms in boolean expression
      input variable names to be used and assign to var_list
      number_of_variables = length of var_list
      for (each term)
            input term
            restore(term)
            convert_to_binary(m_term)
      end for
      to_minterms()
      fill_min()
      prn_min()
end main()

module restore(term)
      j = k = m = 0
      while ( k <number_of_variables)
            c = term[j]
            m_term[m] = c
            if (c == var_list[k])   /* input character in var_list */
                  j = j + 1
                  k = k + 1
            else if (c == prime)    /* input character is prime symbol */
                  j = j + 1
                  else              /* missing input character, add '-' */
                  m_term[m] = '-'
                  k = k + 1
            end if
            m = m + 1
      end while
      add trailing prime if needed
end restore()

module convert_to_binary(m_term)
      j = 0
      while (j < length_of_term)
            if (m_term[j] == '-')
                  insert '-' in binary form
            else if(m_term[j + 1] == prime)
                  insert '0' in binary form
                  j = j + 1
            else
                  insert a '1' in binary form
            end if
            j = j + 1
       end while
       store binary form in left_table
end convert_to_binary()
```

Figure 14.30 Second-level pseudocode for Boolean expression to minterm conversion.

```
module to_minterms()
      right_count = 0
      for (each variable position)
            for (each term in left_table)
                  if (char == '-')
                        expand into two terms in right_table
                        right_count = right_count + 2
                  else
                        copy term as is to right_table
                        right_count = right_count + 1
                  end if
            end for
            terms_right = right_count
            copy right_table to left_table
            terms_left = terms_right
      end for
end to_minterms()
```

Figure 14.30 (continued).

have been examined, the **right_table** is copied back to the **left_table**, and the next variable position is considered. After completion of the last pass, the entries of **right_table** will constitute the minterms of the input expression in binary array format.

The modules **fill_min()** and **prn_min()** are not included in the second-level pseudocode since they are relatively simple to implement. **Fill_min()** simply converts the binary arrays of **right_table** into decimal form. **Prn_min()** then prints the converted minterms.

Figure 14.31 presents a **C** program that implements the pseudocode. Notice that the maximum number of variables, defined as **MAX_VARS**, is set to 7. The maximum number of minterms, **MAX_TERMS**, is then defined as 128 or 2^7. The maximum table size can exceed the maximum number of minterms due to duplicates in the minterm list. Therefore, **MAX_TBL_SZ** has been set to **10*MAX_TERMS**.

The function **restore()** has two arguments, **term** and **m_term**. Since **m_term** is local to **main()**, it must be passed to **restore()** so that function will know where to place the processed contents of **term**. The function **to_binary()** also has two arguments. Its first argument, **m_term**, identifies the location of the array containing the term to be converted into binary form. The second argument, **i**, tells **to_binary()** where in **left_tbl[]** the converted term should be placed.

```
/* noncanonical to canonical form (minterms) */
#include <stdio.h>
#include <math.h>
#define MAX_VARS 7               /* maximum number of variables in expression */
#define MAX_TERMS 128                       /* maximum number of minterms */
#define MAX_TBL_SZ (10*MAX_TERMS)           /* maximum table size */

char left_tbl[MAX_TBL_SZ][MAX_VARS], right_tbl[MAX_TBL_SZ][MAX_VARS];
int terms_l, terms_r, n_vars;
int minterm[MAX_TERMS];
char var_list[2 * MAX_VARS];
```

Figure 14.31 Program to convert a Boolean expression to minterm form.

```
main()
      {
      int terms, i;
      char term[2 * MAX_VARS];
      char m_term[2 * MAX_VARS];
      void restore(), to_bin(), to_min();
      void fill_min(), prn_min();

      printf("Enter number of terms in the boolean expression\n");
      scanf("%d", &terms);
      printf("Enter single character variable names in correct left to right
      order\n");
      scanf("%s", var_list);
      n_vars = strlen(var_list);
      printf("Enter ' after a variable to make it primed\n");
      printf("For example: a'is a primed or not a\n\n");

      for (i = 0; i < terms; i++)
            {
            printf("Enter term %d: ", i);
            scanf("%s", term);
            restore(term, m_term);
            to_bin(m_term, i);
            }
      to_min(terms);
      fill_min();
      prn_min();
      }

void restore(term, m_term)
char term[], m_term[];
      {
      int j, k, m, t_len;
      char c;

      t_len = strlen(term);
      for (m = 0; m < 2*MAX_VARS; m++)
            m_term[m] = '\0';
      j = k = m = 0;
      while (k < n_vars)
            {
            c = term[j];
            m_term[m] = c;
            if (c == var_list[k])
                  {
                  j++;
                  k++;
                  }
            else if (c == '\'')             /* an " ' " */
                  {
                  j++;
                  }
            else
                  {
                  m_term[m] = '-';
                  k++;
                  }
            m++;
            }
      if (j < t_len)
            m_term[m] = '\'';
      }
```

Figure 14.31 (continued).

```
void to_bin(m_term, i)                    /* convert to binary image */
char m_term[];
int i;
      {
      int j, m, t_len;
      char c;

      t_len = strlen(m_term);
      j = m = 0;
      while (j < t_len)
            {
            c = m_term[j];
            if (c == '-')
                  {
                  left_tbl[i][m] = c;
                  }
            else if (((j + 1) < t_len) && (m_term[j + 1] == '\''))
                  {
                  left_tbl[i][m] = '0';
                  j++;
                  }
            else
                  left_tbl[i][m] = '1';
            m++;
            j++;
            }
      }

/* expand binary to minterm form */
void to_min(terms)
int terms;
      {
      int i, j, k;
void to_r_tbl(), r_to_l();

terms_l = terms;
for (i = 0; i < n_vars; i++)
      {
      j = k = 0;
      while (j < terms_l)
            if (left_tbl[j][i] == '-')
                  {
                  /* expand into two entries */
                  left_tbl[j][i] = '0';
                  to_r_tbl(j, k);
                  k++;
                  left_tbl[j][i] = '1';
                  to_r_tbl(j, k);
                  k++;
                  j++;
                  }
            else
                  {
                  to_r_tbl(j, k);
                  j++;
                  k++;
                  }
      terms_r = k;
      r_to_l();
      }
}
```

Figure 14.31 (continued).

```
/* move jth element of left table to kth element of right table */
void to_r_tbl(j, k)
int j, k;
      {
      int i;

      for (i = 0; i <= n_vars; i++)
            right_tbl[k][i] = left_tbl[j][i];
      }

/* move right table to left table */
void r_to_l()
      {
      int i, j;

      for (i = 0; i < terms_r; i++)
            for (j = 0; j <= n_vars; j++)
                  left_tbl[i][j] = right_tbl[i][j];
      terms_l = terms_r;
      }

/* fill minterm table */
void fill_min()
      {
      int i, j, n_min;
      for (i = 0; i < (int)pow(2.0, (double)n_vars); i++)
            minterm[i] = 0;

      for (i = 0; i < terms_r; i++)
            {
            j = to_dec(i);
            minterm[j] = 1;
            }
      }

/* convert binary string to decimal */
int to_dec(i)
int i;
      {
      int j, dec = 0;

      for (j = 0; j < n_vars; j++)
            if (right_tbl[i][j] == '1')
                  dec = dec + (int)pow(2.0, (double)(n_vars - j - 1));
      return (dec);
      }

/* print the minterm table */
void prn_min()
      {
      int i;

      printf("%8s%8s%\n", "TERM", "OUTPUT");
      for (i = 0; i < (int)pow(2.0, (double)n_vars); i++)
            printf("%8d%8d\n", i, minterm[i]);
      }
```

Figure 14.31 (continued).

```
Enter number of terms in the boolean expression
3
Enter single character variable names in correct left to right order
abc
Enter ' after a variable to make it primed
For example: a'is a primed or not a

Enter term 0: ab
Enter term 1: ac
Enter term 2: bc
    TERM  OUTPUT
      0       0
      1       0
      2       0
      3       1
      4       0
      5       1
      6       1
      7       1
```

Figure 14.31 (continued).

14.8 SIMPLIFICATION OF BOOLEAN EXPRESSIONS

The last section dealt with the process of finding the minterms associated with an arbitrary Boolean expression. Another important process is that of finding the most simplified representation of a Boolean expression that is presented as a series of minterms. These are almost inverse processes. (They are not exactly inverse since the input to the first is not necessarily a most simplified representation of a Boolean expression.)

Let's assume that we wish to represent our simplified Boolean expression in a sum-of-products form. A procedure called the *Quine–McCluskey method* finds a set of simplified terms called *prime implicants*. The minimum sum-of-products form will consist of a subset of the prime implicants. None of the prime implicant terms can be further reduced. However, in most cases, some of the prime implicants may be eliminated to form the minimal sum. The theorem

$$\mathbf{AB + A'C + BC = AB + A'C}$$

can be used to eliminate nonessential prime implicants. Another method for eliminating nonessential prime implicants is to remove one term at a time and reconstruct the minterm list with that prime implicant missing. If the resulting minterm list matches the original, the prime implicant was nonessential. The order in which the prime implicants are removed is significant. Some sequences will result in a minimal sum, while others will not.

In this section, we will only consider the solution for prime implicants and not the minimal sum. The process involves applying the theorem

$$\mathbf{AB + AB' = A}$$

which is the reverse of the one used in the previous section to find minterms. The first-level pseudocode for finding prime implicants using the Quine–McCluskey method is given in Fig. 14.32.

```
/* pseudocode for Quine-McCluskey minimization */

Enter variable names in left to right order
Calculate number of variables being used
Enter the number of minterms in the original equation
Enter minterms as decimal numbers
Convert minterms to binary form
Enter binary form into left_table
for (number of variables in equation)
      for (each line in left_table)
            compare line to all others
            if (different by one bit)
                  add combination line to right_table
            if (equal)
                  delete duplicate
            if (different by more than one bit)
                  add line to right_table
      end for
      copy right_table to left_table
end for
print right_table in equation form
```

Figure 14.32 First-level pseudocode for Quine–McCluskey solution for prime implicants.

The inputs for the process are the minterms. These are entered as decimal numbers. We also enter the variables used in the expression to permit printing the prime implicants in equation form. The minterms are converted from decimal to binary form. A two-table method similar to that used in the last section then eliminates terms by combining pairs of terms that differ in only one position into a single term. For example, the two terms **AB'C** and **AB'C'** would combine to form **AB'**. After all possible combinations have been made, the resulting terms are the prime implicants corresponding to the original minterm list. These are printed in equation form.

A more detailed level of pseudocode will not be presented since the process is almost the inverse of the one used in the previous section and the programming techniques are very similar. The **C** program is given in Fig. 14.33. You may wish to make use of the program with some knowledge of its workings. A good number of students will undoubtedly be inspired (or required) to analyze it completely.

```
/* Quine McCluskey reduction of Boolean expressions */
/* yields prime implicants in sum of products form */
#include <stdio.h>
#define MAX_VARS  8            /* maximum number of variables in expression */
#define MAX_TERMS 256                       /* maximum number of minterms */
#define MAX_TBL_SZ (10*MAX_TERMS)           /* maximum table size */
#define YES 1
#define NO  0

char left_tbl[MAX_TBL_SZ][MAX_VARS + 1], right_tbl[MAX_TBL_SZ][MAX_VARS + 1];
char var_list[2 * MAX_VARS];
int terms_l, terms_r, n_vars, prime;
int minterm[MAX_TERMS];
```

Figure 14.33 Program to find prime implicants using Quine–McCluskey method.

```
main()
    {
    int terms, i, j, k, m, p, t_len;
    char term[2 * MAX_VARS], c;
    char m_term[2 * MAX_VARS];
    void comp(), prn_sp(), to_bin_arry();
    void to_r_tbl(), r_to_l();

    printf("Enter single character variable names in correct left to right
    order\n");
    scanf("%s", var_list);
    n_vars = strlen(var_list);
    printf("Enter number of minterms in the boolean expression\n");
    scanf("%d", &terms);

    /* Enter minterms and convert to binary array */
    printf("Enter minterms as decimal numbers:\n");
    for (i = 0; i < terms; i++)
          {
          printf("minterm %d: ", i);
          scanf("%d", &minterm[i]);
          to_bin_arry(&left_tbl[i], minterm[i]);
          }
    terms_l = terms;
    terms_r = 0;
    /* Quine-McCluskey reduction */
    for (i = 0; i < n_vars; i++)
          {
          j = 0;
          while (j < terms_l)
                {
                k = 0;
                prime = YES;
                while (k < terms_l)
                      {
                      if (j != k)
                            comp(j, k);
                      k++;
                      }
                      if (prime == YES)
                            to_r_tbl(j, terms_r);
                      j++;
                      }
                r_to_l();
                }
          /* print the minimized sum of products expression */
          prn_sp();
          }

    /* compare two lines in left table */
    void comp(j, k)
    int j, k;
          {
          int i, diff = 0;
          void delete(), merge();

          for (i = 0; i < n_vars; i++)
                if (left_tbl[j][i] != left_tbl[k][i])
                      diff++;
          if (diff == 0)
                delete(k);
          else if (diff == 1)
                merge(j, k);
          }
```

Figure 14.33 (continued).

```
/* delete duplicate entries */
void delete(k)
int k;
      {
      int i, j;

      if (k != terms_l)
            {
            for (i = k; i < terms_l - 1; i++)
                  for (j = 0; j < n_vars; j++)
                        left_tbl[i][j] = left_tbl[i + 1][j];
            }
      terms_l--;
      }

/* merge two entries that differ in one position only */
void merge(j, k)
int j, k;
      {
      int i;

      for (i = 0; i < n_vars; i++)
            {
            if (left_tbl[j][i] == left_tbl[k][i])
                  right_tbl[terms_r][i] = left_tbl[j][i];
            else
                  right_tbl[terms_r][i] = '-';
            }
      terms_r++;
      prime = NO;
      }

/* print minimized sum of products results */
void prn_sp()
      {
      int i, j;

      printf("The prime implicants are:\n");
      terms_r = terms_l;
      for (i = 0; i < terms_r; i++)
            {
            for (j = 0; j < n_vars; j++)
                  if (right_tbl[i][j] != '-')
                        {
                        putchar(var_list[j]);
                        if (right_tbl[i][j] == '0')
                              putchar('\'');
                        }
            if (i < terms_r - 1)
                  printf(" + ");
            }
      }

/* convert decimal to binary character array */
void to_bin_arry(b, dec)
char b[];
int dec;
      {
      int i = 0, j;
      void str_rev();

      while (dec != 0)
            {
```

Figure 14.33 (continued).

```
        b[i++] = dec % 2 + '0';
        dec = dec / 2;
        }
    for (j = i; j < n_vars; j++)
        b[j] = '0';
    b[j] = '\0';
    str_rev(b);
    }

void str_rev(s)                          /* string reverser */
char *s;
    {
    int i, len, last;
    char temp;

    len = strlen(s);
    last = len - 1;
    for (i = 0;  i < len / 2;  i++)
        {
            temp = s[i];
            s[i] = s[last - i];
            s[last - i] = temp;
            }
        }

    /* move jth element of left table to kth element of right table */
    void to_r_tbl(j, k)
    int j, k;
        {
        int i;

        for (i = 0; i < n_vars; i++)
            right_tbl[k][i] = left_tbl[j][i];
        terms_r++;
        }

    /* move right table to left table */
    void r_to_l()
        {
        int i, j;

        for (i = 0; i < terms_r; i++)
            for (j = 0; j < n_vars; j++)
                left_tbl[i][j] = right_tbl[i][j];
        terms_l = terms_r;
        terms_r = 0;
        }
```

```
Enter single character variable names in correct left to right order
wxyz
Enter number of minterms in the boolean expression
8
Enter minterms as decimal numbers:
minterm 0: 2
minterm 1: 3
minterm 2: 5
minterm 3: 6
minterm 4: 7
minterm 5: 9
minterm 6: 11
minterm 7: 13
The prime implicants are:
w'y + x'yz + w'xz + xy'z + wx'z + wy'z
```

Figure 14.33 (continued).

PROBLEMS

14.1. Use the Gauss–Jordan elimination program of Fig. 14.6 to solve the following set of simultaneous equations:

$$5x_1 + 10x_2 + 20x_3 = 0$$
$$-10x_1 + 8x_2 + 12x_3 = 0.5$$
$$6x_1 - 3x_2 - 2x_3 = 0.3$$

14.2. Solve for the three loop currents in Fig. 14.34 using the program of Fig. 14.6 or Fig. 14.8.

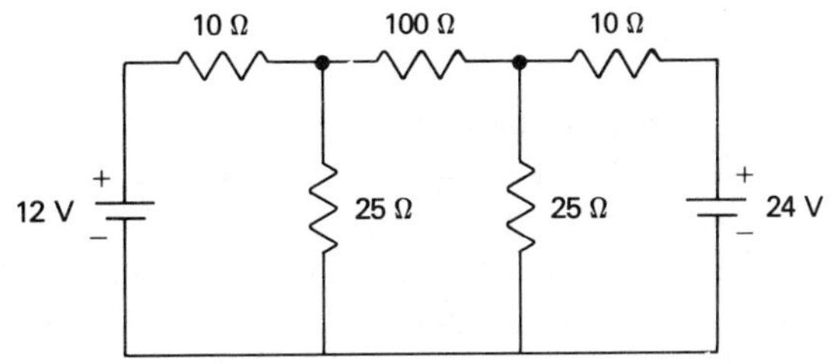

Figure 14.34 DC circuit of Problem 14.2.

14.3. Use the program listing of Fig. 14.16 to solve the following set of complex equations:

$$(0 + j2)x_1 + (1 - j3)x_2 + (2 + j5)x_3 = 0 - j10$$
$$(3 - j1)x_1 + (6 + j8)x_2 + (12 - j10)x_3 = 5 + j0$$
$$(4 + j4)x_1 + (3 + j0)x_2 + (i + j1)x_3 = 2 + j2$$

14.4. Solve for the three loop currents in the circuit of Fig. 14.35 using the program of Fig. 14.16.

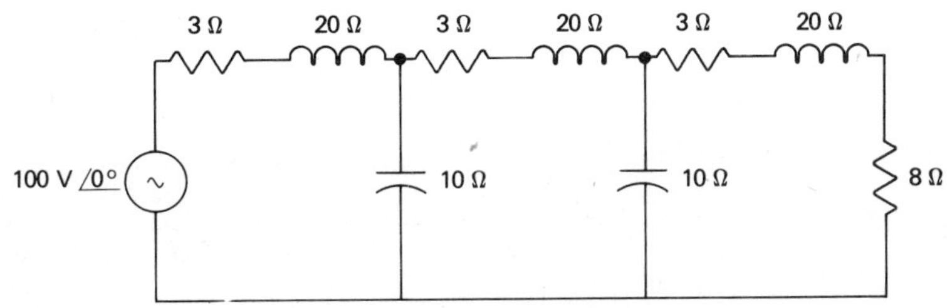

Figure 14.35 AC circuit of Problem 14.4.

14.5. Write a program that finds the area under the curve of Fig. 14.36.

14.6. Write a program that computes the derivative of $\mathbf{e^{-0.15t}}$ from $\mathbf{t} = 0$ to 20 at intervals of 0.5. It should tabulate the results. If your computer has graphics capability, have the program plot the function and its derivative.

14.7. Repeat Problem 14.6 for the expression $\mathbf{2x^2 - 15x + 25}$ for $\mathbf{x}$ ranging from 0 to 10 at intervals of 0.25.

14.8. Change the duty cycle of the pulse train in the program of Fig. 14.22 to 1/4 and observe the effect on the spectral output.

14.9. Modify the program of Fig. 14.22 to find the DFT of a 100% amplitude-modulated sine wave having one cycle of the modulating signal and sixteen cycles of the

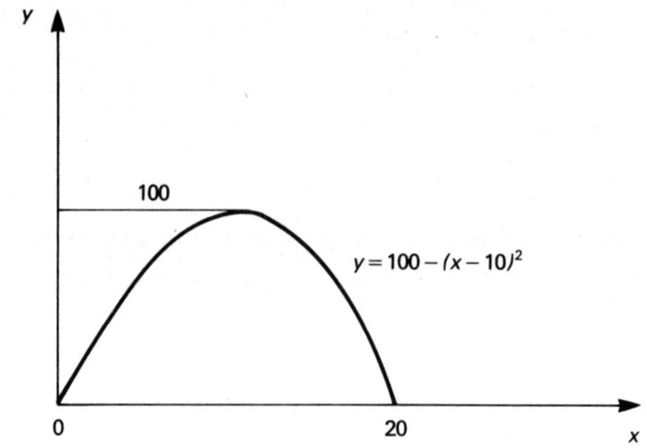

Figure 14.36 Curve of Problem 14.5.

carrier within the sampling window. Repeat for 50% modulation. Compare the output spectra for the two cases.

14.10. Modify the program of Fig. 14.22 to find the spectra of a phase shift keyed (PSK) signal having eight cycles with one phase and eight cycles shifted by 180 degrees within the sampling window. Compare to the FSK spectra.

14.11. Use the program of Fig. 14.27 to find the base address and address space of the decoder shown in Fig. 14.37. The bus width of the system is 16 bits.

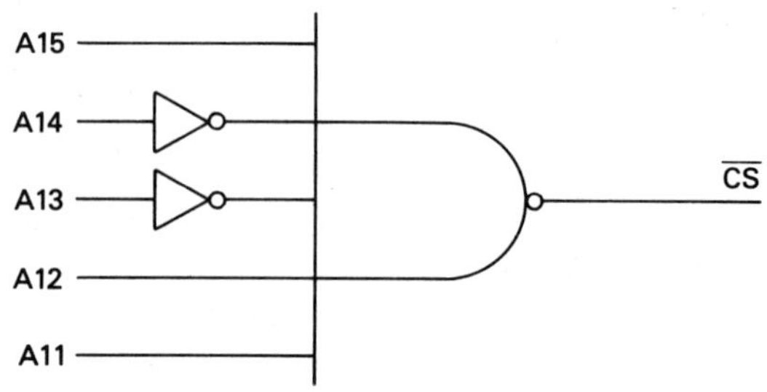

Figure 14.37 Address decoder of Problem 14.11.

14.12. Use the program of Fig. 14.28 to design a decoder that maps a device with an address space of 64K (65536) at a base address of 0b0000. The system has a bus width of 24 bits.

14.13. Use the program of Fig. 14.31 to find the minterms of the following Boolean expression:

ab'cd + ac + ad

14.14. Use the program of Fig. 14.33 to find the prime implicants associated with the following minterm list.

F(A, B, C, D, E) = Σ (0, 2, 4, 6, 12, 14, 17, 23, 27, 29, 31)

PROGRAMMING PROJECTS

14.15. Modify the program of Fig. 14.16 to output the complex results in both rectangular and polar form.

14.16. Modify the program of Fig. 14.22 to find the largest spectral component of the output, and scale the plotting of spectral lines based on its value. It should scale the plot for any given spectra.

chapter 15

System Interfaces

15.1 INTRODUCTION

The **C** language is ideally suited for interfacing into the system in a variety of ways. It does not present the closed or restricted environment that might be found in other languages. Some of the most common ways in which we can communicate with the system from **C** include:

1. Making function calls to our own assembly language subroutines
2. Calling operating system (OS) or basic input/output system (BIOS) routines.
3. Accessing hardware devices, such as CRT controllers, serial or parallel ports, and disk controllers

In this chapter, we will look at how to implement these system interfaces using **C**. Each topic will be introduced independent of any particular hardware or operating system. Specific examples will then be given for the IBM PC and Microsoft **C**. This will facilitate an understanding of the general concepts involved and still provide concrete examples of implementation.

15.2 C CALLING CONVENTIONS

Whenever a function calls an assembly language routine, whether it is our own code or an operating system feature, the function arguments must be passed to the routine in a manner prescribed by the compiler or interpreter. We must also consider how the compiler or interpreter expects to receive a returned value, if there is one. This format for data interchange is referred to as the *calling convention*.

In **C**, function arguments are passed on the *stack*. The stack is a last-in first-out (LIFO) type of memory. Data are accessed by sequence rather than address. We store data on the stack with a *push* operation and retrieve it from the stack with a *pop* operation. Figure 15.1 illustrates the location of arguments on the stack when the function **system** (*arg1*, *arg2*, *arg3*) is called. Notice that the last argument is pushed first and the first argument is pushed last. The *return address* is pushed on top of all the arguments. It is the value contained in a register called the *program counter*. The return address is used to resume execution at the proper place after a return from the function call.

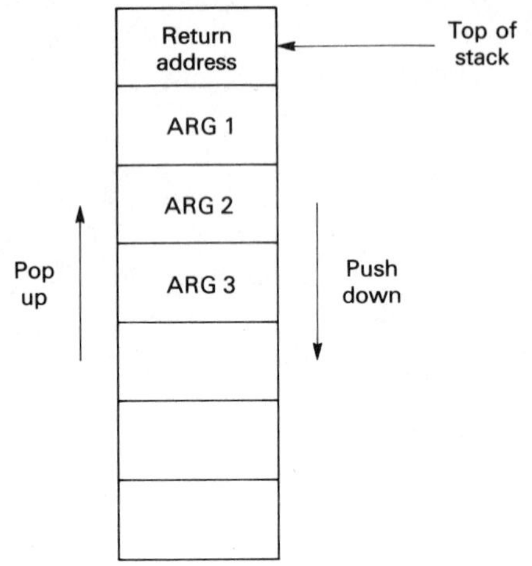

Figure 15.1 Location of arguments on the stack.

The number of locations of stack memory occupied by one argument depends on the machine architecture and the data type. The same can be said for the return address value. The language user's manual will contain specific information for a particular compiler and system. Although the calling conventions are similar for all **C** compilers, there are minor but very important differences that must be adhered to.

If there is a return value from the assembly language routine, it will be passed back to **C** via a register. The specific register used depends on the compiler and the data type being returned.

15.3 ASSEMBLY LANGUAGE ROUTINES AS FUNCTIONS

Assembly language routines may be called as functions. This is usually done for maximum speed of execution, compactness of code, or for access to some system feature that cannot otherwise be accessed from **C**. The structure of an assembly routine being used as a function is prescribed by the compiler.

Some machine registers may need to be saved on the stack during the execution of the assembly routine. The function name, as well as all the variables to be accessed by **C**, must be declared as global. Assembly language variables to be accessed by **C** are usually tagged with a leading or trailing underscore. Thus, a **C** function **peek()** may be named in the assembly subroutine as **_peek** or **peek_**.

A register called the *stack pointer* stores the address in the stack where the next value will be pushed. When function arguments are passed on the stack, the stack pointer is adjusted to reflect their presence. After completion of the function call, the stack pointer must be restored to its condition before the call was made. Some compilers adjust the stack pointer after a return from a function call. Others force the assembly routine to adjust the stack pointer before a return is made.

To write assembly language subroutines as **C** functions, you must be familiar with the assembly language for the system being used. It is not the objective of this text to present assembly language programming details. Yet it is very instructive to see some examples for a specific system. The assembly language subroutines presented in this section and the next are written for the Intel 8086/88 family of central processors used in the IBM PC and its compatibles. If you are not familiar with the assemblers for these machines, focus on the program comments (at the end of each line) to learn the general concepts involved in writing these programs.

Creating a Peek() Function with Assembly Language

In Chapter 7, we saw how a pointer could be initialized to a specific memory location. Not all **C** compilers and interpreters permit access to the full memory space of the system. **Peek()** and **poke()** functions can be added using assembly language to perform the equivalent task. These terms are borrowed from the BASIC language. *Peek* refers to reading a byte from a specified memory location and *poke* refers to storing a byte at a specified location. Let's look at the design of a **peek()** function.

A peek function must pass the memory location from which a byte is to be read. For systems with a *linear* address space, this simply involves specifying the memory location as an **unsigned** or **long** type. The Intel family of processors use a *segmented* addressing scheme in which a memory location is specified using a *segment* value and an *offset* from the beginning of that segment. Therefore, two arguments must be passed to the function, the segment number and the offset. Both of these arguments are **unsigned**.

The return value must be stored by the assembly language routine in a register that is determined by the compiler being used and the data type being returned. For simplicity, let's assume that the return value is an **int** type. Microsoft **C** expects to find this value in the accumulator or **ax** register.

Our assembly function must then perform the following:

1. Save registers that must be preserved
2. Get the address arguments from the stack
3. Use the address arguments to load the peek byte into the Accumulator
4. Restore the saved registers
5. Return control to **C**

The assembly language peek function in Fig. 15.2 is written for Microsoft **C** and the IBM PC and its compatibles. Lines 10 through 13 are part of the program prologue. They do not generate any code but are directives to the assembler telling it how to handle this code segment.

The **bp**, **di**, and **es** registers are saved on the stack. The stack pointer, **sp**, is moved to **bp** as a reference to access the arguments on the stack. The first argument, **offset**, is found at **bp + 6**, or 6 bytes from the top of the stack. It is loaded into the **di** register. The second argument, the **segment** address, is found at **bp + 8**. It is loaded into the **es** register. Line 22 moves the byte specified by **es** and **di** into the low-order byte of the accumulator, or **al**. The high-order byte of the accumulator, **ah**, is cleared by loading it with a zero. After restoring the registers that were pushed onto the stack, a return is made to **C** with the return value stored in **ax**. Microsoft **C** adjusts the stack pointer to clear out the arguments after the return is made.

A **C** program that calls **peek()** is given in Fig. 15.3. It peeks at the first 12 lines of the monochrome video memory in the IBM PC and prints the data to the

```
;***********************************************************************
;PEEK.ASM
;***********************************************************************
;an assembler subroutine called from Microsoft C (or QC) on the IBM PC
;that returns a byte from the address to be peeked
;called as peek(offset,segment)
;where offset and segment are unsigned integers that identify
;the memory location as an offset from a segment value
;
;PGROUP    GROUP _TEXT
_TEXT      SEGMENT WORD    PUBLIC 'CODE'
           PUBLIC  _peek
           ASSUME cs:_TEXT

_peek      PROC  FAR                        ;identify as a far procedure
           push  bp                         ;save base pointer, bp
           mov   bp,sp                      ;initialize bp to sp
           push  di                         ;save di
           push  es                         ;save es
           mov   di,[bp+6]                  ;get offset from stack
           mov   es,[bp+8]                  ;get segment from stack
           mov   al,es:[di]                 ;move peek byte to al
           mov   ah,0                       ;clear ah
           pop   es                         ;restore registers
           pop   di
           pop   bp
           ret                              ;return
_peek      ENDP
_TEXT      ENDS
           END
```

Figure 15.2 **Peek()** function for Microsoft **C** on the IBM PC.

screen. The segment address for the start of video memory is **0xb000**. **Seg** is therefore initialized to this value. Since the characters are stored in alternate memory locations, the **offset** increment is set to two.

```
/* peek at screen memory block using Microsoft C on the IBM PC */
#define BLOCK_SIZE      1920
#include <stdio.h>
main()
      {
      unsigned seg, offset;
      extern int peek();

      seg = 0xb000;
      for (offset = 0; offset <= BLOCK_SIZE; offset += 2)
            printf("%c", peek(offset, seg));
      }
```

Figure 15.3 **C** program that calls **peek()**.

15.4 USING OPERATING SYSTEM AND BIOS RESOURCES

The concepts used in the preceding section may be applied to access powerful routines available in the system BIOS or the operating system of the computer. To make use of these features, technical information relating to the BIOS or OS must be referenced. This information is available to programmers through technical reference manuals supplied by the system manufacturer. Third-party literature may also be available as an alternate source for technical information.

For the IBM PC, hardware and BIOS details are available in the hardware *Technical Reference* manual. Operating system details are available in the *Disk Operating System* and *DOS Technical Reference* manuals. A wealth of third-party paperbacks also describe the hardware and software of the IBM PC.

System resources are accessible via calls to specific system routines whose entry addresses are known or via *software interrupts*. The latter method is safer since it is less system dependent and guaranteed to be supported in future versions of the system.

In the IBM PC, software interrupts numbered **0** through **1FH** are used by the BIOS. Interrupts **20H** through **3FH** are used by the DOS. These routines are well documented and available for user application programs.

To illustrate the utility of the routines in the BIOS and operating system, we will consider a function that writes a dot to the graphics screen. BIOS software interrupt type **10H** is for video I/O. The contents of the high-order byte of the accumulator (**ah**) upon entry determines which of the 15 video I/O operations will be called. For the "write dot" function, the **ah** register must contain a decimal 12.

Other registers that are used for the write dot interrupt are **al**, **cx**, and **dx**. Each of these registers must be initialized before calling the interrupt. The **al** register contains the color to be used for writing the dot. The **cx** register contains the **x** coordinate and the **dx** register contains the **y** coordinate of the dot.

The **C** function to set a dot on the graphics screen will be called **pnt(x,y,c)**, where **x** and **y** are the screen coordinates of the dot and **c** is its color. All the arguments are unsigned. The assembly routine that calls the BIOS interrupt for writing the dot must perform the following:

1. Save registers that must be preserved
2. Move the function arguments from the stack to the appropriate registers
3. Call interrupt type 10H
4. Restore the saved registers
5. Return control to **C**

The program listing of Fig. 15.4 implements the **pnt()** function. It is written for Microsoft **C** and the IBM PC. Notice that the arguments are read from the stack in an order different from that in which they were pushed. This is perfectly acceptable, since we are not popping the arguments but merely accessing their values. After loading the registers with the function arguments, the type **10H** video interrupt is called by line 21 as **int 10h**. **Pnt()** does not return a value to the calling function.

15.5 ACCESSING I/O PORTS

I/O Ports

I/O ports are addressable interfaces between the computer system and external devices. I/O ports may either be *serial* or *parallel*. Data travel through a single line on serial I/O ports and through parallel lines on parallel ports. The number of data lines in a parallel port is usually a byte multiple, such as 8, 16, or 32. Simple input and output ports are attached to a system in one of two basic configurations. A *memory-mapped I/O port* is addressed in the same manner as any location of main memory. An *isolated I/O port* is attached to an address space that is separated or isolated from main memory. It must be accessed by special processor commands.

```
;**********************************************************************
;PNT.ASM  (Microsoft C calling convention )
;**********************************************************************
;call from C with pnt(x,y,c)
;where x,y are coordinates for the point and c is its color
;all arguments are unsigned
;
PGROUP      GROUP _TEXT
_TEXT       SEGMENT WORD      PUBLIC 'CODE'

            PUBLIC _pnt
            ASSUME cs:_TEXT

_pnt        PROC  FAR
            push  bp
            mov   bp,sp
            mov   ax,[bp+10]              ;set the color in al
            mov   ah,12d                  ;set write dot routine in ah
            mov   cx,[bp+6]               ;set x plotting coord in cx
            mov   dx,[bp+8]               ;set y plotting coord in dx
            int   10h                     ;call BIOS video I/O
            pop   bp
            ret
_pnt        ENDP
_TEXT       ENDS
            END
```

Figure 15.4 **Pnt()** function using the IBM PC BIOS resources.

We can address a specific memory-mapped I/O port either by initializing a pointer to the port location (see Chapter 7) or by using **peek()** and **poke()** functions. A **C** compiler written for a system with isolated I/O ports will usually have library functions for accessing these ports. If not, short assembly language routines may be written to communicate with the ports.

The Intel family of microprocessors uses isolated I/O. The 8086/88 processor instructions **IN** and **OUT** are used for port access. They transfer data to and from the accumulator and a designated port. Microsoft **C** provides the library functions **inp**(*port*) and **outp**(*port*, *value*) for I/O operations. For these functions, *port* is **unsigned** and value is an **int**. The **inp()** function reads a byte from the specified port. The returned value is an **int** type. **Outp()** writes the byte *value* to the designated *port*. The function returns *value*.

Whenever a programmer wishes to communicate with an I/O port, he or she must know the address or address range where the port is located and also the details about the architecture and programming of the port. This information is obtained from hardware reference manuals for the system.

Parallel Ports

To illustrate the access and programming of parallel ports, we will consider the ports associated with the parallel printer adaptor (LPT1) for the IBM PC and its compatibles. There are actually three ports used to implement the printer interface. They are the **DATA** port, the **STATUS** port, and the **CONTROL** port. Figure 15.5(a) shows these ports and provides information about their address locations, signal names, and pin numbers. All the signals are brought out to a DB25 shell connector at the rear of the computer. Any given pin number can be found by referencing the diagram given in Fig. 15.5(b).

We can demonstrate the use of these ports for input and output by sensing switch closures and controlling light-emitting diodes (LEDs). Figure 15.6 gives a wiring diagram for interfacing the ports to LED displays and switches. Notice that

Port (Address)	*Signal name*		*DB25 Connector pin number*	*Comments*
	D0		2	All Outputs latched
	D1		3	
	D2		4	
Data	D3		5	
(OX3BC)	D4		6	
	D5		7	
	D6		8	
	D7		9	
	ERROR	(BIT3)	15	Input
	SLCT	(BIT4)	13	Input
Status	PE	(BIT5)	12	Input
(OX3BD)	ACK	(BIT6)	10	Input
	BUSY	(BIT7)	11	Inverted input
	STROBE	(BIT0)	1	Output
	AUTOFEED	(BIT1)	14	Inverted Output
Control	INIT PRN	(BIT2)	16	Output
(OX3BE)	SELECT	(BIT3)	17	Inverted Output
	GND		18–25	

(a)

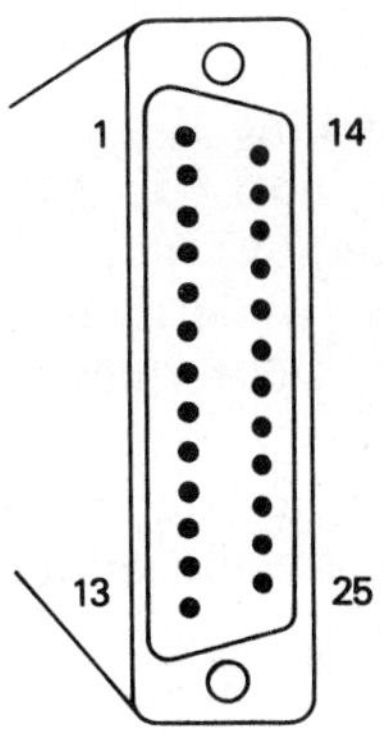

(b)

Figure 15.5 Parallel ports associated with LPT1 on the IBM PC. (a) LPT1 port signals and pin numbers; (b) DB25 connector diagram.

the LED displays are driven from an output port, while the switches are connected to an input port. A digital logic trainer may be used for the entire interface circuit. We will consider a program in Microsoft **C** that will read the status of the switches and control the LED displays accordingly.

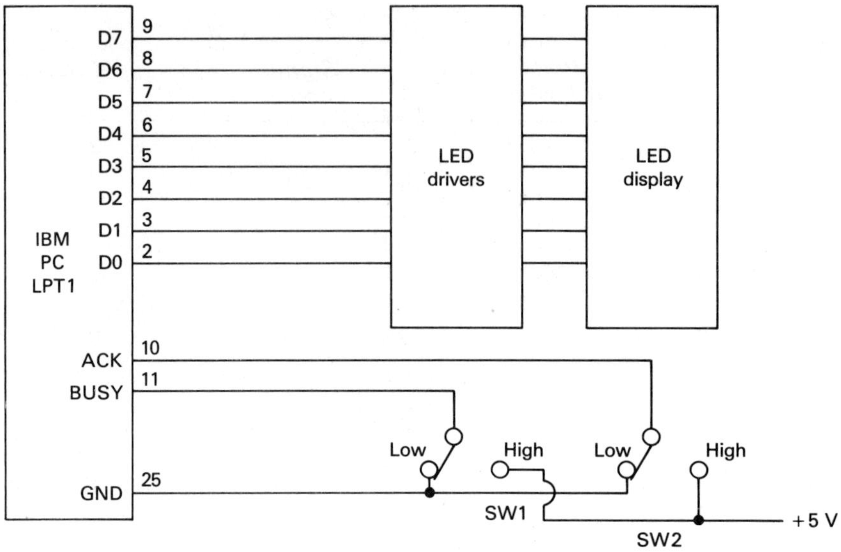

Figure 15.6 Schematic for LED and switch interface to LPT1.

The program will read the status of switch **SW1** and execute a **while** loop as long as this switch is set low (note that **BIT7** value is inverted in hardware). If switch **SW2** is low, the program will flash the LEDs. Otherwise, it will cause them to display the binary value of an incrementing count.

The program listing of Fig. 15.7 defines the addresses for the data port (**LPT1_DPORT**) and status port (**LPT1_SPORT**). It also defines the rate (**FLASH_RATE**) at which the LEDs will be flashed and the rate at which they will display the binary value of an incrementing count (**COUNT_RATE**). Other definitions include **LED_ON** and **LED_OFF**, which define the on/off status of the LEDs, and the **BIT6** and **BIT7** decimal equivalents.

The **inp(LPT1_SPORT)** statement reads the input from the status port. A bitwise and (**&**) with **BIT7** will be true if **SW1** is low (remember the **BIT7** inversion). The **while** loop continues for the condition **SW1** being low. Thus setting **SW1** high will terminate the program after completion of the currently selected task.

BIT6 is tested in the **if** statement. It reads the value of **SW2**. If **SW2** is high, the display count option will be selected. Otherwise, the flash LED option will execute.

The count routine uses the outer **for** loop to count from 0 to 255. The inner **for** loop establishes the time delay between counts or the count rate. Each value of **i** (the count) is output to the data port by **outp(LPT1_DPORT,i)**.

The flash LED routine turns the LEDs on by an all 1's output. A delay determined by **FLASH_RATE** is then introduced. Next, the LEDs are turned off by an all 0's output. A second delay is then introduced. After completion of this delay, the **while** loop test determines if the program will continue or terminate.

```
/* count or flash */
/* exercises the parallel output port at 0x3BC on the IBM PC */
/* and the parallel input port at 0x3BD */
/* using Microsoft C */
/* sw1 low for run, high for quit */
/* sw2 low for flash, high for count */

#include <stdio.h>
#define LPT1_DPORT      0x3BC   /* lpt1 data port */
#define LPT1_SPORT      0x3BD   /* lpt1 status port */
#define FLASH_RATE      10000
#define COUNT_RATE      500
#define BIT7            128
#define BIT6            64
#define LEDS_ON         255
#define LEDS_OFF   00

main()
    {
    int i,j;

    while (inp(LPT1_SPORT) & BIT7)
        {
        if (inp(LPT1_SPORT) & BIT6)
            /* count */
            for (i = 0; i<= 255; i++)
                {
                for (j = 0; j <= COUNT_RATE; j++)
                    ;
                outp(LPT1_DPORT, i);
                }
        else
            {
            /* flash */
            outp(LPT1_DPORT, LEDS_ON);
            for(i = 0; i < FLASH_RATE; i++)
                ;
            outp(LPT1_DPORT, LEDS_OFF);
            for (i = 0; i < FLASH_RATE; i++)
                ;
            }
        }
    }
```

Figure 15.7 Program to control LEDS on LPT1.

Serial Ports and Asynchronous Communication

A serial port may be nothing more than a single addressable line over which a binary stream of data passes. Such is the case with the speaker port of a microcomputer or terminal. The operation of a serial port used for data communication is considerably more complex. In this section, we will look at the simplest type of serial data transfer, referred to as *asynchronous* serial communication. The name derives from the fact that each byte being transmitted is not synchronized to any particular timing source.

A byte consists of 8 bits. To transmit a byte over a serial communications link requires converting the data from a parallel to a serial format. The rate at which the serial bits are transmitted is called the *baud* rate. It must be the same at both the transmitting and receiving stations. Standard baud rates are 300, 1200, 2400, 4800, and 9600 bps, or *bits per second*. Other baud rates are less frequently used.

An *asynchronous communications adaptor* is a hardware module used to provide a serial port for communication. It takes care of the parallel/serial data format conversion, baud rate regulation, and a variety of other tasks needed to ensure reliable communication. The heart of the adaptor is a UART, or *universal asynchronous receiver/transmitter*. An 8250 type UART is used in the IBM PC and compatibles. The registers of the 8250 and their addresses are given in Fig. 15.8.

We will select the minimum number of registers that must be programmed to provide a communications link. The **MSDOS mode** command will be used to set communications parameters including baud rate, number of data bits, type of parity, and number of stop bits. This approach will keep the application simple. If you wish to consider the programming of the other registers, refer to the *technical reference* manual for the IBM PC or some alternative source for details of the 8250 UART.

The UART contains two parallel buffer registers. The **Tx** buffer stores a byte to be transmitted to an external device. Another byte cannot be written into the **Tx** buffer until the last byte has been completely transmitted. At that point, the **Tx** buffer is said to be empty.

ADDRESS	REGISTER	READ/WRITE
3F8	Tx buffer	W
3F8	Rx buffer	R
3F8	Divisor latch LSB	R/W
3F9	Divisor latch MSB	R/W
3FB	Line control	R/W
3FC	Modem control	R/W
3FD	Line status	R/W
3FE	Modem status	R/W

Figure 15.8 8250 UART registers and addresses.

We can check the status of the **Tx** buffer by interrogating the **line status** register. The **Rx** buffer contains a completely received byte. We cannot correctly read a byte until it has been fully received and transferred to the **Rx** buffer. Again, checking the **line status** register will tell us whether a byte is waiting to be read.

When asynchronous communication is to occur to a remote site, a **modem**, or *modulator/demodulator*, is used to transmit and receive the signals over a phone line. It is installed between the computer or terminal and the phone line. To communicate with the computer or terminal, the **modem** will itself contain an asynchronous communications adaptor with its own UART. The computer or terminal is referred to as the **DTE** or *data terminal equipment*. The modem is referred to as the **DCE** or *data communications equipment*. The hardware configuration, signals, and protocol for the link between the **DTE** and **DCE** are prescribed by the Electronics Industry Association (EIA) RS-232-C standard.

Two signals that the **DTE** must provide to the **DCE** to indicate it is ready and requesting to transmit are called **DTR**, *data terminal ready*, and **RTS**, *request to send*. These signals are activated through the **modem control** register within the UART. The four registers that we have considered and their functions are summarized next.

Register	*Function*
Tx buffer	Holds the byte to be transmitted
Rx buffer	Holds the received byte
modem control	Tells modem (or other device) the DTE status
line status	Indicates when transmit buffer (**Tx**) is empty and when the receive buffer (**Rx**) has a byte that is ready to be read

Since the **Tx** and **Rx** registers share the same address, we will refer to them collectively as **TxRx**. A write to **TxRx** will go the **Tx** register. A read from **TxRx** will come from the **Rx** register.

The **modem control** and **line status** registers must be programmed at the bit level. Their internal configurations are given in Fig. 15.9. Bit **0** of the **modem control** register must be set to **1** to indicate that the data terminal is ready. Likewise, bit **1** must be set to **1** to indicate that the data terminal or **DTE** is requesting to send. The other bits of this register will be left in the **0** or reset state.

The **line status** register contains 2 bits that are important for our application. Bit **0**, the **DR** or data ready indicator, is automatically set to **1** whenever a received byte is ready for reading. After reading the **Rx** register, **DR** is automatically reset by the UART. Bit **5** of this register is the **THRE**, or transmit holding register empty, indicator. When a byte is loaded into the **Tx** buffer, **THRE** will be set to **0**. After the byte is transferred from **Tx** for transmission, the **THRE** bit is automatically set to **1.**

Modem Control Register

BIT NUMBER	SIGNAL	DESCRIPTION
7	0	always zero
6	0	"
5	0	"
4	loop	a 1 forces xmit shift register loop back to rcv register
3	OUT2	a control output
2	OUT1	a control output
1	RTS	Request to send
0	DTR	Data terminal ready

Line Status Register

BIT NUMBER	SIGNAL	DESCRIPTION
7	0	always 0
6	TSRE	1 = Tx shift register empty
5	THRE	1 = Tx holding register empty
4	BI	break interrupt
3	FE	framing error
2	PE	parity error
1	OE	overrun error
0	DR	receive data ready

Figure 15.9 Modem control and line status registers.

15.6 DUMB TERMINAL PROGRAM

Now that we have examined all the essential features of the asynchronous communications adaptor, let's look at a simple communications program, often called a *dumb terminal* program. Such a program is used to provide basic communications capability between a computer or terminal and a remote computer. In a system where multiple users are connected to a central computer system, the central computer is referred to as a *host*.

Communication may occur in one of three basic modes. In *simplex mode*, data can flow in one direction only. This arrangement is rarely used for computer communication. In *half-duplex mode*, data can flow in either direction, but not at the same time. Half-duplex is used to a limited extent. The most popular arrangement is referred to as *full-duplex mode*. Here, data can flow in either direction simultaneously.

The full-duplex mode is often used to send characters in one direction and instantly *echo* the same characters in the reverse direction. This procedure, called *echo-plex*, is used primarily in terminal/host types of communication links. It provides verification to the sender that the data were received correctly by the host. In such cases, the characters displayed on the sending terminal or computer are actually those that were echoed by the remote system. In half-duplex communication, characters must be locally echoed.

The basic functions of a dumb terminal program are:

1. Initialize communications parameters such as transmission mode, baud rate, parity, number of data bits, and number of stop bits.
2. Accept keyboard characters and send them to the asynchronous adaptor for transmission. If local echo is being used, the characters must also be printed to the display.
3. Read incoming characters from the asynchronous adaptor and display them.
4. Provide options such as adding a linefeed (auto linefeed) after a carriage return.

In our applications, the initialization step will be accomplished via an operating system command. Specifically, the MSDOS mode command will be used to set up all the parameters. It has the format:

```
MODE COMn: baud[,parity[,data-bits[,stop-bits]]]
```

where *n* is the communications adaptor number, and *baud* is the baud rate. *Parity* is the error detection scheme, which is:

E for even parity
O for odd parity
N for no parity checking

The parity scheme must be the same at the transmitting and receiving ends. The number of *stop bits* is either 1 or 2. It identifies the length in bits of the character termination code. To initialize the **COM1** adaptor for 1200 baud, even parity, 7 data bits, and 1 stop bit, the **mode** command is

```
MODE COM1:1200,E,7,1
```

The pseudocode for a dumb terminal program is given in Fig. 15.10. The addresses of all the UART registers that will be accessed are defined. Here, **TxRx** defines both the **Tx** and **Rx** register addresses, since they are common. **STATUS** defines the **line status** register address and **MCTRL** defines the **modem control** register address.

Since the communications parameters are being established through the operating system, the only initialization required by the program will be for the **modem control** register. Specifically, **DTR** and **RTS** must be asserted. This indicates to the **modem** (or other equipment) that the terminal is ready and requesting to send.

```
/* dumb terminal program pseudocode */
define TxRx       /* transmit/receive register address of UART */
define STATUS     /* status register address of UART */
define MCTRL      /* modem control register address of UART */

module main()
      intialize modem control register
      while (1) /* do forever */
            /********** receive routine **********/
            input a character, stat, from STATUS
            while(stat indicates receive register has a character)
                  input a character, c, from TxRx
                  print c
                  input a character, stat, from STATUS
            end while
            /********** transmit routine **********/
            while (keypress character c is not NULL)
                  output c to TxRx
                  print c
                  if (c == carriage_return)
                        wait for TxRx register empty
                        output a newline character to TxRx
                        print newline
                  end if
            end while
      end while
end module main()
```

Figure 15.10 Dumb terminal pseudocode.

There are two routines that the dumb terminal program repeats until communication is terminated. The receive routine inputs a character from **STATUS** and tests it to see if a character is present in **Rx**. If a character is present in **Rx**, it is read and printed to the display. Another read then occurs from **STATUS** to test for the presence of another character in **Rx**. The **while** loop repeats until the **Rx** register is found to be empty. Control then passes to the transmit routine.

The transmit routine tests for a keypress. If a key has been struck, the character is output to **Tx**. For local echo, the same character is printed to the display. If the keyboard character is a carriage return, a linefeed (newline) character is output to **Tx** and the display. The system must wait for **Tx** to be empty before the linefeed character can be written to that register.

A program that implements the dumb terminal pseudocode in Microsoft **C** on the IBM PC is given in Fig. 15.11. The UART address definitions are for the **COM1** adaptor. **RCV_RDY** and **XMIT_RDY** are *masks* to test **STATUS** for **DR** (bit 0) and **THRE** (bit 5). **Inp(STATUS) & RCV_RDY** will be true only if the **DR** bit is true or a byte is ready in **Rx**. Likewise, **inp(STATUS) & XMIT_RDY** will be true only if **THRE** is true or the **Tx** buffer is empty.

The function **kbhit()** is a Microsoft **C** library routine that tests for a keypress. It returns an **int** that is nonzero if a key has been pressed. Otherwise, it returns a zero. **Kbhit()** is used to test for a keypress without waiting for a carriage return or the presence of a character in the keyboard buffer. If **kbhit()** is true, a character is read from the keyboard buffer with **getch()**. Otherwise, the transmit routine is not executed.

```
/* dumb terminal program for Microsoft C */
#include <stdio.h>
#define TxRx          0x3f8
#define STATUS        0x3fd
#define MCTRL         0x3fc
#define RCV_RDY       1
#define XMIT_RDY      32

main()
     {
     int c, stat;
     void tx_wait();

     outp(MCTRL, 3);
     while (1)
          {
          stat = inp(STATUS);
          while (stat & RCV_RDY)
               {
               c = inp(TxRx);
               printf("%c", c);
               stat = inp(STATUS);
               }

          while (kbhit())
               {
               c = getch();
               outp(TxRx, c);
               putchar(c);
                    if (c == '\r')
                    {
                    tx_wait();
                    outp(TxRx, '\n');
                    putchar('\n');
                    }
               }
          }
     }

void tx_wait()
     {
     while ((inp(STATUS) & XMIT_RDY) == 0)
          ;
     }
```

Figure 15.11 Dumb terminal program.

The **getch()** function reads a character from the keyboard buffer without requiring a carriage return. It cannot be used without **kbhit()**, since an empty buffer would force **getch()** to wait for a keypress.

The **tx_wait()** function simply tests **STATUS** continuously until the **THRE** bit is **1**. While **THRE == 0**, the **Tx** register is not empty and a write to **Tx** would cause the loss of the original character in that register.

appendix A

C Language Reference

COMMENTS

A comment field begins with the **/*** character sequence and ends with the ***/** sequence. Comments may span more than one line. Examples include:

```
/* A one line comment */

/*****************************
     A multiline comment
*****************************/
```

EXPRESSIONS

Expressions may consist of a single operand or multiple operands connected by operators. The operands may include constants, macros, variables, function names, function return values, an array name or element reference, structure member or pointer. Examples include:

```
i++
(a+b)/2
(ch = getchar())
x >> 2
y == TRUE
```

STATEMENTS

A *simple* statement consists of an assignment, declaration, keyword expression, or function call followed by a semicolon. Examples include:

```
i = 12;        /*assignment */
char ch;       /* declaration */
while (i);     /* keyword statement */
putchar(ch);   /* function call */
```

A *compound* statement consists of multiple statements included within braces. The collection is treated as one statement.

DECLARATIONS

All variables must be *declared* before they are used. The declaration specifies the storage class and data type of the variable. Variables may be declared outside a function or within (see storage class and data types). The default type for variables declared outside a function is **extern**, while for those inside a function it is **auto**. Variables declared within a function normally appear after the function opening brace. The format of a declaration is:

```
storage-class type-specifier variable-name;
```

Examples include:

```
int     i;
char    ch;
static double data[MAX_X][MAX_Y];
extern long   address, base;
```

DATA TYPES

Fundamental Data Types

Type	*Description*
char	A byte, contains one character of data
short	A short integer (see **int**)
int	An integer number, usually 2 bytes long
long	A long integer, usually 4 bytes long
unsigned	An integer without a sign bit; largest value is twice that of a type **int**
float	A floating-point number
double	A double-precision floating-point number

Data-type Conversion

Any binary operator having two types of operands will promote the lower type to the higher type. The result will have the higher type. In any assignment, the type of the right side is converted into the type of the left side, if it fits. Therefore, care must be taken when demotion occurs in an assignment. The ranking of data types from lowest to highest is:

Type	*Comment*
char	Always converted to **int**
short int	Always converted to **int**
unsigned short int	Always converted to **int**
int	
unsigned int	
long int	
unsigned long int	
float	Always converted to **double**
double	

Derived Data Types

Type	*Description*
Array	An array of elements of some data type
Pointer	A variable (or constant) whose value points to an address
Structure	A collection of mixed data types
Union	Different data types occupying the same memory area
Function	A function may return a data type

OPERATORS

Binary Operators

Precedence	*Name*	*Symbol*	*Associativity*
1	Parentheses	() []	L to R
1	Structure access	-> .	L to R
2	Unary	! ~ ++ -- -	R to L
2		(type) * & sizeof	R to L
3	Multiply, divide, modulus	* / %	L to R
4	Add, subtract	+ -	L to R
5	Shift left, shift right	<< >>	L to R
6	Less than, less than or equal	< <=	L to R
6	Greater than, greater than or equal	> >=	L to R
7	Equal, not equal	== !=	L to R
8	Bitwise AND	&	L to R
9	Bitwise exclusive OR	^	L to R
10	Bitwise OR	¦	L to R
11	Logical AND	&&	L to R
12	Logical OR	¦¦	L to R
13	Conditional expression	? :	R to L
14	Assignment	= += -= *= %= %=	R to L
14		>>= <<= &= ^= ¦=	R to L
15	Comma	,	L to R

Unary Operators

Name	*Operator*
Unary negative	!
One's complement	~
Increment	++
Decrement	--
Unary minus	-
Cast	(type)
Indirection	*
Address of	&
Size of	sizeof

CONSTANTS

Type	*Examples*	*Comments*
char	`'a' '\n' '\07'`	Characters or escape sequences within single quotes
char	`"Enter data"`	A character string is an array of **char** followed by a **NULL** ('\0')
int	`250 -300`	Whole number starting with a nonzero digit
int	`07 0250`	Octal integers start with 0
int	`0xAF5`	Hex integers start with 0x or 0X
long int	`2000000L`	Long integers end with l or L
float	`2.2 1.5e-6`	Include decimal point
double	`3.14159265`	Include decimal point

VARIABLE AND FUNCTION NAMES

Variable and function names are called *identifiers*. The following rules apply to naming identifiers:

1. The first character must be a letter or the underscore (_).
2. An identifier may include letters a to z, A to Z, or digits 0 to 9. Upper- and lowercase are differentiated. Normally, variable names use lowercase and symbolic constants use uppercase.
3. Any number of characters may be included within an identifier. The compiler may recognize eight or more characters. The linker may recognize fewer characters.

KEYWORDS

Data type	*Storage class*	*Statement*
char	**auto**	**break**
double	**extern**	**case**
enum	**register**	**continue**
float	**static**	**default**
int		**do**
long		**else**
short		**for**
struct		**goto**
typedef		**if**
union		**return**
unsigned		**sizeof**
		switch
		while

KEYWORD STATEMENTS

Statement	*Description*
break;	Stops execution of the current loop or **switch** and continues with the statement immediately following the loop. May be used with **for**, **do**, **while**, or **switch**.
continue;	Continues execution of a loop, ignoring statements that follow it within a **do**, **for**, or **while** loop.
do **statement;** **while** (*expression*);	Executes **statement**, then evaluates *expression*. Repeats until expression is FALSE or 0.
for(*expr1*;*expr2*;*expr3*) **statement;**	*expr1* is used to initialize variables. *expr2* is the test condition that must be TRUE for **statement** to execute. *expr3* is used to increment or decrement some variable(s). Multiple expressions separated by commas may be used for *expr1* and *expr3*. The **for** loop repeats until *expr2* is FALSE.
goto *label*;	Causes an unconditional transfer of execution to a statement prefixed by *label*: in the same function. *Label* is an identifier.
if (*expression*) **statement;**	If *expression* is TRUE, **statement** is executed. Otherwise, **statement** will be ignored. **If** statements may be nested.

if (expression)
   statement_1;
else
   statement_2;
	If *expression* is TRUE, **statement_1** executes. Otherwise, **statement_2** executes. The **if-else** statement may be nested.

return *expression*;	Returns to calling function with value of *expression*. *Expression* is optional. If present, it will have the type of the function in which it occurs.

switch (*expression*)
  {
  case (*const expr1*)
      statement;
  case (*const expr2)*
      statement;
      .
      .
  default:
      statement;
  }
	The integer *expression* is compared to the *const expr* (constant expression) for each **case.** If a match occurs, control is transferred to the statement following that **case.** Otherwise, the **default** is executed. To execute only the statement following the selected **case**, a **break** must follow that statement.

while (*expression*) **statement;**	Executes **statement** while *expression* is TRUE (nonzero).

STORAGE CLASS

Type	*Comments*
auto	The default storage class within a function. An **auto** variable lasts until the function call is completed; then it disappears. It cannot be referenced outside the function in which it is declared. **Auto** arrays cannot be initialized. **Extern** or **static** arrays can be initialized.
extern	An **extern** variable is *defined* by a declaration, outside any function, that omits the **extern** storage-class specifier. It can be referenced from the point where it is defined to the end of the same source file. An external variable is defined only once. We can *declare* a variable as being external by using the **extern** storage-class specifier in a declaration. The **extern** declaration is needed when an external variable is to be referenced before it is defined or when it occurs in a different source file.
static	A **static** variable may be internal to a function or external. Internal or local **static** variables, unlike **auto** types, are permanent. They remain in existence from one call to another. External **static** variables can be accessed from the point where they are declared through the rest of the same source file. However, they are hidden from or not available to other source files.
register	A **register** declaration requests the compiler to store an automatic variable or formal parameter in a machine register, if possible. This is done for speed of execution.

PREPROCESSOR

#**define** *identifier string*	Replaces *identifier* with *string* throughout program before actual compilation occurs.
#**define** identifier(id1, id2,...) *string*	Replaces *identifier* with *string* and places the arguments *id1*, *id2*, etc., in the corresponding argument definition of *string*.
#**include** "*file*" or #**include** ⟨file⟩	Includes source code of *file* for compilation. Used frequently for including header files having a **.h** extension.
#**if** *const expr* . . #**endif**	If the constant expression is TRUE, all lines between #**if** and #**endif** will be processed.

FUNCTIONS

Functions have the following format:

```
type name(arg1, arg2, . . .)
    argument declarations
          {
        declarations

        statement;
            .
            .
        return(value);
        }
```

The type of a function is the type of the return *value*. If no value is returned, a **void** type is assigned and **return** is omitted. If a type is not assigned, the default is **int**. All the arguments (formal parameters) must be declared before the function open brace. All the function declarations usually follow the open brace of the function.

POINTERS

A declaration such as

```
type *ptr;
```

declares **ptr** as a pointer to type. Pointer variables must be initialized before being used. The statement

```
ptr = &variable;
```

initializes **ptr** so that it points to **variable**. Pointers may point to basic data types as well as arrays, structures, unions, functions, and so on. Examples of pointer declarations follow:

int	***pi;**	/* pointer to type **int** */
double	***pd;**	/* pointer to type **double** */
float	***fctn();**	/* function returning pointer to **float** */
int	**(*f)();**	/* pointer to function returning **int** */
int	**(*a)[];**	/* pointer to an array of **int** */
char	***i[];**	/* array of pointers to **char** */

ARRAYS

type data[i];	/* declares **data** to be a one-dimensional array of **type** having **i** elements. */
type data[i][j];	/* declares **data** to be a two-dimensional array having **i** rows and **j** columns. */
type data[i][j][k];	/* declares **data** as a three-dimensional array. */
type *ptr= data;	/* declares **ptr** as a pointer to **type** and initializes it to the array **data**. */

An array name is a pointer constant. **data** points to **data[0]**, the first element of the array. Arrays are passed by reference only. Examples of initializing **static** and **extern** arrays follow:

```
static type data[] = {val1,val2,val3,...,valn}; /* Initializes data with n elements of type.*/

extern type data[][] =                           /*Initializes the two-dimensional array data*/
            {                                    /* with m rows and n columns of data */
            {val11,val12,...,val1n},             /* data is an extern array */
            {val21,val22,...,val2n},
            ...
            {valm1,valm2,...,valmn}
            };
```

STRUCTURES

A structure is a data object that can store more than one data type. A structure *template* defines the arrangement of data within a structure. In the following structure definition

```
struct primitive
        {
        char    command;
        int     param[4];
        } line;
```

the name **primitive** is the structure *tag* name. This particular structure has two *members*. The first, **command**, is a type **char**. The second, **param[]**, is an **int** array of four elements. The variable **line** has been declared of type **struct primitive**. The tag name or the variable declarations may be omitted within the structure definition, but not both. The following declares **circle** as being of type **struct primitive** and initializes it.

```
struct primitive circle = { 'c', 100,120,50,2};

struct primitive *ptr = &circle; /* declares ptr as a pointer to type struct primitive */
                                 /* and initializes it to point to circle. */
ptr -> param[0]                  /* accesses param[0] of circle through ptr */
circle.param[0]                  /* accesses param[0] of circle through the structure name */
```

USING PRINTF AND SCANF

```
printf(control string,arg1,arg2,...);   /* prints formatted data to standard output */
fprintf(control string,arg1,arg2,...);  /* prints formatted data to a file */
scanf(control string,arg1,arg2,...);    /* inputs formatted data from the standard input */
fscanf(control string,arg1,arg2,...);   /* inputs formatted data from a file */
```

Control string includes text and a number of *conversion specifiers* equal to the number of arguments that follow *control string*. For **printf**, *conversion specifiers* locate where arguments will be inserted into the control string and how they will be formatted. The text of the control string and the inserted arguments are printed in the prescribed format. For **scanf**, *control string* usually includes only the conversion specifiers. (It may also include additional input controls.) The arguments are pointers to the storage location for the input data. The conversion specifiers are:

Specifiers	Description	Used with Printf	Used with Scanf
Numeric			
%d	Decimal or base 10 integer	×	×
%o	Octal or base 8 integer	×	×
%x	Hexadecimal or base 16 integer	×	×
%u	Unsigned decimal integer	×	
%f	Floating-point decimal	×	×
%e	Exponential (scientific) notation	×	
%g	Shortest of %e or %f	×	
%h	Short integer		×
Character			
%c	Single character	×	×
%s	String of characters	×	×

Conversion modifiers are placed after the % symbol and before the specifier. They control field width, justification and precision.

Printf() Examples

```
printf("The answer is %8.4f volts\n",v_out); /* prints v_out with 4 decimal places and */
The answer is 127.2333 volts                 /* a field width of 8 */

printf("%ld\n",big);       /* prints big as a long int type */
printf("%x\n",address);    /* prints address as a hex number */
printf("%20d\n",num);      /* prints num right-justified inside a field width of 20 */
printf("%-5d\n",num);      /* prints num left-justified inside a field width of 5 */
```

Scanf() Examples

```
scanf("%d %lf",&i,&dbl);       /* inputs int i and double dbl using whitespace as a separator */
scanf("%x,%x",&hex1,&hex2);    /* inputs two hex numbers using a comma as a separator */
scanf("ld",&big);              /* inputs big as a long type */
scanf("%s",word);              /* inputs the character string word[] */
```

THE STANDARD C LIBRARY

Math Library Functions

Group	*Math function*	*Description*
Arithmetic	ceil(x)	Returns the nearest whole number above **x**
	fabs(x)	Returns the absolute value of **x**
	floor(x)	Returns the nearest whole number below **x**
	pow(x,y)	Returns **x** raised to the **y** power
	sqrt(x)	Returns the square root of **x**
Trigonometric	acos(x)	Returns the arc cosine of **x**
	asin(x)	Returns the arc sine of **x**
	atan(x)	Returns the arc tangent of **x**
	atan2(y,x)	Returns the arc tangent of **y/x**
	cos(x)	Returns the cosine of **x**
	cosh(x)	Returns the hyperbolic cosine of **x**
	sin(x)	Returns the sine of **x**
	sinh(x)	Returns the hyperbolic sine of **x**
	tan(x)	Returns the tangent of **x**
	tanh(x)	Returns the hyperbolic tangent of **x**
Logarithmic	exp(x)	Returns the value of the exponential e^x
	log(x)	Returns the value of the natural logarithm **ln(x)**
	log10(x)	Returns the value of the common logarithm **log(x)**
Random number	frand(x)	Returns a pseudorandom number between 0.0 and 1.0
	rand(x)	Returns a pseudorandom whole number
	srand(x)	Reseeds the random generator with a value of **x**

Character Test/Conversion Library Functions

Character test

Function	*True if character **c** is*
isalpha(c)	Alphabetic
isdigit(c)	A digit
isspace(c)	A blank, tab, or newline
islower(c)	Lowercase
isupper(c)	Uppercase
isalnum(c)	Aphabetic or a digit
iscntrl(c)	A control character
isgraph(c)	A graphics character
isprint(c)	A printable character
ispunct(c)	A punctuation mark
isxdigit(c)	A hexadecimal digit

Character conversion

Function	*Converts character **c** from*
tolower(c)	Uppercase to lowercase
toupper(c)	Lowercase to uppercase

String/Memory Library Functions

String functions

The following entries fall into two categories. The first group having names starting with **str**, perform basic operations on strings. The second converts strings of digits into a numeric data format. The variable names used in the table have the following definitions:

```
char *str,*str1,*str2;
int n;
char c;
```

strcat(*str1,str2*)	Appends *str2* to *str1*
strchr(*str,c*)	Returns pointer to first occurrence of *c* in *str*
strcmp(*str1,str2*)	Compares *str1* and *str2*, returns 0 if equal
strcpy(*str1,str2*)	Copies *str2* to *str1*
strlen(*str*)	Returns number of characters in *str*
strncat(*str1,str2,n*)	Appends *n* characters from *str2* to *str1*
strncmp(*str1,str2,n*)	Compares first *n* characters of *str1* and *str2*
strncpy(*str1,str2,n*)	Copies first *n* characters from *str2* to *str1*
strpbrk(*str1,str2*)	Returns first occurrence in *str1* of any character in *str2*
strrchr(*str,c*)	Returns pointer to last occurrence of *c* in *str*
atof(*str*)	Convert *str* to double
atoi(*str*)	Convert *str* to int
atol(*str*)	Convert *str* to long

Standard library memory buffer functions

The arguments used in the memory buffer functions are defined as follows:

char *buf, *buf1, *buf2;
char c;
int n;
unsigned size;

where **buf**, **buf1**, and **buf2** are pointers to the beginning of a buffer.

memchr(*buf,c,n*)	Returns pointer to first occurrence of *c* in first *n* characters of *buf*
memcmp(*buf1,buf2,n*)	Compares first *n* characters of *buf1* and *buf2*
memcpy(*buf1,buf2,n*)	Copies *n* characters from *buf2* to *buf1*
memset(*buf,c,n*)	Sets first *n* characters of *buf* to *c*
malloc(*size*)	Allocates and returns a pointer to a memory block of *size* bytes
calloc(*n,size*)	Allocates memory for *n* elements of *size* bytes
realloc(*buf,size*)	Changes size of previously allocated memory
free(*buf*)	Deallocates memory block referenced by *buf*

File Library Functions

The arguments used by the standard library file functions are defined as follows:

FILE *stream;
char c, *filename, *type, *string, *format;
char *pathname, *buffer, *old, *new;
int n, size, origin;
long offset;

The argument **stream** is a pointer to an opened file. Another commonly used name for this pointer is **fp**, which stands for *file pointer*. You may use any valid name for this pointer provided that it is declared as being of type **FILE**.

Function	*Description*
fopen (*filename, type*)	Opens *filename* for access *type "r"*, *"w"*, or *"a"*
getc (*stream*)	Reads a character from file pointed to by *stream*
fgetc (*stream*)	Reads a character from file pointed to by *stream*
putc (*c, stream*)	Writes character *c* to file pointed to by *stream*
fputc (*c, stream*)	Writes character *c* to file pointed to by *stream*
ungetc (*c, stream*)	Pushes character *c* back onto input *stream*
fclose (*stream*)	Closes file pointed to by *stream*
fgets (*string, n, stream*)	Reads a string of up to *n − 1* characters from *stream* and places them into *string*
fputs (*string, stream*)	Writes *string* into file pointed to by *stream*
fscanf (*stream, format, arg, . . .*)	Reads data from *stream* using *format* conversion specifier into address specified by *arg*

fprintf (*stream*, *format*, *arg*, . . .)	Writes *arg* into *stream* using *format* conversion specifier
fread (*buffer*, *size*, *n*, *stream*)	Reads *n* items of length *size* from *stream* into *buffer*
fwrite (*buffer*, *size*, *n*, *stream*)	Writes *n* items of length *size* into *stream* from *buffer*
fseek (*stream*, *offset*, *origin*)	Locates file pointer for *stream* at *offset* bytes from *origin*
rename (*old*, *new*)	Renames file specified by *old* to that given by *new*
rewind (*stream*)	Sets file pointer for *stream* to beginning of file
remove (*pathname*)	Deletes file specified by *pathname*
clearerr (*stream*)	Clears error and end of file conditions on *stream*
freopen (*filename*, *type*, *stream*)	Closes current file and reassigns *stream* to *filename*
setbuf (*stream*, *buffer*)	Assigns user-specified *buffer* to *stream*
fflush (*stream*)	Writes buffer contents to file pointed to by *stream*
ftell (*stream*)	Returns current position of file pointer for *stream*
feof (*stream*)	Detects end of file on file pointed to by *stream*
ferror (*stream*)	Detects a read/write error on *stream*
perror (*string*)	Prints *string* error message to **stderr**

Miscellaneous Library Functions

void exit (*int status*)	Terminates program, flushing all open buffers and closing all open files. *Status* is optional. If present, passes status to system. A **0** status value indicates no errors.

appendix B

ASCII Code

ASCII	*Decimal*	*Hex*	*Octal*	*Binary*	*Key**	*ASCII*	*Decimal*	*Hex*	*Octal*	*Binary*
NUL	00	00	00	000 0000	^@	SP	32	20	40	010 0000
SOH	01	01	01	000 0001	^A	!	33	21	41	010 0001
STX	02	02	02	000 0010	^B	"	34	22	42	010 0010
ETX	03	03	03	000 0011	^C	#	35	23	43	010 0011
EOT	04	04	04	000 0100	^D	$	36	24	44	010 0100
ENQ	05	05	05	000 0101	^E	%	37	25	45	010 0101
ACK	06	06	06	000 0110	^F	&	38	26	46	010 0110
BEL	07	07	07	000 0111	^G	'	39	27	47	010 0111
BS	08	08	10	000 1000	^H	(	40	28	50	010 1000
HT	09	09	11	000 1001	^I	)	41	29	51	010 1001
LF	10	0A	12	000 1010	^J	*	42	2A	52	010 1010
VT	11	0B	13	000 1011	^K	+	43	2B	53	010 1011
FF	12	0C	14	000 1100	^L	,	44	2C	54	010 1100
CR	13	0D	15	000 1101	^M	−	45	2D	55	010 1101
SO	14	0E	16	000 1110	^N	.	46	2E	56	010 1110
SI	15	0F	17	000 1111	^O	/	47	2F	57	010 1111
DLE	16	10	20	001 0000	^P	0	48	30	60	011 0000
DC1	17	11	21	001 0001	^Q	1	49	31	61	011 0001
DC2	18	12	22	001 0010	^R	2	50	32	62	011 0010
DC3	19	13	23	001 0011	^S	3	51	33	63	011 0011
DC4	20	14	24	001 0100	^T	4	52	34	64	011 0100
NAK	21	15	25	001 0101	^U	5	53	35	65	011 0101
SYN	22	16	26	001 0110	^V	6	54	36	66	011 0110
ETB	23	17	27	001 0111	^W	7	55	37	67	011 0111
CAN	24	18	30	001 1000	^X	8	56	38	70	011 1000
EM	25	19	31	001 1001	^Y	9	57	39	71	011 1001
SUB	26	1A	32	001 1010	^Z	:	58	3A	72	011 1010
ESC	27	1B	33	001 1011	^[	;	59	3B	73	011 1011
FS	28	1C	34	001 1100	^\	<	60	3C	74	011 1100
GS	29	1D	35	001 1101	^]	=	61	3D	75	011 1101
RS	30	1E	36	001 1110	^^	>	62	3E	76	011 1110
US	31	1F	37	001 1111	^_	?	63	3F	77	011 1111

* The ^ is the CTRL (control) key pressed simultaneously with the other indicated key.

ASCII	*Decimal*	*Hex*	*Octal*	*Binary*	*ASCII*	*Decimal*	*Hex*	*Octal*	*Binary*
@	64	40	100	100 0000	‘	96	60	140	110 0000
A	65	41	101	100 0001	a	97	61	141	110 0001
B	66	42	102	100 0010	b	98	62	142	110 0010
C	67	43	103	100 0011	c	99	63	143	110 0011
D	68	44	104	100 0100	d	100	64	144	110 0100
E	69	45	105	100 0101	e	101	65	145	110 0101
F	70	46	106	100 0110	f	102	66	146	110 0110
G	71	47	107	100 0111	g	103	67	147	110 0111
H	72	48	110	100 1000	h	104	68	150	110 1000
I	73	49	111	100 1001	i	105	69	151	110 1001
J	74	4A	112	100 1010	j	106	6A	152	110 1010
K	75	4B	113	100 1011	k	107	6B	153	110 1011
L	76	4C	114	100 1100	l	108	6C	154	110 1100
M	77	4D	115	100 1101	m	109	6D	155	110 1101
N	78	4E	116	100 1110	n	110	6E	156	110 1110
O	79	4F	117	100 1111	o	111	6F	157	110 1111
P	80	50	120	101 0000	p	112	70	160	111 0000
Q	81	51	121	101 0001	q	113	71	161	111 0001
R	82	52	122	101 0010	r	114	72	162	111 0010
S	83	53	123	101 0011	s	115	73	163	111 0011
T	84	54	124	101 0100	t	116	74	164	111 0100
U	85	55	125	101 0101	u	117	75	165	111 0101
V	86	56	126	101 0110	v	118	76	166	111 0110
W	87	57	127	101 0111	w	119	77	167	111 0111
X	88	58	130	101 1000	x	120	78	170	111 1000
Y	89	59	131	101 1001	y	121	79	171	111 1001
Z	90	5A	132	101 1010	z	122	7A	172	111 1010
[	91	5B	133	101 1011	{	123	7B	173	111 1011
\	92	5C	134	101 1100	¦	124	7C	174	111 1100
]	93	5D	135	101 1101	}	125	7D	175	111 1101
^	94	5E	136	101 1110	~	126	7E	176	111 1110
_	95	5F	137	101 1111	DEL	127	7F	177	111 1111

Index